Genie's Bottle, a rich and rewarding novel, invites us into the lives and struggles toward self-realization of believable characters created by the author's insight, imagination, and stylistic charm. Kara, Rikk, Dutch, and the supporting characters ring true and engage reader empathy. *Genie's Bottle* welcomes readers aboard for a fine sailing trip.

Ralph Latham, retired English Professor,
Kirkwood Community College, Cedar Rapids, IA

We root for Bauer's likeable characters as they struggle through turbulent ups and downs of joy, sorrow, hurt, and love, as they seek connection while trying to protect themselves. Bauer puts voice to the inner critics—the 'saboteurs'—that chatter in our heads. The plot twists kept me interested until the very end.

Melissa Creede,
Sapis Insight, Career and Leadership Coach

Genie's Bottle

BERTA BAUER

BALBOA PRESS
A DIVISION OF HAY HOUSE

Dear Eney & Woody)
Rau and sacred our friendships
likes yours, when time and space
apart are irrelevant. Once together
we pick up where we left off as if
it was yesterday that we hung out.
Please always know how important
you are in my life and how much
fun to be your friend.
May you enjoy the
mysteries that are within.
Be in Choice,
Berta

Balboa Press books may be ordered through booksellers or by contacting:

Balboa Press
A Division of Hay House
1663 Liberty Drive
Bloomington, IN 47403
www.balboapress.com
1-(877) 407-4847

Because of the dynamic nature of the Internet, any web addresses or links contained in this book may have changed since publication and may no longer be valid. The views expressed in this work are solely those of the author and do not necessarily reflect the views of the publisher, and the publisher hereby disclaims any responsibility for them.

The author of this book does not dispense medical advice or prescribe the use of any technique as a form of treatment for physical, emotional, or medical problems without the advice of a physician, either directly or indirectly. The intent of the author is only to offer information of a general nature to help you in your quest for emotional and spiritual well-being. In the event you use any of the information in this book for yourself, which is your constitutional right, the author and the publisher assume no responsibility for your actions.

Any people depicted in stock imagery provided by Thinkstock are models, and such images are being used for illustrative purposes only.
Certain stock imagery © Thinkstock.

ISBN: 978-1-4525-4349-9 (e)
ISBN: 978-1-4525-4350-5 (sc)
ISBN: 978-1-4525-4351-2 (hc)

Library of Congress Control Number: 2012901422

Printed in the United States of America

Balboa Press rev. date: 03/08/2012

For Tim, Scott, Kate. Life is rich and good because they travel this world with me.

For Mom, Jean Leirich Morris. She raised her children repeating the wisdom and idioms of my grandfather, Jack Leirich. Mom inspired me by how she lived her life. She embraced and accepted the diversity of others while maintaining her commitment to her own beliefs and values.

For Ralph Latham. His gentle guidance and kindred spirit touched me in a way that gave me confidence to release *Genie's Bottle* to the world. I am honored that he granted me permission to include a poem he wrote that resonates so deep within me and depicts my life journey. That poem was also synchronistic to the voyage the characters of *Genie's Bottle* traveled as their story entered my head and heart and flowed through my fingertips onto the page.

Lake Lesson

Just like Lake Superior,
We sometimes storm and rage,
Thrash wildly, out of control.

Just like Lake Superior,
We sometimes grow smooth,
Regaining serenity and poise.

Unlike Lake Superior,
We spend great stores of energy
In recrimination and regret.

Lake Superior, show us how
To forget storms when they've gone by
And, like You,
    Sit Still
        Listen
            Learn.

Ralph Latham

Acknowledgments

My mom raised her children with affection and respect while instilling independence. She gave us the tools to make our own decisions and held us accountable for our actions. Following her passing, I am blessed with Mom's continual guidance and love that continue to grow stronger as time speeds by. I'm amazed how many of her gifts have seeped into Genie's Bottle.

My husband, Tim, has praised, encouraged, given suggestions, and provided "a word that means—" when my brain and thesaurus failed me. He has served as my technical sailing advisor, and helped me put my characters into peril and to bring them safely out. My son, Scott, dedicates himself to living his life authentically by following his internal compass. He motivates me. My daughter, Kate, challenges me—directly—to be authentic and live my passion. She inspires me I continually learn from them.

Karina Hipp, my coaching classmate and coach, listened attentively and repeated back to me the words I spoke, "Be in choice." I thank her for hearing my words and making sure that I heard them too.

My coach, Melissa Creede, exposed my saboteur with tenacity. When I didn't have faith in my ability to know what to do, she gave me an assignment to find an editor within one week. I found Ralph Latham, and he edited with wisdom, gentleness perfect for a beginner, and tons of encouragement. Later, Melissa read the manuscript and convinced me to keep working on scenes that, in her words, were "chunky." I trust her frank and sincere comments, not only as my coach, but as my friend who offers invaluable feedback to me.

Jamie Block's eye for detail, accuracy, and consistency made publishing Genie's Bottle happen. She polished my manuscript while preserving my writing style and at times challenged me when she came across something that wasn't consistent with the voices of the characters.

Several years before I began writing *Genie's Bottle*, my friend, Anna Hess, created for Tim and me an oil painting. Sixteen months ago, she granted me permission to use it for the front and back cover. I had her read Genie's Bottle, and I continue to be awed with her ability to tell me what I often know but try not to heed.

Thank you to Maryl Skinner, Denny Fitzpatrick, Kelly Rauzi, Jetty St. John, Jim Boyd, Lois Wiley, Diana Heston, Pamela Faye, Eileen Tollefson, Kelly Summers, and my writing group for the encouragement, comments, and suggestions during my voyage writing and revising *Genie's Bottle*.

The staff at Balboa Press, with their professionalism and dedication to help create a beautiful book has been wonderful, especially Jennifer Slaybaugh for her attentiveness and quick response to my questions, emails, and requests.

Preface

I believe all things are possible. In 2006, when I pledged to sit at the computer and release the story brewing inside me, *Genie's Bottle* was born. It is a story that refused to be contained any longer. It was a six-year journey filled with doubts as well as accomplishments. I can't help but remember when I revisited my first draft of *Genie's Bottle* after letting it sit for few months. I detested it. However, it opened my eyes to what was going on inside my head and heart. The first draft I wrote of *Genie's Bottle* was my catalyst for changing my life, and together we have grown and transformed.

The story pointed to those things in my life that were no longer serving me. I freed myself of limiting beliefs as I freed my characters of theirs. I discovered my purpose in the world and learned how to be at peace with others and myself. Two years after I typed the first words in *Genie's Bottle*, I was led to life coaching. It was a much needed and wanted career change, and it showed me how to be happy with what I have, where I am, and how to manifest what is next.

The lessons I was learning about conscious choice began to sneak into *Genie's Bottle* while I revised it, and before long, I realized that the purpose of this book was to uplift as well as entertain. I share my own beliefs in *Genie's Bottle*, and through the story, I encourage everyone to choose their own path in this world. I see much of Kara, Rikk, and Dutch in myself—their imperfections as well as their perfections—and my spirit resonates in all of them. Like them, I have my own saboteurs to grapple with and my authentic self to thank when its wisdom prevails. Publishing *Genie's Bottle* has been my greatest triumph over my saboteur's relentless doubt-inducing chatter.

May *Genie's Bottle* give you the knowledge that you can "Be in choice."

May 1, 2007

"Excuse me," Vincent said, "Do you want the car brought around this morning?"

Her somber eyes gazed out the sitting room window at the sea of tulips blooming in dazzling colors. Throughout the seasons, the brook meandering through the garden captivated and held her eyes, but never as long as it did each spring. He watched her eyes retain their stare while they reluctantly turned towards him. At last, they blinked and refocused on him, yet he could tell she hadn't a clue what he had just asked.

His eyes dropped as he said, "I was wondering if you want the car brought around this morning." He looked back into her lucent blue irises and watched astonishment replace the grave stare. He stammered, "To, to take you to the, to the river?" The incensed glare he received made him realize that the annual May Day trip to the isolated and overgrown riverbank was not something he should've brought up. Even though he had made the trip every May Day since he had come to work for her eleven years ago, it was a mistake to let on that he was aware of the pattern.

"Yes, Vincent." Her eyes held their stare before they turned back to the window.

This was the best job he could ever ask for 364 days a year, but an eerie mystery shrouded every May Day. Vincent had no idea that this would be the last May Day he'd spend wondering what secrets lay buried at the riverbank, nor could he have imagined the changes to come when those secrets were exhumed.

Chapter 1

Rikk

Rikk didn't wake up from his dream. He was awake when it ended and his eyes were wide open as he watched her leave. How bizarre it was for him to find himself fully awake from what began while he slept. It was the most surreal feeling that he'd had yet, and lately he had a lot of them. He was lying on his bed and staring at the ceiling, feeling the most ethereal calm he had ever experienced in his life. He was with her, talking to her. It wasn't a dream of something that happened in the past, nor was it a bizarre dream full of impossible circumstances. It was today, May 1st. It was this year, 2007, and Lauren had been gone for about a year and a half. But Lauren visited him this morning. It wasn't a dream. *She was real*. She was transparent—glowing in a brilliant and iridescent pure white light.

She floated through their bedroom, pausing at the side of their bed. She said, "Happy May Day, Rikk."

"Lauren," his whispered word was filled with incredulity and love.

"You've picked her out; now it's time you buy her." Lauren's voice was clear and soft.

"The boat?"

"She'll not be your mistress for long. Oh, Rikk, she'll bring you so much more than companionship." Lauren's compassionate smile comforted him, yet he was unnerved by her words.

"But Lauren, all I want is you." That was all he had time to say before she floated away. She left him staring at the ceiling in the rising amber dawn that filled their bedroom with warmth. He wondered if she'd heard him. It somehow didn't matter. Although he couldn't explain what he had just experienced; his whole being felt as if it were vibrating—vibrating so fast that he felt perfectly calm and filled with awe.

But what did she mean by, "She'll not be your mistress for long. She'll bring you so much more than companionship?" How could that be? To Rikk those statements were a paradox. Even though it didn't make sense, he found peace with Lauren's message to buy the boat. He had been stalling, waiting for something to reassure him that it was the right boat to buy. Or maybe he was still uncertain about buying any boat. Now, after Lauren's visit, it was clear. She told him that he'd picked out the boat. At last, Rikk knew buying it was the right thing to do.

Lauren's appearance lingered on his mind. Rikk was having a hard time wrapping his analytical brain around her presence this morning. He wanted to bounce this apparition off someone. But who? Surgeons, after all, believed in science. Miracles supposedly had occurred in his practice, but for him they were nothing more than unexplainable recoveries. Lauren had been the only person with whom Rikk could ever share something so inexplicable—so mystifying as her visit. *She* wouldn't question his competence or his sanity.

Rikk sighed, what a shell of an existence he had lived these past nineteen months since her death. He turned his thoughts from Lauren to the sailboat. With surgery all day, he had better email the purchase confirmation to Ocean Sail Quest before work or he wouldn't get another chance until this evening.

Rikk crawled out of bed and went directly to the computer. He opened up the email addressed to OSQ that was sitting in his "Drafts" file. It was the only message in the file, and it had been there for weeks—waiting to be sent. When he pushed send, he felt a rush of euphoria, much like what he felt when he first met Lauren on May 1, 1983. Today was the anniversary of the day he spilled coffee on her in Dinky Town. Late for class, he had barreled out of the second-floor door of McDonald's with his to-go bag, coffee, and books when he crashed into Lauren. If she hadn't attempted to catch the books slipping out of his hand, they never would've met.

With that thought, every cell of Rikk's body felt the same vibration that he felt as he laid awake and watched Lauren float away and disappear just minutes ago. He felt strange, but peaceful. He also knew that this boat was right. He looked forward to getting it. This was Rikk's first flicker of hope for contentment since the cancer consumed Lauren's body and stole her life. At last, Rikk thought he might have a chance to feel alive again.

Chapter 2

Kara

Kara set the ladder up against the hull of *Genie's Bottle* and climbed onboard her sailboat that she had last slept on three nights ago. The following morning she watched it leave Marathon, Florida on the flatbed of a truck heading for Duluth, Minnesota. This morning she walked to *Genie's* bow and looked over all the other boats sitting on stands and cradles in the marina. She wondered how many other owners would come out on May Day, a Tuesday, to prepare their boats for spring launching into the lake.

The lake—Lake Superior—the largest freshwater lake in the world was *her* lake. Kara remembered all the times when the moment her car crested Spirit Mountain her whole being relaxed upon spying *her* lake. The Duluth and Superior cityscapes hugged her lake's western tip. After being away for even as short a time as a weekend, she always felt like she had already arrived home—even though her house in Bayfield was still an hour and a half away. Today she stood on *Genie* and inhaled deeply, soaking in the entire city. The breeze carried the springtime aroma of the grass lawns beginning to green up. The earth's scent would be the predominant smell of her very near future. She would miss being on the water, but at least she had a view of the lake. So many changes had occurred since she lived there, and so many were to come now that she was moving back. The wildest thing was that she only had a vague clue about what to expect. She remembered what Connor had said years earlier, "Don't worry; we'll sail by the seat of our pants." He was right, but it wasn't with reckless abandon. Now with Connor gone and their boat sold, would she fly by the seat of her pants as fearlessly and courageously as they had during the five years they sailed and lived aboard in the southern latitudes? Could her life ever be as fulfilling as it was with Connor? *I guess it's your choice, Kara McKee.*

It had been two years since Kara had last seen Lake Superior, and though it felt like home that time, it had pushed her away. Or did she run away? She had stayed long enough to tie up most loose ends after Connor's death. With their boat on the hard in a marina in St. Vincent, *Genie's Bottle* called Kara back to her and placated her sorrow as she acclimated to life as a widow. Now what was calling her? She shivered at the uncertainty of her answer and rubbed the chill bumps off her crossed arms. This question haunted her and made her doubt her intuition.

Intuition was something Kara had learned to trust implicitly. It plotted her and Connor's course to make the lifestyle change that gave them five years of sailing the Caribbean. With his death, she lost the internal compass that her intuition provided. During much of the past two years, she aimlessly floated throughout the Virgin Islands, alone. Several months ago, she had rediscovered how to follow her intuition, and it put her back on course. That course had brought her to Duluth. Although her new course wasn't crystal clear, every step so far left Kara in a place that felt better than the one she'd just left. She contacted her old friend Dan, who managed Minnesota Point Marina, and he promised to squeeze painting *Genie's* hull into the schedule if Kara would get her scraped and sanded. A newly painted hull was one of the terms of the sale of *Genie's Bottle*—her vagabond home of the last seven years.

※⊙⊛⊙※

Kara looked across Minnesota Point toward Lake Superior. She couldn't wait to be back on her waters, even if launching *Genie's Bottle* commenced Kara's last trip on the lake. It marked her re-emerging into her new life—her new *old* life. Going back home, unclear about what drew her there, Kara sensed she was in for a change that was about to blindside her. *Weird analogy—blindside. Is that my intuition suddenly changing its mind?*

No, it was Kara's saboteur, her inner critic's voice yapping in her head, creating doubt in her decision to sell *Genie* and return home.

Kara had learned to listen to her intuition, and today a feeling arose that something auspicious was looming. Her intuitive instinct hinted her future would unfold in ways she'd never imagine, but she had learned to expect the unexpected.

Kara's saboteur squawked, "Blindsided—oh yes! You *better* expect the unexpected!"

Work was the best way to silence Kara's saboteur, and she had thirty-five feet of Genie's hull to scrape, sand, and have painted before launching her. She needed to get it done by the end of next weekend—six grueling days of labor. That ought to keep her saboteur at bay. She opened the hatch and crawled down the companionway stairs to retrieve her tools.

⁂

Kara shut off the orbital sander, then pulled off her dust mask and let it dangle around her neck. She reached her aching arms overhead, interlaced her fingers, and stretched backwards. A deep inhalation revived her with scents of fresh-cut grass and lilac blossoms being carried on a cool, off shore breeze. She listened to the seagulls screech as they fought over the abandoned donut on the picnic table a few yards away. No doubt, they'd chased the owner away. To Kara, gulls were nothing more than winged rats preying over anything from delectable ducklings to human cuisine that was easily procured with dive-bombing missions. *Sky rats!*

Kara heard the voices of the couple that accompanied a boat broker when she first started scraping *Genie's* hull. The couple was alone now, standing in the cockpit of the freshly painted, midnight green sailboat cradled next to *Genie's Bottle*. The gal, in her blue paisley dress, pressed her opened checkbook onto the back of the fellow's black t-shirt and began to write. She shook the ink down to the tip of the pen then continued writing while in a jubilant voice she said, "May 1st, 2007." Kara watched her tear it out of her checkbook and wave it at the fellow. "It's May Day!" She tousled his curly, red hair, then stepped on the cabin deck and stood holding onto the mast. Her dress rustled in the breeze, and her smile invited the fellow to join her. She spread her hands to the sky and announced to the world, "Some guys buy their girlfriends flowers on May Day, but my beau is buying me a sailboat!"

He said, "Careful what you say, Sophie! 'Mayday' is not a term that you want to casually throw around on the water." Kara noticed that his tall, lanky frame disguised his strength. The sleeves stretched taut around his biceps when he picked Sophie up and flung her around in a circle.

Sophie held on and leaned back. Her long, straight, flaxen hair twirled through the air as did her dress' flounced hem. The celebration was ill suited for the deck of the boat, and Sophie shrieked, "Pete!" and clutched onto him as he bobbled her to keep his footing on the curved topside.

Pete regained his balance as he released her. He clutched her close and nuzzled her behind her ear. "We'd better be careful, or we'll have a 'Mayday' call before she is even ours."

Sophie stepped to the bowsprit; holding onto the forestay, she looked out over the marina. "I'm glad we moved here."

"Even though you miss our friends back home?"

"Yes. We'll make new friends, probably right here from the marina." Sophie flashed Pete an impish grin. "Friends who can help us figure out how to sail this boat."

Pete wrapped his arms around her, drawing her close to him. "Are you afraid?"

"No! Well, kind of. Yeah, it's a little intimidating to think about all we need to learn. Being an eager mate when you were ten and pulling on a rope to bring the sail to the other side doesn't make you a sailor."

"You do think we can do this, don't you?"

"I do. I just need you to promise me that we will take lessons. No matter how busy we get at work, we'll learn how to sail before we make any excursions onto Lake Superior."

"I, Peter Joshua Thomas, do so promise. But you have to promise me something too."

"What?"

"Promise that you'll be a co-captain, not just a first mate."

"So I can ferry you in front of all those Victorian houses along London Road, and you'll be inspired to design great buildings and become the highly-sought-after and successful architect, Peter Joshua Thomas," Sophie said. Pete laughed and kissed the top of her head. She turned to face him and wrapped her arms around his neck. "I promise I'll learn to sail this boat and be the co-captain," she rose onto her toes and kissed him, then said, "and one day we'll own one of those houses?"

"There is nothing I'd like more than to buy you your favorite Victorian house on London Road."

"And start a family?" Sophie's voice had turned mushy and her eyes filled with tears. "You'll be a great dad. We'll be great parents."

"I love your eyes, Sophie Thomas."

"You love my eyes?" Sophie sounded utterly confused, and Kara assumed that Sophie, like her, wondered how Pete jumped from the subject of parenting to her eyes. Kara worked hard to stifle her mirth at their conversation and chastised herself for even listening—although she couldn't wait for his answer.

"I love seeing the world through your eyes," Pete said.

Kara swallowed; she only hoped Sophie was as touched by Pete's gentle and loving response as she was.

"What does the world look like through my eyes?"

"Full of dreams that we both share."

"Yeah?"

"Yeah. You keep reminding me of our dreams, so I don't lose my focus. I love that about you, Sophie. How you see us having everything we want, all our dreams coming true."

"I hope it is more than just a dream, Pete. I really do want to live on the lakeside of London Road in one of those Victorian houses—a small one to raise a couple of incredible children that we always have time to play with while they grow into great adults."

"And they'll be great little first and second mates." Pete kissed her again and hugged her so tightly she gasped for air.

"Then we better buy this boat and figure out what we're doing so we can teach our little mates how to sail."

Kara felt guilty about eavesdropping on the couple. She also could see how secure Sophie felt in Pete's arms and how unbelievably excited they were standing on the boat they were about to buy. It was as if she were watching Connor and her years earlier when they were their age—happy, free, in love. When she overheard their intention of having children, Kara thought, *Oh, please don't buy that boat. If you only knew how possible it was for that boat to cause a 'Mayday' hail, you wouldn't buy it.* That's why she had to stop them. *Not this boat—a boat for sure, just not this one.*

After Kara brushed fine dust and white paint chips off her faded, teal camp shirt and threadbare jeans, she ran her hands through her hair shaking free a cloud of dust from her head. Kara walked over to them and called up, "I'm sorry for intruding, but I overheard the broker and you talking while you were looking at this boat and again just now. I heard you say you're going to buy it. I know it isn't any of my business, but I've been around boats for twenty-five years, and I would never buy *this* boat." Kara read surprise followed by disillusionment on their faces, but she was sure that stepping in was the right thing to do. When they both asked why not, Kara asked permission to board the boat where she pointed out several major problems, some masked under a fresh top coat of paint.

Although Sophie had showed her disappointment that they had not bought that boat on May Day, she did thank Kara for sharing her knowledge. The three had made a bargain. Pete and Sophie would return later this evening and evenings during the week to help Kara scrape and sand *Genie's* hull. In exchange for their labor, Kara agreed to spend the next weekend boat hunting with them and to give them a few lessons whenever they found the right boat. Sophie and Pete also agreed to research brokerages online to locate all potential boats from Knife River to Ashland before next weekend.

※⊙⊙☙↞

Kara said goodbye to Sophie and Pete, then glanced at her watch. She spent almost two hours with them, but she didn't feel panicked about lost time since they'd be back soon to help her. As she pulled her dust mask over her mouth and nose, she noticed an older fisherman staring at her again. It wasn't a menacing stare, more sad. He seemed well known in the marina and well liked by the jovial greetings he received.

"Dutch!" one boater shouted, "How the hell are you?" He returned this greeting with a polite nod and a subdued hello, just like he'd done with everyone else that Kara saw greet him. It was so odd to see this man, Dutch, refuse to engage in the spring reunions with boater friends he hadn't seen all winter. "Not your day, huh?" the fellow said to Dutch. "Hey, tomorrow remind me to tell you about the fish I caught this winter in the Florida Keys." These friends seemed to accept his unresponsiveness; somehow, they all knew he'd join in tomorrow. However, today, every time Kara caught a glimpse of him, he stood brooding in the cockpit. He appeared to be drinking up the sights and sounds of boaters doing their pre-season projects.

His boat certainly could use some scrubbing to remove the winter's dirt from her deck. *So odd*, Kara thought, Dutch's boat appeared to be home-built and cared for reverently, which was evident right down to the lines coiled in perfect shape, hanging with a rolling hitch knot to the rail. But then there was *Miss Sea's* hull—it needed to be painted much more than *Genie's* did. Maybe the reason why Dutch didn't scrub *Miss Sea* was to preserve some of the paint on her hull.

Chapter 3

Dutch

"Hey, you're the lady that has that double-ender sailboat, *Genie's Bottle*," Dutch greeted Kara when she walked into the marina's lobby. "Saw her as soon as I drove into the marina yesterday. What's she, thirty-four, naw, must be least thirty-five feet long? From the looks of it, she's a salty. Just get here?" He didn't wait for Kara to reply, "Wasn't here a couple of weeks ago when I drove into the marina. Them snow banks were scattered through the parking lot—too deep to drive up to *Miss Sea*. Always feel like a kid again in the spring when the sun bakes the snow off *Miss Sea*."

"Um, I guess I forgot how long the snow lingered up here in the spring," Kara said.

Dutch grinned, then said, "Yep, should've had them paint her over the winter. Needs a paint job bad—had it scheduled for next week, but Dan said someone needs to get their boat painted 'fore they sell it. That wouldn't be you, would it?"

"Uh, um, yeah, it probably is me. My buyer wants *Genie's Bottle* painted before he writes the check. I hope that hasn't caused you any inconvenience?"

"Naw, I've been a monkey on Dan's back because I wanted *Miss Sea* painted this week so I can launch her. Couldn't get her fit in till next week, and that didn't settle with me. That's too long before I'm catching the first lake trout of the season. Don't think Dan meant it when he asked me if I wanted *Miss Sea* launched Friday and painted in July. Should of seen his eyes when I said, 'Hell yeah.'" Dutch laughed and was glad to see she laughed with him. "Least then the fishing bug ain't so strong in July. Told me last night he's going to launch it tomorrow. Don't know who got moved

11

back, but that's two days early. Good news for me, I'll be out catching fish tomorrow. You like fish?"

"Yes. I love fish. By the way, I'm Kara McKee, and you are Dutch, right?"

After a hearty laugh, Dutch said, "Yeah, guess you heard my name a couple of times yesterday. Didn't feel much like talking, but I'm over it now. Just my day with *Miss Sea*—always been, always will be."

"Really. Every May Day?"

"Yep. For forty-five years."

"Why, or is that too personal?"

"Naw. It was forty-five May Days ago that Pa and my brothers gave me their interests in her. We all built her when I was just a kid, called her Miss Sara after my little sister. I changed her name to *Miss Sea* after I got her."

"So you don't buy the sailor superstitions of doom when you change a boat's name?"

"Naw, figure she needed a new name since they was going to sell her anyway."

"How does your little sister feel about your changing the boat's name?"

"Don't know. Ain't never asked her."

"Why did you choose Sea to replace Sara?" Kara said.

Remorse washed over Dutch, and he wondered if she realized how tempted he was to answer her question, and that shocked him. Nobody ever made him even consider answering it before. He wasn't stumped for words often, but he couldn't think of one thing to say.

Kara broke the uncomfortable silence and in a caring yet light-hearted voice when she said, "Hey Dutch, do you remember that song, *Brandy* by Looking Glass? The chorus was: 'Brandy, you're a fine girl, what a good wife you would be, but my life, my lover, my lady is the sea.'"

Dutch grimaced and stared out the window at *Miss Sea*, perched on her jack-stands, and wondered how it'd feel to answer her question. As Dutch returned his gaze, he caught Kara looking at him as if he was a lost puppy. That good feeling rushed through him. Kara was one of the decent people—really cared about others and wasn't standing here talking to him cause she felt she had to be polite either. He gave no reply.

Kara smiled and bit her lower lip. "Hmm. I think it came out in the late sixties. Maybe your *Miss Sea* inspired the song?"

"Maybe," Dutch gave a rueful smile and contemplated her words.

"Actually, I came up here to use the restroom, so please excuse me." Kara said as she walked past Dutch.

"Oh. Sorry. I'll catch you later." Dutch scratched the top of his head and watched her walk into the ladies' room, then crossed his arms. He wondered if she had any idea how her questions cut to the bone. She was the first person ever that he almost told his story to—the story of why forty-five May Days ago his family gave him their interests in the boat.

Dutch lost himself in his memories of when he returned from the Indochina War and found himself standing in front of the boat. His older brother, John, was in Duluth on behalf of the others to list the boat for sale, and he stumbled on Dutch sitting in the cockpit. Dutch was trying to figure out what he would do now that he was out of the service. John saw the tear in his eye that morning, and probably thought his little brother was choked up about the boat, and that was fine with Dutch. He'd never admit what caused that tear because it's what Dutch hoped none of them would remember. Two years before that Duluth morning, Dutch left Marshville for the navy. That was May 1st, 1960; he was just seventeen— and on the run. All the townspeople had probably gotten over the scandal by the time his enlistment was up, but he never returned home. He could never forget—nor forgive himself.

While in the navy and merchant marines, Dutch spent every May Day alone as much as he possibly could. Every May Day since he retired he spent secluded on *Miss Sea* brooding over those things he could never change. He shook his head; reminding himself his annual day of reverence was yesterday. *Ain't gonna change nothing moping over the past either.*

Yesterday the classic lines of *Genie's Bottle* stole more of his attention than he intended. Or was it her—the slender attractive woman that appeared to be the sole owner, scraping her hull? He still didn't know anything about her, but that'd soon change.

"Hey, Jessie, I need another cup of coffee."

Kara

Kara didn't expect later to be a few minutes after she emerged from the ladies' shower and bathrooms. Dutch held out a cup of coffee he'd bought at the ship store for her.

"I buy coffee here every morning, find out what's new and see if anyone needs help. You got those kids helping you with your boat. They coming back today?"

"Thank you for the coffee, and yes, they are coming back after work to help me." Dutch walked with Kara to *Genie's Bottle*, talking the whole way. She wasn't surprised when he picked up a scraper and started scraping on *Genie's* hull.

Kara had no idea that this was just the beginning—that Dutch would dote on her every chance he got. He would fill her in on all the marina activities and report on the boaters who had arrived and who wouldn't be back this year. He'd tell her who was new and what couples changed partners over the winter. Kara didn't know these people, but she found Dutch fascinating. A gossip, sure, but always in a no-shame, no-blame way. She could imagine him saying, "Just the facts, ma'am," after he recounted the news.

"So they ain't buying it, are they?"

Dutch's question hijacked Kara from her thoughts. "What?"

"Those kids, you set them straight about that boat yesterday, didn't you? They buying the other one you showed them?"

"No, I just showed it to them to compare the two. I thought it'd help them figure out how to find a sound boat."

"Good. I could've showed them a couple of things too."

Dutch kept on scraping, but Kara turned to watch him. When he finally stopped and faced her, she said, "Then why didn't you?"

"It wasn't my day to save anyone." Dutch's words growled out, and he turned his gaze back to *Miss Sea*. He ended the conversation, taking powerful strokes with the scraper.

She looked out over the marina's nearly empty docks and the parking areas filled with boats sitting on the hard and wondered what he meant by that. Kara went back to scraping, sneaking peaks at Dutch as she contemplated the baffling paradox of his actions.

Dutch brought his ladder over on Wednesday when he got in from his first fishing trip of the season. He worked alongside her until lunch time and then a couple of hours that afternoon. It became his schedule over the next three days. He quizzed her about her life, family, and her and Connor's travels in the Caribbean. Kara didn't know if they got more done together than she did alone since they often stopped while Dutch told his sea-going stories and gave marina updates—all nonjudgmental except for one. Today he clearly didn't approve of the teenage girl who was too obviously interested in Ted, the young sailor who worked summers at the marina preparing and launching boats. "You see that hussy chasing after Ted, making a damn fool of herself—worse than a wild cat in heat," Dutch said pointing at her.

Kara stopped scraping the bow and could see the girl was fawning all over Ted, who seemed to be disinterested. Kara looked at Dutch—her jaw dropped. "Dutch, I've never heard you say one disparaging word about anyone. I'm shocked. I guess, I didn't think you were capable of speaking unkindly of others."

"Never liked it when girls chased after me. Not that I don't like girls. I do. I just never found anyone that compared to Ch—" Dutch looked out over the marina, and his eyes seemed to land on *Miss Sea*. His furrowed brow deepened and his voice mellowed. "Girls I knew acted like ladies. You'd never see them putting on a burlesque show out in public and humiliating themselves and the poor devil they was after." His scraper swept across the hull as if it was motorized and gouged through the bottom paint.

The raw nerve Kara's comment struck was the only time Dutch resembled the man whom she first witnessed on May Day, purposely alone, in what she now understood to be a solitary suffering he endured annually

15

on his boat. But why? Kara watched him furiously gouge through the paint and decided it would be a great time to bring up a new subject that would change Dutch's focus—and save *Genie*'s hull.

"Dutch, you told me that your Pa and brothers *gave* you *Miss Sea* forty-five years ago. I'm wondering if they were going to *sell* it, why didn't you buy it?"

Dutch stopped scraping and gave a sigh. His mood seemed to lighten, but the spark wasn't back in his eyes. Kara crawled down the ladder and said, "Time for a break."

Kara watched Dutch hesitantly descend the ladder. She grabbed her water bottle and took a swig from it while Dutch sat down on the stepladder. She passed the bottle to him and sat down on the ground, preparing herself for a long story that would derail often but would provide understanding to his life story. Kara sensed it was a story Dutch was long overdue telling, and he seemed comfortable—or maybe just resigned—to tell it now.

Dutch paused often to carefully choose his words that were steeped with sadness, yet he seemed reconciled with their truth. "I returned from the Indochina War with no intention of reuniting with my family. I come to Duluth to see if Miss Sara was launched but she was still on the hard, so I put the ladder up to her and crawled aboard. That was May Day, 1962. I was just sitting in the cockpit when my oldest brother, John, climbed up the ladder and caught me sitting there. He'd been sent by Pa and the others to list the boat. John was gonna pull everything they wanted off the boat before he met the broker. He didn't know what to expect when he found a ladder leaning against the hull. John never expected to see me sitting in the cockpit. Said so, and said I looked clean. Still don't know what he meant. Guess my windbreaker and faded navy work pants didn't look so bad. That was a change—John used to say I only wanted things I couldn't afford. Said the worst was I wanted friends who outclassed me. Hell, my family could never afford much more than the necessities, but we was always clean and well kept, even if our clothes were hand-me-downs. They first were handed down from my cousins and then through my four big brothers, until nothing remained to be handed down. I was at the tail end of the family. Every once in a while I was lucky enough to get a pair of jeans that didn't have patches on them. They'd never last though. Seems like the first time I wore them my knees poked through." Dutch laughed at this. "Now days I give my pants away when the knees start to fade. Wonder what John thinks of that."

Kara watched him slap the scraper on his knee. She knew he was uncomfortable with wherever that thought took him. Gently, she said, "So, John gave you the boat?"

"John took me to breakfast, and it didn't take long for him to figure out that I wasn't ever going back home. He excused himself, said he had to go to the bathroom, but he didn't come back for a long time. I was about to go find him, then he slid back into the booth. He told me he called Pa. They was giving the old boat to me. I guess they thought they'd least have a way to find me."

"In forty-five years you've never gone home?"

"Nope."

"Do you see your brothers and sister often?"

"Nope. But they come see me here, and I take them and their kids out fishing."

"Why haven't you ever gone back?"

Dutch stood up and extended his hand to Kara. Helping her stand was more than a kind gesture, it was a clear message that the conversation was over. His mood brightened and out of nowhere said, "What's your plan?"

"My plan?"

"Yeah. When you get back to Bayfield? You got someone you moving back for?"

"What? No. No, I—I guess I have a pretty loose-knit plan right now."

"What you mean—loose-knit plan?"

"I guess it will take some time to get settled into our house—my house, then I'll amp up my business and let life lead me."

"Let life lead you?"

"I'm open to what life brings. I'll be happy with what turns up."

He shook his head and rubbed his whiskers below his crumpled nose. "You'll be happy with what turns up? What the hell does that mean?"

"I don't know. It's my belief, I guess. I choose to live in full appreciation of every moment, even if in this moment I'm scraping my boat. I appreciate talking to someone I just met about, well, about my plan—even if I don't have a completely clear plan."

"No plan! Sounds like you plan to plant your nose in *amping* up your business. Hell, you'll end up an old widow. You're going to live all alone in the house that you and—what's his name, Connor—built and raised kids in. You're going to be lonely."

Probably, Kara thought, and she began climbing her ladder. Dutch just stood there shaking his head, scratching his chin, and waiting for her to respond. She stopped halfway up the ladder and said, "You know, for someone I just met a few days ago, I like you—a lot. Even if you don't understand how I live. I've never known change to not have some lonely moments. But lonely is a choice just as much as anything else is. I don't plan on being lonely." Kara leaned her hip into the ladder and pushed up her sweatshirt sleeves, then smiled at him. "Don't worry about me, Dutch. If I ever get too lonely, I'll come visit you."

"Maybe I won't be here. I'm not that young."

"You're not that old either, and my guess is that you're going to be around for a long, long time."

Dutch handed her the scraper. "If you ain't planning on being lonely, then you better start planning on finding someone." Then he stomped away.

⚜

Kara watched him go and knew he'd be back again. She looked at her watch and snorted a laugh. In only three days she had come to know Dutch and feel his fatherly kinship. Instead of being put off by Dutch's disapproval of her acceptance lack of a plan and acceptance of being lonely, she was drawn to him. She was drawn back to Duluth, drawn back to Minnesota Point Marina, drawn back to her old hometown, drawn back to—what? What was it? Duluth, the marina, and Bayfield all seemed reasonable, but there was something bigger. Being drawn to Dutch didn't make it clearer.

Kara blinked her eyes to clear those often-repeated and answerless questions from her head. She expected that some of those answers would be clear to her by now, or at least clearer. *Why do I need to return?* She had a plan, and she hadn't been blindsided yet even if it was a loose-knit plan.

She'd deliver *Genie's Bottle* to the new owner and teach him how to sail her. Then Kara would build up her coaching clientele, and settle into her house. OK, there weren't many details to her plan, but things would fall into place.

Her stomach growled and rumbled, carrying on as if it were rioting against Kara's belief that her loose-knit plan would come about as simple and straightforward as it currently was spelled out.

Kara refused to worry about it and instead practiced what she had learned before she and Connor set out on their cruise. It had changed their lives and made their cruise possible. Since then she always tried to practice it—to think about what she wanted, feel how it would be to have what she wanted, and visualize having what she wanted right now rather than bemoaning the past and worrying about the future. Worrying was just praying for what you didn't want. After Connor's death, it became a struggle to practice it, but it was getting easier.

Kara knew what she didn't want—she didn't want to give any energy to worrying about what else drew her back here. As she'd done so many times before, she changed her worrying to consciously thinking about what she did want. But since she didn't know exactly what that was, for now she would change her thoughts to something she appreciated. Kara also knew enough to let go of figuring out the details and allow her loose-knit plan to firm up by some synchronistic occurrence.

It was a beautiful Friday morning, and with Sophie, Pete and Dutch's help, Kara still had the port side of the bow to finish by Monday—only three days away. She had to get busy since she agreed to help Sophie and Pete with their search for a sailboat over the weekend.

Kara thought of Dutch; what an old salt. For sixty-four, he maneuvered swiftly on his trawler, with more agility than many men half his age. His thick, silver hair highlighted his deeply wrinkled and tanned face. Dutch was about six feet tall and must have been over six feet as a young man. He lovingly and meticulously maintained *Miss Sea*. From the merchant marine tales he told, she figured he must have been quite young when they built her. She knew little of Dutch's early years, and she didn't expect to learn details about it any time soon.

The second day Kara was in the marina, Dutch invited her onboard *Miss Sea* for a late afternoon beer. This gave Kara the opportunity to get a closer inspection. Her eyes looked past the sun-scorched hull to the immaculately clean and orderly condition that he kept her cabin. She was impressed by the impeccable care he bestowed to her interior; everything shined and was perfectly stowed, as it was topsides. Dutch was a treasure, and she got a sense that he was part of her reason for coming home.

Chapter 4

Kara

Over the weekend, Sophie and Pete picked up Kara and together they looked at one more sailboat in Duluth and two in Superior, and then they traveled to Cornucopia. There they found their perfect starter sailboat.

The fiberglass boat had a two-foot draft, tiller, and outboard motor; and it was equipped with necessities such as a compass, marine radio, wind speed and direction indicators, and depth finder. The sails had to be raised on the deck, common with a twenty-year-old boat this size. Its cabin was small and convenient, and the head separated the V-berth from the cabin, but it was just large enough to accommodate a port-a-potty. The hanging locker had only enough space for their foul-weather gear, and the table collapsed down to make a cramped double berth.

When Sophie and Pete pulled their boat into the marina parking lot, Kara was waiting to congratulate them. After helping them step the mast, rig the sails, and launch the boat, she noticed how nervous they appeared. They had been humble and eager learners so far and had expressed their respect for the water, especially for Lake Superior. They were relieved when Kara told them she wouldn't take them out onto the lake until they were ready for it.

Today they'd sail the St. Louis River basin. "Time for your maiden voyage," Kara said and removed the dock line from the cleat. They motored out of the marina into the basin towards Spirit Lake, feeling the warm eight-knot breeze blowing off the land. It was a perfect evening for sailing. Kara instructed Sophie to steer their twenty-five foot boat into the wind while she helped Pete hoist the main sail and then the jib. They went back into the cockpit, and Kara told Sophie, "OK, you are going to fall off, which means you are going to steer the boat away from the wind. You can go either to port or to starboard. I would suggest we go to port and just take a nice leisurely sail and get used to the feel of her. To go to port you need to push the tiller to starboard. So whenever you are ready, push it slowly, and you'll feel the wind fill the sails. Pete, you are going to sheet in the jib on the port side as soon as the wind starts to fill it." She helped them through the motions and trimmed the sails, explaining the process as they went.

Kara couldn't help but smile at Sophie's thrilled expression as the boat began to move under the power of the wind. Pete gave Sophie a victorious look when he shut off the motor. Then he hugged Sophie and stole a kiss. The boat drifted back upwind in their celebration moment. The sails began to luff and sounded like flags snapping in the wind, and sheer panic spread on their faces. Kara laughed. She pushed the tiller to starboard, and the sails refilled as the boat resumed its silent course.

Kara explained how to tack and jibe to change course and then guided them through several of both as they spent three hours sailing until the golden dusk ended their lesson. Kara walked up to the forestay to give them some privacy as they steered their boat on a long tack toward the marina.

When they got close to the marina's entrance, Kara walked back to the cockpit. Pete announced, "Sophie just thought of the perfect name for our boat. She whispered to me that we can whisper and hear each other. We're naming her *Whisper*."

Sophie started *Whisper*'s motor and Pete and Kara dropped the sails just before they got to the marina entrance. They agreed to meet the next evening for another lesson.

⁂

As Kara watched the sun set over the St. Louis River basin, she remembered her initial conversation with Sophie and Pete. She glanced back at them and waved while they got into their car, and she laughed at the effervescent Sophie hanging out her window and blowing her a kiss. She had just given them their first sailing lesson, and although they didn't know it, they provided Kara with the perfect reason to stay in Duluth while *Genie* was being painted. Sophie wanted to pay her hotel bill to compensate Kara for staying in Duluth and giving them sailing lessons, but Kara refused and was happy for the excuse not to go to Bayfield. It wasn't so much she didn't want to be there; she just didn't want to arrive in Bayfield by land. She had always envisioned her return sailing up to the Bayfield city docks. It would be her last voyage ever on *Genie* and her first time back home since Connor's funeral. Maybe it was silly, but it was important to her that she arrive back home in the same way that Connor and she had left.

Kara walked back to her hotel and thought about the May Day twenty-five years ago when Connor brought her flowers, and she gave him a sailing magazine. Was it then that Connor had set his intention to blue-water sail? She laughed when she thought about how frustrated she was with all the new sailing terms Connor started to use. He had to explain that blue-water was sailing jargon for the open ocean.

Kara remembered a couple days before Connor's sudden death they decided to live-aboard permanently, and sail to Polynesia. Their next trip to Bayfield was supposed to be to sell their house. She shuddered at the recollection of their plan. The reality was that her next trip was for Connor's funeral. She never imagined that two years later she would be moving back into their house without him and would be selling *Genie* to acquaintances in Bayfield.

Kara sighed. As she walked past *Whisper*, she purposely turned her thoughts back to Sophie and Pete's joy and excitement in sailing. It was good to share her knowledge with a couple who seemed to rekindle Kara's memories of the fun she and Connor experienced with their first boat. It reminded her to feel the joy that she wanted in her future as if she already had it now. It would come only then.

She didn't expect that giving Sophie and Pete sailing lessons would grant her a new nickname. Though Kara did not have her license, she soon became known as Captain Kara among the boaters in the marina who were busy readying their boats for launching. Though she had been the captain of *Genie's Bottle* ever since Connor's funeral, she just never thought of herself with that title. How odd for that label to come at the *end* of her sailing career.

But then, maybe it wasn't the end. A chill ran through her. Kara's intuition told her she was in for a surprise.

Chapter 5

Rikk

Rikk read the email twice, just to make sure he got all the information. The truck would deliver his Ocean Sail Quest boat on Thursday morning, provided transit from Maine happened without a hitch. Thursday was three days away, and it was perfect timing. He wouldn't have to rearrange his schedule, as that was his day off. He sat in his office in the Duluth Clinic, staring in disbelief that his dream of owning a sailboat was becoming a reality. Exciting, yes, but it was equally frightening, maybe more so.

A knock on Rikk's door interrupted his private moment and the department's newest surgeon, Dr. Heidi Norris, stepped into his office. *Damn it, what stupid reason does she have for consulting me today?* Her constant and blatant attempts to win his affection irritated him and kept him on constant guard. What else could he do to send a polite message that he was not interested? He hoped he wouldn't have to be blatant and tell her he wasn't attracted to her, but she had missed all the signals he'd already sent. She was a beautiful young woman that had no clue how to handle rejection. Everything she wanted she worked tenaciously for until she got. With a stellar performance through medical school, she was an outstanding surgeon and an asset to the practice.

Now, that Heidi was well on her way to establishing her career, men became her current conquests—or more accurately, casualties. Her reckless voyages with men ended soon after they committed to dating exclusivity. Heidi always moved on to bigger and better catches. Rikk wasn't interested in an escapade into her fantasies, no matter if, at times, her lithe body and alluring advances tempted him. He wasn't attracted to the immature games she played. But worst of all, even with the intentional distance he kept from her, his strict professional association with her seemed to increase her desire to make him her latest conquest.

"Rikk, I'm sorry to bother you, but I was wondering if you'd take a look at these test results. I wonder if I'm missing something." She walked into his office as if it was her own and stopped behind his desk with her hip cozy against his arm.

"Heidi, I've been looking at your patient's charts and results for months now. You proved yourself competent the first day you arrived. I trust your judgment."

Heidi flashed a charming smile at him and held the chart out and said, "Please, just take a look."

Rikk couldn't believe he felt sorry for her, even when Heidi irritated the hell out of him. Grabbing the chart from her seemed the only polite thing to do, but it was done with haste. "Let me see it." He shook his head in the slightest way and frowned at her, partly because the way he'd barked out his words would've dismayed Lauren, who always told him he didn't accomplish anything with rudeness. Now, Lauren was gone, and gone with her was the invisible barrier that kept women like Heidi Norris at bay. He didn't want her attention, but avoiding her had become a burdensome part of his days. He scanned the reports that accompanied the lab results and x-rays. He clenched his teeth to hold back his impatience with her, but regretted it because it gave her a moment to get to the point of her visit.

"Is it true that you just bought a sailboat? I grew up sailing the—"

"Dr. Norris, what is your question about your patient?" His words reprimanded her. For Lauren he held his tongue and didn't say all the things welled inside of him that would curtail all Heidi's future advances. Rikk's tried patience was further tested as he listened to Heidi's concerns and even more as he agreed with her care plan. He looked at his watch and told her he had patients to see and was relieved that his phone rang. He had been informed his first patient was waiting in the exam room. "I'll be right there," he said into the phone and scowled at Heidi. She thanked him and strode out into the hall, holding the door for him. He had noticed that the office staff had begun to detect Heidi's attention had turned to him; he only hoped they also observed his attempts to thwart it.

Chapter 6

Kara

Even though *Genie*'s hull was ready to be painted on Monday, she couldn't get painted until Tuesday because of the marina's backlog of work. The marina launched *Genie* and set her mast Wednesday morning, leaving Kara the rest of the day to rig *Genie*. Dutch insisted on helping her. Although she could have done it herself, the extra hands made the process speed by. She, in turn, insisted on helping him pull a wire from his marine radio to his cockpit speaker. Kara enjoyed Dutch's fatherly attention, and he seemed to enjoy treating her like a daughter.

Kara wondered if he had always been a bachelor. Dutch's romantic involvement, or lack thereof, was the only area of his life that was never discussed. More than never discussed, the mere mention of it was a sure method to shut him down. She wondered if Dutch would ever let his guard down with her enough that he'd be able to release that apparently painful slice of his history. She guessed there was a woman he had fallen in love with, and no other woman ever came close to win Dutch's heart. Kara's gut instinct made her believe it was the one unresolved issue in his life. She also knew it was Dutch's choice to hang on to it or release it.

⁂

Kara awoke Thursday to the sound of early morning traffic, mostly coming from U.S. Intestate 35. She rolled onto her back and fluffed her pillow; then she shut her eyes and allowed her imagination free rein. This practice helped Kara see and then get what she wanted. She visualized *Genie* motoring out of the canal into the westernmost tip of Lake Superior. Kara saw *Genie*'s main sail luff as she pointed her into the wind and hoisted the sail to the top of the mast. Kara imagined herself steering and felt

Genie lurch as she began to fall off and gain speed as the wind filled her main. She listed comfortably as she sliced through the waves with ease and grace. Kara saw herself pulling out the jib and setting *Genie*'s course east into the rising sun. She would glance back at the gentle wake cutting through the lakes' glassy surface mirroring the diffused billowing clouds and magenta sky.

Squawks of seagulls scavenging for whatever they could find yanked Kara back to reality. She squeezed her eyes tight, hoping it would keep her fixed in her vision of sailing home. However, the moment passed. She crawled out of her berth and looked out the porthole.

Today is a perfect day for a crossing. High winds and possible thunderstorms were forecasted to move in and out of the region later tonight, followed by fair weather on Friday. Later a low pressure system would move in, bringing a couple of days of rain and isolated and severe thunderstorms.

Kara was in a great mood after her first good night's sleep in weeks, which she credited to *Genie's Bottle* rocking her to sleep. She stretched. *God, it's good to sleep in my own bed.* Her words froze as their reality stung. Her mood faded as she said aloud to herself, *Geez, it'll only be my bed for two more nights.* Kara shook her head. She was determined that her saboteur would not spoil her mood this beautiful morning. In fact, she was determined to continue with her plans, loose-knit as they may be. They had served her fine so far, and she knew they'd continue to do so if she would relax and let them lead her.

Kara wasn't really feeling that fine about her loose-knit plans. She was tired of all these twinges of doubt. Whatever that gut-wrenching feeling was, it didn't feel good. She'd have to figure it out later and, in the meantime, keep her thoughts on it all turning out even better than anything she imagined.

Kara dressed, made her punch list, and gathered her rolling carts. Her first mission was to go to the beach for meditation, journaling, and yoga. Then she'd head to Bay Side Market for provisions. After stowing them, she'd recheck the rigging and do all the maintenance required just before *Genie*'s final voyage.

In an effort not to disturb Dutch, Kara quietly opened *Genie*'s hatch. She peeked to see if he was up yet. *Miss Sea* was docked closer to the shore with only the finger dock and one open slip separating their boats. Kara smiled at the fact that *Genie* had been assigned a slip near *Miss Sea* and understood Dan put her in this slip instead of a transient slip on another dock because Dutch and she had become fast friends over the week.

Dutch usually was up by this hour, but they talked late into the night after they shared Dutch's fried Lake Superior lake trout he caught that morning and her vegetable salad she marinated in a fresh herb vinaigrette.

As quietly as Kara could, she left *Genie*, carrying the rolling carts until she got to the sidewalk. It was almost eight when Kara walked through the marina entrance. She had to wait for a semi-truck before crossing the street. What appeared to be a brand new sailboat was loaded on its trailer. Road grime dulled its hull, but Kara had seen enough new boats to know that when it was cleaned up its navy blue topcoat of paint would glisten. With its brass dorades and portholes, it was a classic styled boat. Kara only had seen a couple Ocean Sailing Quest sailboats, but knew OSQ's were stout blue-water cruisers. She scanned the parking lot to see who would emerge to greet the vessel. She always enjoyed watching boat owners as they took possession of their new boats. Typically, they burst with pride while caressing its hull, climbing up the ladder, rummaging around the cockpit, inspecting and fiddling with the hardware, and spinning all the winches. She couldn't wait around to watch this boat's new owner's arrival if she planned to be ready to sail tomorrow.

Walking towards the beach, Kara thought about how perfect her week and a half in Duluth had been, especially how the last few days gave her time to help Sophie and Pete with *Whisper*. She was grateful for the gift they'd unknowingly given her—they reminded her to dwell on what she wanted rather than to dwell on the past. Kara wanted to be happy again, as she was with Connor, and knew that it would only come by starting within herself. Sophie and Pete made her feel happy and now she had started to attract other joyful people into her life, including Dutch, and hopefully many more.

Dutch

Dutch woke to the sound of Kara's carts clattering up the sidewalk. He was going to miss her. He pulled himself out of his berth, dressed, and headed for the marina men's room. After using it, he made his usual stop at the ship's store to buy coffee and then banter with Jessie, the store's clerk, as they did every morning while Dutch drank his coffee. He noticed a semi parked near the boat lift with a navy-blue-hulled sailboat loaded on its trailer. Other than road dust, the boat looked shiny new as if it just rolled off the showroom floor. When Jessie finished taking a slip reservation by phone, Dutch said, "Hey Jessie, who's got the new boat?"

"I don't know, Dutch. I find out all the gossip around here from you."

"I don't gossip. If it's all true, it ain't gossip."

Dan, the marina manager, walked by them on his way out to meet the truck driver. Dutch dashed out and caught up with him.

"Hey, Dan, looks like we got a new boat in the marina. They gonna stay here the year?"

"Should've known you'd be the first one to hit me up for news on the boat's owner." Dan never broke stride, and Dutch matched his pace as together they marched across the marina to the truck. "I suppose you're going to tag along until you snoop out what you want to know, so I might as well give in, so I can get my work done."

"I ain't snooping out nothing. Us sailors are family. Always ready to lend a helping hand. What boat is he stepping up from?"

"This is his first boat."

"Humph! Fancy boat for a first. He sail much?"

"You know, Dutch, from what I can tell he doesn't have that much experience, but he is a quiet guy and I think he likes it that way. Don't bug him today." The truck driver was getting out of the cab when Dan greeted him, "Good morning. I'm Dan Johnson. I've just called the owner, and he'll be here in a few minutes with the check. You can park the trailer over there, and we'll get it lifted first thing."

"Sounds good, but the paperwork has to be finished before I take the straps off the boat."

"Yes, of course."

"So, just to be sure, this is for—" The driver looked for the buyer's name on the bill of lading, "Dr. Rikkert Harmon."

"Yes, Rikk Harmon." Dan said. They stepped aside while the truck driver got back into the cab and started to pull away.

"He's a doctor?" Dutch said.

"Yep, he's a doctor."

"What kind?"

"I don't know—a surgeon or something. Dutch, I got work to do and don't have time for all your questions. I can't stop you from hanging out. Just do me a favor, and give the doctor some space."

"If he ain't got much experience, then he probably could use a hand getting her docked. Forecasting a mighty blow coming tonight. Where you putting her?"

"Actually, I was thinking about the slip between you and Kara for just that reason."

"Then I'll stick around to be introduced," Dutch saw impatience cross Dan's face, "After the paperwork's done and the boys are lifting her."

"Sounds good." Dan walked after the truck, leaving Dutch to mull around and chat with other owners preparing their boats for launching.

Dutch spied a black, two-door BMW convertible drive in and park. The fellow was new to the marina. He headed down to the new boat, giving Dutch an opportunity to size him up. Dutch was talking to Sophie and Pete, who dropped by to grab Sophie's purse that she'd left on *Whisper* last night. As the new owner walked past, Dutch said, "Good morning."

"Good morning."

"We was just admiring your new boat. She's a beauty."

"Thank you." Rikk smiled and waved a check at them, "I guess they need my check before they unload it."

"Unload *her*," Dutch said, "Vessels are ladies of the sea. Even those big lakers with men names are ladies of the sea. Awe, you better go pay for her, or Dan will chew me out for holding everybody up."

⚓

Dutch walked down to the lift slip where Dan and the owner were talking.

"Rikk, this is Dutch. Dutch, Dr. Rikk Harmon. Dutch is a fisherman who has spent most his life on the water."

"I'm pleased to meet you, Dutch. You can call me Rikk." Rikk reached his hand out to Dutch.

"Likewise."

Dan said, "I'm going to put your boat in the slip next to Dutch's. He'll help you dock her and help you with anything else you want to know. Just don't be afraid to cut him off, or he'll chew your ears off with his merchant marine stories."

Dutch took the good-natured ribbing well and laughed with the others. Then he said, "Captain Kara will be on her other side, and she's just back from sailing the Caribbean. She'll know the answers to all your sailing questions."

Surprise flashed in the Doc's eyes, followed by a hint of a smile. Dutch didn't know what it meant, but he sure as hell was going to find out.

"Ain't many women captains around, Doc, guess you're lucky to be docked next to one."

Rikk nodded and fixed a stoic expression.

"Got a funny feeling that there was something about a woman captain that makes you uneasy, Doc. Hope you don't mind me calling you Doc?"

"Not at all, and I'm not uneasy about a woman captain, either. I guess I never gave any thought to captains being men or women until you mentioned Captain Kara."

"She ain't no she-man, either." The Doc was pinching back his laughter, but Dan snickered and shook his head. "She's a real good sailor and nice about it. Pretty too. Kara can tell you anything you need to know about sailing. I'm always around to tell you anything you want to know about boat handling and the water. Happy to give you a hand whenever you need one."

"I appreciate your offer, Dutch, and will try not to take up too much of your time. I will take advantage of your boat-handling knowledge."

"Doc, one thing you ought to know about sailors. We watch out for each other, no matter how long we've known you. Once you're in a boat, your part of our kin."

The loudspeaker bellowed, "Dan, you have a call on line four." Before he left he said, "Just be careful, Rikk, or Dutch will forget to go fishing."

"I was just heading back to *Miss Sea*; she's my boat. I'll be watching for you, Doc."

"Thanks. I'll see you later," Rikk said.

Kara

Kara left the beach after her yoga salutations and morning meditation and walked to the Bay Side Market, the only grocery store on Minnesota Point. Kara loved the store and its perseverance, holding on as one of the few neighborhood grocery stores still open in Duluth. It had a clean and bright atmosphere for such a small market. Kara filled her cart with sandwich makings, fruits, vegetables, nuts and other snacks for her crossing. She couldn't believe they still had her favorite local gourmet coffee–Lake Superior Morning Blend. She steered her cart to the checkout lane.

A fellow who had just finished pumping gasoline entered the store. "Good morning," he handed his credit card to the clerk and looked at the *Duluth News Tribune's* cover story about road maintenance and construction that would be starting on the following Monday.

"Good morning," said an older woman who was standing behind the counter.

He pulled a paper off the rack and set it on the counter. "Add this in too, will you? I guess I better figure out a new route to work before Monday."

"Can you believe they just got the work on the Lift Bridge done, and they are starting to tear up the downtown streets?" she said.

"It's going to be a pain, but they sure need to do some major repairs. Yesterday I followed someone who dropped his tire into a pothole the size of a Volkswagen. Their bumper nearly bottomed out, and I thought for sure they'd have a flat," he said while signing his receipt.

"Well, no use complaining about it. It does need to be done," she said and handed his credit card back. "Have a good day."

"Thanks. You have a good one too."

Kara placed her groceries on the counter and gazed around the checkout one last time. Her eyes fell on a dark chocolate bar. Dark chocolate was a vice that she was unwilling to give up, and she tossed a couple of the bars onto the counter.

The woman checked her out while Kara packed her groceries into her canvas shore bags and placed them into her carts. "It's been seven years since I've been here, and I love that you've kept your store so much the same; always looking fresh and clean. It feels like I'm almost home."

"Where is home?"

"Bayfield. I'll be there by tomorrow night."

"Tomorrow night? You must be taking a slow boat. Sailing?"

"Yeah, it's about a ten-hour trip."

"The weather forecast is for storms tonight. When are you leaving?"

"I've got a small weather window tomorrow. If I don't leave early tomorrow morning, I will be socked in for a few days." Kara dug cash out of her pockets and handed it to the cashier.

"Well, if you're from Bayfield, you know enough to respect Lake Superior. Have a safe trip."

"Thanks." Kara rolled her carts out of the store and down the sidewalks.

Rikk

It was midmorning when Rikk steered the boat into the slip between *Miss Sea* and *Genie's Bottle*. Dutch was standing on the dock when he motored down the channel. Rikk was cautious, steering her slowly; with no wind yet today it was going to be an easy landing.

"Hey, Doc, throw me a dock line," Dutch yelled over the motor. "Looks like you been doing your studies, or did the yard hands help you draw the bowline back to the cockpit?" Dutch caught the line Rikk threw and spun it around the dock cleat, and together they secured her to the dock. With that finished, Dutch said, "She's got all the equipment, looks like she's set up pretty good too. Of course, Kara would know more about that than I do." This time when he mentioned Kara the Doc looked away. "So, what's she look like below?" Dutch stood there waiting for permission to board. Finally, he said, "You're supposed to say 'come aboard' or something."

"Oh, um, come aboard."

Dutch gave admiring looks at the teak and holly trimming throughout the cabin. He reviewed the use of the steaming and running lights and rules of the waters with Rikk. "You got yourself a damn efficient and cozy cabin. Even though you ain't spent much time on the water, you know more than some of the beginner sailors I've seen. Hell, I've rescued some." Dutch related the story of a young couple who got caught out on building seas that he had towed into the harbor last summer, then abruptly said, "Your missus like to sail?"

Rikk looked down and said, "My wife passed away a year and a half ago."

"I'm sorry."

Rikk watched Dutch grow despondent. Or had he imagined Dutch's reaction? He wasn't about to share his story with Dutch or anyone else at the marina. Those lonesome feelings rushed through him excessively. He dodged the subject—it was something he'd perfected. He didn't know Dutch well enough to know what subject to bring up to reroute the conversation.

Almost inaudibly, Dutch said, "She must've been something special."

Dutch's voice sounded familiar, as if it was coming from the same part of his heart where Rikk's pain resided. Rikk's hollow voice said, "She was."

"So this here lovely little vessel is your new mistress?"

Astonishment filled Rikk at the mention of mistress almost as much as when Lauren said it. Time passed before he formulated his response. "Something like that."

"What you escaping from? Her memories?"

"That, and my well-intentioned friends and family."

"Oh, they always got a sister or friend who'd be perfect for you, huh?"

The truth in this statement registered on the Rikk's face. He had a gut feeling about Dutch, a good one, but he didn't have any response.

"What's her name?" Dutch said.

"Who?"

"Your wife."

"Lauren."

"You gonna name her after your wife?"

"Who?"

"Your boat!"

"No. She wouldn't like that."

"Humph! Then what you gonna name her?"

"I haven't given it any thought." Rikk sighed and felt uncomfortable with this subject. "I've been too busy with finding a boat I wanted to buy to think about what to name it—I mean her."

Dutch heard the wheels from Kara's cart labor over the dock planks, "Sounds like Kara's back from the market. You got to go topside and meet her."

"I think I'll just stay down here and get to know my boat."

"Kara ain't been here long, but she's spent just about same time on the water as me, sailing in the Apostles for years before going to the Caribbean. She's a great sailor and a friendly one who'll help anybody. She ain't gonna be here long either; she's leaving in the morning. Come up and meet her, then you got any sailing questions you know somebody to ask."

Rikk sighed while he was trying to find an excuse to stay down in his cabin. Dutch ignored his reluctance and scampered up into the cockpit. Rikk followed him just to be polite.

"There she is," Dutch winked at him as he trudged out of the cabin in time to see Kara pulling carts spilling over with groceries alongside *Genie's Bottle.*

Chapter 7

Kara

Kara was pulling the over-filled carts down the dock and mulling over the list of chores she needed to complete before setting sail early tomorrow morning. As she neared *Genie*, she discovered the OSQ was in the slip between *Miss Sea* and *Genie*. Maybe she would have a chance to meet the owners of the newest boat in the marina. She parked her carts next to *Genie's Bottle* and heard Dutch bounding off the OSQ. Kara looked up to see him emerging from the cabin with the new owner shadowed behind him. She hefted the canvas bags over *Genie's* hull into her cockpit and wondered how many seconds before Dutch would make introductions.

Dutch shouted, "Hey Kara, what do you think of our new dock mate's fine little vessel?" Turning to the new owner, Dutch continued, "Doc, this here's Captain Kara McKee, owner of that little beauty, docked on your starboard side. She's the *Genie's Bottle*. Yep, she's what you call a double-ended sailboat." Then turning to Kara he said, "Doc here ain't come up with a name for his sailboat. I told him he should talk to you. You've heard as many boat names as I have, sailing the southern latitudes over the last few years, and you know all them fancy and foreign words that'd sound romantic for such a charming little vessel."

Kara laughed at Dutch while turning back towards the new boat. "Dutch, I think naming a boat is personal and has to come from within each captain's soul." As she said this, her eyes floated from Dutch and landed on the face of the new owner as he stepped out of the OSQ's cabin and up into the cockpit. He extended his hand to her, and that's when Kara got the first clear glimpse of him. She recognized him at once. She flushed and felt herself fill with embarrassment. *Oh God, did I just say that? What a bunch of lame passionate bullshit!* She closed her eyes and inhaled. Kara stepped forward and offered her hand. His familiar gaze unnerved her.

"Rikkert Harmon," his serene baritone resonated as his strong hand clasped hers. Kara held his direct stare for a moment and then diverted her eyes to Dutch. Maintaining her composure, she lifted her chin, met his stare, and managed a polite smile. Dr. Harmon's cerulean eyes locked onto hers. She hadn't forgotten their intensity. They matched the ocean water of the Caribbean near the beaches she had left a little over a month ago. His jeans were worn, and somehow that didn't fit her image of him; dress slacks and oxford shirt with a conservative tie were planted in her mind's eye. The azure-blue polo shirt didn't fit her image of him either; but, God, it brought out his compelling eyes. Until now, she thought she may have imagined his physique better than it was. Memories tend to fade and change over time. Kara stood paralyzed, staring at him—she was transfixed. Did the flesh and blood standing before her match the strong, fit, and agile body she remembered? Kara's eyes glanced down over him. *Damn it!*

Damn it—what? Damn it—she conceded to her curiosity and looked him over? Or, damn it—she found his physique matched her memory of him? Or, damn it—did his physique match her imagination of him? Or, just damn it—she was affected by his presence? Her throat was dry, and she felt catatonic. She noticed the wind sweep his graying brown hair against his face. It needed to be trimmed, but he looked affable with his hair a little longer. She noticed the kindness in his face seemed to have hardened a bit. He was still handsome in an earthy way. Yet, somehow, his vibe seemed defeated. Mostly, he was the same. So was her reaction to him. Mostly. But there was a difference in him—in both of them, Kara admitted. She did *not* want a chance to figure out what these differences were.

⁂

"Hi, I'm pleased to meet you." Her perfunctory greeting, sure and affable, contrasted the sudden retraction of her hand from his. Attempting to hide her faux pas, she rushed to brush free a strand of hair clinging to her lip. She knew he noticed her quick withdrawing of her hand from his and bristled at how he leisurely drew his hand to his side. He seemed to enjoy seeing her crimson cheeks. She didn't know why he took so much pleasure in her discomfort. Kara's stomach churned at his arrogance.

Dutch said, "I was just telling the Doc here about the time I rescued this young couple on a sailboat—"

Kara's head shuddered involuntarily at the sound of Dutch telling a story. She felt Dr. Harmon scrutinize her while she strained to hold her attention on Dutch's tale. Even though Kara concentrated her gaze on Dutch, the more Dr. Harmon's eyes studied her, the more rigid she stood. When she did steal a fleeting look at Dr. Harmon, it was just long enough to telegraph her discomfort at his self-satisfied leer. Kara burned as he casually glanced back at Dutch, only to shift his gaze back on her a moment later. She held little hope that her aversion to him would be respected.

Not one word of Dutch's story registered in Kara's head, and from the haughty look on Dr. Harmon's face Kara was certain he had paid little attention to Dutch either. Dutch laughed after he finished his story, and Kara jumped at the opportunity to leave.

Kara was not about to let her unease around Dr. Harmon show, so with all the grace and confidence she could muster, she turned to him and said, "I have ice and perishables to stow. It was nice to meet you, Dr. Harmon. Congratulations on your new boat." With that she stepped onto *Genie's Bottle* and opened the hatch. Her feet skimmed the companionway stairs as she carried the two ice blocks down. Luckily, she didn't fall or drop the ice onto the cabin floor. Kara then sat down to catch her breath.

Dutch

Dutch eyed the Doc watching Kara disappear into *Genie's Bottle*. He wondered what the Doc was thinking, but didn't know him well enough to ask. "Come on, Doc, I'll show you *Miss Sea*. She might look a sorry sight from here, but she's a beauty below." Dutch tapped his arm and crossed over to *Miss Sea*, not giving him a chance to refuse.

"OK, but only for a quick tour. I want to spend some time getting to know my boat."

"Sure, and then Kara will have her provisions stowed, and we'll get a quick tour of *Genie's Bottle*."

"That'd be interesting." Rikk said with sarcasm and chuckled. "I'm not sure she'd want to be confined with me in the tight quarters of any boat."

"What you mean, Doc?" Dutch was surprised at his tone. Although he must've been hurt bad by his wife's death, he had no reason to think that of Kara.

Rikk shrugged. "She practically flew down into the cabin. I'm not sure she'll want to meet me again, much less give me a tour of her boat."

"Her ice was melting. She's just got to take care of stuff, and then she'll be happy to show you *Genie*. Seen her do it to others she just met."

"Really? I didn't get that impression of her."

"Naw, you got her all wrong. Sure, she works when there's work to be done. She got ice and cold stuff to put away. Once she got that done, she'll invite you aboard herself, tell you anything you want to know about sailing too. Hell, she took Pete and Sophie under her wing—steered them away from buying a sieve and helped them find *Whisper*—a honey of a boat. She's been giving them sailing lessons too. Just teaching them 'cause she wants to."

"Well, let's have a quick look at your boat. I'm curious if your boat is the beauty you say she is."

"Yeah, I'm going to paint her hull this summer, just never can wait to catch fish after being on the hard all winter." Rikk looked confused, so Dutch added, "On the hard means on land instead of in the water."

"Oh, that makes sense."

Dutch finally dismissed Rikk so he could acquaint himself with his new boat. Rikk was glad to be alone but frustrated that Kara McKee distracted his thoughts. He wanted this boat to be a refuge from people, and now he was staring hopelessly at his owner's manual. He was reading words, but they had no meaning because his mind focused on Kara. Her striking smile and high cheeks still accentuated her intelligent eyes. Sun-bleached strands streaked through her shoulder-length, brown hair. It was a familiar look, though her hair was lighter than he remembered. Her sunglasses, worn like a headband, pulled her gentle waves back and framed her face. When the wind blew, wisps of Kara's hair whipped her cheeks and fused to the corners of her mouth veiling her tetchy and distracted gaze. When Kara brushed the strands of hair away from her face with her deeply tanned hands, Rikk noticed her long fingers free of any jewelry. She crossed her arms in front of her; her rolled up sleeves revealed her sculpted arms. Kara wore her ivory, button-down, Henley shirt tucked into her slim, faded blue jeans. They hung loose at her waist and over her slender hips. Her suntanned ankles peeked out between the fraying hem of her jeans and her Sperry Topsiders when she stepped onto *Genie's Bottle*. He also noticed the strength in her arms when she lifted the ice blocks up and flew down into her cabin. She obviously recognized him. Most people he'd known in a similar manner at least admitted that he looked familiar. Rikk had given her no reason for this slight. From her, he expected at least common courtesy.

Rikk's cell phone rang startling him out of his thoughts. It was the hospital, and his offer to be available when an associate's wife went into labor was accepted. Unfortunately, she was five weeks early, and they needed him now. Of course, he would leave right away; he wasn't getting much acquainting with his new boat accomplished anyhow. He ran into Dutch as he left the dock.

"How long you gonna be, Doc? Cause you gonna need more lines and fenders on her before the wind begins to blow tonight."

He looked at his watch, "I should be back in a couple of hours."

"You want me and Kara to add some lines to her for you? It'd only take us a few minutes. Wind's starting to pick up already."

"Are you going to be around in a couple of hours? I'd rather you help me, and that way I'll sleep easy knowing she's safe and know exactly how to leave her next time."

"That's thinking, Doc. The wind ain't supposed to be howling 'til close to sunset. You gonna be back before then?"

"Three hours tops." Rikk wished he felt as certain about getting back as he told Dutch he was. Only a severe emergency would keep him tied up in the hospital longer than two to two and a half hours. Still his gut felt queasy when he said that, like it knew something he didn't.

Kara

Earlier in the day, Kara watched Dutch and Dr. Harmon cross over the two feet of water that separated the doctor's OSQ and *Miss Sea*. She snatched the opportunity to grab the groceries from the cockpit and stowed them before she escaped off the dock undetected by either of them. She went for a long walk on the beach, but neither the walk nor meditating eased her mind, much less helped her purge her thoughts of Dr. Rikkert Harmon.

✥

Now, a few hours after her unexpected reunion with Dr. Harmon, Kara found herself walking through the marina on her way back to *Genie's Bottle*. She hoped Dr. Harmon had left, or at least was inside his boat. Dutch was in the ship store; he raced out and caught up to Kara. They talked briefly, but Kara cut it short. She had to get her punch list done and had wasted too much time on her walk avoiding contact with Dr. Harmon. She couldn't help but notice that the new boat needed more dock lines, and a couple of fenders would be a good idea too. "Did the doctor leave?" she tried to ask without expression.

"Got called to the hospital but said he'd be back in a couple of hours. Doc didn't want us to add lines and fenders 'cause he wants to learn how. Told him that you and I would help him when he gets back."

"Huh." Kara couldn't contain her disgust.

"The Doc's coming back. I ain't gonna guess what's eating at you, but you could act a little more friendly to him. He don't know much, and you could help him out."

Kara didn't like feeling scolded even when she knew she had been snide and deserved it. "I don't get it, Dutch. You could sit in your boat and watch Sophie and Pete almost buy a boat that should be salvaged for parts and then tell me it wasn't your day to save anyone. Today you're in a snit because I'm not jumping up and down to help Dr. Harmon when you are so eager and capable to help him by yourself! Maybe today's not *my* day to save anyone." Dutch said nothing, but Kara knew she crossed the line as she watched red rise up his face. She didn't want to continue down this road. She shook her head and looked at her feet. "Of course I'll help,

Dutch. I just have to get *Genie* ready, and I'm—" She squeezed her eyes shut and exhaled. "I'm fine with lending a hand." She waited for Dutch to speak, anything would be better than his silence.

After a moment's standoff, Dutch said in a resigned voice, "Do you need help? I got time to help you."

"No, I have little projects to do. Check the oil, top off the water tanks, stow things, make sandwiches—little things that don't require extra hands. But thanks for the offer."

"OK, I'll give you a holler if you ain't out on deck when the Doc gets here."

"All right," Kara said and stepped into *Genie's* cabin. It took a couple of hours for her to cross everything off her list.

❦

When Kara looked at her watch; it was two thirty, and she was surprised that Dr. Harmon still hadn't showed up. It agitated her. She reminded herself to stop worrying about his new boat; after all, it was his responsibility. She also reminded herself that she could choose her thoughts and she should use her agitation from his surprise reappearance to cue her to choose consciously what she did want. But Kara didn't know what she wanted. So, if nothing else, she could always resort to thinking about things she was thankful for.

Genie's Bottle listed to port in the wind gust and squeezed the fenders against the dock. The fenders squealed and moaned in protest until the wind passed and *Genie* righted herself. The dock lines creaked as they held *Genie* tight. *With that gust of wind, I am thankful I know enough to check dock lines and fenders, tie off my halyards, and secure the hatches and everything below.* She looked out *Genie's* hatch over the marina and observed the front moving in, still in the distant northwestern sky. She turned on her instruments, and she zipped up the companionway.

Kara checked her wind speed and found the wind was blowing a steady ten knots with gusts registering up to fifteen. Daybreak had started out calm with temperatures in the fifties and warmed with the May midday sun to seventy-one degrees. The old adage proved true once again; if you don't like the weather on Lake Superior, wait an hour—it will change. However, the change isn't always what sailors wish for. This wind resembled an Alberta clipper, common in the winter months when winds escort low-pressure systems down into the Great Lakes and usher in the Canadian arctic chill. The temperature had already dropped to forty-eight degrees.

The docked boats chattered in the marina, which was only a quarter full because most boaters were waiting for the warm and calm June weather to launch their vessels. A few sailboats complained by slapping their halyards to their masts; more experienced sailors tied their halyards off to prevent unnecessary chafing and noise. As the wind blew, the boats on the hard hummed on their cradles and stands. Their chatter sounded like pleas for the comfort and support the lake provided, which was so much better than on the hard, except in the most wicked of gales. Kara listened to the waves lap against *Genie*'s hull, and felt safe and at home on her while she danced in the water.

The early evening sun saturated the Duluth hillside revealing the multitude of vivid-colored houses, Central High School's bell tower, and the coppertop church, now oxidized to verdigris. Kara adored this city, awash in spring green from trees budding out. Golden light skimmed over the marina and illuminated the few boats in their slips with their smooth and mostly white hulls reflected in the jittering blue-gray water where they bobbed and swayed.

On *Genie*'s deck, Kara began to recheck the lines. She added another spring line on *Genie*'s starboard side, readjusted the fender heights, and checked the tension on the bungees tying off halyards. She stood on the deck and leaned against the mast. This may be her last night on a sailboat forever. Thank God, it was in Duluth.

Kara decided a cup of tea and a nap would be good for her. Even though napping wasn't on her to-do list, it was a good preparation for her final voyage home, now only a few hours away. She wanted to start out tomorrow rested and ready for the fast sail to Bayfield that it was sure to be.

Chapter 8

Kara

Kara bolted up from the settee. A nearby crash startled her awake from her nap, and she glanced around, trying to determine where it came from. Something nearby continued to bang around, but it was not coming from Genie's Bottle. She looked out the porthole at Dr. Harmon's brand new OSQ sailboat and discovered the cause.

Novices! What the hell am I, a novice magnet? Do I have to save every boat from their new owner's incompetence the first time the wind blows? Damn it! Can't just one new owner know something about boats? Kara threw on her polar fleece jacket, slipped on her Sperry Topsiders, and raced up the companionway steps out into the grey dusk.

She stepped down onto the finger dock between Genie's Bottle and the OSQ sailboat. The OSQ was as seaworthy as Genie's Bottle, but it had a glitzy showpiece appearance. She wondered if Dr. Harmon was as worthy of the OSQ as the OSQ was of Lake Superior. Kara also wondered why, with all the open slips in the marina, his boat was assigned the slip between Genie and Miss Sea. Kara blew out a short breath, irritated by her snipe-ridden thoughts. She was better than this—at least she always tried to be.

Dutch scrambled out of Miss Sea's cabin and jumped across his boat to the OSQ as Kara boarded it from the dock.

The boom had somehow worked free of the topping lift cable and now rumbled around on the cabin deck. The cable whipped about wildly in the gusting wind, swinging dangerously close to Kara's head. Immediately, they began to rescue the boat from further damage. As Dutch reached for the cable, Kara could not contain her scorn, "Where is he, Dutch? I thought you said the doctor would be back in a couple of hours. What

44

kind of time does his clock keep? It's been over six hours!" She clenched her teeth and turned to follow the cable.

As Kara grabbed for the cable, she sputtered under her breath, "I've imagined many things about Dr. Rikk Harmon over the years, but I never thought he'd turn out to be just another arrogant wannabe sailor who knows someone will bail him out whenever the wind blows." The cable jerked away just as Kara grasped at it. She yelled, "God, he is nothing like the man I imagined him to be."

"What'd you say?" hollered Dutch.

Facing Dutch as the cable flew back at him, Kara shouted over the wind, "He's probably having a drink in his warm den, watching TV in front of his gas fire place. Just flip the switch and instant fire. Here *we* are, rescuing his brand new boat!"

They continued to grab for the cable as it flailed and whipped past them, but the now inky sky complicated tracking it.

Dutch took his eyes off the cable and scowled back at her. "Geez, Kara, the Doc got called to the hospital for an emergency. He said he thought he'd be back in a couple hours. Why the hell are you acting so strange? I ain't known you long, but you never been so quick to sneak away as you was when you met the Doc. It's like you got something against him, and you just met him."

Kara knew he was right. She wasn't acting normal around Dr. Harmon. She turned away and reached for the cable, glad for a reason not to answer Dutch.

"What's up with you anyways? I've seen you charm all kinds of boaters you just met these past couple weeks. Hell, Sophie and Pete would be at the bottom of the lake without you. The Doc's got you hiding away in Genie's Bottle. You're acting like he's evil." Dutch's voice trailed off as he ducked, but the cable's shackle grazed his head. He caught it when it swung back towards him. Dutch struggled against the wind's determination to jerk the cable out of his hands. The dock lights provided enough illumination to see the shackle was intact, but scratches covered its surface from the keeper pin wiggling free.

"I'll get a line to tie it off," Kara said as she jumped onto the dock. As she grabbed a worn dock line out of Genie's Bottle, she thought about what Dutch had just said. She had never thought of Dr. Harmon as evil, although he was shrouded in mystery. She imagined him to be—what? So many things, but never evil. Maybe this time his piercing gaze was recognition of her, but then what was the cause of it the previous time they met? Everything about him made her bristle. The one person she never expected to see again—and sure didn't want to see again—was the brooding and irresponsible doctor whose surprise reappearance this morning was so opposite from her impression of him seventeen years earlier. Fortunately, tomorrow morning she would sail out of this marina and never have to see him again.

❧❀❧

Dutch and Kara lashed the topping lift to the lifeline. The repair was simple: connect the boom to the topping lift's shackle and insert the keeper pin. The fierce wind would make it difficult, but without deliberation, Kara and Dutch began the repair. Dutch yelled, "I'll see what I got for pins."

"I'll bring a few spare fenders and lines to add to his boat. We've got to move this boat ahead so the side stays don't get tangled with Miss Sea's outriggers."

Dutch yelled, "I'll get a flashlight and a couple of fenders too." He disappeared into his cabin while the boom rumbled around on the OSQ's deck. Kara grabbed a life jacket and some old worn fenders and lines from Genie's Bottle. She set the end of the boom on the life jacket to protect the boat before she added three fenders to the boat's starboard side. The wind howled past in a violent blast, and the OSQ listed perilously close to Miss Sea again.

The flashlight beam arced through the sky, and two fenders swung like pendulums from their lines, bouncing against Dutch's legs as he jumped back onto the Dr. Harmon's boat. He set the flashlight down and started to untie the topping lift.

Kara yelled, "We've got to move her ahead a couple feet, NOW! *Before* we fix the boom!"

Another wind gust bore down, blowing the two boats dangerously close together. Without a word, he added the two fenders to the boat's port side. Fighting the wind's incessant attempts to crash the OSQ into Miss Sea, they waited for the gust of wind to pass before Dutch eased the aft dock and spring lines on the cleats, while Kara took up slack on the bowline. They maintained tension on all the lines to keep the OSQ close to the dock. With it repositioned, they secured the OSQ with two more spring lines.

Dutch pulled the keeper pin out of his pocket and clenched it between his teeth. Kara lifted the boom up and spotted the flashlight on the cable as Dutch took the boom from her and hefted it with one hand onto his shoulder. With the topping lift thrashing about in his other hand, Dutch flexed his knees to ride out the pitching boat. Kara stood on the cockpit seat, took the boom onto her shoulder, and held it as still as possible. With his hands now free, Dutch began to line up the shackle and insert the keeper pin. While they worked, neither Dutch nor Kara noticed Dr. Harmon running down the dock toward his boat.

The wind gusted, and the OSQ lurched to the port side at the same time Dr. Harmon stepped onboard, weighing it down and counteracting the port list. The combination threw Kara off balance and propelled her onto the cockpit floor. Dutch caught the boom and hefted it onto his shoulder. Kara stepped back onto the seat, but as she reached for the boom, it slipped off Dutch's shoulder. He caught the boom in the crook of his elbow as it collided with Kara's forehead. She watched it come down but didn't have time to dodge its path. She shut her eyes as it glanced off her head and heard the thud echo in her ears over the wailing wind. She crumpled backwards and saw Dutch bobble the boom.

Dazed from the crack on her forehead, she became aware of someone holding her upright, securing her tight against his torso. She held her breath and time slowed; Kara fought to remain conscious. She had to help Dutch secure the boom. When she opened her eyes, a sharp pain surged through her head. Then Dr. Harmon's calm voice resonated, "Kara, hold still," and a tide of exasperation flooded Kara as her eyes fell shut.

Dr. Harmon held her jaw and head against his chest. Or was she dreaming? *Please, let this be a bad dream.* Kara opened her eyes and glanced at Dutch. She watched relief replace the concern covering his face and noticed him struggle to hold the boom and topping lift on the pitching boat. *Oh, damn! This is real.*

Dutch yelled, "Doc, grab the light!"

Rikk didn't respond to Dutch's demand and said, "Kara, I need to get you sitting down. Slowly bend your knees." He talked her through the motions until she was sitting on the seat while he knelt behind her on the deck, still holding her body and head stable against him.

She said through clenched teeth, "Help Dutch."

Rikk glowered at Dutch and said, "Let those damn things go and help me get her lying on the seat."

Dutch set the boom down and with swiftness of a skilled seaman, he lashed the cable to the lifeline. His eyes watered when he looked at her. "You got a pretty nasty bump there, Kara. You better do what the Doc tells you."

Kara uttered, "I'm fine. Please, Dutch, let's fix the boom first."

"Screw the boat. You just got a hard blow to your head, and you may have damage to the cervical region of your spine. I need to get you immobilized first, and then I can either examine you to see if you are fine or call an ambulance, and they can determine that."

"NO! I've been through this before. I'm fine. I don't need an ambulance."

Dr. Harmon took a deep breath and blew it out slowly with what seemed to take immense effort. In a quiet, yet unyielding, tone, he said, "Kara, you got injured on my boat, and for that reason alone I need to make sure that you are *fine*—and make sure you don't do anything that will cause any further injury. I am the best-qualified person here to do that. However, if you refuse to let me examine you, I will call an ambulance."

"I don't need an ambulance, and I can refuse it."

"Yes, you can refuse treatment if you are coherent, and you are coherent. I saw your head get hit hard, and you were knocked down. I'm not sure why you are on my boat, but it looks like you were trying to fix the boom. I am going to call an ambulance if you refuse to allow me to examine you. Are you going to cooperate?" He strained his neck to catch her profile and tried see her expression.

Kara started to shake her head, but Rikk tightened his hold on her and said, "Hold still."

Kara was irritated with Dutch as he stood motionless and watched her spar with Dr. Harmon. "Dutch," her voice pleaded, and she hated that she sounded desperate.

"Kara, you gotta do what the Doc tells you. It's for your own good. I ain't gonna side with you."

"Dutch, you are going to lift her legs and swing them up onto the seat while I turn her body." Dr. Harmon nodded to Dutch's left. "I'm going to hold her head stable while you get her feet up onto the seat. Then you will help support her back, and we'll ease her down onto the seat. Are you ready?"

"Yeah," said Dutch.

"Kara, you need to relax and let us do all the work for you. Do you understand?"

"Yes." Kara hissed her answer, and she rolled her eyes but stopped when the pain from the movements stabbed her brain.

"Anger and aggression are symptoms of head injuries, and your reaction could indicate it is more severe than you think," Dr. Harmon said in a calm, authoritative voice as Dutch and he helped her lie back on the seat.

The litany of medical questions Dr. Harmon asked irritated Kara. She thought he must have honed them over the years. She told him her name, the date, where she was, and what happened.

Kara held up her hand to stop his questions and the examination, "Why do you doctors assume that everyone is near death? This isn't the first time I've bumped my head in my life. It probably won't be the last either."

Dr. Harmon glared at her as he shook his head. "Doctors are trained to be thorough, so they do not overlook anything and make the injury worse by being careless." Dr. Harmon's calm words tinged with bitterness as he added, "Over the years I've witnessed people reacting to severe pain in many different ways, and agitation is very common."

Kara shut her eyes when Dr. Harmon leaned away from her and sighed. She spoke slowly and clear, "My head is throbbing, and I know I need to stay awake for at least an hour." *How hard could that be?* she thought. She blew out her breath, and said, "I'll probably be awake all night." Kara tried to stand but when she pulled herself forward, she felt Dr. Harmon restrain her.

"Are you nauseated?"

"I'm lying in a rocking boat and looking up at the mast swaying through the sky. Wouldn't you be nauseated?"

"I suppose I would," Dr. Harmon said. He glanced around the boat as if he were making a plan. "I want to examine your neck before I allow you to move. I *will* follow medical protocol."

"Protocol? Is that what this is about? Dutch and I are rescuing your brand new boat while you were—God only knows where you were—and you're worried about medical protocol? Maybe you should have been more concerned about seamanship protocol earlier, and I wouldn't have this—" She stopped herself, took a deep breath in, and slowly exhaled. Tears pooled in her eyes, and she glanced over to Dutch.

"Guess she don't like being injured, Doc. Stubborn that way, I imagine," Dutch's eyes misted. "Damn, Kara, if the Doc says you need an ambulance, then that's what you need."

With Dutch and Dr. Harmon uniting against her, and her inability to overcome the unsteadiness that kept her from getting up and walking to *Genie's Bottle*, she could think of no other choice than to cooperate. She looked up at the white mast swaying through the murky sky and breathed. It was the best choice, and given any other doctor, she'd gladly cooperate. God, she was being stupid. It wasn't his fault she didn't want to see him again—it was hers.

"Kara, I know it must be hard for you to be injured. We need to get you off the boat because even I'm feeling a little nauseated on it. I still would like to call an ambulance. They'll stabilize you and carry you off on a back board—"

"But an ambulance cannot do anything unless I agree, and I know that I'm hurt but not bad enough to call an ambulance."

"Then we need to work together."

She pinched her eyes closed, and pain swept over her face. She whispered, "OK."

"I would like to examine your neck; then if you are able to sit and stand, we'll get you to the marina lobby. If not, I'll call the ambulance. Are you willing to let me do that?"

Kara felt bad about her uncooperative behavior. She realized that she was allowing her past to cloud the present and acting in a way that she was embarrassed to admit she was capable of doing. Her voice cracked as she spoke, "I'm sorry. I really am sorry for my bad attitude. I'm frustrated because I won't be leaving at dawn. Really, I'm sorry I've been so uncooperative; I'm just disappointed."

"I'm sorry you're disappointed too—that you won't be able to leave when you want to." He paused. "I'm sorry that you have a bump on your head from my boat."

"I want to go to the lobby, so what do you need me to do?"

Rikk examined Kara's cervical spine, asking her if she had pain as he worked his way down each vertebra. She did not, so he then checked her arms and legs for feeling and asked if she had any tingling in them. He asked Dutch for the flashlight to check her pupils and noticed the eye below the bump was slightly dilated, but she was able to track the light. She had a minor concussion, and Rikk told her that they were going to help her sit; if that went well, they would help her walk to the lobby.

❦

Kara imagined a melon-sized bump on her head and knew from previous experiences that her body would require her to lie low for a few days to heal. Despite her intent to sail home tomorrow, she'd be sitting at the dock for days as the weather was forecasted to sour up most of the week following tomorrow's narrow crossing window. *Why now? What is the point of this delay?*

From neglect of his boat to over-attention paid towards her, Dr. Harmon's actions left Kara wanting to be alone to sort out her feelings about him. Unfortunately, her physical condition dictated her compliance with his directions and his company. Glad that she passed all the requirements, Kara accepted their assistance since the nausea she was feeling gave her incentive to get off the bronco ride from the boat pitching wildly in the wind. Kara mustered all her control to walk to the lobby. Dutch and Dr. Harmon were on either side of her as she took about three steps. The wind's blast rocked the dock and caused her to lose her balance. She swayed and fell against Dutch. Despite her protests, Rikk took her hand and pulled it over his shoulder, then placed his arm around Kara's waist. Dutch followed his lead, and they flanked her as they all maneuvered down the undulating dock.

Chapter 9

Rikk

While they walked, Rikk asked Dutch, "What happened to the boom?"

"The keeper pin must've worked its way out of the shackle, and the boom fell. I damn near spilt a full cup of coffee on me when I heard the crash," Dutch said. "Had no idea what it was till I came out of my cabin. Kara was already on the dock."

When they got to the end of the dock, they released their support of Kara. Rikk peered into her scowling face at the familiar, independent, olive eyes that had intrigued him over two decades earlier. When Dutch introduced them on the dock this morning, Rikk's self-isolation *wasn't* the only reason that prevented him from disclosing their previous encounters. But what about her? Most of his past patients and their families acknowledged him, even though he himself didn't always remember them.

The marina yard lights cast a dusty illumination over the marina's grounds. Through the wisps of Kara's hair that veiled her forehead, Rikk saw a goose-egg-sized bump had already formed.

Kara looked to Dutch and said, "I can walk on my own." Turning away from their stares, she took slow and careful steps to the lobby door.

Rikk followed behind Kara, ready to catch her if she began to even wobble. He held the door open for Kara, and as she entered, she looked directly into his eyes. She muttered a thank you, but her look had him concerned. Oscillating in his opinion of her, intrigue replaced Rikk's irritation. What were her eyes seeing in him? Even more, what were they conveying to him? Why did Kara McKee vex him so much? She now appeared almost appreciative, but minutes ago Kara had been angry. He guessed her anger was less about her injury than about something else. But what? And what reason would she have for ignoring him this morning? Her mysterious reentry into his life simultaneously fascinated and aggravated him.

≈≈≈≈≈

Kara shivered when she felt her bump with her fingertips. "I want to see it," she said and turned towards the ladies' room. Before she reached the door, Rikk caught her arm and carefully rotated her to face him. "Kara, I don't want you in there alone; you have a minor concussion. You can resist and refuse all you want, but you agreed to be compliant. I am coming in with you."

Kara silently conceded with a nod. She knocked on the ladies' room door and called out, "Is anyone in here?" She only waited a second before she pushed the door open.

Dutch

As Dutch watched Kara and the Doc walk into the ladies' room, he remembered the first day he talked to Kara. He had vowed to find someone for her, so she wouldn't suffocate in the loneliness he knew all too well. His inner voice spoke to him again. *I have no blood right to be worried about her, but I ain't gonna see her doing what I did. I don't know what's up with them two, but this gut tells me something's going on.* He muttered in a disgusted low voice, "She may think she knows what being alone is like, but she don't. Neither does the Doc."

"What?" Rikk said and looked back at Dutch.

"Nothing. I was talking to myself."

≈≈≈≈≈

Dutch stood in the doorway and saw that Kara only got a peek at her forehead before Rikk turned her towards him and brushed strands of her hair back for a better view of her bump in the bright dressing-room light. He watched the Doc examine the tiny lacerations from where the boom made impact on her forehead. The Doc cautiously touched the wound, and when Kara grimaced and pulled away he muttered, "Sorry." Doc lifted

53

her chin and looked at her eyes, then said, "Dutch, can you get some ice in a bag?"

As he charged out of the lobby, Dutch mumbled, "Them two get along like oil and water." He'd never seen two people take such an instant dislike to each other who was so meant to be together. "Well, hell, they're just making my job harder." He wouldn't let neither of them follow in his dumbass footsteps.

Rikk

Rikk turned back to see the look of resignation spread across Kara's face as she slouched and looked at the mirror. She didn't say a word as she held her bangs off her forehead, but her sigh resonated through him as if she held him responsible. In his gut, he knew he was.

"What did Dutch say?" Kara said.

"I don't know. He's been talking to himself."

"I'm ready to go back to the lobby." Kara turned to face Rikk, and he moved out of her path but stayed close as she walked past him. She opted to sit on the arm of the lobby couch.

Rikk looked out the window and saw Dutch jump aboard *Miss Sea*, and he studied the wooden trawler covered in blistering paint. He liked Dutch, even though the first thing he had done this morning was invade Rikk's private sanctuary that he intended his boat would provide. Initially Dutch had seemed meddlesome, but Rikk soon appreciated his free-flowing and unsolicited boating knowledge. When Dutch had insisted that he step onboard *Miss Sea* and have a look in the cabin, Rikk had hesitated. Once he had stepped into the cabin, his opinion of Dutch transformed. The shabby exterior of his boat contrasted with the meticulous condition of the teak-and-holly-inlayed cabin. Dutch said he gutted the boat and upgraded it by himself. It reminded him how often looks were deceiving. Dutch's rough outward persona deceived his multifaceted and colorful character. He was far from Rikk's first impression of him.

Rikk's thoughts turned back to Kara. She was opposite from the women his friends had been setting him up with. Rikk was so far from knowing himself these days that he didn't know if he was just cynical, or if these women were more interested in being kept than in him. Kara wasn't interested in him in the least. As Rikk watched for Dutch to reappear, he realized his eyes were fixed past *Miss Sea* and past his boat onto *Genie's Bottle*. He almost chuckled aloud as he wondered if the immaculate exterior of *Genie's Bottle* was completely opposite of the condition of her interior; just as Kara's radiant exterior contradicted her hostile and challenging behavior.

Rikk watched Kara slide her fingers over her forehead. A sharp cry escaped from her as she gasped and stifled it with a controlled exhalation. Rikk was astounded at his reaction to her pain. He had seen patients in much worse condition than Kara without feeling the sharp pang of sympathy that overtook him. He shook his head in disbelief and thought his reaction was caused by his guilt. *Why didn't I accept Dutch's offer to help me tie her off, especially with his warning about this wind? Damn, I'm over my head with this sailboat.*

Raking his hand through his hair, Rikk furrowed his brow and looked down at her. He cleared his throat as he pushed the coffee table further from the couch, "Kara, why don't you sit down on the couch. You'd be more comfortable."

"Thank you, but I'm fine here, Dr. Harmon."

"OK, but please call me Rikk. I'm sorry about all of this." Kara looked surprised at his offer of first-name familiarity. He wondered if she thought he was attempting to protect himself because of what he said earlier—that she was injured on his boat. He found himself torn between his unexplainable and conflicting feelings toward her and fear of her. He wasn't maneuvering to protect his assets; he was feeling bad about causing her injury. But the sneering voice inside his head reminded him, *you already have been sued.*

Kara sighed, "OK, I will call you Rikk." She stood and started to walk to the window. When he followed her, she turned towards him and stopped. "I was just going to look out the window." Hesitating, she added, "I guess you'll want to come with me. I am capable of standing here alone. I just want a little space."

Dutch burst into the lobby. He hung onto the door to prevent it from blowing wide open in the wind. "I got your ice," Dutch said as he hurried over to Kara, but she didn't break her stare even with his entry. He looked past Kara and said, "Ain't you going to put the ice on her head, Doc?"

Kara pulled her gaze to Dutch and conceded her independent stance, "Thanks, Dutch."

Rikk took the ice from him and followed Kara to the couch. She again sat on its arm. He wrapped the ice in the towel Dutch brought. "This is going to hurt," he brought it close to her head. "The slightest pressure on your abrasion will be painful, but the ice will numb it pretty quick. Here, hold it just above the bump until the ice starts to numb the area," Rikk said.

"Thank you," Kara accepted the ice pack and brought it directly to the bump. "Either way, it hurts like hell."

"Are you feeling any nausea?" Rikk said.

"No."

"But you did earlier?"

"Earlier I was being jerked around on your boat as the wind whipped to thirty-five knots. I would expect to feel nauseated from the wind gusts and from getting beaned on the head," Kara retorted. She cleared her throat and spoke, "I'm sorry for my short fuse. I'm feeling pretty good now, but yes, I was nauseated earlier. I appreciate your concern and yours too, Dutch. I'm just disappointed. I'm dealing with a throbbing headache."

Dutch said, "Awe, Kara, you can't blame the Doc for the boom falling on your head. I had you fix it instead of lashing it down on the life jackets you wrapped around it. You should be mad at me for being a stubborn old cuss and making you help me fix it."

"Dutch, I'm not blaming either you or Dr. Harmon or holding anyone responsible except myself. I don't recall either of us discussing whether to fix it or not; we just did. It was an accident." She directed her gaze to Rikk. "I'm sorry I didn't wait until daylight and for the wind to stop, and I wish I would have left the life jacket under the boom. I don't hold you liable for this bump. But I really could use some ibuprofen."

Rikk's face froze at the word liable, and an anxious wave rolled through him. *Could this be the next bogus malpractice lawsuit?* His gut ached at the thought of it. No, he'd seen the boom strike her head, and she refused an ambulance. It was an accident, although that didn't mean a thing as far as the law was concerned. What little he remembered about her, she always seemed like a woman of integrity. She didn't seem the type to sue him or anyone else. Rikk tried to convince himself of that, and then he thought of Lauren. Maybe she was right; maybe he was jaded.

"I got some in *Miss Sea*, Kara. I'll get them for you," Dutch spun on his heels and scurried for the door.

"No ibuprofen! Do you have Tylenol?" Rikk said.

"Yeah, got some of that too. I'll get you some, Kara," Dutch raced out of the lobby and down the dock to his boat again.

⁂

Kara broke the silence, "I need to go to the bathroom—but not to see my bump, Dr. Harmon."

Kara must have noticed the disappointment wash over his face because she corrected herself. "I mean Rikk." Her lame smile conceded to his request, but he saw her grimace in pain from raising her eyebrows. Rikk watched her ignore her pain as she moved slowly to stand.

Rikk furrowed his brow. "I'm going in with you."

Kara gave a rueful laugh and whispered, "OK Superman. I must be Lois Lane."

"What?"

"Oh, nothing. I just made a bad attempt at humor."

"Humor? What did you say?"

"I'm glad you didn't hear it. It wasn't bad, just stupid. But, on the bright side, humor is good for healing. Right? You know—Patch Adams?"

Rikk relaxed, and a subtle smile spread over his tired face. "Yes, Patch Adams encourages humor to speed up recovery."

"Um, Rikk? I would like to go in alone and want to negotiate a compromise. How about you wait at the door and listen. If I have any problems, I will call you."

"That won't do you any good if you lose your balance and fall. It is for your safety, Kara."

"I know your only concern is my safety, so would you reconsider it if I walk from here to the door on my own—without wobbling?" She drew in a deep breath and then blew it out as she took a step towards the restroom door.

Rikk was fascinated as he watched Kara stand her ground. Her resilience astounded him. She stepped towards him as if he would step out of her way, but he didn't move. She was so close to him that he could feel heat radiate from her. He once again found Kara and himself standing in each other's personal space. This time he was sure she was responsible for invading his. Although she hadn't intended to put herself there, she seemed stuck there—as if there was an invisible force holding them together. He watched her eyes trace down his face, neck, shoulders, and body and land on the floor. Rikk flashed back to another awkward moment when they stood so close to each other. Flustered in the feelings that again swept over him, Rikk did not understand the attraction that held them together. Nor did he understand the repelling words they exchanged. *God, I can't read her.* This thought made him flinch.

Kara said, "You've got goose bumps." She touched his elbow, then swallowed and said, "You need a coat."

Her light touch broke his penetrating stare. Rikk glanced at his arms, then back at Kara as he stammered, "I—I left it in the car. I'll get it when Dutch gets back."

The sound of the straining door hinges opening and bringing in the howling wind drew them out of their awkwardness as Dutch entered the lobby. Rikk took the Tylenol bottle from Dutch and dispensed two tablets to Kara. She was about to step towards the ladies' room, but before she'd took a step he said, "I'm sorry, Kara. I'm going into the bathroom with you."

Chapter 10

Kara

Kara gazed at the floor feeling beaten. She looked up at Dutch and broke the unnerving moment when she whispered, "Thank you, Dutch. I'm OK. Really I am." Then she retreated to the ladies' room with Rikk in tow. "I need to use the bathroom and would prefer privacy. Would you mind staying out here?" she asked when they reached the first lavatory stall.

Rikk shook his head slightly with a look of disbelief before consenting, "Only if you leave the door unlocked."

Inside the lavatory stall, Kara unfastened her jeans and fumbled with her zipper. Finally, she sat down and tried to relax. Her elbows braced on her knees, she cradled her chin in her palms and sat there long after she could have left. Her mind raced with a million questions why this damn accident happened now, and she agonized over how long it would be before she could escape Dr. Harmon's presence. His guilt-ridden face did not give her any satisfaction. She mused about Dutch's comment accusing her of acting as if Rikk were evil. *Is he evil, or just an egoist peppered with spurts of compassion? Why now have I attracted him into my life? I know why, but it isn't supposed to work that way. All those memories and all I imagined about him should be purged by now. What's the lesson I need to learn? Is it his true identity, so all my suppositions will finally be dispelled?* She searched for the answer to why they were meeting again after all these years since her previous encounter with Dr. Harmon. No, now it was Rikk.

Before any inkling came to Kara, she heard a metal garbage can outside, lofted by the angry wind, crash to the ground next to the lobby door. She heard it clank as it rolled off the sidewalk and thud across the lawn. They all had been silent for a long time. Now she heard Rikk step toward her bathroom stall door.

"Kara, are you all right in there?"

Kara lifted her head off her chin but couldn't suppress her tetchy inflection as she answered Rikk. "I'm done. I'll be out in a second." She was exasperated with herself, and she regretted her tone. She was determined to hush her saboteur that was busy polluting her speech and mind with menacing thoughts and reasons to fear Dr. Harmon. She admonished herself: *Good grief, Kara, what are you attracting now with your insolence? You're letting your imagination run wild about Dr. Harmon—Rikk. This reappearance was the furthest thing from your intentions, but you still get to choose in this moment what you think about it and what you want to attract because of it.*

Dutch

Dutch stood at the window and watched the garbage can spill its contents over the grounds. The wind blew the paper plates, cups, and dirty rags in front of the window and scattered them around the marina's yard. He heard the Doc and Kara talking, but he didn't know what they'd said to each other. They stopped, and he looked through the braced open door of the ladies' room and saw the Doc leaning against the wall, just staring. Doc reminded Dutch of himself—too damn prideful, but honest and good at heart. Doc was doing what Dutch had done almost fifty years earlier and what Kara was doing now too. Just like Dutch, they both were hiding away in their pain and shutting themselves off from finding someone to be with the rest of their lives. They both had too much life left to live for Dutch to allow that to happen to either of them. It was different for Kara and the Doc; their spouses died, and nothing they could do would change that. Dutch figured he had damned good reasons to let his love die, though he often questioned his decision. Maybe he was gutless, just like Charlie told him years and years ago. Well, he wouldn't be gutless with Kara and the Doc. They had something going on; he knew it instantly. He looked back at Doc; his eyes were shut and his head faced the ceiling. "I'm gonna get them off their high horses. Damn sure they gonna open their eyes and see each other," Dutch said.

Rikk

Rikk leaned his head back on the wall. *Oh shit, now I have an old man making blind dates for me.* He laughed a little. No, Kara McKee wasn't a blind date; she was barely civil. His mind drifted, and he saw his new sail boat—the marine-blue hull of his twenty-five foot Ocean Sailing Quest—his OSQ sailboat. She was beautiful, and he felt comfortable alone in her cabin this afternoon. She provided him freedom from the constant painful memories of Lauren that every object in their home brought up. She also provided the solitude that he coveted since Lauren's death. But tonight, as Rikk listened to the wind that was beating against her hull, his focus drifted past her to *Genie's Bottle* who was resisting the same wind. *Huh, Captain Kara McKee? That's a surprise. I never would have expected this from her. Hell, I never expected to see her again.* He pushed himself off the wall and went to the lavatory door and raised his hand to knock.

Kara

"Ahhh!" Kara screamed when she stepped out of the stall and almost collided with Rikk. "You scared me."

"I'm sorry." Rikk said and nodded, "You were quiet in there for a long time."

"I didn't hear you." Kara's startle morphed into irritation. "I didn't expect you to be standing right outside the door." As she washed her hands, she inspected her weary face in the mirror once more. She glanced at Rikk's uncomfortable reflection and considered how difficult this must be for him too. If only *Genie* would've been ready to leave this morning, she wouldn't ever have seen him again. Why had Dutch been so adamant about her meeting him? The wind gave out an eerie howl that rattled the lobby door. Kara felt Rikk's eyes leave her and noticed that he looked out into the lobby. She wondered where Dutch was and what he was doing that temporarily distracted Dr. Harmon from his constant observation of her. Kara paused in front of the mirror to reexamine the goose egg that had formed on her forehead. She tried to ignore Dr. Harmon's reflection in the mirror, but she couldn't help wondering what he was thinking, and specifically what he thought of their encounter. She drew a long breath in as she purposely changed her thoughts. Even if tomorrow's weather window was as perfect as forecasted, with this head injury she wouldn't be leaving for awhile. In fact, the weather would keep her single-handling *Genie*'s final voyage back to Bayfield at least a few days out because she wasn't going to get a crew together to help her leave by tomorrow. *So here I am.*

Kara activated the hand dryer before considering that its motor would sound like a jet landing. Her head reacted to its noise just as if she had a bad hangover. She held her temples as she walked to the door.

Rikk took Kara's arm and asked, "Are you dizzy?" while he assisted her back to the couch.

"I chose poorly. That hand dryer is too loud for my already throbbing head." This time she sat in the middle of the couch, and Rikk sat on the coffee table opposite her. Kara looked into his guilt-laden eyes and smiled. She guessed he was about to start asking her the irksome questions checking her consciousness, and wondered if they were test questions on the first exam med school students ever took. "How do I say this without offending you? I know you want to ask me a whole litany of questions, and your questions are important to assess your patient's condition and treat them, but with all due respect, I'm not your patient. I'm just a fellow sailor. So let me tell you what is going on, and you will see that although I'm injured, I don't have a concussion. I'm fine. Really, I'm fine."

Rikk's scowl prompted Kara to talk faster; she needed to prove that she was all right. "I was nauseated when I was on your boat, but that stopped when I got into the lobby. Today is Thursday; my name is Kara McKee, and I'm docked at Minnesota Point Marina in the slip next to yours. Your slip is between Dutch's and mine. Dutch is the captain of *Miss Sea*, and together we came to the rescue of your new OSQ. By the way, it is a beautiful, classic-looking boat. I won't be heading home to Bayfield tomorrow even if the weather is perfect, but I'll be finding crew to help me take *Genie* to her new owners who are waiting for her arrival in Bayfield." Pausing for a breath, she added, "Yes. My head throbs, but I did just get whacked on the head by your boom." Her nervous laugh gave way to the grin that spread over Dutch's face. She was hoping that Dr. Harmon would lighten up and realize that she was OK, but no amusement registered on his face. After a short silence she added, "Zero."

"Zero?" Rikk asked.

"The number of fingers you are holding up is zero. But if you hold some up, I will tell you how many."

Dutch broke out laughing, "Doc, she's a feisty one, ain't she?"

Kara began to laugh even though it made her head pound. She held her hand up to Dutch and pleaded, "Stop, Dutch. It hurts my head to laugh."

Dutch turned away as he attempted to contain his laughter. Both Rikk and Kara watched his shoulders convulse from his silent chuckle. Kara looked at Dr. Harmon. He was glaring at her, and his face turned port red. "You think this is funny?" Rikk said.

Kara slumped and shook her head, "No. I'm sorry. It is my belief that there is humor in every situation, even the most devastating, but this isn't devastating. Look, I'm just trying to save you from asking all those questions that doctors usually ask by beating you to it with the answers. I don't want you to call the ambulance because I don't need it. I'd rather donate the money spent on an ambulance ride and emergency room visit to someone who can't afford it and really needs it. I won't waste the time of medical personnel on this bump."

"Your condition does not warrant an ambulance at this time." He turned and walked to the door. His hand grasping the handle, he stopped and turned to Dutch who now was wide eyed. "Keep her awake for at least another hour. If she gets lethargic or agitated, has tingling in her extremities, or is nauseated or vomits call 9-1-1 and have them send an ambulance. Get that ice on her head. If you have any questions, call 9-1-1." He pushed the door open, and the wind sprung the door wide, banging it against the outside wall. Instead of leaving, he struggled to hold the door so the wind wouldn't rip it off its hinges.

Dutch rushed to help Rikk close the door. "Doc, I ain't no good at this medical stuff. I got a queasy gut for it. You got to come back, Doc. Kara needs you looking after her. Hell, I can just barely gut a fish, I ain't watching over Kara by myself. You said yourself anger and aggression are signs of bad injuries. She's hurt more than you're treating her."

"I'm not so sure." Rikk glared at Kara.

Kara's mouth dropped opened and despair spread over her face as she acknowledged Rikk's glare. "You are so different than—" She bit her tongue to stop herself as her eyes fell shut, then covered her face and pressed her fingertips against her eyelids.

Rikk pulled the door shut but didn't release the knob. He was peering up at the ceiling and shaking his head. Time passed before Kara stood up and approached Dr. Harmon. He didn't look at her until she stopped a few feet away. Kara bit her lower lip, and her eyes scanned the room before she began, "I'm sorry. I really am. I will honestly and respectfully answer any question you ask. I know I've been difficult, and I didn't intend to offend you although I know I have." He did not answer, but his glare changed into what? Curiosity? Kara finally asked, "Can we start all over?"

Staring down at her, Rikk said nothing. As Kara watched Rikk's anger dissipate, she noticed that Dutch seemed to be holding his breath. Kara didn't understand his anxiety. For the first time Dutch appeared tired and old, but she didn't buy his queasy-gut argument. She knew something was bothering him, but she had no idea what. Since she had never witnessed him in a stressful situation before, Kara tried to convince herself that his uncharacteristic behavior was stress-induced. *Why am I even thinking about Dutch's stress?* Kara rolled her eyes, and the sharp, stabbing pain pierced her head. How long had it been since the boom landed on her head? She wanted nothing more than to lie down, shut her eyes, and let the Tylenol at least subdue her aching head. She turned and looked at her watch, but found she couldn't read it. *Damn, this is going to take some time to heal.* Kara walked back to the couch. Turning to sit, she felt Dr. Harmon's hand grasp her bicep. Startled, she looked up into his face and was relieved to see the serene expression back in place. He sat across from her on the coffee table.

"You can't read your watch, can you?" he asked.

"No."

"Has the throbbing diminished at all?"

"A little."

"What time did the boom fall on your head?"

Kara breathed in as she formulated her answer. "I don't know. I was napping. The boom woke me when it crashed onto your cabin deck. I jumped up to see what happened and never did look at my watch, but the sun was setting, so it must have been around eight or eight fifteen." After a long silence she asked, "What time is it now, Dr. Harmon?"

"Rikk," he corrected her as he looked at his watch then added, "Nine o'clock."

"Sorry, I will try to remember to call you Rikk. It's just that I've known you—I mean, been introduced to you, and, well, Dutch said you were a doctor and," Kara bit her lip and glanced over to Dutch, giving him a pleading look.

"You need to stay awake at least an hour and a half longer. I would like someone to stay with you for twelve hours and talk to you every two hours."

Rikk was watching her, almost anticipating her response to his order. Kara just nodded, but stopped as any motion by her head stabbed her with pain.

"Do you have anybody that you could stay with? Friends, or family—children?"

Dutch sighed, and when Kara looked at him, he was a million miles away. She wondered if he was thinking about his family—maybe he had children or he wished he had. Who was this woman he never got over? She wondered if he ever trusted anyone enough to reveal his deepest regrets. Her intuition screamed that those regrets were tied up with his family by how quickly he changed the subject every time it was broached. He seemed tempted to spill his heart when she'd asked him about *Miss Sea*, but instead he changed the topic. She suspected there was more to *Miss Sea*'s name than he was capable of sharing.

"Kara?" Rikk prodded her to answer.

Kara's voice cracked, "It'd take my kids more than twelve hours to fly here, and my Bayfield friends that know I'm coming back are out of town." She turned to Dutch, and with a hollow voice, she said, "Will you stay with me, Dutch, here in the lobby?" Dutch tilted his head, but said nothing. Kara wasn't sure what to make of his lack of response—she had expected him to agree without consideration.

"This afternoon Dutch said you sailed in the Caribbean. Tell me about the towns you sailed to," Rikk said.

"Towns by land, ports by sea. I hope you don't mind me correcting your sailing lingo."

"I don't mind. Ports."

"Um, Charlestown, Nevis—and—um." She was watching his face and wondering why he asked about sailing to ports in the Caribbean.

"Can you remember the ports?"

"Yes. Um, I was just looking at your face to see if I could—this is going to sound crazy, but I guess I can't sound much crazier than I already do." Kara blushed and felt oddly vulnerable.

Rikk's voice softened, and he said, "Let me decide if it sounds crazy. What were you trying to see on my face?"

"Oh," Kara sighed and deliberated while attempting to form a sensible answer. "Um, I was trying to—to read your expression—" She watched his eyebrows rise. "I was just trying to see if you really were interested in this, actually listening—or just hearing me—keeping me talking, so I would stay awake."

"I was listening."

"Hmm, listening," Kara repeated. She whispered to herself, "Or being in choice."

"What?"

"Oh, I said listening."

"What did you whisper after that?"

"Being in choice." Kara couldn't decipher the meaning of Rikk's grin. That made her nervous. "It means making conscious choices in what we listen to as well as what we say—and watch and do and how we act, and especially what we choose to think about. To some it sounds a little crazy. I mean, of course we choose our words, but we can choose our thoughts too."

Finally, he said, "I'm not sure I know what you mean."

"At least you didn't say that sounds crazy," Kara said.

Rikk's smile was as sincere as his question, "What did you mean by 'Being in choice'?"

"I meant that you—well, everyone, has the choice in every moment to listen or to hear. There are three levels of listening. One is where you are hearing but preoccupied with your own affairs. You know, when you ask someone a question and while they're answering it, you're thinking about something else."

"Is that what you thought I was doing?"

"I wasn't sure, but the only reason that I could think of you asking me those questions was to keep me awake."

"What are the other two levels of listening?"

"The next is where you solely focus on listening to the person and are unaware of any background noise or activity. The third is when you are listening intently while still aware of what is going on around in your environment, and you're taking in the person's unspoken communication as well as what they are saying. Whatever we do, it is always our option. Being in choice is a conscious state where we deliberately make the choice about what we focus on. It applies to everything, not just hearing and listening." Kara felt strangely comfortable after disclosing her belief, even though she also felt very uncomfortable being in such close proximity to Rikk. He was studying her. She stared at his knees, which were practically touching hers. She stiffened, looked away, and then forced herself to relax. She cleared her throat and continued listing ports, "Basseterre, St. Kitts— Port of Spain and San Fernando, Trinidad, and Scarborough in Tobago. Do you want me to go on?"

"No." He looked at his hands, and Kara didn't know if he was contemplating what she said or trying to come up with another question to ask.

Kara smiled at Dutch, relaying she was fine. She relaxed and shut her eyes for a moment, then set the ice back on her forehead and winced, shutting her eyes tighter.

Rikk said, "Kara, are—"

"I keep forgetting to be gentle with my forehead. I stabbed myself with the ice bag. I know that it will take a few days for that to stop. At least that is what my previous experiences have been."

When Kara opened her eyes, she saw Rikk shake his head but did not comment. At last, he peered deep into her eyes and in a hushed tone loud enough that only she could hear, he asked, "I'm so different from what?"

Taken aback with Rikk's return to this question, Kara squirmed as she looked away. Her brain sprinted to come up with an answer. Her voice faltered as she spoke, "Different from—you are different from—how you were this morning." Kara cleared her throat, "When Dutch introduced us." Kara had just said to him "Being in choice." Now she needed to choose her words with care. Even if Dr. Rikkert Harmon attempted to pry out of her the real completion of her sentence, she had the ability to choose her response. The truth was that he was different from how she remembered him. Or was it her imagined truth?

Chapter 11

Rikk

Rikk knew that Kara's answer was orchestrated to avoid telling the truth. A minute ago, he'd been amazed at her strength and honesty. Now he was annoyed with her transparency, and he didn't know how to respond to her lie. He was angry—hell, that didn't even begin to describe the ravaging effects of her oscillating behavior. What surprised him most was how good anger felt. At least anger was a diversion from the emptiness that had consumed him since Lauren's death. He thought of Lauren and wondered why the hell she made him promise to get a sailboat.

Why has Kara come back into my life? OK, that is just crazy to ask you, Lauren; you never had any reason to know Kara ever existed anyway. Rikk sighed and slumped; he thought he was crazy for talking to his deceased wife. His head ached from confusion between his scientific brain and mysterious dreams and feelings that had been overwhelming him lately when he felt Lauren's presence. Tonight he felt her presence as if she were still alive, and she seemed to be calming him down and keeping him from walking away from Kara McKee.

To hear Kara say "Being in choice" was eerie. That alone would keep Rikk here, riveted by the similarity of her beliefs to ideas Lauren had explained in her last days. *Be in Choice* was the title of the last book Lauren read before the cancer took her. It was sitting on his fireplace mantle. Lauren shared some of its passages with him, and he was certain Kara paraphrased something Lauren read to him from the book. He shuddered. He guessed it must have made a similar impact on Kara as it did on Lauren.

Rikk finally broke the awkward silence, "What is your previous experience with goose-egg-sized bumps on your head?"

"I'll tell you my experiences after you get your coat. You've got to be freezing, and I'm not going to tell stories to anyone sitting around with goose bumps covering his arms."

"OK, I'll get it."

Before Rikk left, Kara said, "Dutch, I made sandwiches for my crossing today. They are in a plastic container in my icebox. I have a gallon jug of ice tea in the cabinet to the left of the oven, glasses—oh, you'll find them. Would you mind getting them for me? Bring the grapes in the strainer—they're in the sink. You might as well eat since we'll be spending the next hour and a half together."

"You shouldn't eat for awhile," Rikk said.

"I'm not eating, Dr. Harmon. I'm feeding you and Dutch."

"That isn't necessary," Rikk replied.

"Naw, you don't have to feed us, Kara," agreed Dutch.

"No, I don't have to feed you just like you don't have to sit here with me. But you are here, and I have some great sandwiches that you might want to look at before you refuse my offer. Oh, yeah Dutch, there's a shore bag tucked in the bottom drawer toward the back to carry it all in."

Dutch and Rikk were motionless except for their eyes that darted between each other and Kara. Finally, Kara shut her eyes and let out a loud sigh. She rested her head back and held the ice pack to her forehead. They remained as still as statues watching her until she said, "Geez!" Rikk got up and strode to the door with Dutch following close behind.

"I ain't known Kara long, Doc, but known her long enough to know she's always thinking of someone else," Dutch said as he followed him out the door.

"She does seem full of surprises," Rikk said.

Kara

Kara wondered if she heard Rikk correctly. *What did he mean by full of surprises? I would rather get tumbled around in Genie with this enormous headache than spend another minute in his insolent company.* She blew a cleansing breath out. *Oh, geez!* Kara just recognized that her saboteur had awakened and was offering her all kinds of negative comments that made her feel miserable. Kara's training as a life coach gave her skills in recognizing and calling out her clients' saboteurs when they started dictating their lives. It is always harder to identify your own saboteurs than someone else's, let alone quiet them. Tonight hers spewed its venom, and she conceded that the saboteur could win this round. She would just sit back for the next hour or so and watch Dutch and Rikk eat. She would talk when asked a question and then excuse Dr. Harmon when the time was up. At least Dutch's personality was consistent and most always pleasant, and she'd just have to convince Dutch to babysit her through the night.

Oh, stop, Hisser! That was the name Kara had made up and given to one of her saboteurs years ago. She pictured him as a snake slithering onto her shoulders and incessantly hissing vile comments into her head, disseminating fear. Kara taught her clients to identify their saboteurs when they discovered them lurking in their heads, then to get to know them through recognizing the fears they activated. She had them imagine their saboteurs as a person, animal, or even a monster, then imagine a way to hush them. When Kara found Hisser slithering around, she envisioned tying the snake into knots until it was a tight ball and kicking it off a high cliff into a dark, bottomless cavern. Now envisioning Hisser falling endlessly, Kara's thoughts diverted from what might happen, based on past experiences or imagined worst-case scenarios, to what was real in this moment.

Even if Rikk Harmon said she was full of surprises, his sardonic belief didn't change her. Kara remembered a wise mantra. *It only matters what I think of myself.* Kara contemplated those words and knew all people must live their lives for themselves, as they alone know what is right for them. She knew she would feel disappointment and frustration by trying to control the thoughts and actions of others. Her pep talk was over. She didn't know why she attracted this gigantic bump, but here she was, so she better make the best of it. Who knows, maybe there was some reason she needed to be detained. With that last thought, Kara shuddered. *Was it Dr. Rikkert Harmon? Why? What was the lesson?*

Just then, Rikk entered the lobby, wearing a navy, fleece pullover jacket. Kara grinned. He looked himself over, pulling forward his arms as he checked his sleeves. "What? Do I have something on my jacket?"

"No. It's silly, I just imagined you wearing a tweed blazer."

Dutch sprang through the door with the food stuffed into a canvas bag. Rikk helped him set the items out on the coffee table. Dutch opened the plastic container, took out a sandwich, and took a giant bite. Kara closed her eyes and rested the ice pack on her forehead, then heard ice tea being poured into a glass.

"Kara," Rikk called quietly.

Kara opened her eyes to see him holding the glass out for her. "Oh, thank you." What a contrast this man was—sometimes generous and compassionate as Kara had imagined, but other times he came across sarcastic and controlling. Dutch was devouring his sandwich while Kara watched Rikk pick his up and inspect it for a second before biting into it. He closed his eyes and moaned, "Mmmmm." She smiled at his obvious enjoyment.

Rikk swallowed and held his sandwich up as if he was using it propose a toast. "You were right. We should've looked at what you offered before refusing. This is the best sandwich I've had in a long time. Thank you."

"I'm glad you like it."

"Kara, you agreed to tell us about your previous bump experiences," Rikk said.

"Yeah, I guess I did. Well, let me think. First, I'm a Type A personality. Even as a kid I believed that I could move faster than my body really could. I got a couple bumps in the school yard, just running into things."

"Weren't you watching where you was going?" Dutch chortled.

"Most often I was watching where I was going. When I was in first grade, I would eat my lunch as fast as I could and then run to the playground to get on one of the three teeter-totters. One day another girl and I were racing out of the school doors to get the last one. She pushed off me like I was her starting block, sending me a few feet back, but I was fast, and I caught up to her. We were neck and neck, I had the inside lane, so to speak. Since she already pushed me to get ahead, I was afraid she would hip check me out of the way when we got to the last one. My scheme was to dodge under the other two teeter-totters while they were up in the air and slide onto the last one before she did. I cleared the first teeter-totter but not the second. I remember trying to duck out of the way while I watched it come down on my head. WHACK! I stood there wavering like Wile E.

Coyote for what seemed to be forever before I toppled. It must've been a scene straight out of a cartoon to all the kids watching."

"Did you see stars while you was wavering?" A raucous laughter overtook Dutch.

"I don't remember seeing stars, but it brought me to my knees. As a matter of fact, I got smacked in about the same place on my forehead as I did tonight."

Dutch choked on his sandwich from laughing at Kara's story. After he coughed, downed some ice tea, and regained his breath, Kara said, "OK, Dutch, story hour is over. If you keep laughing at my stories, Rikk will have to perform the Heimlich maneuver on you."

Kara was happy to see Rikk lighten up. He even chuckled before he replaced the levity with his serious question, "Did you see stars tonight?"

"No, Dr. Harmon, it was overcast tonight." Kara regretted her answer the second Rikk grimaced. "Sorry, bad attempt at a joke." Kara deliberately changed the subject back to the playground. "I do remember the playground monitor said she wasn't surprised that it happened to me. It took me years to figure out what she meant by that."

"How many more bumps did it take for you to figure out how to dodge out of the way?" Dutch said with laughter in his eyes. "Oh, yeah, I guess you haven't learned about large falling objects yet."

Rikk laughed, really laughed. Why that surprised Kara, she didn't know. She'd have laughed too if it didn't hurt her head to do so. "I don't tempt fate by purposely putting myself in the path of objects that are sure to come down on me. I thought you had a good hold of the boom—believe me I'd have jumped into the lake to avoid it if I knew it was going to slip off your shoulder."

"You'd have jumped into the lake in this weather?" Rikk shook his head and pressed his lips together.

"Well, the negative effects of wet and cold are only short-term, unlike a crack to the forehead," Kara said.

"Can't wait to hear about your other bumps you said you got over the years," Dutch said, goading her back to more stories.

"I've had a few—and some cuts, bruises, and scrapes too. I also remember the playground monitor took me to the nurse's office, left, and then came back with a butter knife from the lunchroom. I just looked at it and didn't know what I was supposed to do with it. I guess the school kitchen didn't have ice cubes, because they had me hold the knife on the bump."

"A butter knife!" Dutch burst into a new round of laugher. Rikk joined him to Kara's relief.

"I never knew a knife could be so cold," she said.

⁂

While Dutch and Rikk finished eating, they coaxed Kara into telling them about a couple of other good-sized bumps she had gotten during her life, although none caused the ruckus of her first story. It did lead all of them into sharing stories of stupid and silly things they had done in their youth, some resulting in injuries, and some resulting in shame and embarrassment. Dutch's stories were rich with easily pictured details but void of specific locations. Kara wondered how hard it must have been for him to delete all locations from his vocabulary permanently. The conversation lulled, and Kara asked, "Dutch, what was the name of that 'small town' you grew up in?"

Dutch hesitated then said, "I ain't thought about that poor, swampy, little town in years."

"You're from central Minnesota, right?" Kara said.

"Pretty much central."

Kara pondered Dutch's aversion to her question, but decided to press forward anyway. "Central Minnesota narrows it down to just a few-hundred-thousand-square-mile area, and poor swampy pinpoints it right to—?"

Dutch squirmed. "Ah, hell, Kara, the past is the past and don't matter where you come from, just what you make of yourself that counts."

"Sorry, Dutch, I didn't mean to pry." Kara shut her eyes and quivered from the chill that ran through her. She reminded herself that she wasn't his life coach; even though her intuition told her that Dutch's aversion to his past held him captive in pain. She had helped many of her clients heal and move on to live fulfilled lives by asking questions that encouraged discovery of their answers and allowed their repressed hurts to surface. What you resist persists. If Dutch would only let his secret out of the vault

74

he had constructed around it, he would free himself of his self-imposed bondage to his past. Then he could start to allow what he really wanted to enter his life. She wanted to tell him that he, like most people, might have something that causes guilt, anger, resentment, or some other negative emotions that keep him stuck doing the same thing and getting the same unwanted results. She wanted to coach him—she had been able to ask the difficult and direct questions that so many of her clients needed to answer for themselves in order to move forward. She wanted that for Dutch. She also knew that coaching only worked if the clients wanted to be coached, and Dutch hadn't expressed any desire for coaching.

Kara noticed Rikk watching her and wondered what Rikk had buried. He mystified her; who was he anyway? Were all her assumptions about him wrong? Maybe he had some devastation in his life that caused him to close down, yet she saw glimpses of compassion in Rikk. She thought about Dutch's accusation of her acting like Rikk was evil, but she wasn't sure how she felt about him. Kara believed good existed in all people. Although some were consumed with their fears and insecurities, they allowed their negativity to emerge. She believed everyone was capable of releasing that negativity to live a joyful and authentic life.

Kara caught herself in a self-coaching moment. She too had a fear about Dr. Rikkert Harmon, one that made her feel insecure and ridiculous. She wondered why it was so hard for her to walk her talk when it came to him. Her heart told her to release the secret she kept, to free herself. Her brain said not tonight; not with this headache. It also told her to wait, and maybe she could avoid it altogether, or at least she could choose whom she released it to. Her long-time friend, colleague, and often times coach, Robin, came to mind.

Rikk broke the silence, and he cleared his throat. "Thank you for the sandwiches. I didn't know how hungry I was."

"You're welcome."

"Yeah, thanks, Kara. So what you think, Doc? Where you think Kara should spend the night?" Dutch blurted out.

"Dutch!" Kara protested.

"Well, you can't stay on *Genie* in this blow!" Dutch said.

"That's what you call the wind, a blow?" Rikk laughed.

"When it's a gale force wind," Kara saw little humor in Rikk's question and even less in Dutch's suggestion. "I'm perfectly capable of making the decision where I spend the night, and I will stay here in the lobby until the wind dies down. I can't believe that you think it's up to you or Rikk to decide where I sleep tonight." She closed her eyes and took a deep breath, "You're going to stay with me, aren't you?"

"Well you'd be more comfortable in a house than in this here lobby. Why don't you take Kara to your place, Doc?

"DUTCH! You don't impose on someone and his family by volunteering his house for refuge." Kara was furious.

Rikk looked as though he was stunned speechless and sat immobile as he listened to Kara defend her position.

"Doc here's widowed, Kara, just like you are, so you won't be imposing on nobody."

Stunned, she sat back and stared out the window but only saw the reflection of the three of them sitting there. "Except him," Kara said.

Dutch took the last bite of his sandwich. Rikk stared at her in what seemed to be a similar state of disbelief. What should she say first? She turned to Rikk and said, "I'm so sorry to hear you lost your wife. I know what it's like."

"Yes, I know you do. Dutch told me that your husband died recently too." His somber expression and silence quelled the discussion of their loss. "It doesn't make any sense to insist someone go some place where they are uncomfortable, Dutch, and Kara would not be comfortable going to a complete stranger's house. Given the situation, I agree that the best place for you is here in the lobby. But I do insist that someone stays here with you through the night, unless you have friends nearby to—"

"Well, it ain't gonna be me," said Dutch with an insulted tone, and he stood up, stomped out of the lobby.

Dutch's abrupt retreat left Kara bewildered. She brought the ice bag back to her head and took several deep breaths. *Think, Kara, think.* She tried to come up with a rational argument to dismiss Dr. Harmon. Several seconds passed before she finally dropped the ice bag from her head. Rikk was sitting in a chair across from her, slouched forward with his elbows on his knees. He peered at his feet. Kara cleared her throat, and he looked up at her. "Dr. Harmon," she said, "I don't want to—you don't have to—I mean. I've had bumps like this before. I really don't think—"

"Stop, Kara. It's clear that you don't want to be here or have me stay with you. But I'm going to stay here with you anyway. You can go to sleep any time now, and I'll be waking you up every two hours. You can argue about it all you want, but in the end if you insist that I leave, or if you try to go to *Genie's Bottle*, I will call the ambulance. I'd have any patient with a bump like yours watched through the night, and since you don't have anyone to come stay with you or take you to their home, this is the best option you have."

Chapter 12

Kara

Kara slumped back and placed the ice bag on her head. She squeezed her eyes together tight to contain the tears that welled up, but that caused too much pain. When Connor died, she learned to allow herself to privately let her emotions surface and release them by crying, sometimes yelling, and even punching a pillow. Her favorite release was to beat the tar out of a rock with a stick while taking a long walk on a secluded trail. Tonight, as hard as she tried to squelch her tears, they came streaming down. While she silenced her sobs, she could only muffle the sniffling.

Rikk found a box of tissues and set them on the coffee table. She felt his presence but did not open her eyes. She couldn't bear seeing the discomfort in his face caused by her crying.

"You know, given the circumstances, it is probably right that I stay with you. After all, it was my boat that caused this in the first place." Rikk sat on the coffee table across from her again.

Her defenses were melting, and she found his guilt disarming, which just increased her vulnerable feelings. Kara hadn't had a good cry for quite awhile, but this was not the place to have it and not the person to have witness it. God, she wanted to evaporate. She remembered the television show *Star Trek*. She wanted Scotty to beam her up out of this time-and-space realm. She wanted to be alone, especially in her present state of mind.

"I'm sorry, Kara, that all this happened to you. I feel responsible for all of it. I wish I could make it all disappear."

Kara slid the ice bag from her head and looked at his remorseful blue eyes. She didn't know where it came from, but she felt a twinge of laughter sprouting inside of her. *Well, this will just be weird. He doesn't know me, and I go from inconsolable crying to uncontrollable laughter.* That did it. She started to grin, and soon the nervous laugh burst from her. "I'm so sorry for laughing, Rikk. It is not what you said, not exactly. I mean, I just was thinking—did you ever watch *Star Trek*?" Rikk nodded. "I just remembered my favorite line, 'Beam me up, Scotty, I'm in a hell of a lot of trouble here.' Then you said you were sorry that you couldn't make this all disappear. That may not sound funny to you, but it felt like we were on the same wave length." Kara could tell he didn't understand. "I want to disappear as much as you want to make the fact your boom hit my head disappear."

Rikk

A grin spread over Rikk's face, and he was thankful that Kara's mood had shifted, at least for the time being. "Same wave lengths. Hmm. I wish I was Scotty."

"Me too!" Kara's reassuring smile relaxed him.

They sat in silence. Some of the discomfort with their strange situation had melted away. Kara shut her eyes and returned the ice to her head. Rikk watched her and lost himself in the thought of what it would've been like to take her home as Dutch suggested. Of course, he would've had her sleep on the couch, and he would've stayed awake. Probably he'd have dozed in the recliner. He felt lighter as his thoughts dwelled on Kara. She was alluring, even with a bump on her forehead and tears staining her cheeks.

She shivered. *Damn.* He had been so drawn into studying her that he overlooked her comfort. He leaned forward and touched her arm, "Kara, can I get some blankets off *Genie's Bottle* for you?"

Kara smiled at him and joked, "Until now I thought you were a better doctor than nurse. I guess there is hope for your nursing skills after all."

"There is only hope for me if I can find some blankets and maybe a pillow for you."

"You'll need a flashlight to open the hatch lock, and find the cabin light switch on the control panel."

"Your boat wasn't locked when Dutch got the sandwiches."

"Sometimes, when I run through the companionway too fast, the doors slam shut, and it jolts the tumblers enough to lock them. Dutch doesn't know that, and it may have locked behind him. It might still be open. But just in case, the combination is—"

Rikk saw Kara's distant look full of deep sadness. He cleared his throat before he asked, "Do you remember the combination, Kara?"

Kara blinked her eyes then said, "Of course, I'd never forget it." Her voice quavered as she recited the numbers to him.

"I'll be right back." Rikk hesitated and felt awkward about searching around in Kara's boat. "Um, anywhere I should look for them?"

"Grab them off the settee." Rikk was turning for the door when Kara added, "Rikk? Bring some for yourself. You might as well be comfortable too."

⚓

When Rikk returned, Kara placed the pillow behind her head. Rikk spread the blanket over her, and she pulled it up around her neck. Kara sighed, "I don't suppose it'd do any good to tell you that you can go home?"

"I thought I made it clear that I'm staying."

She kicked off her Sperry Topsiders and rested her feet on the coffee table. Rikk tugged the blanket over her feet and noticed Kara's appreciative smile. She said, "You did."

"Are my nursing skills improving?" he said. Rikk regretted his foolish-sounding question, but noticed some of Kara's tension dissipate that seemed to have been trapping her since they first saw each other this morning.

"Yes, but your real gift is your doctoring." A quiet moment passed before Kara said, "Rikk? Thank you for your sense of humor. I really appreciate your concern, and, well, I guess for staying with me tonight."

Rikk's smile acknowledged her gratitude.

Then Kara simpered, "Even if I think it is unnecessary."

Rikk smirked but didn't respond. He decided that he wasn't going to open up negotiations on this matter. His mind returned to *Genie's Bottle*. While getting the blankets, he discovered it was as neat on the interior as the exterior. Maybe more—the cabin was beautiful and inviting. The walls behind the shelves were upholstered with fabric that looked like an old-world map drawn on parchment paper, containing two hemispheres of the earth. King Neptune guarded the oceans with his spear, and tall ships sailed the seas between the east and west hemispheres. The cushions were upholstered in a brocade of burgundy, marine, and forest green with bronze accenting the pattern, and a matching bronze rope-braid edged them. Rich teak finished in high gloss covered the ceiling, cabinets, and shelves. Turned teak spindles enhanced the shelf railings, striking an elegant look.

He looked at Kara, her legs sprawled onto the coffee table and the blanket draped over her. At this moment, she resembled both her boat's exterior and interior. Rikk thought about the framed photo he saw on the shelf of Kara and her husband sitting in the cockpit of *Genie's Bottle*. Kara's husband had his arm wrapped around her, and they were clinking wine glasses together in front of their beaming smiles. He wore a Panama Jack hat that almost hid his sun-bleached blond hair and a worn t-shirt and shorts. Kara wore a straw hat with a wide brim pressed against his cheek, and her long-sleeved t-shirt scantly covered her navel. Below bikini bottoms, her slender, long tanned legs stretched out and rested on the wheel.

Rikk felt like a snoop, stealing a peek at her picture when his mission was to gather blankets and a pillow. The picture had sent a rush through him, stirring warmth inside that no other woman had since he'd met Lauren decades ago. That surprised him.

⚓

Rikk cleared his thoughts and changed the subject, "You have a beautiful boat. Is it hard for you to sell it?"

"Wow. I haven't been asked that question before. Um, yes and no. It is hard to imagine not having a boat, but I can get another if I want. The fellow purchasing it is an acquaintance through a mutual friend and part of the deal is that I help him learn to sail it. My transition will be gradual from boat owner to land lubber. It will be hard to go back to our house and refurnish it just for me, but," Kara furrowed her brows then said, "no, that is only true if I believe it to be."

"What is true only if you believe it to be?"

81

"Oh," Kara looked like she was carefully choosing her words, "I believe, and have—I've experienced that you always get what you talk about, think about, and feel. So it will be hard to move back into our house if that is what I manifest with my feelings, thoughts, and speech."

"Manifest? You believe that you manifest things by what you say, think, and feel?" The concept wasn't foreign to Rikk, but he found this idea scientifically unsubstantiated.

"You just admitted that a sense of humor helps people to heal—Patch Adams would certainly agree with that. Keeping a sense of humor and belief that you will heal are only a part of how people can manifest a return to health. I believe that we can manifest anything we can think of, including things we don't want, like it being hard to return to my old home. I can always choose something different, like returning to my house will be easy and full of incredible surprises. I'm not trying to convince you of anything—it's just how I feel. I think everyone is manifesting all the time and in all aspects of their life whether they know it or not."

"Whether they know it or not?"

"Yes, people are doing it all the time without knowing it. When they consciously control their thoughts, they control the outcome of those thoughts. It isn't new. You've heard the saying, 'Good associations bring good deeds,' haven't you? Well, just expand that into every realm of life."

"You seem sure of your conviction on manifesting." Rikk smiled even though he didn't subscribe to her beliefs.

"I used to be. I got lost for awhile though."

⚜

Rikk broke the silence that filled the room for the last few minutes, "I would like to look at your pupils again."

"Of course." Kara looked down, let out a measured breath, and in quiet voice said, "Rikk." She hesitated and then said, "I will be a gracious and compliant patient."

"Are you manifesting now?" Rikk saw the quick flushing of her cheeks and regretted teasing her. His next words erupted without a moment to consider them, "I will be a considerate and empathetic doctor."

Kara didn't respond. Rikk took the flashlight and looked into her pupils, only muttering instructions where she should look. At last, he asked her if she wanted to lie down.

Kara began to nod her head yes but stopped as this movement caused a piercing pain in her head. "Yes," she said almost inaudibly. As she swung her legs up onto the couch, Rikk adjusted the pillow for her. With a retiring voice Kara asked, "Do you think—that Dutch is coming back?"

Rikk covered Kara up with another blanket and thought about her question. It was so foreign for him to be with someone so uncomfortable in his presence. Kara was an anomaly; their paths crossing up until now had been amicable, at least in his view. Yet this time she acted as if she'd rather be in a leper colony than in his presence. He sighed and said, "I think Dutch has other ideas."

"Other ideas? Do you think he has a hidden agenda?"

"I think he has an exposed agenda of match-making the widow and the widower. I guess he is doing what he thinks is best for you, Kara. His overt fatherly gestures are—" Rikk couldn't think of a word that he felt accurate to finish his sentence. 'Nice' sounded patronizing and 'compassionate' sounded like pity. Kara's smile warmed him while he groped for a word to finish his sentence.

"Well, I concur with your diagnosis of Dutch." Kara shut her eyes and said, "You did give me the OK to go to sleep, didn't you Dr. Harmon?"

"Rikk," he reminded her while a smile covered his face. "Yes, but just so you know, I will be waking you up in a couple of hours, and sooner if I think you are too sound asleep."

Kara's eyes opened and she wore a gleeful expression. "That won't get you a considerate and empathetic doctor endorsement, Rikk." She emphasized his name.

Rikk saw a sparkle back in her eyes. Damn, she was vexing and infuriating! Kara McKee provoked more contradicting emotions than he thought possible. He mentally started a list of her attributes: resilient, independent, pretty, caring, intriguing. But that manifestation thing was flaky. Besides, how often—and fast—did she yo-yo from pleasant to irritable? He looked down at her lying peacefully, eyes shut, and holding a bag of ice over her left eye, her hair tangled over her cheeks. *Why in God's name am I continually drawn to this woman who's so conflicting?*

Chapter 13

Rikk

Rikk glanced around the marina lobby and noticed a small bookcase with a sign posted on it, "Book Exchange." He wasn't going to get any sleep tonight with Kara mulling around in his mind, so he went over and scanned the shelves until he came across a book, *Be in Choice*. There it was again, the book that Kara paraphrased earlier this evening—Lauren's book.

Lauren had made him promise to read *Be in Choice*; but every time he tried his grief overwhelmed him. He remembered the times she would read him passages in the book as she struggled to pretend the chemotherapy was not wreaking havoc in her body. He had picked up the book hundreds of times after Lauren's death, only to set it back down again. He could never get past the inscription in the front cover that Lauren dictated to her best friend, Barb, when she became too weak to write it herself. He had read the inscription repeatedly, and every time Lauren's words reopened his wounds leaving him feeling hopeless, lost, and alone. Rikk always promised himself that the next time he picked it up he would read it, but his brain could never convince his heart to turn the page.

Rikk sat down and clenched the book in his hands. He had a strong need to feel connected to Lauren, and for the first time he had a strong urge to find out what about this book caused her to want him to read it. He opened the cover and stared at the blank inside page. This is where Barb had written Lauren's inscription in her book. Rikk had memorized Lauren's words. He'd read them at least a thousand times. He shut his eyes and could see them as clearly as if they were written on the inside page of this book.

Dear Rikk,

You've loved me, even during times when you had no reason to even like me. You've blessed my life, and helped me to become whole and fulfilled. Leaving now is the hardest thing I'll ever do. You have so much more to live, and even more to give. I know this book was written to help you on your journey after I'm gone.

Please, read it for me, and see all that I see in you.

I love you,
Lauren

For the first time, Rikk felt peaceful enough to turn the page. He began to read. The preface was intriguing, very different from what he expected. He read the first chapter, and Kara rolled onto her side. He did not get up but watched her until she was still and asleep again before he continued to read.

The next time Rikk looked at his watch it was ten thirty. Kara was resting so silently that he put the book down and went over to check her. Her color was good, her breathing was slow and steady, and she rested peacefully. The ice bag was still full so he decided to let her sleep undisturbed. Rikk sat back down and resumed reading.

Awhile later Kara was mumbling in her sleep. Rikk could not make out what she was saying but could tell her dream was not distressing. He yawned and laid the book on the table. He glanced at his watch; it was eleven thirty. Rikk went over to her and put his hand on her shoulder as he called her name. As Kara woke, she reached her hand up and stroked Rikk's cheek, and through squinted eyes she whispered, "Oh, Connor, is it my watch already? Can I sleep just a few more minutes? I have such a throbbing headache." She dropped her hand to her forehead, and when her fingers grazed her bump, she scrunched her face in pain and awoke. Kara squeezed her eyes tight, and when she opened them, she gasped, "Oh, I'm sorry." She clasped her hands together. "Dr. Harmon. Um, Rikk, I was dreaming. I thought you were Connor."

"I know. I'm glad you know who I am; and why you are here?"

"Why I'm here? OK, but just the highlights." Kara sighed, closed her eyes, and said, "My nap was interrupted by a loud crash, your boom met my forehead, and Dutch ditched my slumber party." Kara grinned as she said this. "I hope you won't make me fill in all the details."

"You forgot the sandwiches," Rikk replied, "I think they are worthy of the highlights."

"Hmm, watching you and Dutch eat my sandwiches was definitely a highlight," she said. "What time is it? Oh, wait, that's your question."

Rikk looked at his watch as he stood and backed away. "Eleven thirty-five." One minute Kara stroked his cheek with tenderness and the next she annoyed him with teasing. Why did she trivialize the basic protocol that he and other doctors used to determine patient awareness? "You said you had a headache," he barked at her.

"What? I—I don't remember saying that."

"When you thought I was Connor, you said you wanted to sleep longer because you had a headache."

"Oh. When I was waking up? Um, yeah, I still have a headache," Kara's stunned eyes darted around the room as they moistened. "I guess it is a little too early for more Tylenol?"

"Yes, it's too early." Rikk reminded himself that she had the real injury and real pain; he merely suffered a bruised ego. Oh, hell, maybe she didn't recognize him, maybe he was the only one affected by this unexpected reunion. More now than ever Rikk missed Lauren—none of this would matter at all if she were still with him.

Kara sighed and rolled onto her side and readjusted the half-melted ice pack. Her voice strained through tears as she said, "Dr. Harmon, I'm sorry that I don't have anyone to stay with me. I can tell that this isn't how you want to spend the night. Maybe you should just take me to the hospital. But no ambulance." Kara shut her eyes and blew out a cleansing breath, relaxing her tense shoulders. "Will you drive me to the hospital?"

"I'm sorry I was terse. You really don't need to be admitted. Staying with you for a few hours is the least I can do." Rikk walked toward the door and stared out the window. He could feel her eyes watching him, but he couldn't look at her—but God, how he wanted to.

"You remind me of Connor when he was preoccupied in his own world. I used to bribe him to break into that world."

Rikk at last turned toward Kara. She looked weary—drained even more than he felt. He had no clue what to say, nor how she'd interpret it.

"Penny for your thoughts," Kara said.

"What?"

"That's what I used to say to Connor to entice him to tell me what he was thinking."

Rikk could never tell Kara what he was thinking. His mind muddied in a myriad of conflicting thoughts, and most were of her. He said, "I was wondering what your lock combination number means."

"Oh," Kara answered, "if I told you, it would expose how illogical I am."

Rikk gave her a curious smile. "I don't think you are illogical."

"Or crazy! I guess I'm keeping my crazy, illogical, and romantic self at bay—oh, shit." Kara clamped her eye lids shut and bit her lower lip as her cheeks blushed.

"Romantic?" He held his laughter.

"This is a time that I wish I had a delete key and the ability to erase my words and all memory of everyone who heard them. Connor used to tell me he loved it when I anchored my controlled self in the bay and set sails to the crazy, illogical, and romantic Kara that he loved."

Rikk chuckled softly, "I don't think you are crazy or illogical. I guess the circumstances haven't provided an opportunity to see if you are romantic."

"Thank you."

"For what?"

"For not making me feel more uncomfortable or embarrassing me about my silly remarks."

All Rikk could do was look away. When he finally turned his eyes back to Kara, she held up the sagging bag of ice cubes now half water.

"Dr. Harmon, my icepack has suffered from global warming. The polar ice is melting at an alarming rate from the heat generated from the mountain that just erupted on my forehead. Do I have your permission to drain some of the ice water out of this bag?"

Rikk laughed, surprised at her analogy. "Permission denied. Let me do it for you." He also was surprised by his mood shift on the heels of Kara's request. He hardly remembered the last time that he had laughed, let alone twice in one night. It felt good, especially since as of late he'd wondered if anything would make him laugh again. As he took the bag that she held up, he asked, "Do you always use analogies?"

"Actually, I use them often. It just seems to give people a visual way to help them grasp and apply a concept or idea." Kara grimaced and back-pedaled, "Not that I thought the melted ice was a hard concept for you, I mean—"

"How often do you use the melting polar ice caps for a visual?" inquired Rikk steering away from Kara's slight.

"Just once—now," Kara smiled. "But I do have some favorites that seem to come to me over and over. I modify them to fit my client's situation, and sometimes the client modifies them, and I gain a new perspective from them."

"Clients? What do you do?"

Kara

Kara contemplated her standard reply that showed rather than told about coaching and often brought her new clients. She didn't want to elicit any questions from Rikk. Instead she explained, "I help people transition from where they are to where they have always aspired or dreamed to be."

"How?"

"People often are stuck putting up with something that they no longer enjoy or that no longer serves them. They have grown so comfortable or complacent with being stuck that they just can't find the courage and confidence to make the change to realize their dreams and goals. I help them remove their limiting beliefs. I help them stop buying into others' expectations of them, and help them go all-out for what they truly want. Some transitions are huge, like a new career or taking up something new that everyone they know thinks is impossible or crazy. Sometimes they are more subtle like changing their focus to accept things that are beyond their power to change." She explained way more about coaching than she intended. Almost inaudibly she added, "Or finding peace within themselves."

"Are you a counselor or therapist?"

Kara grinned, "I guess I told you what I do; you were asking what my job is. I'm a life coach." Kara sensed Rikk was waiting for her to continue, but she shut her eyes; she'd said enough. She heard him open the bag and pour water down the drinking fountain drain. When he brought it back, Kara lay still and kept her eyes closed.

Rikk bent down next to her and cleared his throat. "Kara, here is the ice."

"Thank you." Kara managed a smile.

"Did you coach while you sailed the Caribbean?"

"Yes, um, with a telephone you can coach anywhere there is modern technology available." Rikk's nearness discomforted her. She didn't understand how he could go from surly to tranquil so fast. She liked his tranquil side, but damn, her attraction to it frightened her. A shiver ricocheted through her, and she hoped he hadn't seen it. Kara was petrified that she was as attracted to his serene demeanor now as when they first met. She needed him to step back, or she would need to escape; and that wasn't likely, "Dr. Harmon, do you think it would be all right for me to rest again for awhile?"

His wry smile grew as he said, "Yes, of course."

Kara closed her eyes, then said, "Talk to you in a couple of hours?"

Looking at his watch, he said, "Yes, around one forty-five."

⚜

The heat Kara felt inside her was generated from his presence, and it would dissipate as soon as he stood back. It seemed like hours before he moved away. The antagonistic voice of Hisser chattered in her head. *Dr. Harmon's frequent terseness is his frustration with you.*

Hisser's sole mission was to keep her from following her heart and listening to her intuition; and it had always proved to be the voice of bad choices. Hisser sneered, "He's a doctor, and his attention is purely professional. If anything, he watches you because he doesn't trust you." Kara sighed and decided that her saboteur could win this battle. Anyhow, despite Hisser's bad intentions, maybe this time he helped her by making sure she looked before she leapt into a complicated situation. Kara heard Rikk stand and walk away, and she relaxed. She glanced at him as he settled back into his seat, picked up the book, and flipped the pages. Now and then she peeked to see if he was reading before she dozed off.

Chapter 14

Kara

Kara awoke to Rikk's hushed snores. It again took her a few minutes to assimilate the events leading to her sleeping in the lobby with someone snoring in a chair a few feet away. Her headache had subsided, and she slowly pushed herself up. The ice pack was now tepid water. She had to go to the bathroom, and she wanted to have another look at her head.

Kara moved slowly to stand and maintain her balance, and then walked to the bathroom. Passing Rikk, she saw the book on his lap and realized that he must have been reading most of the night. *God, what time is it?*

The bathroom wall clock said five after two. What a story this night would be to retell. The bump hadn't changed any. She expected the next couple of days to be slow going with a gnawing headache, followed by a black and blue bruise draining into her eye. She would be a sight when she got to the Bayfield harbor with a shiner. Leaving the bathroom, she opened the door slowly so she wouldn't wake Rikk. She paused when he rolled over to his side and the book slid between the chair arm and the end table.

Kara tiptoed across the room and grabbed the Tylenol off the coffee table. As she neared Rikk, Kara noticed the room felt chilly. She looked around and found an afghan Rikk had brought from *Genie's Bottle* and draped it over him. It was a small gesture, considering the burden her injury had created. His snoring subsided, but she had not awakened him.

Kara was curious about what Rikk was reading, but the only part of the book visible was the edge of the pages. The cover of the book lay wedged between the chair and table. Being a compliant patient, she decided to let him know what time she had the Tylenol, since the afghan would disclose that she had been up. She found a pen and pad of paper next to the lobby computer. She wrote, "2:05 took 2—KMK" and then drew an arrow and set the Tylenol bottle on the paper at the tip of the arrow.

Although Kara's head still had a dull and persistent pain, it was a huge improvement to the previous wakeful time. She touched her bump, and although it was less painful than before, it still pummeled her head. She felt emotionally and physically exhausted but not sleepy. Kara returned to the couch and settled herself under the blankets. She shut her eyes and breathed the pranayama yoga method until she eventually drifted to sleep.

Rikk

Rikk squinted, yawned, and stretched, feeling somewhat disoriented until he spotted Kara on the couch. She appeared to be sleeping soundly, and he was feeling bad about having to wake her. He found himself restricted by the afghan he'd brought from *Genie's Bottle* and realized that Kara must have gotten up and put it on him.

Looking at the afghan, Rikk was reminded him of the prayer shawl that Barb Watson gave to Lauren when her cancer was diagnosed. He had mixed feelings about it. He remembered the sad times when he covered her with it when she was too weak to do it herself, and the times how good it felt when Lauren persuaded him to snuggle with her under it. Because his memories of wrapping it around both of them had a slight positive edge over the reason that it was given to her, he kept it around. When the Watsons would visit Barb would always walk over and stroke it.

It was two twenty now. Rikk remembered looking at his watch at one twenty-five. Kara must have woken up and covered him. Then he spotted Kara's note under the Tylenol bottle. She had been up shortly after the two-hour interval passed when he was supposed to check on her. Rikk stood up, stretched, and walked over to wake Kara. He considered letting her sleep but decided he needed to make sure she was coherent. He sat on the coffee table across from her, not sure if he should call her name or nudge her shoulder. Her breathing was deep and relaxed; her color was good. The bump on her head hadn't gotten any smaller, but it hadn't gotten any larger either. A black bruise was setting in from the contusion, and the scraped skin looked red and tender. Kara stirred, squinted her eyes open just a slit, and rolled from her side onto her back. Rikk watched her eyes gradually open. "Kara, why didn't you wake me up?"

"I figured you needed to get some sleep since you have to work in a few hours."

Rikk didn't reply to this and proceeded to ask the same questions he'd asked before. Kara complied with answers. Then he said, "I want you to wake me up when you're awake."

"OK, fine. But I didn't wake you up because you looked so tired earlier."

"The point of me staying here with you is to help you, and I can't do that when I'm sleeping."

"So, let me get this straight. If I wake up, but don't get up, you still want me to wake you?"

"That's right."

"Fine. I can do that." Kara shut her eyes. "Can I go back to sleep?"

"Yes." Though civil enough, Rikk felt her chill. He shook out a couple Tylenol tablets from the bottle, and swallowed them before he settled back into his chair. This time he didn't pick up the book, just stared out the window and noticed that the wind had subsided. He dozed off again.

At four in the morning Rikk woke up. He checked Kara and then decided to wait at least fifteen minutes before waking her. He stepped outside and felt the diminishing breeze blow fresh air in his face. He paced the sidewalk in front of the lobby, drinking in the sight of shimmering yard lights dancing on the water with the various shades of white boats swaying and bobbing, all against the bashful backdrop of early dawn. The squealing fenders rubbing against the docks and halyards clanking on the sailboat masts created a surreal performance. Rikk felt like he was in a music video where the boats were the musicians, and he was the surreptitious observer. Rikk pulled himself away from his daydream and went back inside. He sat on the coffee table across from Kara.

"Kara, Kara." He set his hand on her shoulder and said louder, "Kara."

"I'm awake. I need some water."

"How does your head feel?"

93

"Still hurts." She sat halfway up, bracing herself on her elbow. "What time is it?"

"A little after four. Do you have any numbness or tingling in your arms or legs?"

"No."

"Why don't you sit up? I'd like to check your neck for any pain or discomfort." He examined her and was glad that she had minimal stiffness. He held the blankets while she settled back onto the couch and then covered her.

"I really appreciate your staying with me all night, but I'm fine. You can go home and get a little sleep."

"Kara, I'll stay with you at least until six, and then Dutch can check in on you." Rikk needed to leave by six if he was going to get home, shower, and get ready for work on time. He sat back down, put his feet on the coffee table, and covered himself with the afghan. He picked up the book again and read a few more chapters before he fell asleep.

✦✦✦✦✦

Rikk drifted out of his deep slumber. The sun had climbed above the horizon, and daylight gradually filtered into the lobby illuminating it with its warmth. The sun beamed into his eyes; he yawned and stood up.

"What time is it?" asked Kara, peering out from under the blanket.

"It is—oh, geez, it is six fifteen," Rikk's voice was anxious.

"What time do you have to be at work?"

"I'm usually showering now, but I don't have to be there until seven. I have to hurry."

"I should pick up my stuff and head back to *Genie's Bottle*," Kara said as she pushed herself up.

Rikk watched the cautious and steady effort she exerted to stand. She stretched and winced when she brushed her bruised forehead with her hand. He replied, "How do you feel?" as he helped her pick up the blankets, pillows, and containers from last night's sandwiches.

"OK, all things considered."

"I'll talk to Dutch and ask him to look in on you."

"I thought I only needed a babysitter through the night."

"I said twelve hours, but I guess it's close enough. I will walk you to your boat."

"Really, I'm fine and can get there on my own. I—"

"Kara, do you still have a headache?"

"Yes, a dull constant ache, but the Tylenol has helped it, Dr. Harmon." Kara emphasized the word doctor. "It is still pretty tender; but I heal fast, and it is much better than it was last night. If you don't leave now you'll be late for work."

Although Kara was moving slower than usual, Rikk wasn't about to mention it, at least she didn't refuse to let him walk her to *Genie's Bottle*. They walked in awkward silence. He helped her step up on *Genie's deck,* and then handed her the canvas bag. She thanked him as she opened the hatch.

"I can make it from here. Thank you for, well, for staying with me last night. God, that sounds so pathetic," Kara said as she slid the hatch open.

"Sure. Thank you for taking care of my boat." The whole situation was as uncomfortable for him as he thought it was for Kara. He took a few steps, then turned abruptly and said, "I'll be back later today to check in on you." He caught Kara admiring him, and her mortified expression that followed. Rikk grinned and sauntered down the dock, listening to her careful flight into her sailboat's cabin.

Chapter 15

Rikk

As Rikk drove home, he wondered what was going on between them, or if anything was going on—he wasn't sure. If nothing was going on, why did he have an underlying fear about his role during the night? Then he remembered one of the last conversations he'd had with Lauren, and her words replayed in his head with her clear voice telling him to trust his intuition and keep his heart open. Somehow, that eased his anxiety about Kara.

When he arrived at the hospital, he ran into Joe, who was holding an empty coffee cup and heading for the staff lounge. Rikk asked him if he had a few minutes to talk. Before he could close the door behind them, Joe's wife, Barb, caught the door and walked in. "Hi, Rikk. Did you get your boat?" she asked.

Rikk smiled but felt less happy than he should have when he replied, "Yes, it was delivered yesterday." Barb just scowled a quizzical look at him, which was enough encouragement for Rikk to begin. "You might as well hear this firsthand, Barb. I know that Joe will fill you in anyhow." Rikk relayed the past twenty-four hours to them. When he ended the tale and walked to the window overlooking Lake Superior, silence filled the room. Joe and Barb said nothing. He turned to face them and then admitted what plagued him the most. "I couldn't let her stay there alone. I must be an idiot for not insisting she go to the ER"

Barb walked over to Rikk and stood next to him, resting her hand on his back. "Rikk, you know you cannot force someone to accept treatment. Besides, I've always known you to make sound decisions. I do know that

96

if Lauren were alive, she would've insisted that you bring Kara home with you, so you both could watch her. Given the circumstances, I'm sure Lauren would've wanted you to stay with her last night. It's funny, though, that Dutch didn't stay with both of you." Barb pursed her lips together and added, "So how does that make you an idiot?"

"I don't know. I guess I've been pretty gun shy about helping anyone since the lawsuit."

Joe said, "Rikk, the lawsuit was bogus, and you know that. You took the advice of the insurance company because it would be cheaper in the end for you and them to avoid the litigation costs, not because you had any fault. As far as last night, I'm not sure what I would've done in that situation, but I have to agree with Barb. If Lauren could talk to you now, I'm sure she'd tell you in this situation you were right to spend the night."

Rikk appreciated their support, but continued to stare out the window. He omitted revealing their past acquaintanceship and the resurfacing conflicted feelings Kara's presence evoked. Rikk also knew his fear of a lawsuit was unfounded, even though he'd felt cuffed when Kara said "liability."

"Rikk, it sounds like she is all right and everything is going to be fine. Who knows, maybe she is supposed to teach you something," Barb said.

Rikk was stunned, and he knew he showed it.

Barb smiled and said, "Maybe about sailing?" She shrugged. "I bet you'd love to show off your boat to us tonight. Afterwards we can go out for dinner. What time should we arrive, and how do we find it?"

It took a couple of seconds for Rikk to catch up to the new topic before he answered, "Of course I would, Barb. How does six thirty sound?"

"Sounds great." Barb walked towards the door flashing Joe a grin.

"Sounds like you didn't have a choice," Joe snickered and winked at Barb. "Barb has an uncanny way of proposing ideas she has packaged with something she wants. The good thing is that it is something everyone else wants too."

"And might I inform you, Rikk, that I got my way with Joe when we first met by offering him dinner and dancing," Barb said.

Joe laughed and countered, "Dancing or there would be no dinner is the way I remember it."

"Rikk, relax. Spending the night with someone who may have had a minor concussion is not worth your worrying. Go be the great doctor that I know you are." Barb paused, and then reiterated, "Rikk, you did the right thing; now give Joe the information we need to find your boat. I have an appointment. I've got to dash. See you tonight."

Rikk gave Joe the dock and slip location and then started his rounds. He first went to the room of his patient whose emergency surgery kept him at the hospital much later than he had anticipated the night before. His patient's hair was the same color that Kara's hair was when he first met her over twenty years ago. Now it was lighter, filled with sun streaks. Why was he thinking about the most ridiculous things, like how the sun had bleached streaks into Kara's hair? Later in the morning, he pulled the chart of a new patient off the door whose last name was McKeon. All morning everything seemed to make his mind wander to Kara—and that irritated him. He hadn't had time to call the marina and talk to Dan about why the boom fell and what repairs were needed. He saw patients in the clinic until twelve thirty. After checking his schedule, Rikk found he had a cancellation, which gave him time to drive to the marina. *God, I haven't even looked at my boat yet.*

⚓

As Rikk slowed and made the turn into the marina, he spotted Kara walking about a block away heading toward the beach, which was on the other side of Minnesota Point. The twinge in his stomach made Rikk realize that he wanted was to check on Kara first, then his boat. He stopped at the marina office and was directed to the lunchroom to find Dan. While Dan finished his lunch, he told Rikk that they had heard about the accident from Dutch and already checked it out. The extent of the damage was cosmetic. Unless they could find the keeper pin, they wouldn't be able to determine if it was faulty or improperly installed. Together they walked to Rikk's boat and spent a couple minutes looking at the shackle. Rikk agreed to have Dan get the repairs on the schedule even though it would be mid-summer before they would be able to get his boat into the shop. Dan left Rikk standing next to his boat when the office paged him.

Miss Sea was not in her slip, which relieved Rikk. He stood quietly listening to hear any sounds from *Genie's Bottle*, but everything was quiet. He knocked a couple times on *Genie's* hull, but Kara wasn't back yet or wasn't answering. He would check on her after work, and that would be better because it would give him more time to figure out her strange behavior.

⁂

Rikk intended to drive back to the clinic to finish his afternoon appointments, but on a whim, he turned toward the beach. From the parking lot he couldn't see the beach over the sand dune. He parked and walked down the boardwalk, feeling like he was on a reconnaissance mission to find Kara.

Rikk spotted Kara a few hundred feet down the beach, sitting crossed legged with her palms facing up and the backs of her hands resting on her knees. She held her thumb and middle finger together in a classic meditation pose. He was about to turn and leave when he saw her stretch and watched her deliberate effort to stand. Rikk checked his watch and found he still had fifteen minutes to get back to the clinic, and it was a ten-minute drive. He could ask her how she was feeling in less than five minutes. Besides, if she spotted him walking back to his car, it would appear that he was spying on her. He came toward Kara, watching her and waiting until she noticed him. When she spotted him, her expression was a combination of surprise and apprehension, followed by a weary smile. She waved at him, although it seemed that it was more of a reflex since she stopped abruptly.

"You must be feeling pretty good to be walking on the beach," Rikk smiled and called to her from fifteen feet away.

"I'm feeling pretty good."

"I saw you meditating. I hope I didn't disturb you."

"No, you didn't disturb me, Dr. Harmon. But I thought that is what doctors do best."

"How is that?"

"Don't you know that doctors have perfect timing to walk in and ask their questions, poke, prod, and disturb their patients exactly one minute after they have finally fallen asleep?"

99

"I guess I'd be foolish to argue with you after last night, except the one-minute part of your theory. I know of no scientific study proving that it takes exactly one minute before the doctor disturbs the patient."

"I guess you are here to quiz, poke, and prod me. Did you bring your flashlight to look at my pupils?"

"No, but since you brought it up I'll take a look." Actually, Rikk didn't need to, but he wanted to look. Anyhow, he wasn't her doctor. Kara made that clear last night. He stepped in front of her, and she lifted her chin to him. Kara swayed a little, so he rested his hand behind her head and neck. He paused for a moment to see if she would resist his help, but she stood almost motionless. He said, "You've got quite a black eye." Rikk noticed Kara's reserved smile. "But I guess you must have seen that this morning."

"I've got a shiner and no one to show it to." Kara started walking toward the waves lapping the sand, and Rikk followed half a step behind. "I guess I should be glad for that."

"Have you made those calls to arrange for help sailing your boat back to Bayfield?"

"I made a couple and left messages; I'm waiting to hear back from people. It's funny, though. We have been gone for so long that it is hard to ask for help. Many of our friends have moved or have dropped out of contact with me, especially since Connor died. So calling to ask for help is harder than I expected."

"Most people love to come to the aid of old friends in need."

"Yes, but my intentions were to sail back into Bayfield unnoticed and let our old friends find me on their own volition to re-engage in our friendship. I'm not being elite; it's just that I was half of the Connor and Kara Show when I left, and now I am returning as a solo act. I don't want to impose on them, especially when so many changes have taken place over the years for everyone."

"Are you worried about finding help?"

"No, this morning Dan said he'd help me find crew. I'll need to pay them for the delivery, but as I meditated—I guess you saw me—I got the feeling I should not enlist the help of old friends. It just feels right to hire my crew instead."

"It sounds like you aren't sure you want to go back to Bayfield?"

"I am. I've been thinking more about it these last few months—more than ever since Connor's death. I just want to go back there standing behind the wheel with the sails filled." Kara looked out over the lake towards Bayfield and then took slow steps to the water's edge.

"Is that why you didn't have your boat delivered to Bayfield?" Rikk kept an arm's distance between them as he walked beside Kara, now a half step in front of her to read her expressions.

"Mostly no. Dan is an old friend. Connor and I used to sail *Genie* to Duluth and stay in the marina every summer to go to the Bayfront Blues Festival. Dan came down to visit us a few times while we cruised in the Caribbean. When I decided to move back, I called the yards in Bayfield, and they couldn't get *Genie*'s hull painted until late summer. So I called Dan, and he promised to squeeze *Genie* into the shop for at least the painting if I got her shipped here by the first week in May. After those arrangements were made, I just began to love the idea of sailing her back to Bayfield single-handed."

"Is it that important for you to be independent?" Rikk asked, and he picked up a piece of driftwood and inspected it.

"Yes. I don't want to land there looking like a forlorn widow. Maybe that is the reason for this bump. When I do get there, I'll have a story to tell that will show everyone that I'm fine and capable of taking care of myself."

"Don't you think you've proven that already?"

"I think that those friends who are still close see it. But from some of the comments I've heard, I think a lot of them feel I'm returning to the comfort of the womb, so to speak."

"Why do you care what those people think?"

Kara's eyes widened, and she stopped walking. "Ahhh!" She squeezed her eyes shut, looked skyward, and cupped her palms upward to beckon an answer.

"Hit a nerve?" Rikk said.

"Yes. You hit a nerve I didn't realize I still had. Well, I guess I've been caring too much. Thank you for the reminder that it only matters what I think of me, not what anyone else does."

Rikk gave the driftwood a sidearm toss into the lake. "Do you really believe that?"

"What side of this topic are you on?"

"I'm just wondering if you really don't care what others think of you."

"I believe that if you care too much about what others think, you are living your life for them and not yourself. Essentially, you can't live authentically when you are trying to live in a way that is acceptable to everyone else. Besides, it is impossible to please everyone, especially everyone at the same time. Pleasing yourself by listening to your intuition and following your heart is being real—authentic. Those who share your values and beliefs will find you attractive and gravitate to you. In that way you please others, not by trying to please them, but by being real."

"If others don't share your values and beliefs, you don't care about them?" Rikk found this thought incredible.

"That is not exactly what I said or meant. I do care very much about others—sometimes too much. I try not to base my decisions and actions on what others want from me or what I think they want from me." Kara looked annoyed and turned toward the boardwalk.

As Rikk watched Kara's agitated response, he felt a strange glee that he had irritated her. He sighed and softened his stance. "So you do care about others; you just don't live for them."

"Yeah, that's right. I don't live my life to meet their approval, or to meet my approval or disapproval of them."

"What do you mean by your approval or disapproval of them?"

"It's the opposite side of the same subject. An example is hate—or envy. If I'm envious of a person's wealth or status, and live my life to have everything they have—or more, to have equal status, then I'm living my life to meet my approval of them. I can't live authentically living up to someone else."

"What about hate?"

"If I'm saying and doing things to hurt someone I hate, I'm living for them too. If my hate is covert, played out in my thoughts only, the person I hate isn't even aware of it. So all the hate I feel eats me up and does nothing to them."

"What about overt hate? Where I work, I've seen people have no problem showing their hate behind other people's backs and even right to their faces."

"Then I hurt myself by going public with my hate. I believe that hate often stems from insecure feelings and manifests in the form of aggression. People who display hate publicly, or privately, create problems in their lives. I think it limits their careers and their friendships—and their personal relationships. Either covert or overt, hate controls the hater—possesses them just like a demon."

"You don't seem the type to hate others." Rikk admitted to himself he'd tried a few times to hate her. *But why?* He looked back at the lake as if his answer would roll in on a wave.

Kara said nothing for a moment; then said, "I am human and capable of all human emotions."

"I've heard that before. Who said that?"

"I don't know. It's humbling, isn't it?"

Rick's smile confirmed agreement. "You don't seem the type to envy, either."

"Rikk, my demons may not be hate and envy, but I do have demons. I'd just as soon not list them right now."

"Hmm," Rikk nodded as he contemplated that.

"When you said that you would be back to check on me, I thought it would be later, after work. Are you off early today?"

"No, I'm due back," Rikk looked at his watch, "soon."

"Do you have patients waiting for you?"

"No, not yet."

"But you will have patients waiting by the time you get back." Kara's accusing tone and scowl telegraphed her disapproval.

Rikk was angry at Kara's tone and did not try to hide it from her. "It is rare that I'm late for my appointments." He turned away and walked fast to his car.

"I'm sorry," Kara called out to him, "that was judgmental."

Rikk turned and shot back, "Is judgment one of your demons?" He felt smug, but only for a moment. It ended when he glanced back and saw her stand there looking dejected. That only made him feel—hell, he didn't know. Empty, yes, it made him feel empty.

Chapter 16

Kara

Kara regretted passing judgment as she watched Rikk flee. He was angry and had a right to be. She had given him a hard time without real cause. For someone she was not planning to see again, Kara decided she had spent much more time with Rikk Harmon than she ever intended. She didn't want to go back to *Genie's Bottle*. Sitting out in the cockpit on this warm spring afternoon would probably end up like earlier this morning when she caught herself numerous times staring at Rikk's boat. His boat was beautiful, yet a constant reminder of the man with a reserved, calm demeanor she observed years ago. The irritated and antagonistic side of him she had never witnessed before, nor had she expected to. She walked along the beach for a while until her dull headache had resumed, and she wanted to nap.

Kara was happy to see that Dutch was still out fishing when she reached the dock. She hadn't spoken to him since the night before when he stormed out of the lobby leaving Rikk alone with her. She wondered if she and Rikk were right about Dutch's agenda, and even more why it mattered so much to him. For now, though, she would escape to the comfort of *Genie's Bottle* and nap the afternoon away. She'd find an old friend that she never tired of, *To Kill a Mockingbird*, and read it while she snuggled under a blanket.

Kara woke to the sound of *Miss Sea* coming into the marina. She decided not to rush out to greet Dutch. She was certain he'd check in on her today. She looked at her clock and was surprised to see she had indeed slept the afternoon away, but sleeping kept her thoughts from sneaking back to Rikk. It was five o'clock, and she needed to get up, if for nothing more than to be able to sleep tonight. Kara heard knocking on the hull and assumed it was Dutch, so she yelled, "Come on in." Dutch would've come in, but whoever it was kept knocking. When she opened the companionway hatch, she was surprised to see Ted standing in her cockpit. She had only talked to him when he helped launch *Genie's Bottle* two days ago, and then he seemed reserved. He looked nervous and stammered as he told her that Dan had mentioned she was looking for crew.

Kara grabbed her sweater and stepped out into the cockpit. She arranged with Ted to help her sail *Genie* to Bayfield on Monday, providing the weather cooperated. He said he'd ask around and see if anyone else might want to crew. Kara thanked him and watched him walk down the dock. She was wrong about Dutch's boat; it wasn't *Miss Sea* but another fishing boat that sounded like her. The only boat near *Genie* was Dr. Harmon's boat. She wondered if Rikk would be back tonight, and if he did come back, if he would ignore her for chiding him about keeping his patients waiting.

Kara walked up on *Genie's* deck, and as she passed the side stays, she noticed that the one she grabbed seemed a little loose. She checked all of them and found three that needed to be re-tuned. Kara was glad for something to do to break up the monotony of the day and grabbed a crescent wrench and large screwdriver. Back on *Genie's* deck, she kneeled down and adjusted the tension of the stays, standing to check them as she worked. She finished with the stay on *Genie's* port side next to the dock. She forgot about her injury and consequently stood up too fast. Dizziness overcame her, and she grasped onto the stay as she teetered over *Genie's* lifelines. *Hang on, breathe, hang on,* she told herself in rapid succession. *Genie* dipped to port, and she heard someone stepping aboard. Strong arms grabbed her and held her steady until the dizziness subsided. In the process, she again found herself leaning on a person she couldn't see.

Rikk's husky voice gave her a chill, "I've got you, Kara. Just let me get on the boat."

Kara managed to stand still and desperately fought to regain control of both her equilibrium and dignity. *God, what message have I been sending out all day? Why haven't I been able to purge him from my thoughts after so damn long?* As Rikk held her between him and the side stay, he took his time to swing his feet over the lifeline. He held her much too close. His face grazed her head, and Kara felt him inhale as if he was consuming her.

She shuddered despite her efforts to stay motionless. Kara knew he felt her involuntary action, and hoped he interpreted it as dizziness. With a dry throat, her voice croaked, "I'm OK now. I just stood up too fast."

"I saw that," Rikk said as he turned Kara to face him. "Let's get you sitting down." His hands cradled her rib cage as he lowered her to the cabin's deck. Rikk still held onto her while she sat there. Kara wouldn't look into his face until she gained control. She held her breath and began to feel dizzy again.

Rikk moved one hand to lift her face to his, but Kara's eyes remained fixed on her feet. He waited, then in a hushed voice he said, "Breathe, Kara."

Kara gasped as she looked into Rikk's eyes, trembled, and felt the crescent wrench and screwdriver slip out of her hands. Her reflex action to grab them before they slid into the lake failed. Rikk snatched both items just before they slipped off the deck. In a hoarse whisper, Kara managed to say, "I need to sit in the cockpit." With one hand holding the tools, he helped her to her feet and then wrapped his arm around her waist and assisted her from mid-ship to the cockpit.

The fact that Kara was so affected by Rikk's close presence tonight seemed to enthuse him—like he was winning some sophomoric courting contest. When they got to the cockpit, he helped her sit, set the tools down, and then asked if she wanted some water. Kara nodded yes. Rikk disappeared into *Genie's* cabin and provided Kara a moment to compose herself. She rested her head on her knees, which she clutched close to her chest. He came back out too soon, and put his arm around her back, offering her the glass of water. "Kara, here, drink this."

Kara finally gathered courage to look into Rikk's face, the handsome face that once again was too close to hers for comfort. She cleared her parched throat to utter a thank you. Kara took a long drink. He continued to hold her shoulder, and Kara knew she needed to make conversation for no other reason than to gain control over her growing desires that contradicted the impossible circumstances she hid from Rikk. "I'm surprised you came back tonight after I criticized you for being late for your appointments."

"It didn't set well."

"I'm sorry for moralizing. I guess I find it frustrating when clients don't call me on time; but then I've been late for appointments too," Kara said.

Rikk glanced at his boat, then back to Kara and said, "Dizziness is common after concussions for a couple of weeks, especially if you stand or move suddenly."

Kara gave a cynical smile. "Is that your way of asking me if I've been dizzy today?"

"Actually that is my way of asking you that, and other questions too."

"What other questions?"

"It doesn't sound like you're open to any questions regarding your injury—"

"Ask away. I'll honor my pact to be a gracious and compliant patient." Kara was surprised at how her reply disarmed Rikk; he actually looked remorseful.

"And I'll honor my pact to be a considerate and empathetic doctor."

Rikk sounded sincere, almost apologetic, and Kara realized that she didn't know him at all. Maybe the man she had imagined Rikk to be all these years was standing here right now. She forced a smile and set her head back on her knees.

"How's your headache?"

"For the most part it is gone, although it is back now. I mean, I have a slight headache, but I just got it when you got here." Rikk's quizzical look made Kara laugh. "Not because you are here, because I stood up too fast." She guessed Rikk was aware of and enjoyed how edgy she was in his presence. Why else would he stay planted in her personal space? She wanted to tell him to back away. Her intuition screamed at her to tell him that they had met years ago. It was time to reveal her secret, though not all of it.

"Well, I'm glad I'm not the cause of your headache."

"No, you aren't."

"I suppose I am, indirectly, since my boom hit your head."

"Well, it'd be easy to blame you, but I chose to put my head where your boom could crash down on it. So, we could argue who's to blame all night."

"I thought Dutch's words were so strange; that boaters look after each other, as though they have an inclination to do so."

"Foul weather makes the water the foe and all of us adversaries."

"Then you acted as my adversary, not on a whim?" Rikk asked in a way that Kara couldn't discern if he was teasing or serious.

"A whim? No, more like an impulse."

"Aren't impulses the same as whims? Reactionary?"

"They can be, but not always." Kara considered every word as she spoke, "Rikk, have you ever had a—oh, geez, a feeling so strong—" She blew out her breath and then searched for right words. Meeting his direct stare she resumed, "Have you ever had an impulse that you logically knew would be disastrous, even though you wanted to act on it—one with no guarantee how it would turn out. One that if you carried it through, you would risk losing everything you knew, everything you had, and everything you loved. Yet an impulse so strong that over time you questioned what would've happened if you *would* have—" She stopped and shook her head. She had said too much. Kara was irritated that she let her guard down and intrigued at how Rikk's benign question triggered her to spew out way more than what was safe. She had to change the subject. She heard an incoming motor boat and looked out to spot *Miss Sea* coming toward them.

Dutch waved at them, slowed as he approached his slip, and yelled out, "I caught dinner. Got lake trout for all of us. Come take a look at 'em." His face was beaming.

"Either he's caught the biggest fish of his life, or—" Kara bit her lip and exhaled.

"Or Dutch is extremely happy to see us together tonight?"

"More like jubilant."

Rikk and Kara went over to look at the fish, and Dutch tossed *Miss Sea*'s dock lines to Rikk. Before they could say anything, Dutch said, "Kara, you got something to go with the trout with all those provisions you loaded on *Genie's Bottle* yesterday? Don't think the Doc's got anything, do you, Doc?"

Dutch's arrival saved Kara from finishing a conversation she regretted starting, and even though she would've preferred to eat alone, she took the easy way out and acquiesced to his plan. "I can make some pasta and a salad."

"I've got a bottle of wine in the car that I forgot to bring to my boat," Rikk said. Then he glanced at Kara and added, "Dutch, do you need any help cleaning those fish—with that queasy gut of yours?"

Kara smiled as Dutch defended himself, "Awe, I just said I almost get sick cleaning fish. I'll do it myself; and Doc, you help Kara with the other stuff since you ain't got nothing else to do."

"Dutch, here you go again, calling all the shots. I'm capable of preparing pasta and throwing together a salad," Kara said just before turning towards *Genie's Bottle.*

"Since I don't have much to offer except the wine, why don't we eat on my boat? It's the least I can do. But I don't have dishes. Maybe I can borrow them from you, Kara?"

Kara longed for distance from Rikk, but she recognized that both Dutch and Rikk were conspiring to prevent that from happening. She shrugged and agreed, figuring that she would gather plates, silverware, wine glasses, and napkins first thing and set them in the cockpit for Rikk, so she could cook in solitude.

When Rikk got back with the wine, he saw the tableware sitting in the cockpit but came onboard and asked, "Do you have a corkscrew, Kara?" She replied yes, but before she could get it, Rikk added, "I'm pretty skilled at making salads."

"That's OK. It gives me something to do, since I haven't accomplished anything all day."

"I'd really like to come down to give you a hand, and I have some other questions I'd like to ask you."

"Oh, more questions?"

He came down the companionway and took the corkscrew that Kara dug out of the drawer and opened the wine. "This wine needs to breathe."

Kara said nothing and continued to gather salad ingredients from the icebox and drawers. She placed them on the table alongside a bowl, cutting board, and knife.

"Kara, besides the headache and dizziness just now, how are you feeling?"

"Good. I've iced my bump most of the afternoon while I napped. I've basically lain low all day."

"Have you found your crew yet?"

"I'm waiting to hear back from a couple of people and have one crew now. I'm sure that I will be able to leave Monday or Tuesday." She didn't look up from the pasta she was measuring, but out of the corner of her eye she noticed that he was watching her more than he was preparing the salad.

"Kara, what were you saying about a strong impulse? You weren't finished when Dutch came. Do you have regrets about something now because you didn't act on an impulse?"

"No, just the opposite. Years later I now know that following my impulse would have been a mistake, yet it's strange how some things stay with you and haunt you and some you forget immediately." Kara spoke as unaffected as possible, and regretted every word she said earlier about impulses. She did not intend to revisit that discussion now. Rikk stopped cutting the lettuce and stared at her. "Here, these are for the salad too." She handed him the pear, pecans, and gorgonzola cheese. She sensed that he was once again irritated with her. She knew she was going to call her coaching colleague, Robin, tomorrow to get some coaching and a new perspective on all the events that occurred since Dr. Rikkert Harmon's boat was delivered.

"What made you ask me if I ever had an impulse that I didn't act on?" Rikk's impatient and controlled voice demanded.

"Rikk, I was uncomfortable and was just blabbering and blundering."

"Uncomfortable about what?"

"You must know about personal space, especially in your profession."

"What?"

"You were invading my personal space."

"I recall you were dizzy, and I caught you and helped you sit down."

"Yes, and I am grateful for that. You may have saved me from toppling into the lake, but you have to admit that you could've moved away when

I was sitting in the cockpit. You certainly don't always remain so close to your patients."

"You are not my patient," Rikk shot back. "That is what you told me."

Rikk

Rikk finished making the salad while Kara tossed the fettuccini noodles in basil pesto and freshly grated Asiago cheese. Their conversation was minimal and limited to the food they were preparing. *Damn her! She isn't going to finish what she started to say.* Spending time with Kara was like riding a roller coaster. Their ride was filled with brief peaks followed by exhilarating descents, like catching her when he arrived tonight and feeling her awareness of him. But the excruciating struggle of the ascents always followed. He found himself back on the ascent as he worked to melt her coolness. *Hell, she was like ice again.* The bottom of the ride was always underscored with the nagging question. *Why does she treat me like a complete stranger?* He was never sure if the ride was over or beginning the next ascent. Now, a new question nagged him. What did the impulse she mentioned have to do with him?

※◎※

When they had finished preparing food, Kara suggested that they bring it along with the tableware and wine to his boat and set up the cockpit table. Dutch finished frying the fish and crossed over onto the OSQ from *Miss Sea* right after Rikk had put the cockpit table up.

Rikk toasted, "Here's to Dutch for catching fish and Kara for the rest of the meal."

Kara added, "And to you for the wine."

"And for the Doc's boom landing on your head, Kara, that kept you here today to eat with us," Dutch said, bellowing his jovial toast, and then he clinked his wine glass with Rikk's.

Kara feigned shock and shook her head in mock disgust, "I'm not sure I can toast to that, Dutch."

"I can! I'm sorry that you got hurt, but it has given me a chance to try to figure out why you look so familiar." Rikk said. He watched Kara flush and squirm—she looked almost panicked. Rikk smiled at his timing at exposing her former acquaintanceship with him, and with Dutch's presence, he'd be sure to extract an admission. Instead, she took a bite of pasta and chewed slowly, a ploy, no doubt, to avoid divulging their prior association.

Dutch's eyes darted from one to the other, and he huffed. "You two still at it? You're feuding like school kids pretending not to be smitten with each other; that I know for sure. What I don't understand is how you both got too damn much pride—keeps you from admitting it."

Rikk noticed Kara was shocked at Dutch's brashness, and he wondered if she felt as guilty as he did for the truth of Dutch's words. Kara looked over at *Genie's Bottle* as if she were ready to run for refuge. Rikk said, "Dutch, that's a strong accusation, don't you—"

"Hell, the way you two are acting reminds me of my friend, Johnny." Dutch likely had plenty of tales to draw them back into an amiable conversation, and Rikk could see Kara felt as uncomfortable as he did. Dutch started on a tirade. "When I was in the merchant marines, we was in Zihuatanejo, Mexico, loading bananas. We spent the last night ashore drinking tequila. Johnny, a buddy of mine, was positive that he spotted his girlfriend in a bar dancing with some local. The poor bastard's eyesight was crap. He went swinging both fists after the guy. By the end of the fight, the bar was full of tipped over chairs and tables. Some broken ones too. There was blood splattered all over the floors—and cerveza and tequila everywhere. The policia broke it up and threw the whole crew in jail. Let the locals all go. As the girl walked out, Johnny got a closer look at her. All he said was 'Shit, you ain't Myra!' She spit in Johnny's face. The captain spent most of the next day bailing us out of jail. I guess we deserved the scrubbing duties he assigned the whole lot of us. We scrubbed the sun's shadows off the ship the entire trip back to the States!"

Dutch's story succeeded in getting them relaxed and into an amiable conversation. While they ate, Rikk quizzed Kara about places she'd traveled. She teased him about getting up to speed on his sailor lingo; reminding him that sailing all alone is called single-handed.

"Have either of you ever been to the Port of Altamira?" Rikk said.

"Nope," Dutch said.

"Yeah, but quite awhile ago. Were you there?" Kara said.

"Lauren and I went for a month on a working vacation four years ago. I volunteered in a rural hospital, and Lauren did anything that was needed. She had such a way with people that they gave her a hand-carved mask when we left. I think it's very old and valuable." Rikk reflected momentarily before saying, "Value never really mattered to Lauren. She loved it because it was beautiful, and it reminded her of her favorite vacation."

"It sounds like Lauren's memories meant more to her than the mask itself," Kara said.

"They did," Rikk said, sounding more melancholy than he'd expected. "I'd love to show it to you."

"I'd love to see it."

Rikk didn't expect her quick acceptance to his invitation. The conversation lulled until Dutch gave the latest near and offshore weather forecasts for the next few days, ending it with, "Rain called for all weekend. You know, sometimes you just got to get wet since you ain't going to stop the rain by fighting it."

Kara laughed as she repeated, "You aren't going to stop it by fighting the rain. When I was a kid we had a two-week rainy period that kept everyone in a bad mood. I was so sick of being stuck inside that I went outside in a downpour. I just stood out in the middle of the yard facing the sky with my eyes shut and let the rain drench me. I was doing the opposite of a rain dance."

"Did you stop the rain?" Dutch asked.

"Not instantly. But it did stop, and I got some crazy neighbor stares."

"Were the neighbors crazy or the one standing in the rain?" said Dutch.

"The neighbors' stares were crazy—the neighbors were fine. I actually think they would've joined me if they'd been living in the moment."

Rikk contemplated her answer, and he recalled, "I was much younger when I got my mom into trouble for playing in the rain. My mom and I were visiting my grandparents, and it had been raining for days. Mom had done everything she could think of to keep me entertained and out of my strict grandma's hair. Grandpa worked in a bank, and Grandma had gone to a luncheon one afternoon. My mom caught me digging in my grandpa's forbidden desk drawers, and she scolded me. I begged her to go outside. She reminded me that it was raining, but I persisted, and she finally gave in. It was one of those hot Minnesota rains, where you sweat in your raincoat. My mom took hers off and then took mine off. She threw a rock into a mud puddle, and we had a contest to see who could make the biggest splash. The next thing I knew, we were both jumping into the mud puddle and splashing each other. We were covered with mud when Grandma got home and caught us. She yelled at my mom," Rikk punched his fists onto his waist, hunched his shoulders forward and stuck his chin out. His eyes squinted and out of his tightened lips came a shrill voice, "Charlotte Marie, what on earth have you and Rikkert been doing?"

Kara laughed and said, "Your mom sounds like someone who knows the value of adults being childlike and having fun. You should have splashed your grandma!"

"Oh, no! That would never happen." Rikk laughed at the thought of splashing his grandma, and said, "Not that we didn't consider it—or regret not doing it ever since."

"Well, sometimes visualizing that sort of thing ends better than actually doing it."

"Lauren used to say she and Lotte were kindred spirits. You'd like my mom, Kara."

"Lotte is your mom?"

"Yes." Rikk said. He noticed Dutch's sudden withdrawal from their conversation and his empty stare fixated on *Miss Sea*.

Chapter 17

Kara

Kara looked at Dutch and was confused by his hollow stare. Whatever memory it brought up for him was a mystery. She started to ask him about it when a beautiful, younger woman walked down the finger dock towards them.

The cuffed, short-sleeved, marine-blue crew polo hung loosely on her slender body, and the top three buttons were unfastened revealing a stunning gold chain and sextant pendant. She pulled her hand out of the side cargo pocket of her putty-colored Capri pants and waved to Rikk. Her perfect complexion, powdered cheeks, and alluring smile glowed below her over-sized sunglasses. Her melodious voice sung out, "Hi, Rikk. Surprise! I wanted to be the first to congratulate you on your new boat—and help you mark this happy occasion. I'm so glad you had your sailboat delivered to our marina." She propped her sunglasses on top of her head and peered around the marina with familiarity of its amenities and confidence of her status as a member of the marina. "Oh, I see you already have company on her. Hello." She gave Dutch and Kara an obligatory glance and then transferred the shore bag to her other shoulder. Bottles clattered in the bag, and Kara knew they indicated this young woman's intentions of spending the evening with Rikk. "I brought you a couple of gifts to celebrate your new boat." Her eyes fixed on Rikk, and she sent him a luminous smile and then rolled her eyes before she glanced at Dutch and Kara—just long enough to force a spurious smile at them. "Your dock neighbors already paid you a visit?" Her perfect tone didn't conceal the snipe that preceded her fake laugh. "Everyone wants to see the new boat." She looked directly at Dutch and Kara, gave a heavy sigh, and turned her attention back to Rikk. "Everyone wants a piece of you all day at the hospital; I sure hope people don't make those demands on you here with your leisure time with her."

Rikk appeared confounded before he managed to ask, "What?"

"Now, I suppose I'll have to address you as Captain Harmon, instead of Dr. Harmon. Do I also need to follow maritime protocol and ask for permission to come aboard?" she said with a sophisticated, yet seductive, lilt.

Kara, watching in disbelief, couldn't fail to notice Dutch's growing irritation. She assumed he scorned Rikk's friend for her overt sensuous display, remembering how Dutch criticized the young woman who worked so hard to attract Ted a week ago. She didn't blame Dutch, either. Many times she had seen women use similar obvious lure tactics, yet never as supercilious as this woman. She always found it interesting to watch those chasing, be it man or woman, as well as those being chased. Kara realized she was staring at this woman, astounded more by her insolence toward Dutch and herself than by her overt pursuit of Rikk. Kara looked back at the woman, who was years younger than Rikk, and then eyed Rikk as he ran his hand through his hair looking stunned and sheepish.

"God damn Sirens," Dutch muttered. He glowered at this woman and then at Kara before he grabbed his fry pan and jumped from Rikk's OSQ onto *Miss Sea* in haste.

Kara, stunned by Dutch's comment and abrupt departure, yelled after him, "Dutch! Geez! Dutch?" But nothing slowed his instant retreat. She watched him stomp down *Miss Sea's* companionway and heard the pan slam on the counter.

Kara saw Rikk's mouth hanging agape as he stared at *Miss Sea*, and then he turned slowly to her. She could see his scowl matched her own. Was he embarrassed to be seen with her and Dutch, or did he expect her to make as fast a get away as Dutch just had? She felt like she was in the middle of a living puzzle. The words and actions of everyone were ripping the pieces out of the picture instead of putting it together. What the hell was he scowling at her for?

"Fuck!" he whispered, and then looked as if he hoped neither Kara nor this woman had noticed.

Giving Kara a fleeting look, the woman continued her pitch as if Kara were not there. "My parents insisted I take sailing lessons at a week-long sailing camp in Bayfield every summer, before our family's sailing vacation. Then we chartered a sailboat from this marina, and we'd spend a couple nights hanging out in Duluth before we sailed to the Apostle Islands for two weeks. I had to take my turn as captain during the mandatory man-overboard drills. Then Dad bought a Sunfish for me. I loved sailing on Lake Minnetonka all summer long when I was a kid. I sailed every day I could, except when I was at science or language camp. You know, I never had time to figure out how much I missed sailing while I was in med school and interning. When I started working at the clinic, I realized that sailing is part of what lured me back to Duluth. It's great to have some time to do it again; all I need is a boat." She flashed Rikk her smile and pulled her sunglasses back over her eyes. "These last two summers I crewed on *Pulse Rate* a few times when they were short handed on race nights. This year, I've committed to sail more often. I love racing." She sighed then laughed. "Do you know that I have a colleague who just got a new sailboat? As far as I've heard, he doesn't have crew lined up to help him sail her. I am hoping he'll accept my offer."

Her smile was charming, although her tactics anything but subtle. She had taken a step closer to Rikk's boat and set down her shore bag with the marine-blue number fifty-five printed on the recycled and worn white sail that made up the bulk of the shore bag. She unzipped the zipper along the red, top edge of the bag and dug out a box covered with nautical wrapping paper with a narrow, yellow ribbon tied in a shoestring bow. She turned away from Kara but her waist-length, blond hair didn't completely block Kara from her vision.

Kara noticed her Dansko deck sandals revealed perfectly manicured feet with glossy crimson toenails. They matched her glistening lipstick, but her fingernails were short and unpolished. *Who is she, and what does she do?* Even though Kara felt unwelcome, she couldn't pull herself away—this woman was so far from respectful that she couldn't help but study her.

The woman handed her gift to Rikk. "Am I going to have to request a boarding pass again, or am I going to have to write you up for violating the Naval Courtesy Regulations?"

"Naval Courtesy Regulations?" Rikk frowned and shook his head as he accepted the box from her.

Rikk's glance at Kara confirmed she'd failed to stifle her guffaw that exposed her astonishment of his colleague's lack of etiquette. This woman had already violated every common courtesy Kara had learned before kindergarten. Kara took a deep breath and then selected words sufficient to make a gracious escape. "We just finished eating. I'll grab my stuff and go." Kara gathered the dishes and stood to leave.

The woman's focus remained in her bag, while she said, "I guess I interrupted your dinner." Her words were as insincere and abrupt as a parent-forced apology. She pulled a bottle of champagne shrouded in a net out of her bag, and smiled at Rikk, "This is for christening your boat." She pulled another champagne bottle from her bag, "And this one is to toast her and her new owner, Captain Harmon. Open the box. Oh, I can't wait that long—it's a couple champagne flutes." She flashed an artificial smile at Kara and said, "I didn't know you'd have company so soon. I never thought to bring extra champagne flutes. However, I couldn't exactly call ahead to see how many flutes to bring, or I would have spoiled my surprise. But then, you said you were leaving." She glanced at Kara.

Kara blinked, astonished at this woman's impudent behavior. "Yes, I am leaving."

"Then I brought the perfect number."

Kara eyed Rikk; his shoulders slumped as he combed his fingers through his hair again. When he at last said, "Heidi," his voice was strained and harsh.

Kara's temper nearly flared, but before she would give Rikk a chance to introduce this woman, who so obviously didn't want Kara present this evening, she said, "You were right. I am Rikk's dock neighbor. Kara McKee. It was nice to meet you." She extended her hand to the woman, "I'm sorry; I didn't catch your name."

With a obligatory smile and practiced congeniality, the woman volunteered, "Dr. Heidi Norris. I'm a surgeon and colleague of Dr. Harmon's." She studied Kara's extended hand as if it was below her to shake hands, and then accepted Kara's hand for only a moment. She handed the netted champagne bottle to Rikk. "Rikk, I would love a tour of your sailboat. I've contacted the race admiral, and he gave me information on the Wednesday night races. You would love racing her. I started racing sailboats with my family on Lake Minnetonka when I was eight. When I was at Stanford, I was crew on—"

Kara glimpsed a confounded and immobilized Rikk, who cringed as she jumped to the dock. She teetered and held onto the OSQ's lifelines to steady herself.

"Kara, slow down." The champagne bottle made a loud thud when he set it and the gift box down, and jumped off the boat behind her. He clasped her bicep and rotated her to face him. With his teeth nearly clenched and an unmistakable warning tone he said, "Slow down. You need to move slower."

Kara bit her lower lip to refrain from sniping at him. She looked down at his hand grasping her arm and wrenched it from him. Drawing on her experiences with antagonistic customs agents, she changed her glare to a feigned pleasant expression. She agreed, "Yes, *I* need to move slower." She over emphasized I and stepped past him. He was telling *her* to slow down! This came from the man who didn't move at all, not even an introduction of Dutch or her. *Who in God's name are you to tell me to slow down?* Once again she was disappointed in him. She also was disappointed that Dr. Heidi Norris was apparently the type of woman Rikk found attractive. Why else would he just stand there and watch his colleague's brazen insolence? Maybe the two doctors had more in common than their professions.

⚜

"Well, well, well, what do we have here?" said an older gentleman approaching them, along with his wife.

"Joe," his wife sang out a warning. She smiled at Kara and said, "Hello, Rikk. Heidi." She acknowledged Heidi with a forced courteousness and turned her attention back to Kara. "Rikk, is this the sailor who rescued your boat last night?" As she said this, she let go of Joe's arm and offered to take some dishes out of Kara's hand. She raised her eyebrows at Rikk and added, "Rikk, aren't you going to introduce your friend to us?"

This time it was Heidi who looked more astonished than Rikk or Kara. Rikk let his breath escape before he said, "Kara, this is Joe Watson and his wife Barb. Joe is another colleague of mine and good friends. Uh, Barb and Lauren were best friends. Barb, Joe, this is Kara McKee, and she is the captain," making an obvious glance to Heidi as he said this, "of *Genie's Bottle.*" He gestured to Kara's boat.

"It is very nice meeting you, Barb and Joe, and Heidi—uh, Dr. Norris. I was just taking my dishes back and, well, I've got things to do. Good night," she said as she stepped toward *Genie's Bottle* and took the dishes back from Barb.

119

"Just a minute," Joe stopped her from stepping onto *Genie's Bottle*. "I'd like to take a look at the lump you have on your head. Rikk said you got knocked pretty hard last night on your rescue mission."

Kara stopped, glared at Rikk, and then said. "Really, I'm all right. I don't need a second opinion."

"She got injured rescuing your boat?" said Heidi. Her sharp voice rang with incredulity as her eyes scrutinized Rikk.

"I didn't come here to look at your head or give you an opinion at all, Kara. I came for a tour of Rikk's boat and to take him out to dinner," said Joe as he glanced at Barb.

"Oh, fuck." Rikk moaned and raked his fingers through his hair. "I forgot. Barb, I'm sorry. I forgot all about dinner."

"You've already eaten dinner with Kara?" A smile appeared on Barb's face as she looked between Rikk and Kara.

"And Dutch," Kara blurted. "Dutch caught lake trout today and insisted on sharing it with us." Kara winced, exasperated with her defensive explanation of being in Rikk's company tonight.

"And Heidi just showed up," Rikk said.

Heidi turned her charm on again, and said, "Rikk, maybe we can do this tomorrow night? I had no idea, Joe, that Rikk had already made plans for tonight. I was hoping to surprise him and brought champagne to christen his boat." She extended the champagne bottle she held to Rikk. "I'll call you tomorrow, and we can make a date to christen your boat later. By the way, what have you named her?"

"Who?" Rikk said and rubbed his forehead.

"Oh, Rikk," Heidi gave him a reassuring smile.

Kara wondered if his head was reeling as much as hers was from Dr. Heidi Norris' incessant babble. She hardly believed herself capable of empathy for Rikk having to work with this woman.

"Who are you talking about?" Rikk's voice sounded perplexed.

Heidi's embarrassed laugh preempted her congenial explanation, and she politely nudged Rikk's hand with the bottle until he took it from her. "What have you named your boat?"

"Why?" barked Rikk.

"Because you need to name your boat in order to christen her."

"Oh," Rikk snarled at Heidi, "naming this boat seems trivial at the moment."

"Trivial? You have to name your boat; you'll need a name to hale others on the radio. I've got a few ideas of great names for her. It's been awhile since I've christened a boat. Good night, Barb. Good night, Joe. I'll call you tomorrow, Rikk. I'll have a list of names for you to consider too." Heidi turned to Kara, nodded while she said, "*Mrs.* McKee." She smiled at Rikk, and then sashayed down the dock.

Kara noticed Barb and Joe resisted snickering as they watched her leave. Heidi must be in her early thirties, going on fourteen.

"Fuck!" Rikk breathed the word as he turned, grimaced, and faced the Watsons.

"Favorite word?" Kara said audible only to Rikk as she turned toward *Genie.*

Rikk glared at her; then guilt washed over him when he looked at Joe and Barb. "I'm sorry about dinner."

"That's OK, Rikk. But since we're here, how about showing off this boat of yours?" Barb asked.

Kara was about to step onto *Genie* when Joe said, "Not so fast, young lady. I still haven't had a look at your head." Kara froze. She was about to protest when Joe shrugged and said, "Occupational hazard. This old surgeon always has needed to examine every bruise, scrape, and bump that he can, especially if it has been caused by his very accomplished surgical colleague but incompetent sailor friend."

"Incompetent? Why do you call him incompetent?" asked Kara. She set the dishes down on *Genie*'s deck and brushed her bangs off her forehead.

"Yes, why do you call him incompetent?" echoed Barb.

He looked over his glasses at Rikk and said, "Because that is what Rikk called himself when he told us about this accident; because he didn't secure the boat well enough, the—what was it, the boom? The boom fell on your head."

"The boom fell because the keeper pin came out, and unless we find that keeper pin, no one will ever know if it was inferior, or if it wasn't properly installed by the manufacturer. It wasn't because Rikk was incompetent."

Kara looked at Rikk and saw him watching her carefully. "You do know that, don't you?"

"Yes, I guess," he said looking away as if he wasn't convinced.

"Dr. Watson, thank you for my exam, and it was nice to meet both of you. I'm exhausted and have dishes to do before I turn in, so I better be on my way."

"Don't you want to know my diagnosis?" teased Joe.

"Now, Joe, let Kara go. Good night, Kara," Barb said and shot Kara smile.

"Well, honor me with one request then, Kara. Help our friend learn how to sail this boat," Joe said.

Before Kara could answer, Rikk offered to help her with dishes. Kara refused, reiterating that she was tired, and reminded him that he had a tour to give. She also suggested that he join the Watsons for dinner and at least have dessert with them afterwards. Then she said good night one last time and escaped down into the comfort of *Genie*'s cabin.

❧⚓❧

"Fuck!" Kara muttered under her breath. She set the dishes down, turned the cabin lights on, and shut the hatch. "Fuck the dishes! Fuck Dutch for ditching me, and fuck YOU, Dr. Rikkert Harmon!" she said louder than she wanted. She sat down on the settee and buried her head in her hands. *Geez, I'm totally captured by my f-ing saboteur. I can always tell because the F word comes so freely.*

Kara felt defeated, and all she could do was yell, "Enough, saboteur!" She took two Tylenol, shut the cabin lights off, and sat on the settee under a blanket. Kara knew she'd allowed Dr. Heidi Norris to get to her and was perplexed at how that had happened. She could not remember the last time she took someone's offensive behavior personally. She was embarrassed. Kara meditated until her mind was quiet. Then she slid down on the settee and pulled a blanket over her. At last, she drifted to sleep.

Chapter 18

Rikk

Rikk gave the Watsons a tour of his boat. They were curious about Kara and made it known that they liked her. Rikk declined their invitation to join them for dessert as Kara had suggested. As they were leaving, Barb said, "Rikk, do you want to have lunch with us tomorrow afternoon? You could ask Kara to join us. It'd be a nice gesture on your part to compensate for the inconvenience you've caused her."

"Now, Barb, you are bordering on meddling in Rikk's life," said Joe.

"Meddling would be inviting Kara to join us, and I only suggested Rikk invite her." Barb turned to Rikk and added, "If you'd like to. It would be fun for me to visit with someone who has lived such a different and interesting life compared to ours. With or without Kara, will you come to lunch with us? I'll make a reservation at the Boat House in Superior."

"Sure, Barb, that sounds good."

"Should we pick you up at your house at eleven?"

"Yeah, that would be great." Rikk said.

"Good night, Rikk," Barb smiled at him and touched his cheek as she turned and joined Joe, who was already walking down the dock. Then she called back, "Tomorrow is Saturday, just in case you forgot."

Rikk heard Barb snicker as he watched them depart. He stood motionless, debating the idea of asking Kara to join them for lunch. He had come back tonight under the guise of checking in on her, only to allow him time to figure out if he wanted to ask her out to dinner tonight, or have his boat re-assigned to another slip and avoid her until she left. He hadn't expected to have dinner with her and Dutch, or for the evening to end so badly.

Rikk knocked on *Genie's* hull. "Kara, I need to ask you something." He knocked again and this time insisted, "Kara, I need to apologize to you, and I'll go away as soon as I have." Still, there was no answer from her. He felt childlike in his determination as he knocked again and laughed, "I guess I'm acting on an impulse." He heard a muffled stirring and guessed she'd pulled a pillow over her head. He knocked a couple more times and heard her exasperated growl, and though he wasn't sure, he thought she'd said go away. "Kara," Rikk pleaded while knocking non-stop for at least a minute. "Kara, I'm not going to stop until you give me a chance to apologize."

"Damn!" Kara said and groaned. Then she called out to him, "Apology accepted."

"I want to apologize face to face." Rikk was tired of knocking and was feeling about four years old, but he wouldn't sleep knowing what an ass he was to stand back and watch Heidi's disrespectful behavior. He was determined at least to apologize for that. "Kara, please."

Kara got up and opened the hatch. She stood on the companionway step and scowled at him. "You are like a bad toothache. You just won't go away."

Rikk laughed and said, "You are right, I am. Kara, I'm sorry about the way Heidi treated you."

"This is the apology you insisted I get up for? Do you control Heidi?" Kara frowned at him.

"No, I don't control her."

"Then how can you apologize for someone you don't control?"

"I can't. I can't." Rikk heaved a sigh and labored to choose his words, "Heidi's bedside manner has always been poor, but I've never witnessed her treat anyone so impolitely. I'm sorry I didn't stop her."

"Oh, that makes me feel better. She completely lacks manners and leaves people maimed in her wake, and you are rendered speechless." Kara's words snarled out. She looked away, drew in a long breath then forced it out, shook her head, and then looked into Rikk's eyes. In a quiet and even voice, she said, "Apology accepted. Good night, Rikk." Kara started to shut the hatch cover.

Rikk grabbed the hatch and held it open. "Maimed?"

"I've never seen Dutch so upset. I've seen him tease someone about their bad manners, but he has never left in haste."

"He left because of Heidi?"

Kara's exasperation transmitted through her forced sigh. "Good night, Rikk."

"I'm not trying to defend Heidi, but she's been pushed and has pushed herself so hard to get where she is that she hasn't matured socially. It's not uncommon to see young surgeons, especially if they are on a fast career track, to be as competitive in a social setting as they've been all through school and their internships. They just don't have time to develop social skills because their only focus is on their school and careers. She lacks social graces, but she's the best surgeon we have." Rikk huffed as he said, "And she is the worst with people. I'm sorry that I didn't react to her behavior—I was shocked that she showed up here."

Kara smiled and yawned. "Apology accepted, and thanks for the insight on her. It helps me to understand her and see her with compassion. Well, good night."

"Wait, Kara, there is more that I need to say. Earlier you started to talk about not acting on your impulses. I guess that is why I bugged you until I could talk to you; it was an impulse that I just decided to act on. It is driving me crazy that you didn't finish what you were saying about not acting on your impulse."

"Rikk, it's late. Go home and forget it."

"I can go home, but I won't get any sleep."

Kara smiled. "Well, then you will be very tired tomorrow."

"Kara, I've—"

"You've what?"

"I've not acted on impulses and have regretted it." Rikk was not sure what to say next; he'd blow Kara over if he told her his regrets concerning her. Kara's face softened, and she seemed interested in listening to what he had to say. "I—I actually had an impulse to toss Heidi in the lake this evening. I kind of regret that."

Kara laughed. "Now, *that* is an apology."

"What would you have thought of me if I would've pushed her in?"

"You should've asked me what I'd have done, not thought. Because I guarantee that I'd have laughed. But, hmm, what would I have thought?"

"Would you have helped her out?"

"Good grief, Rikk! You're asking hard questions for so late at night."

"It isn't late; it's only nine thirty. I think you would've helped her out."

"Yeah, but I probably would have done a cartwheel down the dock first."

Rikk burst into boisterous laughter. "If I would've known that, I'd have pushed her in just to see you do a cartwheel."

"I was speaking metaphorically." There was laughter in Kara's eyes when she said, "She probably would've pulled me in if I offered her my hand to help pull her out."

"She is so vindictive that she might have, or refused your help and waited for me to offer her my hand."

"So, would you've pulled her out?"

"I'll tell you what I would've done if you let me come aboard. I promise, I'll only stay half an hour. You can be in bed by ten."

"You mean, I can be in my berth by ten, don't you?" Kara's eyebrows rose, and she smiled. "Fine, you have half an hour, Dr. Harmon, before my next appointment."

"I thought doctors never keep their schedule."

"Don't get me started, Dr. Harmon, lest you waste your thirty minutes."

Kara

Rikk stepped on board *Genie* while Kara opened the hatch wider for him. He said, "I never would've pushed her into the lake, but if I somehow got possessed and had the audacity to push her in, I would've helped her onto the dock. Although I'd be slow to move and give her time to think about why I pushed her into the lake in the first place."

Kara shook her head, not knowing how to respond. Kara just hoped Rikk's disapproval of Dr. Norris was true and that he felt no desire for her, for his sake. Even though he had just admitted that, she didn't know him well enough to know if he meant it.

Kara leaned her hip against the dinette table waiting for Rikk to talk, while he sat on the companionway stairs. She could tell he struggled to keep the conversation alive. Kara was relieved that other subjects replaced the subject of Dr. Norris, and he hadn't revisited the impulses-not-acted-upon conversation. Before long, she sat down on the dinette cushions, and Rikk picked up the pillow and blanket and sat on the settee across from Kara. They shared memories of Lauren and Connor; they understood each other's loss. Kara was surprised at the tranquil freedom she felt talking with Rikk about Connor's death, and wished him the same freedom. It seemed Rikk was just becoming comfortable talking about Lauren. From what he did say, she knew his marriage was steeped in love and respect—almost as much as hers and Connor's was.

"I love her memories, even if—" Rikk stopped mid-sentence as if he wrestled with the complexity of working out his grief on his own terms.

"It's good to listen to you share your memories of Lauren. She sounds like an incredible woman. I can tell it's difficult for you to talk about her, but with time it will become easier—that I understand very well." His gaze was warm and unwavering, but Rikk didn't finish his sentence.

⊱⋅☙❦☙⋅⊰

Kara glanced at her watch and was surprised that it was eleven thirty already. She wasn't tired; in fact, she had enjoyed talking to Rikk and hoped he wouldn't think she was hinting that he leave. Even the temporary silence was comfortable, and that is something she never would've expected.

"What are your plans once you reach Bayfield?" Rikk said with a tone of indifference.

"You sound like Dutch. He's in a tizzy about my plans."

"Is that bad?"

"No. I'll be moving back into our house, my house." Kara paused at the thought of this, and saw Rikk watching her but refraining from pressing her for details. "Connor and I built it together." Their story was one she guarded. Kara kept it to herself because letting others know about their love and the life that they built together often resulted in people's pity. She did not feel pity for herself, so she sure didn't want it from others. On the occasions she shared their story, she strived to show that she was not stuck in grief—and mostly she no longer was.

"Are you sure you want to move back there?"

"I've been avoiding going back for so many reasons. Right after Connor died I went back for a short time, but found every bit of the house anchored me in the past that we both had left. So even though it was filled with great memories, I realized that *Genie* was my home, and I needed to get back to her and continue living. It felt like Connor's spirit led and accompanied me back to *Genie* and the Caribbean."

"Why are you moving back here now?"

"I wish I could explain that to you. I don't even completely understand why."

"What do you mean?"

"OK, let me warn you that if you don't meditate, you may not understand this—but you asked." A pensive smile crossed Kara's face, and she fiddled with the dirty dishes sitting on the table. "I meditate daily. Having *Genie* hauled to Duluth was clear. What is odd is that our home in Bayfield keeps coming up in my dreams and meditations, although it's a little hazy. I don't know exactly why or what I'm supposed to do there, but my intuition is so strong that I need to make my way back. I'm ready to let *Genie* go. I'm not sure that I'm ready to quit sailing, but selling her feels right. I can always buy another sailboat. A smaller boat would be great. Enough about me. Have you ever thought about moving since you lost Lauren?" Kara noticed Rikk's eyes dropped to the floor as he contemplated her question. "I'm sorry. That was too personal."

"No, it's OK." Rikk stood up and grabbed dishes off the table and took them into the galley. "Actually, I've been torn with the thought of moving. It seems so conflicting. Friends tell you not to do anything for a year, and that year passes, and you don't have any clearer idea of what to do—and maybe more questions than before. It sometimes feels that moving would force me to move on, but I honestly don't want to. No obvious answer has presented itself, so staying put seems to be the most—"

"Comfortable?" Kara offered a word to finish Rikk's sentence as she walked up to the navigation station to switch on the water pump and water heater. She opened the door under the sink and pulled out the dish soap.

"It will take some getting used to flipping switches when I need hot water," Rikk said.

"It will become second nature before you know it."

"I'll wash, and you can put them away," Rick squeezed dish soap into the sink and turned on the faucet. "Comfortable? I guess staying in our house is more adequate than comfortable. Are you comfortable going back to all the reminders of Connor that your house contains?"

"You know, I think about that often. It sneaks into my thoughts so much that I wonder if Connor is covertly planting thoughts of our house in my brain." Rikk held up a plate dripping water and suds, and she felt his stare. "It feels like he is telling me, 'Kara, you need to go there.' It's weird." She wondered if she looked as embarrassed as she felt. She slipped behind him to get the dish strainer out of the cabinet and set it up on the counter. When he looked down at her, she said, "Now you think I'm crazy."

Rikk shook his head, and he answered, "If you are crazy, then I am too. Lately, I've been feeling Lauren nudging me to do something. The boat is part of it, but there is more."

Kara tilted her head and encouraged him to continue.

"This is weird, but the name of my boat—everyone is asking me what I've named it. It never crossed my mind until Dutch first asked, and now every time I hear a name I keep asking myself if that is what I am supposed to name it. It just seems ludicrous to be so consumed with such a ridiculous aspect of the boat."

"You know that sailors are a superstitious lot, don't you?" Kara said and Rikk chuckled in agreement. "Well, you don't have to buy into it, but you can choose to play along with some of it. That is what I do. I mean, naming your boat can be as simple as picking name, usually it's a female name. Or it can be more of an extension of yourself. Like *Pulse Rate*—I assume someone in the medical profession owns *Pulse Rate*."

"I guess that would be an extension of owner's soul."

Kara blushed. "Or, it can be something more mystical—inspired by the owner's inner desires."

"Is that what you meant by the boat's name coming from the owner's soul?"

"Oh, God, you remembered that." Kara chose to glide over that statement without further explanation. "*Neverland* is a great boat name that gives all kinds of clues about the owner. It probably is an extension of the owner's personality; it leaves so much to the imagination of anyone hearing or seeing it."

"Do you think *Neverland* is owned by someone who never wants to grow up?" said Rikk.

"Yeah. Or the owner feels like a child when he's on her."

"Or the owner has the soul of a child."

"You keep throwing soul out here, and I was embarrassed as soon as I said it yesterday, but I guess that is what I meant. It's silly." Kara flushed again, but with Rikk smiling back at her, she felt content.

"Maybe a little silly."

"So often, the creative names of boats provide the opening of conversations that lead to great friendships."

"Dutch told me the story behind naming *Genie's Bottle*. If it was inspired by *I Dream of Jeannie*, why did you spell *Genie* like the magic genie who grants wishes when you rub on its lamp?"

Kara laughed, "You've been dying to ask that, haven't you?"

"I have," admitted Rikk.

"Well, there is a long story, but at this late hour I will give you the abridged version. The interior of the boat reminded us of *I Dream of Jeannie* because it looked like the decor of Jeannie's bottle. With a room like that, who wouldn't want to be locked in that bottle sometimes? We felt so lucky to end up with her because other boats that were the same model didn't have the elegance or allure that she has."

"But that doesn't answer my question. Was it sailor superstition to use the genie-in-a-lamp spelling?"

"No, it was much more practical than that. I wasn't about to be cajoled into sporting about marinas and villages wearing a belly-dancing outfit like Barbara Eden in *I Dream of Jeannie*." Rikk looked bemused so Kara expounded. "Well, maybe you will understand by the one suggestion I will give you about naming your boat. Don't name her Amazing Grace, unless you've no intention of entertaining any women on it. As soon as the woman is spotted getting on or off, she'll be asked if she is Grace; or worse yet, if she is amazing."

Rikk laughed, "OK, I won't name her Amazing Grace. Does *Genie's Bottle* grant your wishes?"

"Absolutely! The magical part of her morphed from her name. When we wanted something, we would rub on the hull and ask for it."

"Really! What would you ask for?"

"Wind when it was too calm, or calm when the wind was too strong, rain, sun, mangos, avocadoes, a friendly and helpful sailing neighbor. Things like that."

"Did you get what you asked for?"

"Mostly we did. Don't laugh. Rikk, believing you will get what you want, or something greater, really works." Kara was laughing too, but was sincere as she explained, "I mean, sometimes these things were there or would come right away, and sometimes not right away, and often something that was even better came instead—better than what we had ever thought of. The success of asking for what you want comes from believing that it will come true. OK, from your grin I can see I'm sitting on the edge of woo land. But it is more than a positive mental attitude." She smiled at his attentive expression and found her way out of the discussion, "This is too huge a topic to discuss so late at night."

"Lauren bragged that she got what she wanted by believing she would. She'd say, 'If you don't believe, you don't receive.' Did the weather really change for you when you rubbed on her hull?"

"Not always." Kara raised her eyebrows, tilted her smiling face, and said, "Sometimes I had to bare my breasts to the wind!"

"What?" Rikk almost dropped the salad bowl he was rinsing. He turned his grin to face Kara and handed her the bowl.

"Yeah, but that didn't always work either. Then you had no other choice than to hunker down and ride out the storm. You can't imagine how much the weather can push your limits."

"Wait. Did you really bare your breasts to the wind?"

Kara's eyes sparkled as she giggled. "I told you that I have fun with sailor superstitions."

"What is this breast-baring superstition?" Rikk said.

"Why do you think they carved figureheads of mermaids with bared breasts on ship's bows? They were appealing to Anemoi, the gods of the four winds."

"OK, but did you really bare your breasts to the wind, Kara?"

Kara smiled at his determination to wheedle the truth out of her. She was just as determined to keep him wondering. "Excuse me. I need to use the head. Bathro—"

"Bathroom," Rikk interrupted, "I know, head is a bathroom on a boat."

As she walked past him, Rikk stopped her with a question. "Kara, how do you cope?"

"What do you mean by cope?"

"You are way more content than I am, and you seem to look forward to a move that you aren't certain about making. Yet you seem so upbeat."

"You think I'm upbeat?" Kara found his assessment incredible.

"You've been hit in the head, forced to change your plans, and totally insulted by my colleague and then kept awake well past the time I agreed upon leaving." Rikk looked at his watch. "Yet you smile, joke, laugh and keep thinking of others. I would say that is pretty upbeat to keep bouncing back after you get one setback after another."

"If you only knew. I've struggled these past couple days to keep negative thoughts from taking root. It's been difficult. I guess I keep reminding myself that I can always choose a better perspective. I've been back-sliding, though." Kara felt very introspective and added, "Rikk, this may sound bizarre to you, but I believe in the law of attraction and have found it to be true one hundred percent of the time. We attract what we think about, and the more we think about it, the more we attract it to ourselves. When we are full of self-pity or anger and think of those things we don't want, we get them. But when we stop those thoughts by continually replacing them with thoughts of what we *do* want; and believe that we'll get whatever it is by imagining how it feels to have it. Then it comes true—or something better that we may not have even considered."

"So you believe the law of attraction brings you whatever you want? Sounds more like you maintain a positive attitude." Rikk said.

"Hmm. Law of attraction is more than having a positive attitude, but it's part of it. A positive attitude is an outlook that people have. You know—the 'everything is good' sort of attitude. People who have positive attitudes look for the good in all situations, rather than those with negative attitudes who only see the bad in situations. What I do is *intend* to get what I want. For instance, I didn't want to prep and paint *Genie's Bottle* all by myself when I arrived. I kept visualizing that the huge task of prepping her was all done. Then I met Sophie and Pete. I helped them find a sailboat, and they helped me scrape and sand *Genie*. Dutch joined in and helped too. I would've preferred if the marina could have squeezed her in and done all the work, but then I'd have missed getting to know Sophie, Pete, and Dutch. So, I got something even better than I expected."

"You also may have missed getting struck on the head with the boom."

Kara laughed at his comment. "Yes, I may have missed that too. But I may have been here anyhow."

"Don't you think it could just be chance?"

"I don't define chance that way. Most people *unintentionally* attract their experiences into their lives by simply not being aware they can *intentionally* attract what they want. So, as far as the boom falling on my head, I unintentionally did attract that. I confess that I complained about having to save boats from their inexperienced owners when I saw your boom rumbling around on your cabin deck. I had a bad attitude about fixing the boom instead of being happy to help. So, although I didn't really ask to get injured, I didn't intend to help fix the problem without anyone getting hurt. My vibes were low and I was absolutely ungracious when Dutch and I rescued your boat."

Rikk pondered Kara's views, and finally he asked, "So, are you saying you caused the boom to fall?"

"Maybe, but unintentionally."

Then laughter filled Rikk's eyes as he said, "I meant that as a joke. How could you unintentionally cause the boom to fall?"

"I don't know. It's probably too big of a stretch for you to even contemplate." Kara wasn't surprised at his reaction, nor was she feeling any need to explain or defend her views. She shot him a complacent smile and shrugged her shoulders.

"Hey! Since *Genie* grants your wishes when you rub on her hull, what were you and the others thinking about when you were sanding it?"

Kara was spellbound by Rikk's deduction. She contemplated what Dutch, Sophie, and Pete had been thinking while they scraped and sanded *Genie's* hull. What had she been thinking about? She remembered choosing to think about how much she enjoyed Duluth every time she felt uncertain about returning to Bayfield—and she had done that often. That whole idea was too eerie to ignore.

"Kara?" Rikk broke the silence. "Do you think Dutch thought about wanting you to stay in Duluth until he could find an eligible bachelor for you?"

"Maybe, but what about Sophie and Pete?"

"Maybe they wanted you to stay around longer too."

Kara clicked her tongue and remembered Dutch's concern about her being a widow, and Sophie and Pete joked about how they could detain her in Duluth. "And you're proposing their thoughts caused your boom to fall on my head?"

"And your thoughts—when you questioned returning to Bayfield you thought about how much you enjoyed Duluth," he laughed, no doubt at her astonishment and sincere consideration of his observation. "Maybe *Genie's Bottle* has magical powers, and your bad mood along with everyone's thoughts while sanding her made my boom crash down on your head."

Damn it! He's mocking me. She didn't mind being held to her beliefs, except when it was done with cynical condescension. "I'm just saying I didn't have any intentions to fix the problem without getting hurt. Combine that with my irritation that you weren't back and that your boat wasn't moved ahead and tied off better; my attitude and vibration were very low."

"Your vibration?"

"OK, Rikk. Here's more woo for you to ponder. Everything is made up of energy: the human body, the water our boats are sitting in, the teak wood in the cabin, this rock from St. Vincent, that towel you just dried your hands on. Everything is energy and vibrates at different rates. I believe that when humans feel emotionally down, their energy is vibrating at a low frequency, and when they feel emotionally up, their energy is vibrating at a high frequency. When people lose loved ones, they feel despair, grief, and other low-energy emotions. It would be impossible to jump from feelings of grief to feelings of elation and joy in one fell swoop. However, we can choose to step up from our lowest feelings to something that feels a little better by choosing different thoughts. Therefore, by choosing thoughts of anger or maybe loneliness, you choose the thoughts that bring you to the next step up on the emotional scale from grief and despair. By choosing a thought that brings you relief, you vibrate at a little higher frequency and move to a better feeling emotion."

Rikk's smile telegraphed his wonder at Kara's belief. "I agree with some of your reasoning. But it's a hard pill to swallow that I can simply choose to feel better—or recover from cancer or prevent all accidents. If everyone could do that, my career would be eliminated."

"Well, I suppose it would—and that wouldn't be all bad, would it? Except unemployment would skyrocket." Kara was glad to see Rikk smile at her lighthearted answer to his challenge. "OK, how many accident patients come to you with a severe injury and say, 'I was having the best time, and out of the blue this catastrophe struck when everything leading up to it was all roses? And how many say, 'I knew I shouldn't have done that,' or 'I knew I was going to get hurt,' or 'I'm an accident just waiting to happen,' or something like that? All I'm saying is that people attract their circumstances by their feelings and thoughts—maybe not all the time, but more often than not."

"Do you think every injured patient has some negative things going on? What about someone who was walking around having a wonderful day, and something fell on them?"

"I'm sure you have no more conclusive data to support that the people who fall victim to falling objects have had nothing but wonderful thoughts than I have conclusive data that their thoughts were low and they were waiting for the next shoe to drop." Kara didn't want to argue. She shut her eyes, and her voice softened as she said, "Hey, these are just my beliefs, and they have proven themselves true in my life. I have no reason to change them because they work for me. I just believe that the negative feelings are synonymous with low vibrations." She shrugged and smiled at him. "Well, at least we both see that negative feelings cause stress and stress causes disease."

"I agree that negative emotions can cause stress, and that can lead to heart disease, stroke, cancer, and other diseases. But as you said, I do find the idea that negative emotions cause accidents a stretch," Rikk said.

"It was a stretch for me when I first heard it too." Kara sighed. Neither spoke while they pondered each other's views.

"The subject derailed. If you don't mind, I'd like to return to how I choose the next-best feeling when I'm missing Connor."

"OK. You've said you choose the next step up from where you are. So what do you think I should choose?"

"Try choosing anger—it's a little better than despair. Then work your way up."

"How do I choose anger?"

"OK, try this. 'Lauren's gone, and my life has changed. It makes me angry that—'"

"I just fill in the blank?"

"Yeah. Take some time and think about it." Kara decided she needed to lighten the conversation, so with a grin she said, "How about your thoughts yesterday? Were you thinking about your boat while you were gone?" She could tell Rikk mused over her question.

"When I found out that the emergency would take several hours instead of one or two, I worried that the wind might cause damage to my boat. I wished I'd accepted Dutch's offer to add more dock lines and fenders."

"Ah, ha! Then it was you who intended the boom to fall on my head!" Kara jumped at the opening to tease.

Rikk looked despondent and in a flat voice he said, "Kara, I'm not sure what to think of your concepts. I guess I'll consider the possibilities of your arguments because I've seen many so-called miracles in my practice over the years. As I think about it, they all seemed to happen to people I'd describe as having positive attitudes, but I've never correlated the lack of miraculous recoveries to those who have bad attitudes. Do you think positive attitudes come easier to some people than others?"

"I think positive attitudes and setting good intentions work in tandem, and are like an exercised and toned muscle for some. People who practice both know where this muscle is because they use it all the time. Others don't even know they have it, but once they discover it, they have to work hard to build it up. It takes repetition to strengthen it, and that change takes some time. But it is possible for everyone to find it and use it until it is well toned." Rikk crossed his arms and leaned against the galley cabinet. He looked intrigued but not convinced, and that was just fine. "Rikk, to you this is just woo, but there are all kinds of studies you surely have heard about that explain these theories."

"Yes, I've read the technical, analytical studies that explain the physiological reasons."

"Then you probably know more than I do."

"I just don't buy that a person controls their health with their attitude or intentions. My wife did not intend to die of cancer."

"I have no idea why Lauren got cancer. Sometimes people keep their fears to themselves, like secrets. They think about them but never talk about them. I believe sometimes people's fearful thoughts manifest their fears into reality," said Kara. She watched Rikk ponder this, and thought he looked unconvinced—and almost annoyed. "This conversation started when you said I was upbeat. What you don't know is how hard I've been working to strengthen my good intention muscle. In these last couple days, I've been continually talking myself into looking for a more desired perspective. I can always feel better when I remember the people I've met sailing—people who live in destitute situations; but better yet is to be thankful for all the things that are going right for me in this moment. Thanks to you and our conversation, I realize that I haven't been too successful practicing what I preach. You're right, I'm uncertain about Bayfield, and instead of intending anything positive about my return, I've been feeling mystified about my journey. Going home alone is something I never expected I'd do. I feel that I am lower right now than I've been for months, and it's a damn hard battle for me to keep looking for the next step up from where I am. Your boom hit me when I was feeling very irritated and full of self-pity. It isn't always easy to get to the next-best-feeling place, and these last two days, I've fought to keep looking for the next step up from where I am."

"But you do keep looking, and you seem to be getting there. I haven't done that. I'm doing well in my practice, but even that is hard because I shared so much with Lauren. Work just keeps my mind occupied and off of how much I miss her."

"When I felt grief and despair after Connor's death, I worked hard to get myself to feel anger, then forgiveness, then acceptance, and then contentment. I knew that feelings of happiness and joy are steps farther up that I would achieve in due time, but not instantly."

"You make it sound easy."

"It is simple, but it isn't always easy. Like addition and subtraction are simple and easy now, but maybe not when you first learned those skills. Choosing better feeling thoughts does get easier every time you do it, but it doesn't mean that you just tell yourself to get over it and, poof, it's done. You still have to do the work, but you can choose to be angry at Lauren for dying, or God, or modern medicine for not having the cure for cancer. You can also choose to forgive them and accept Lauren's path—her death. You can choose to be happy that you got to share a great part of her life's journey."

"I've accepted Lauren's death; I just want to stop missing her."

"Yeah, I get that." Kara fought the urge to hug him. She would take away his pain if she could, but she knew that was up to him. "Rikk, would you humor me for about ten minutes by doing something that will help illustrate what I mean? It won't hurt or challenge any beliefs you have, and it is simple."

Rikk looked at his watch. It was twelve fifteen, and he was surprised at how fast the time had flown. "Don't you need to use the head?"

"I can wait. It won't take me long to give you the instructions to something I do to help me choose more positive thoughts."

"Sure, I guess I can humor you for ten more minutes. Are you sure you don't mind that I've already stayed past my half hour?"

"I don't mind. I've enjoyed our conversation. I slept most of the day away so I'm not that tired. Anyhow, more than likely, I will humor *you* with this." Kara smiled, rummaged around the navigation table for a pen and paper, then ripped off a sheet from a notebook and folded it in half lengthwise. Giving the paper to Rikk, she instructed, "For the next five minutes, or until you run out of room on this half of the paper only, write what you don't want anymore. For example, I'd write that I don't want to wonder what I am to do once I'm back in Bayfield. You don't have to write complete sentences; it can be phrases, and I'm not going to read it, so be honest. Just free your head of all limitations and write the first things that come to your mind and all the ideas or feelings that you don't want anymore."

"That's it?"

"That is it for the first five minutes," Kara said as she looked at her watch. "Go ahead and start writing." After Kara used the head, she went back to the galley and dug out the grill tong and a lighter.

When Rikk finished, Kara gave him the next instructions, "Now, on the right side of the page write what you want. Use each of the items you wrote down on the left side to guide you. The only rules are that it must be possible; it must be written with positive words—so you can't use any negative words like no, not, or never. Most importantly, it must be written as if you already have it. So if you wrote you want Lauren back, then you can't write, 'It's not possible' or 'It never will happen.' Remember to write these statements positively, and it's vital you write it like you already have it."

"How can I write wanting Lauren back in a positive form?"

Kara bit her lower lip as she pondered how to answer Rikk's question without giving him the answer. "You said you've been feeling her presence more these past few days, and her presence feels good, right?"

"Yeah."

"So use those feelings to write what you want."

"That's all?" Rikk said and sounded unimpressed. She smiled hoping to reassure him. "You aren't going to tell me what to write, are you?"

"No, I'm guessing that you already have your answer but don't trust it," Kara said.

Rikk gave a sheepish grin, and then tentatively said, "I always feel Lauren's presence with me?"

"That's perfect. Just remember to state it as if you already have it—like you just did. Sound simple?"

"I write what I want as if I already have it? So I'm writing a lie?"

"Think of an athlete using a sports-visualization technique. A slalom ski racer is in the starting gate. Before he leaves the gate, he visualizes himself on every part of the run, coming into and out of each gate perfectly, and tucking as he skis to the finish line at course-setting speed. He sees himself winning the race and standing on the highest podium, bending down to receive his gold medal even before he has left the starting gate. I'm asking you to apply the same principle to your life by defining what you don't want, and from that list, defining what you do want. Then just as the ski racer imagines he has already won his race, you write it as if you already have what you want."

"Oh. OK, I can see the logic in that."

"Actually, you can choose to make it your new paradigm. Logically, it might feel like a lie, just as the slalom ski racer is telling a lie at the starting gate. But the racer isn't just telling a lie, he is feeling himself going down the entire course, feeling his speed as he crosses the finish line, and feeling that ribbon with the medal dangling on it being placed on his neck." Kara paused. She hoped her passionate delivery of her belief in this process hadn't been too huge a stretch for his logical thinking. "Rikk, by telling yourself a new story, the one you want, as if you have it, you begin to feel what it is like to have it. You will be astonished at how soon it comes. It's the same principle as 'like attracts like.' Our thoughts attract what we get. The ski racer who thinks he's going to crash and burn usually does."

"So this is your belief in the law of attraction?" Rikk asked.

"Exactly." Kara sighed and bit her lip again. "You agreed to humor me for ten minutes, and I hope you'll do this. Besides, I do have a cool trick up my sleeve if you finish the next part of the game." She raised her eyebrows at him hoping to entice him to play along.

"This is a game?"

"I choose to call it a game rather than work; it makes it feel less like work to me—more like fun. Life is supposed to be fun."

Rick picked up his pen. He read his list and began to write on the other side of the page.

When Kara informed Rikk that his five minutes were up, he said he had a couple left, so she encouraged him to finish those.

Rikk slid the paper to her and set his pen down. "There, I'm done. Now, what is this trick you have up your sleeve?"

Kara took the paper and folded it along its crease with the written sides together, and then tore the paper in half down the center. She held up each piece of paper with the writing side facing Rikk and asked, "Which one is the list of what you DO want?" Rikk pointed to it, and Kara folded it a few times so it was credit card sized. She handed it to him, and asked him to put it into his pocket.

"Now?" Rikk asked.

"Yes, now," Kara replied as she crunched up the sheet listing unwanted items and grasped it in the tong. She handed Rikk the tong and the lighter. "Burning is a cleansing ritual in many cultures. So you are going to light it up."

"You want me to burn this list on your boat."

"Not exactly. You can burn it in the cockpit grill. The point is to purge the items you don't want from your memory—and even more from your life—when you burn this list. From now on, whenever anything unwanted that you wrote on that list pops into your mind, you will remember the list you don't want. Then you'll replace the 'I don't want' thought with what you wrote on the list you carry with you. Then visualize what you do want as if you already have it."

Kara watched Rikk un-crumple and study his list, saying nothing. "I'm going to brush my teeth and hair, so you can have some time alone to mull over your list of what you no longer want. Then burn it up when you are ready to purge those unwanted things from your life. You also should keep that list of things you want some place where you will see and even touch it often. Your pants pocket is best because every time you stick your hands into your pocket it is a constant reminder of what you want. Otherwise, your wallet is OK as long as it doesn't get lost in there. But either place, get it out and read it often, so you will have a frequent reminder of all that you want."

Retreating to wash her face, Kara left Rikk alone. She heard the sound of the hatch slide open, and allowed him privacy with the burning ritual. She gently splashed water over her bump. She was getting tired and spent an extra long time flossing and brushing her teeth. Kara pulled out her moisturizer and applied it to her face and neck. She felt *Genie* list as Rikk stepped off her, and she watched him walk up the dock from the porthole.

⚓

Kara found the tongs and lighter sitting in the cockpit next to the hatch, and brought them into the galley. She wondered what, if anything,

Rikk got from the lists. Yawning, she whispered, "Good night, Dr. Rikkert Harmon, whoever you are." He mystified her, and she was exhausted wondering which side of his Dr. Jekyll-Mr. Hyde personality would show up next. *Damn. That thought just invites him into my life again,* she realized and shook her head. Exhausted, she crawled into her berth hoping *Genie* would instantly rock her to sleep.

Rikk

Rikk drove home deep in deliberation over the list that he had just burned and the one that he had in his pocket. He wasn't sure why he didn't say goodbye to Kara, but the list in his pocket made him want to finish reading the book *Be in Choice*. He finally was in the right place emotionally to find out what Lauren wanted him to know. When he got home, he picked up the book and read Lauren's inscription once again. This time the ache in his heart was bearable, and he thumbed through it until he found the page where he'd left off reading the marina lobby's copy.

Chapter 19

Rikk

Rikk's eyes opened, and he realized that he had fallen asleep on the couch after finishing *Be in Choice*. He stretched the kinks out of his arms and pushed himself up to sit. He stared out the window into the dismal, grey morning and wondered what Kara was doing. It astonished him that his first thought was not of how much he missed Lauren or of self-pity, but of Kara. He briefly pondered the notes that Lauren had scribbled in the margins of the book, first in legible handwriting, then gradually decreasing where Rikk struggled to decipher them. He remembered how wiped out she was from the chemo and radiation treatments. It hadn't occurred to him before that it took the entire time from her diagnosis to her death for her to read this one book, and he wondered if she had held on longer just to finish it and write the notes to help him after she was gone. The last few pages had sentences underlined that he had guessed Barb had done for Lauren. He recalled that Barb had spent a lot of time reading to her while she sat with her the last few days that Lauren was lucid. Before this moment, Rikk never made the connection that this was the book that Barb had been reading to her. The message that Lauren used the book to convey was made in the epilogue. It said:

> "Live fully present in each moment,
>
> Give love freely and unconditionally,
>
> Choose in every aspect and moment of your life
>
> by following your heart and listening to your intuition.
>
> Be in Choice."

Hand written by Barb was this note: "Rikk, Lauren whispered your name and put her hand to her heart when I read this. Lauren's eyes pleaded to me, and I asked her if she wanted me to underline this, and she nodded. Lauren wanted you to know how important this was to her. She wants you to live this."

Today, Rikk would call Barb and ask her why she had never mentioned it to him; although occasionally she asked if he had a chance to read the book yet. He admired her for not prying, and that reminded him of Kara. He pulled out the list he put into his pocket last night and read it over again. Rikk decided to do what he wished he had done the moment he recognized her on Thursday.

Rikk got clarity from the lists he wrote last night, but they also left him with more questions, new questions. One question was why, after all these years, Kara reappeared in his life. He might have the courage to tear down his barriers and tell her what he felt she already knew. He hoped that one way or the other, the mystery around her would be resolved, and he'd be free.

Kara

Saturday morning Kara woke to rain drizzling down *Genie's* windows. The wind was around five knots, and the temps were in the low fifties. She dressed, made a cup of tea, and let it brew while she went to the marina lobby to use the bathroom. On her way back to *Genie*, she met Dutch on the dock and greeted him, "Good morning, Dutch."

"Humph," Dutch stomped toward the lobby with a crater-deep scowl creasing his eyebrows.

Kara was surprised that Dutch was in such a foul mood and guessed it was the interruption of their dinner last night by Dr. Norris. "Your comment about Dr. Norris being a Siren last night was classic, Dutch. Too bad you didn't stick around to meet Rikk's other, and quite normal colleague, Dr. Joe Watson, and his wife, Barb."

"I said Sirens!" snapped Dutch.

"What?"

"You heard me. You both are Sirens. Luring the Doc away—you ain't no better than Odysseus's Sirens luring sailors into their island's rocky coasts, stealing their lives. Dr. Norris might be more obvious, but you're no better with your hard-to-get act." Dutch rushed past Kara leaving her standing alone on the dock, slack-jawed and feeling like she'd been sucker punched.

Kara had no idea what she had done to cause Dutch to put her in the same category with Dr. Heidi Norris, and she sure didn't understand what had caused his change of behavior from cupid to old cuss. She considered chasing Dutch back to *Miss Sea* to find out what was eating him but decided to allow some time to pass before she attempted to talk to him. Kara was confused about so many things, and with Dutch's newly revealed cantankerous character, she wasn't up for round two. She started to walk and soon found herself back on the beach.

The drizzle had stopped, although Kara felt it may as well have continued because it mirrored her mood exactly. Not really raining but certainly not clear, she felt the same way about where she was in her life. She called her friend Robin and left a message telling her she needed to be coached. With nothing else to do, Kara decided that she would try to be as objective as possible and coach herself. She would try to figure out the answer to the question that plagued her the most, what was the lesson to be learned from this delay in her return to Bayfield? She looked for a spot on the beach to examine Dutch's perspective to the question of why she was delayed. Kara knew putting yourself into others' shoes was always tricky, especially if you've never actually heard their perspective. With Dutch's attitude shift, she wasn't sure if she could get insight into his sudden change of heart. She walked to an old driftwood log a few yards down the beach and sat on it while reflecting on Dutch's actions and words from the time Rikk's boat arrived.

Rikk

Rikk showered, dressed, and grabbed the car keys. His stomach rumbled, but he would get coffee and something to eat at the coffee shop and bring Kara something too. Kara could not refuse to see him if he brought her breakfast.

Rikk parked near the marina lobby and grabbed the coffee and bakery bag off the passenger seat. Dutch raced up to the door, opened it for Rikk, and quizzed him about the story he told last night.

After rattling off the answers to Dutch's questions, Rikk said, "Do you know where Kara is?"

"She's just another Siren singing out for you, Doc."

"What?"

"You heard me. She ain't no better than that doctor friend falling all over you last night."

"Dutch? What the hell has come over you? Two nights ago you couldn't get us together fast enough, and now she's a Siren? What's Kara done to change your mind?"

"Ah, hell!" Dutch said and threw his arm down in disgust and turned away as he yelled, "She was walking out of the marina the last time I saw her, and I ain't seen her since." Dutch stomped toward the dock.

Rikk watched Dutch disappear behind the corner of the building before getting back into his car. He drove out to Minnesota Avenue to the stop sign. His gut told him to drive to the beach, and he did without hesitation.

The beach parking lot was empty when Rikk pulled in. He walked down the boardwalk and spotted Kara sitting on a washed up log. She sat still with deep thought painted over her profile, facing the Aerial Lift Bridge and canal. This time she wasn't in the lotus position. He studied her as he walked towards her. Kara hadn't noticed him and abruptly stood up and walked toward the waves. She kneeled down at the edge of the water where it was lapping onto the beach and pushed her rain jacket sleeves up to her elbows. She placed both of her hands lightly on the sand. The next wave swept over her hands up to her wrists and came perilously close to her tennis shoes. She stood up too quickly, lost her balance, and took two rapid steps backwards to regain it. That roused Rikk from of his absorption, and he lunged to catch her before she fell.

"Ahhhhh!" Kara screamed when she noticed someone rushing toward her. She didn't hear or see Rikk approach and was completely startled. She ran a couple steps and ended up in the waves. Her sudden fear seemed to melt into relief when she noticed it was him, but before Kara could breathe again, the next wave rolled over her tennis shoes, drenching the hem of her blue jeans and shoes. Her relief morphed into anger as she bounded out of the frigid water. Dizziness overcame her, and she wavered. Rikk held her arm and placed his hand on her shoulder, steadying her as she scowled and said, "How long have you been here?"

Rikk's attempt to squelch his laughter failed. "I just got here, Kara. I'm sorry I scared you. It's been a long time since I've seen anyone jump that high or move that fast." He burst out in laughter though still trying to rein it in, and he could see that she was only getting more infuriated. "I'm sorry. I'm sorry for laughing and for startling you, and for—" Again his laughter rang out, and he turned away still trying to quell it. "You sprang up like a fawn that's just been startled. How's your head?"

Kara sighed, crossed her arms over her chest, and simpered at him while she backed away. She stood her ground as Rikk wiped a tear of laughter from his eye as another wave rolled up near her shoes. She succeeded to suppress her laughter but not her smile, and he was amused by how hard she feigned anger.

"My head is fine. What are you doing here? And why did you sneak up on me?"

"I didn't sneak up on you. Well, not on purpose. You looked so deep in thought that I was waiting for you to notice me. I really didn't want to disturb you. Then you stood up and started to fall. I was only trying to catch you."

"Then what's so funny?"

Rikk swallowed. "You are! You've gone from fright, to flight, to relief, to trying you're damnedest to be mad even though you're laughing too."

"Next time make some noise." Kara barely suppressed her snicker. "I still don't think it's funny." She covered her mouth as she laughed along with Rikk, and then stuck her hands in her pockets and shook her head. "Anyhow, you seem like you could stand to laugh a whole lot more."

Rikk wiped his eyes as his belly convulsed for the last time. "How do you know I need to laugh more?"

"I'm just guessing. Am I right?"

"Yeah, you're right."

"So why are you here? Are you going to check my pupils, Dr. Harmon?" Kara saw Rikk's expression darken. "I'm kidding. What brings you to the beach this morning?"

"I don't know where to start, and the truth is I'm here—with coffee."

She turned her palms up and said, "Where's the coffee?"

"In the car. I wanted to talk to you about last night."

"What about last night?"

"The two lists that I wrote out."

"Oh. What did you discover?"

"Whoa, no easing into the subject is there?"

"Sorry, old coaching habit of asking direct and hopefully bold questions. Since clients are paying by the hour, coaches need to get to their client's bottom line fast. Clients aren't interested in dawdling around figuring out what changes they need to make to achieve their goals and dreams."

"Are you coaching me?" Rikk's teasing smile and eyebrow wag conveyed his skepticism.

"No, I'm just talking to you," Kara shrugged.

Rikk was amused at Kara's attempt to hide her frustration. "These direct and bold questions sound a little like, how did you put it, 'the litany of doctor questions' you've accused me of asking you."

"Damn! Guilty as charged. However, my questions are tailored to my client's subjects. They aren't rote. Anyhow, what do you want to talk about?"

Looking out at the waves lapping the shore, Rikk sighed and said, "Last night I couldn't sleep, so I stayed up most of the night reading. I didn't bring out my list of what I want until early this morning. I'm not sure what to think about that list."

"Hmm. Well, what *do* you think about the list?"

"I don't know. I mean I have many conflicting feelings about even wanting the things I wrote." He dragged his hand through his hair. "You're the coach. You tell me how I should feel!"

"I'm not your coach, and even if I were I can't tell you or anyone how they feel about anything. I certainly cannot tell anyone what they should or should not feel about things." Kara inhaled deeply, quieting her aggravation. "I wasn't trying to coach you last night. I was just reaching out to you as a friend. I can refer a few coaches. I know one who specializes in working with men."

"You won't coach me?"

"I, uh, I—oh geez. Rikk, I've been taking a sabbatical from coaching for awhile."

"How come your website is still current?"

Kara

Heat rose in Kara's face as she realized Rikk had been interested in her enough to investigate her website. Now she had to carefully choose her words, so she wouldn't divulge anything that would point to the other part of her career casually mentioned on her website. That career she did not want Rikk to learn about because, although well hidden, it gave a clue to her secret. Her intent was to keep that secret hers alone. Stunned, all she could say was, "Oh."

"I read your website this morning, and you offer a complimentary coaching session, so people can 'discover what coaching is.' Why do you still have that offer on your website if you are on a sabbatical?"

Kara was perplexed. She contrived an explanation that she hoped would sufficiently answer Rikk's question and honor her requirement to be truthful. It also would put an abrupt end to any further searching of her website. "I've been doing a minimal and very sporadic amount of coaching since Connor's death, and even less these last couple of months while I have been relocating back to Bayfield. I will start coaching more once I get settled, so I've kept my site current, and it's a place for me to reach my clients and friends when I get an inspiration to blog." He frowned at her, looking suspicious. Kara knew it was driving him crazy and escalating his curiosity. After a long, uncomfortable silence, accentuated with unblinking stares, Kara looked out at the lake.

Rikk pounced at her distraction, "I want a complimentary session."

"What!?"

"Right now."

"*Now?*"

"What else do you have to do in the next thirty minutes?" Rikk smiled and reached down to brush the hair off her cheek. "I really want to know how I'm supposed to never think about the things on the list I burnt and only think about the one in my pocket. You can coach me on that, can't you?"

"Well, yes, but Rikk, I can't be your coach."

"OK, but you can give me a complimentary session."

"I can, but that usually is used for the client to see if they want coaching based on what they get from the session and to see if we are compatible to work together."

"I won't ask you to be my coach. I just want to know what coaching is about, and you opened the can of worms last night with the lists that prevented me from sleeping all night."

"You are persistent when you want something, aren't you?" Kara sighed. "OK, I agree to give you one coaching session right now, right here, but if you want coaching in the future, you will need to find someone else. Agreed?"

"Agreed."

Chapter 20

Rikk

"Well, what do you want coaching on?" Kara said as she looked at her watch.

"Are you timing this?" Rikk was astonished.

"Yes." Kara smiled and her eyes followed a seagull glide overhead and land a few yards away. "As you read on my website, all my complimentary sessions are half an hour, and that is what I agreed to." She looked back at him and said, "You mentioned you had questions about the lists you made last night. What comes up for you around the list?"

"What do you mean by 'around the list'?"

"Rikk, I'm asking you to tell me what thoughts you have, what feelings they bring out, and any memories they bring. What are your questions about this list?"

Rikk reached in his pocket, took out the list, and handed it to Kara. "Do you want to read it?"

"I could read it, but I know that I will learn more if you tell me about it than if I read it."

Rikk took a deep breath. "On the list of things I don't want, the first thing I wrote was, 'I don't want to grieve for Lauren anymore.' That in part kept me awake all night."

"What do you want?"

A seagull stood a few feet away begging for handouts with squawks. It brought Rikk's attention back to Kara, waiting for his answer. His whispered answer had a slight tremor that he couldn't contain. "I feel alive and content without Lauren."

Kara remained silent, studying him as if she expected him to say something. He looked out at the lake, and when he finally brought his gaze on her, she said, "Rikk, what does alive and content mean to you?"

"I'm not sure. I guess I know that I'm sick of everyone trying to match-make Lauren's replacement for me. I don't want to replace Lauren, and I don't want to miss her."

"How would not missing her feel?"

He shrugged, feeling like he'd made a mistake pushing Kara to coach him. He wasn't sure that he wanted to delve into his most private feelings after all. He heard his hollow words and was surprised by them, "I'm not even sure I want to stop missing her." He glanced at Kara standing there, waiting for him to talk. He sighed and looked at her expectant expression, then looked back out at the lake.

"Do you want me to stop coaching, Rikk?"

"No." His answer was abrupt as if someone else had said it. This had happened before in the last few months, and always gave him an eerie feeling.

"OK, but if you do, just let me know at any time. You do know that this is confidential, don't you?"

"Yes, I did read that on your website."

"OK, then the first thing we need to do is find out what the heart of the issue is. Is it missing Lauren or is it friends' match-making? Which one gives you more of a charge?"

"A charge?"

"Do you feel anything in your body? In your heart or stomach or throat or anywhere else when you say you miss Lauren?"

"All those places and my head."

"Describe what you feel."

"Sometimes it's a constant stomachache, dull and almost unnoticeable. Sometimes I can hardly stand it, it hurts so bad. I have a constant tightness in my chest and throat. I usually have a sharp headache too."

"What about your friends' match-making; where do you feel that?"

"I feel that mostly in my stomach, but it's annoying more than anything."

"Which bothers you more?"

"I guess I'm less bothered by my friends than by missing Lauren. I don't want to miss her, and she seems to be slipping away."

"I can hear how much you miss her in your voice and see it in your whole body. Rikk, tell me about her slipping away."

"I don't want to move on as everyone tells me. I accept she'll never be with me, but I don't want to lose her memories." Rikk looked down at the sand. Kara's gentle touch on his arm drew his eyes back to her.

"On your list of wants you wrote, 'feel alive and content without Lauren.' You've said you want to stop missing her, *and* you aren't sure if you want to stop missing her. Tell me about this conflict."

"It drives me nuts. Some days I wish I would forget her completely because I miss her so much, and other times I get involved with things and feel guilty that I haven't thought about her in several hours. Then I wonder if I will eventually forget her, and I would rather feel the pain of missing her than forget her."

"It sounds like 'alive and content' is a place where you hold Lauren's memories close while being free of the pain of missing her."

"Exactly. I don't want to replace her; I don't want to forget her, and I don't want to be lonely." Rikk's eyes fixed on the horizon as he composed himself. The almost indiscernible line that separated the murky grey sky from the steel blue of the lake gave him a shiver. It was a perfect reflection of the thin line between what was real and what he wanted; because what he wanted was indistinct and so far away. He sighed and looked directly into Kara's eyes.

"What's lonely like?" Kara said.

"I miss her companionship."

"Her companionship? Tell me about it."

"I miss her smile, and laughter—her love. Her disappointment when I've screwed up; her anger when I've ticked her off; and her commitment to always reconcile our differences. I miss holding her, touching her, feeling her soft skin. I miss making love to her. I'm lonely, but I don't want a relationship where I forget all that she was, all that we had. I don't want to forget her."

Kara

Kara held her breath while the silence lingered. She maintained her even tone as well as she could, but it faltered a bit as she said, "On rare occasions, I sometimes give a glimpse of my life experiences if I feel it would help my clients. May I share something with you?"

"Why not just tell me?"

"Coaching isn't about the coach, and anything I say needs to be for the client's benefit. It's protocol to ask permission to leave the coach's role and step into my personal role." He nodded, so Kara continued. "Rikk, does it help you to know that I've often had many of the same feelings about Connor?" Rikk's gaze fixed on the waves lapping the beach. "I haven't wanted to miss him, and sometimes I've wanted to hold onto the pain of his absence," Kara allowed that to sink in and watched Rikk to see when he would be ready to move on. His meager smile and sigh signaled her it was time to continue. "How can you keep Lauren's memories with you and feel alive and content?"

"That's the problem, I don't know." Rikk's dismal response mirrored his drained energy.

"Since you also mentioned friends' match-making, I suggest you look at a few different perspectives. First we need to dig until we find out what's at the heart of your frustrations. I'm hearing you say you're missing Lauren and don't want to ever forget her, and you're feeling that might happen if you were in a new relationship. Is the real issue something around keeping both you and Lauren alive?"

"Me and Lauren alive?"

"Did I get that right? Is that your real struggle?"

"I think so, yeah, Lauren and me alive."

"Rikk, you look as though something has been lifted, like you feel lighter. What does 'Lauren and you alive' mean to you?"

"It is the answer to what I've been asking. I haven't figured out what I want, and it just seems that I keep going around in circles trying to figure it out. I feel like a weight has been lifted off my shoulders just to know what I want. But how do I get what I want?"

"Good question. You get to explore the perspectives of all those people involved as they look at 'Rikk and Lauren alive.' Are you willing to explore their perspectives?"

"Sure."

"Getting to the heart of the matter is the hardest step. Not that stepping into the perspectives is always easy. We have the subject 'Rikk and Lauren alive.' Now we are going to move around a little as we look at you and Lauren alive. So we are going to name this spot," Kara picked up a driftwood stick and drew a big circle in the sand in front of Rikk and wrote the words 'Rikk and Lauren alive' in the circle. She said, "Now let's move to another location and look at your perspective first." Kara walked a few feet away to an area where seaweeds washed up onto the shore, and Rikk followed.

"I thought we *were* looking at my perspective."

"You did tell me some of your perspective when you were figuring out what you wanted to be coached on. But before we move to others' perspectives, I think you might benefit from digging a little deeper to see if there is more to learn about yours." Rikk had caught up to her, and she pointed back to the circle around the words 'Rikk and Lauren alive' she had drawn in the sand, "All my questions and all the perspectives we'll explore will pertain only to 'Rikk and Lauren alive.' OK?" Rikk nodded. "What's wrong in your life right now?"

Rikk

Rikk was not prepared for questions that dug so deep. "I guess I try to avoid thinking about it." He wasn't expecting Kara to stand and wait for him to elaborate. He finally stammered, "I work a lot—too much I suppose." She was waiting again, but he didn't know where to begin, or if he really wanted to begin.

"Rikk, you can stop this any time you want, just tell me."

"No, I'm—I don't know. I want to do this."

"My experience has been that coaching around sensitive subjects like yours most often results in digging up and examining some pretty painful emotional baggage. I won't take you into a thorny spot and leave you there, but I will take you there if that is where your answers lead. Do you still want to do this?"

"I didn't think—I didn't know you would ask such difficult and personal questions right away." He hesitated for a moment. "But I asked for it."

"Life can be difficult and messy sometimes, Rikk. It is also beautiful and joyful when you reach inside of yourself and find your way back to who you are really meant to be. I think coaching would be cathartic for you, but you might feel more comfortable with someone else coaching you."

"No, I want to do this—now—with you."

"OK. What do you avoid by working so much?"

Rikk inhaled deeply, "I avoid roaming around in the house filled with constant reminders of Lauren, and the stillness of the house with her gone. Ha, that's funny. I used to call it home, now it is just a house where I sleep, shower, and wander around aimlessly until it's time for work—time to escape from those empty walls. Everywhere I look, I have a memory of Lauren. I can't dodge her presence there, but with her gone, what once was our home is now just a house."

"Earlier you said that you didn't want to stop missing her, and now you said you avoid the house because it is filled with her memories. What is true about those statements?"

"I suppose they are conflicting. I want to always feel her the way I did when she was alive. But feeling her through memories now that she is gone makes me feel—" Kara was waiting and watching him. It was awkward to be the one questioned.

"Makes you feel?"

"Dead."

Kara nodded. "I felt that 'dead' feeling in you when you said that." She brought both her hands to her heart as if he told her where it hurt the most. "Rikk, what you are doing now is hard, and the fact that you are pushing through is courageous. It is painful to face the feelings that often we would rather ignore and pretend don't exist." Rikk sent her a weak smile. "Do you feel like you died along with Lauren, but nobody let your body know?" Rikk just looked at her incredulously, and she spoke hurriedly, "I guess that is how I felt. I'm sorry; I should've asked you permission to share my experiences. How do—"

"Yes, it is exactly how I feel. I don't feel that way all the time though. Actually, I don't feel as dead anymore, and that scares me too. Sometimes I think that if I start to feel alive and especially if I feel happy then I'll let Lauren slip away."

"This sounds like your saboteur talking."

"What?"

"In coaching we call that inner voice a person's saboteur. It's like an alter-ego. It's the voice in your head that creates doubts, fears, and insecurities. It stops you from living authentically. Often your ego takes on the voice of others in your life, like a parent, or a teacher, or a boss, or the boardroom. Your ego can even take the voice of a friend or organization. Basically, when our ego is in control of our thoughts and actions, we aren't being our authentic selves and life isn't going as we want it to go. I refer to my clients' egos as their saboteurs. One of the best results of coaching is when clients learn to identify when their saboteur has a hold on them. Sometimes clients think their saboteur protects them by warning them that they are back in a losing situation again. Saboteurs trick people to play small and impede them from being who they really want—"

"Wait, what does 'play small' mean?" he interrupted.

"It is the opposite of playing full out. Playing small is rooted in fear."

"How is it rooted in fear?"

"Fears make people play small, so they never live up to their potential. Once they've experienced failure, playing small is how they elude the risk of ever failing again. If they quit trying to achieve their dreams or goals, they will never have to face failure. So their saboteur keeps them playing small to keep them safe from the embarrassment of future failures."

"What's wrong with that?"

"We learn from our failures, and those lessons help us later to succeed. I believe all failures are successes. However, if we follow our saboteur, we lose all chances for successful outcomes. The saboteur is more comfortable with people who are stuck in discontentment than with people who discover the lessons of failures and continue to work to realize their dreams. Either way, when clients decipher the motives of their saboteur, they can choose the actions that are innately right. Only you know what is innately right for you; a coach just helps you discover it."

"So what is my saboteur saying?" Rikk was confused.

"Let's find out. You said that you don't feel as dead anymore, and when you start feeling happy you worry that you'll let Lauren slip away; and it scares you. Why?"

"I've started to feel alive again. But then I feel guilty because I haven't thought of Lauren every five minutes. I'm an ass for thinking of something else besides her when I woke up this morning."

"That's your saboteur. What does he gain from keeping you stuck here?"

"I don't know—maybe that I won't lose again."

"Yeah, so if you think of something other than Lauren, you risk losing what?"

"Geez." Rikk looked into the overcast sky and then at Kara. "Joe thinks it's good that I don't think about Lauren so much, but that's easy for him to say. He still has Barb."

"What would you expect from Joe if he lost Barb?"

Rikk grabbed a piece of driftwood tangled in the seaweed and inspected it from all angles. With an outfielder's form, he threw it out as far into the lake as he could. It disappeared into the grey sky. Moments later, he heard it splash into the water. He looked back at Kara, expecting some sort of disapproving expression. He was surprised to see only curiosity. Slowly he formed his thoughts into words. "I'd expect that he would feel how I feel—and I'd expect that he would get to a place where he could get on with his life."

"What have you discovered?"

"I guess that it is OK not to think of Lauren first thing every day and every minute of the day." His eyes scanned the lake, looking for the stick to appear as it washed back to shore. "But you asked what I risked losing. It's not just Lauren I'd lose if I cling to my memories; I lose too. Does that make any sense?"

"What is it that you'll lose?"

"Do you ever worry that you will forget Connor?"

"Yes. I've felt very similar to what you are feeling. But what are *you* losing?"

Rikk listened to Kara's calm voice resonating with strength and sincerity. It seemed to beckon what he struggled with the most. "How did you get through it, Kara?"

"By doing what you are doing now."

"But you did it sooner?"

"We all heal in our own way and time. I had friends who helped me in other ways, and a lot of my friends were coaches, so they helped me get to my answers without imposing their answers on me."

"I'm irritated that friends and some family are trying to find a replacement for Lauren. They are trying to save me from something I don't want saving from."

"What don't you want saving from?"

"Being alone."

"You want to be alone?"

Rikk stood rigid and stared at Kara. She was so self-assured. He somehow knew she wouldn't accept less than the truth from him or anyone else, nor would she retreat from asking the questions he needed to answer. In a hushed voice he said, "No, I just want companionship to feel right. Not pushed on me."

"And it feels like people are pushing companionship on you now?"

"Yeah. I guess your question about what I would expect from Joe helped me to see I need to be all right with moving on with my life."

"Is there more you want to say about your perspective?"

"No."

"Let's name this place before we go look at your friends' perspectives. What word or couple of words sums up the way this place feels to you?"

"Dead and damn depressing. I'm in the spiral of missing Lauren, not wanting to miss her, and then pissed because I didn't miss her. I want companionship, but I want to find it on my own."

"OK, this is 'Dead and damn depressing.' Let's find a new place to look at you and Lauren alive from your friends' perspectives." Kara began to walk to the log she had been sitting on earlier.

He wasn't sure if she was overcome with compassion, filled with memories of Connor, or if her strained voice was purely maintaining professionalism—or was it caused by him. He felt something he couldn't name, but today her affectedness did *not* make him feel smug. "How come we keep moving?" Rikk asked.

"It's quite weird, but it's amazing how exploring every perspective from a different spot will bring back those emotions and feelings when we revisit the spot toward the end of the coaching session. Somehow your feelings attach themselves to the spot. I know that is a hard concept for many people to wrap their brains around, so I ask you to just go along with it and see what happens for you."

Rikk telegraphed his speculation with raised eyebrows. "OK, I'll go along with you and see what happens. So what do we do next?" he asked as they sat on the log. He rested his elbows on his knees and intertwined his fingers.

"In relationship to 'Rikk and Lauren alive,' what are your friends' perspectives?"

"They want me to find someone, so I get over Lauren and act like my old self again. They keep match-making, and I just don't see why they think I'd have any interest in the women they set me up with. I don't even want to see my friends because they won't quit inviting a single, divorced, or widowed woman along."

"Hmm, interfering?"

"Hell yes, interfering!"

"What is their payoff for interfering?"

"What do you mean?"

"What do they gain by setting you up all the time?"

"A sullen and pissed off guest."

"You or the single women?" Kara grinned.

Rikk grimaced, "I never thought about how all those women felt. I guess both."

"Well, there is another perspective to check out—the women who have been the victims of your friends' match-making attempts." Rikk gave a wry laugh and she smiled at him. "I'm glad to see you laugh. What I meant by asking what is your friends' payoff, was why do they keep doing it? I assume you've told them to stop."

"I've told some, but mostly I just decline the invitations. I guess they want me to be happy, like everything was when Lauren was alive."

"So they are attempting to bring you happiness, albeit in a way that you don't want. Is this right?"

"Yeah, I guess they feel that someone new in my life would bring me back to the way it was?'"

"What is true?"

"What is true is I miss my friends, but when I'm around them it is awkward to be the only one without their spouse. It is even worse to be thrown in with someone new that I'm expected to fall in love with when I just want to feel comfortable with my friends without Lauren. I just want to get comfortable being alone. Do you get that?"

"I do. I do get that. Completely."

Rikk smiled at her and felt a rush over take him. He felt understood and connected. "I suppose you do." He had an urge to touch Kara, hold her, but he couldn't stand risking her rejection.

"Is there more to look at in your friends' perspectives?"

Kara's question brought Rikk's attention back to the moment. He felt some peace at last. "No, I know they are doing what they think will help me."

"What would help you?

"For them to be comfortable with me being a widower."

"When will you tell them this?"

"I guess I will have to tell them the next time I get an invitation."

"Good. What should we call this perspective?"

"I don't know. I've only been considering my views in the past, not those of my friends. Maybe call it 'The way it was.'"

"I like that," Kara chuckled as she used her stick to write, 'The way it was' in the sand. "Should we check out the perspective of those women who have been invited to the same functions that you have?"

"Do we have to?"

"No, but you might learn something from looking at their perspectives."

"OK."

"Do you want to pick the spot for their perspectives?"

Rikk scanned the beach, and then walked to the water's edge. "Here, where I can easily douse any hopes they have of getting asked on a date."

Kara faked a shiver. "Brr. You'd douse them in ice cold water! What is their perspective on this new bachelor they have just met—keeping in mind the subject." Kara pointed back at the circle and words scribbled in the sand, 'Rikk and Lauren alive.'"

"I'm like the bachelor on the Dating Game, except I get one bachelorette at a time and always pick going home single to an endless stream of contestants. I'm surly and shut down. I waste their time and effort they put into meeting me. They could start a Rikk Harmon Hate Club."

"Why a hate club?

"I don't know, maybe they don't hate me. I guess I would hate being around anyone who treated me the way I've treated them, so I wouldn't blame them if they did."

"How do you treat them?"

"Disinterested."

"How do you want to treat them?"

"Respectfully disinterested."

"Well, how do you show them you're respectfully disinterested in them?"

"But I don't want to be put in any more match-making situations, so I don't want to even meet them."

"If you find yourself in one, what will you tell the bachelorette?"

"I don't know. I guess I'll have to figure out some way to let her know I'm not interested in dating. But I won't accept the invitations anymore, so this isn't going to happen." Rikk scowled and wondered why she had him looking at the bachelorette's perspective.

"Hmm. I purposely poked you to see how committed you were to telling your friends that you didn't want to be the bachelor in their dating games anymore."

"You purposely poked me?"

"Yep, and you reacted like a snake being poked with a stick. You raised your head and bared your fangs. How does it feel to stand your ground?"

"Good. Do you always poke your clients?"

"I don't have a prescription that I follow when I coach. It's more intuition that leads my questions, and if my intuition leads me to poking, I poke."

He laughed. "Well, your poke got my ire up. I guess I can see the benefit of your poking. What's next?"

"How does the 'Blown away bachelorettes' perspective mesh with what you discovered in your friends' perspectives?"

"I guess I'll tell my friends not to invite a bachelorette and that I want to be with them—not with someone whom I don't even want to know. I'll tell them that I'll leave if they have some woman coming along for me to meet."

"Great. That is your assignment. From now on, will you accept invitations from your family and friends with that stipulation?"

Rikk questioned her, "Assignments? You give assignments?"

"Yes. The way assignments work is, I give them, and you get to accept, decline, or re-negotiate."

"Re-negotiate?"

"Oh, I guess I should've explained. Coaches give assignments to their clients based on what their clients have said about what they want. The assignments help them to get unstuck and progress toward living the life they want. If the assignment is just what they need, they'll accept it. If it is not right, they'll decline it, and if it is on the right track but not quite right, they'll re-negotiate. They modify it to make it more consequential for them. So, do you accept the assignment, decline, or want to re-negotiate?"

"I accept your assignment. I'll only accept my friends' invitations with that stipulation." Rikk felt strong and burden free—that surprised him. He exhaled, stretched his arms out and over his head, then straightened his shoulders.

"Great. How will I know you have told your friends this?"

Rikk's eyebrows raised and without hesitation he answered, "I'll call you." He watched Kara. She bit her lower lip and shut her eyes. He could retract his statement, but he wanted to call her. He felt guilty that he got satisfaction from her noticeable discomfort. Damn, he liked her even though he was annoyed that she resisted him. A water beetle scurried over the sand, and he watched it speed away, then reached down and picked it up.

Kara's eyes were wide with surprise. "That's, um—oh, damn. I wish I could hit the delete key and take back that request. I don't ask for someone's accountability in complimentary sessions unless they've indicated they want me to coach them."

"You asked for accountability?"

"Asking them to report back on their assignment is how I help my clients keep accountable—to help them make progress toward their goals."

"Since I'm not your client, you don't care if I do the assignment or not?" Rikk sighed as he wondered if he had done something to cause her to dislike him. He also wondered why it was so damn important to him that Kara admit she remembered him before he confessed he remembered her. He shook his head.

"No, I do care. It's just protocol—or, or something like that. I guess, since we already established that I'm not coaching you in the future, I didn't want you to misinterpret, or think—Rikk, I'm sorry. I do want you to call."

"What is your number?" Rikk's impatient voice masked the pain he felt. Rikk set the beetle back on the sand and watched it scurry away.

In a quiet voice, Kara gave Rikk her phone number. They looked at each other for a moment before she said, "Rikk, do you want to spend any more time in the bachelorette women's perspective?"

"No. What's next?"

"Let's give it a name first. What do you want to call it?"

"How about 'Hate club?'"

"Ooh, do you hate these women?"

"No, I hate the way I've treated them."

"Hate is such a strong word that's full of negative energy. Do you mind if I suggest a different name?"

"Go ahead."

"How about calling it the 'Dating game?'"

"How about the 'Blown off bachelorettes?'"

"Sounds good," Kara laughed. "The 'Blown off bachelorettes' at the water's edge. They can easily be blown out to sea from this vantage point," She wrote the name in the sand and seemed relaxed again.

Rikk appreciated Kara's humor that lightened up his mood. He had never bothered to consider how these women felt when he brushed them off. He watched Kara write in the sand. "Do you do this walking around and checking out different perspectives every time you coach?"

"No, this is just one of the tools that coaches use to help people see their issue differently. It often helps them to shift or amend their thinking and then take actions toward their goals."

"How do you do this over the phone?"

"If they are working in their office they can stand up, go to the window or door, swivel their chair around and look somewhere else, pick up an object, or just about anything you can imagine. Even just asking them to change their current posture or view works. Now, let's try on Lauren's perspective?"

"Lauren's!"

"Yes. Where should we go for hers?"

Rikk stood immobilized, and he stared at the parking lot and tried to figure out how to get out of looking at Lauren's perspective. Before he came up with anything Kara interrupted his thoughts.

"Rikk, your reaction tells me this may be a hard place for you to explore, but it might be the most important too." Kara was waiting for Rikk to answer, and he guessed she knew he was thinking about bolting for the parking lot. "Do you want to continue?" she said.

Rikk's saboteur was telling him to drive away. He turned to face Kara and nodded. "Lauren's perspective. We need to be near the parking lot; she had a phobia of water." He laid his hand on Kara's arm, and they strolled up the boardwalk, stopping at the edge of the parking lot. Before Kara asked any questions, Rikk's words tumbled out, "Lauren would be disappointed in me. She'd be watching me with her bleak expression until she could no longer stand it, then she'd shake her head and ask me why I was not getting on with my life. She'd tell me that I should at least try; at least give some woman a chance. She'd be furious. She'd let me know how much she doesn't want me to be dead along with her." Rikk was stuck in his thoughts for awhile.

Kara's gentle voice asked, "Why didn't you give any of them a chance?"

Shocked at her question, Rikk glowered at her "None of them held my interest."

"Then why do you think Lauren would be disappointed that you didn't give any of them a chance?"

Rikk kicked the sand off the boardwalk as he considered Kara's question. "She would be mad that I didn't *want* to meet any of them, but she would not be mad that I didn't ask any of them on a date."

"Say more."

"When she was dying, she told me she wanted me to move on, to meet someone—find a companion." He felt so despondent from hearing his own words.

Kara's voice sounded strained, "Hmm, Lauren's wish was for you to find a companion?"

"Yeah. I guess that is what she was saying."

"How can you honor her wish and keep both of you alive too?" Kara pointed to the circle in the sand where they started.

Rikk repeated Kara's question as he deliberated it, then said, "Lauren would not like the man I am now. She wouldn't like being around me. Hell, she wouldn't put up with it. I guess she knew me better than I ever imagined. That is what she was trying to tell me, and I've refused to even consider it." His voice resonated deeply as he said, "I think I'm starting to understand what Lauren was trying to tell me with all the messages written and underlined in the book." He nodded as a relaxed smile spread over his face and he laughed.

"The book?"

"Yeah, the book." He wasn't sure he wanted to share the revelation he just had. He felt lighter and that was enough.

"What just happened? Why the smile? Why the laugh?"

"One of Lauren's last request was for me to remarry, get on with my life without her. I've just been refusing to listen."

"Say more about that."

After deep reflection, Rikk said, "That's all there is. Let's call her perspective, 'Get on with life.'"

"My intuition tells me there is more. Is there?"

"No, that's all." Rikk was impressed that Kara knew there was more, but he also knew that she wouldn't be comfortable hearing it, especially with how she seemed to guard herself from him. He already felt benefits from the insights she had helped him uncover. Thirty minutes had passed since they started, but as long as she didn't mind he'd continue.

After she wrote 'Get on with life' in the sand next to the boardwalk she said, "OK, how about one more perspective?"

"Whose?"

"This may sound a little wacky, but how about the perspective of—" Kara was looking around as if she was searching for something. Her eyes stopped on the patch of sea grass that separated the beach from the fenced off parking lot. "Of the sea grass."

"The perspective of the sea grass!" Rikk snickered. "Sea grass has a perspective?"

"I know this is a stretch for you, but let's walk over there and see if any metaphor or analogy comes to you?"

"And what if it doesn't?"

"Well, I can try another, or we finish by revisiting each of the perspectives and find one that you want to explore possibilities of actions to take."

"What is another perspective we could try?"

"Um," she looked up at the overcast sky and said, "the falling star's perspective?"

"The perspective of a falling star! In this fog, what made you think of a falling star?"

"Oh," Kara laughed. "A few nights ago I stepped off this boardwalk and saw a dark sky full of stars, and I wished I were sailing *Genie* out in the middle of the lake. I wished I were where no city lights illuminated the sky and washed out the stars' brilliance, and then a falling star blazed across the sky and I—" She shook her head and closed her eyes.

"You what?"

"It's not important to our coaching session, I'll tell you later."

"Sea grass, falling stars—do you come up with a wacky perspective every time you coach?"

"No, but I do when I'm using the perspective-coaching method. I throw out the first word that pops into my head. It is crazy how often a random word will give a client a completely fresh and new view on their subject—and even more amazing is how often that perspective is the one that triggers the most insight and learning. It often is the place from which they take action."

Kara and Rikk walked to the sea grass. Rikk looked puzzled, and Kara smiled at him before she explained, "Rikk, sometimes you don't get anything, and then we move to something else like the falling star. But just give yourself a minute to see if anything comes up—if the sea grass reminds you of anything."

Rikk stood gazing at the grass, then squatted, and grasped a grass blade. Kara joined him, descending slow so she would not lose her balance. Once there she mirrored his posture and grasped a blade of grass too. Rikk waited for her to talk, but Kara just smiled.

"Are you copying me for a reason?"

"Yes. Another coaching device is to find out your client's posture and put yourself in it, so you can feel what they are feeling. It helps you better understand their mental and emotional position, and often helps you ask the questions that will benefit them the most. Other times you ask them to move out of that posture when they are stuck. It is like the cliché about needing a change of scenery to see things differently. It works, so I do it."

"So you weren't just trying to annoy me." Rikk smirked at her then looked at the grass.

"No, I'm just trying to feel what you are feeling right now. The sea grass may not give you anything, and that's fine."

Rikk looked out over the sea grass bowing under the weight of the morning's drizzle. Water beads formed and dropped onto the sand. Rikk sighed and ran his fingers through his hair; his solemn gaze returned to Kara. "I'm like this grass that has survived this last storm. I've been blown around, bent and twisted until I almost broke. I've been left alone after the wind and rain passed. I'm like these blades of grass that are weighed down by heavy raindrops. But here I am, still standing, just like the sea grass."

"Yeah, you're like the sea grass, still standing strong *and resilient* in the storm's aftermath."

Rikk looked back over the sea grass; then his deep voice gently vibrated, "Um, hum."

"Rikk? As you look at 'Rikk and Lauren alive,'" she pointed to their starting place, "Where are you in relationship to the storm?"

"The wind has almost stopped, and it is easier to stand."

"Easier? What would make it easy to stand?"

"Shaking off those drops of rain clinging to the grass blades."

Kara waited then said, "Say more about the raindrops."

"The raindrops are falling to the sand, like tears, but I don't cry."

"Never?"

"I just don't feel like crying even when everyone else thinks I should." Rikk issued a dare to Kara to drop the matter, and Kara stared back with compassion. "Don't tell me about therapy and counseling, I know all about them."

"Maybe crying is not right for you."

"What?"

"Maybe it isn't what you need."

"What do you mean?"

"Like I said, everyone has their own way to mourn."

"Everyone thinks they know what's right for me."

"I'm curious how you know what everyone thinks."

"All my mom says is, 'Let it out, Rikk.' What am I supposed to do, cry on command?"

"What do you want to do?"

"I've cried. Not a lot, it just doesn't seem to help me. Sometimes she makes me feel like something is wrong with me because I haven't bawled in front of her. She looks at me with that look, like I didn't love Lauren enough because I haven't fallen apart with her there to comfort me."

"What do *you* want to do?"

"About Mom?"

"Sure."

"I want her to stop worrying about me."

"How can you stop her from worrying about you?"

"I don't know if I can." He shook the raindrop from another blade of grass.

"Looking at the raindrops on the sea grass as if they are tears, whose are they?"

"I don't know. Mom's tears. It's the weirdest thing, but Lauren's death has changed her. Like some ghost was let out of her closet. But I don't know of anyone close to her whose spouse has died, and she divorced my dad when I was young. Hell, I have hardly thought of him in the last thirty years. I can't imagine they are tears for him. He was never around, and she didn't ever seem to care. I suppose they could be the tears of others too. I just know that I'm tired of being the shoulder that everyone cries on. They aren't even crying for Lauren. They're crying for me because I'm alone."

"How do you know that?"

Rikk batted raindrops off a few more blades of grass. "My mom is having a real hard time with Lauren's death, but all her comments are about how lonely I am and will be. She never talks about missing Lauren, but they did things together and talked all the time. They treated each other like mother and daughter. She doesn't cry for herself either, just for me, and she badgers me because I don't whimper along with her. I can't understand her need for me to break down. She tells me not to be afraid to cry."

"Are you?"

"Afraid to cry? No, I'm not afraid to cry, and I already said I have. But I avoid her and other friends because they can't stop crying. I'm just like these blades of grass holding the raindrops. They shed their tears onto me and weigh me down."

"Hmm, you carry the weight of others' tears. How will you shake their tears off?"

"I don't know. I didn't even know how much it bugged me until now."

"This sounds like a great inquiry question."

"What is an inquiry question?"

"It is a question that the client doesn't have an immediate answer for. It is one that often stumps them, and they need to think about it, to digest it over a week or two and see what comes up for them. You can accept, decline, or re-negotiate. What do you think?"

"What was the question again?"

"Um, how will you shake their tears off?"

"I guess I need to think about it. I accept it, but can I ask you something?"

"Sure."

"Are you over Connor's death?"

"Rikk, I'll answer your question because I feel it might help you, but may I share my beliefs about death in general first? It might make it easier to understand where I am with Connor's death."

"Yeah."

"I believe that there is no death—that our bodies are the vessels that we use to grow, learn, and expand on this earth; and then at our earthly defined death we pass back into a non-physical form of energy. I allowed myself to grieve and cry for Connor even with my beliefs, but I had some people who I think expected me to mourn more than I did. I think you and I might view death somewhat the same. When I cried, it was for my memory of Connor and not for Connor himself. I cried because I missed how I felt when he was with me, but I have Connor with me whenever I want. I can choose to miss him and feel lost without him, or I can choose to feel his presence and feel joy for the time I had with him when he was physically here. I guess I work hard to choose the happy memories when I'm missing him the most. Most days I can do this, and a few days I just give in to self-pity and let my tears flow."

"Is your belief that there is no death based in religion?"

"Yes and no. I'm not affiliated with any formal religion, but my beliefs concur with many religious beliefs—at least to some degree. However, in coaching, my beliefs are not important to my client. My job is to help them find their own answers and solutions. Everyone has their own answers. A coach does not give clients any answers or try to persuade them to their beliefs; we just do what is necessary to help our clients find their answers that they've buried within themselves. I'm sorry if I stepped out of my coaching role by answering your question. I don't expect you to adopt my beliefs; I only shared my perspective with you so you might see that everyone has their own unique perspective. My perspectives are right for me, but may be totally opposite from what is right for you and everyone else."

Rikk nodded his head, "I appreciate your openness without attempts to control my views. In my profession, I try to convince patients to follow my opinions."

Kara gave a small laugh and said, "I suppose you do. Now, with my coach hat back on, is there more to explore from the sea grass perspective?"

"No, I'm done." Rikk was exhausted.

"We can be done with this whole session if you want." Kara looked at her watch and said, "We've been doing this for forty-five minutes."

"No, that would be like opening up the patient and spreading their organs out to locate the problem but not fixing it."

Kara laughed. "Great analogy! I might have to use that. So what should we call the sea grass perspective?"

"'Standing tall.'"

Rikk stood and waited for Kara to finish writing in the sand, then offered her his hand and helped her stand. She said, "Now we revisit all the perspectives, and you get to choose the one that you'd like to explore some sort of action to take that will help you keep 'Rikk and Lauren alive.'"

"What about the falling star perspective? You can't close me up with only ninety percent of the surgery done. Anyhow, what do you have to race back to do?"

"Coffee?" Kara smiled, "Cold coffee that you brought but haven't handed out yet."

"Haven't you ever had cold coffee before?" When Kara rolled her eyes and grinned, Rikk said, "I'll buy you a hot cup when we are finished."

"OK, where would you go to watch falling stars?" Kara said.

Rikk walked towards the middle of the beach until he found a level spot in the sand. He sat down on it, and then lay back looking at the heavy, overcast sky.

"What do you see?" Her voice failed to disguise her nerves.

Rikk lifted himself up onto his elbows and chided, "Aren't you going to mirror your client? Aren't you going to lie down and look into the sky and feel what I'm feeling?" He knew his Cheshire Cat grin annoyed Kara, but he didn't care.

"Damn you!" Kara said as she winced. "You can give some people too much information." She accepted his outstretched hand and settled herself onto the sand about two feet away from him.

Rikk enjoyed Kara's discomfort and was confident that she found his ability to locate and push her buttons irritating—and appealing. Rikk noticed a low-lying cloud laden with mist pass over them, then turned his head to see Kara watching it too. He waited for her to look at him with her clear eyes. He felt a warm rush from looking into those eyes that he remembered from decades ago. "I can't see even one damn star." He snickered as he divulged the first thought that raced into his mind, "But I do remember when I was seventeen and out on a date with Debra— Debbie, no Dixie—Dixie Johnson. She was the hottest cheerleader in the school, blond hair, and big brown eyes, with really big—"

"Got it! I got the picture. Dixie was every boy's dream girl come true."

"You don't want to hear about Dixie?"

"As a coach, I get to intrude and direct the client to get to the point. Time is ticking, and I don't need to get all the details to get the picture. Now, what is it about Dixie in the falling star perspective that pertains to 'Rikk and Lauren alive?'"

"Dixie and I had been making out in the car, she said no, and I—um— needed to cool off—so to speak." Rikk appreciated Kara's chuckle, even if she initially clicked her tongue with disapproval. "So I got out and laid back on the car hood. I saw about three falling stars before Dixie came out and joined me. We just laid their saying nothing, until the next falling star shot across the sky. Dixie asked me if I made a wish, and I grumbled that it wasn't going to come true. God, what an ass I was back then."

"How does this relate to 'Rikk and Lauren alive?'" Kara said with impatience as she shook her head.

"I'm getting to that. Back then I was wishing for sex, but now I want more. I want to make love under the stars with someone I love and who loves me too." Both Rikk and Kara lay motionless staring at the now thick mist falling from the sky. He'd wait to say more until she looked at him.

Fear, he supposed, made her voice crack as she spoke, "A love like you shared with Lauren?"

"Yes," Rikk swallowed hard and felt tears pool in his eyes. He'd never expected to at last see what he wanted through all the conflicting feelings he had, much less for anyone to get it. Kara understood. He wasn't sure if that was what made him happy, or if it was that *he* now understood. His voice had a seventeen-year-old enticement to it when he said, "I still haven't made love under the stars." Rikk laughed when Kara's head spun around to him trying to conceal her grin. "Have you?" Rikk stared right at her. She looked away, but he could feel her holding her breath. Her face in profile didn't hide her moist eyes. He wondered what caused them to water.

"Rikk, this isn't about me. It is always about the client."

"With Connor?" Rikk's concentrated gaze never left her.

"I'm not sure how answering this will help your coaching. Um, let's go back to—"

Rikk listened to seagulls squawking in the distance and the waves washing onto the shore, then flowing away. "You're not my coach, and I'm not your doctor. If I can take off my stethoscope, then you can take off your coaching hat. Do you really know how it feels to love someone so much that you want—"

"Yes, under the stars with Connor—and I do really know." She changed her stare from the foggy sky to the opposite side of the beach from Rikk. "Rikk, I think this coaching session has strayed, and it needs—"

"I'm sorry. Please, I don't want to stop now, and I won't ask you any more personal questions." He snorted a sigh. "And I know you really know how it feels to love someone as much as I love Lauren. I *am* sorry I asked that."

Kara didn't make a sound for what felt like an eternity to Rikk. Her voice quivered when she said, "What does the falling star perspective give you in relation to 'Rikk and Lauren alive?'"

Rikk's gaze returned to the sky as he pondered the question. "It's a place where I accept Lauren's death, but still feel her love. It's a place where I hope to make love to someone that I've fallen for. Making love under the stars, and maybe I will see a falling star that is—" He was staring into the dense fog but could feel her turn her head and eyes watching him.

Kara reached out and rested her hand on Rikk's bicep. "That is?"

At Kara's touch Rikk whispered his answer, stunning himself with the rawness of it. "Lauren."

To Rikk's relief, time passed before Kara asked, "And what does that feel like to have Lauren shooting across the sky when you are making love to someone else?"

"Not just making love to someone else," Rikk shook his head and sighed, "It's being in love and sharing my life with someone, like Lauren and I did."

They both were holding their breath, and Rikk was relieved when Kara broke the silence. "The shooting star that represents Lauren, what is she telling you?"

"She is happy to see me in love." Rikk said then shook his head. "But that is the problem; I can't make any sense of thoughts like that. Falling stars are not people's deceased loved ones."

"Rikk, will you humor me again and for a moment allow your scientific brain to take a break and let yourself feel the spiritual and mystical woo? We both know what a shooting star really is, but just allow the star to represent Lauren. If Lauren were that star, how would she feel about seeing you love someone, sharing your life with her?"

Rikk looked up into the sky; the answer came to him quickly, too quickly. He contemplated his answer, wondering if it was him or his saboteur. "You'll think I'm insensitive."

"I don't think you are insensitive, but I do think your saboteur is talking now. What is your answer that your saboteur tells you is insensitive?"

"I'd be free." Rikk looked to the far side of the beach. He wondered if Kara could feel his body drenched with tension.

"Can I share what I think?"

"Sure, as a coach or a friend?" He answered, but he lay as still as a cold marble statue.

"Both I suppose. I think freedom is something that Connor wants for me, and from what you've told me about Lauren, I think she felt the same. That she believes that anyone who truly loves their mate wants freedom for their mate when they depart this world." Rikk's gaze returned to Kara, but he said nothing. "Rikk, tell me about that freedom."

Rikk blew out his breath and released his fears as he spoke. "Lauren would be happy that I was free but had not forgotten her. Her star shooting across the sky would be telling me, 'About time you started to live and love again.' She would be laughing as she sent her message."

"Is there more to her message?"

Rikk took several more breaths, then said, "That she loves me and wants me to be happy, and willing to find someone to spend my life with."

Kara whispered, "Is there more in this perspective, or are you ready to name it?"

"I'm ready to name it. This one is 'Freedom.'"

"'Freedom,' what a great name for the falling star perspective." Kara rolled over and sat up, then wrote 'Freedom' in the sand. "Let's revisit all the perspectives to find one you want to explore further, and then you can find some action to take. OK, let's start with your perspective. What was it, 'Dead and?'"

"'Damn depressing.' Do we have to go there?"

"No, but it just helps to review all the perspectives and—"

"Let's go. I guess I'm not anxious to go back there." Rikk stood up and helped Kara to her feet.

As they walked to the spot of Rikk's perspective Kara explained, "Just see what you feel in your body here in the 'Dead and damn depressing' perspective."

"This is weird." Rikk said as soon as they reached the seaweed spot. "This is like walking into a patient's room who has a very bad attitude or hard angry life. Every time I walk in the room I feel this same gut ache."

"Like a bad aura?"

"Do I have a bad aura?"

"I don't know. What do you think?"

"Yeah, I've been walking around in this funk since Lauren's death. I guess I haven't considered how depressing it must feel to be with me."

"Are you ready to move?"

"God, yes. Get me out of here. Where next?"

They walked to the log where they looked at Rikk's friends' perspectives. "Where does 'The way it was' sit in your body?"

"It is in my gut, but only an annoyance now. I agreed to let my friends know I didn't want them to match-make for me, and tell them I will leave if a bachelorette was also invited. I don't see any other action that I could take from their perspective."

"Let's go to the water's edge and visit the 'Blown away bachelorettes' perspective," Kara said and led the way.

Rikk realized he never wanted those situations to be repeated. Next was Lauren's perspective, 'Get on with life.' It had a good feeling to it, but standing next to the parking lot on the boardwalk is not where he would get on with his life as he knew Lauren wanted him to do, even though he felt more love in his heart. Then they walked to the sea grass and looked at the 'Standing tall' perspective. It was both the burden of everyone's expectations of his grieving process and the relief of realizing that he could shed the weight of their tears and stand tall.

"The falling star is last," Kara said as they left the sea grass and walked back to the falling star.

Rikk sat back down in the spot and extended his hand to Kara, holding it as she sat next to him. "This feels the best. I guess it should, it's 'Freedom.'" He laughed. "I feel about four years old here, or maybe sixteen. It feels good."

"How does four years old feel?"

"Like laughing and not caring about laughing too loud or too long or too much. I don't know, too anything. Just not giving a damn about what anyone thinks."

"Woo who!"

"Did you say woo who?"

"Yes. WOO WHO! It is human's universal instinctive response for awesome! Great! Fabulous! It's all the same. Woo who!"

"Woo who. Ok, what's next, coach? Do you want to know what sixteen feels like?" He enjoyed seeing her blush, and that awoke the sixteen-year-old libido that he'd been suppressing since their reunion on the dock.

"Are you sure you want to continue? Because you are feeling so great now, maybe you just want to stay here."

"Are you afraid of what sixteen looks like?" he asked.

Kara blushed again, and he resisted touching her cheeks, but he knew they were warm. "Maybe I am, but if you need to go there, let's go."

He leaned towards her and murmured, "I think you know what sixteen looks like."

"Do you want to finish this because we can stop this right now." Kara hissed out a breath that penetrated his insolence.

Rikk liked the cautionary tone in Kara's repartee, and didn't regret poking her although he knew it would be wise to sound apologetic. "I made a bad attempt at lightening things up. I guess I didn't expect so much would be brought up. Sorry. I want to finish this."

"It might be better to stop."

Guilt overtook Rikk when he heard Kara's discomfort at his inappropriate behavior. Even more, he was baffled at how he could swing from widower to wanton teenager. He'd win no awards for being decorous. "No, I'm sorry. Please, let's finish. Hey, no walking out of the OR before the patient is stitched up."

"OK. Well, this part usually is lighter, and most people find it fun. Now we get to brainstorm for possible actions that you can take from the 'Freedom' perspective that will help you to keep 'Rikk and Lauren alive.' So we both just say anything that pops into our heads. Just shoot them out as soon as you get them and don't be concerned about taking turns coming up with ideas. So what do you have?"

"Something I can do?"

"Yes, some action that you can take to find the freedom while keeping you and Lauren alive."

"Oh."

"I got one. You could watch a YouTube video of toddlers laughing."

"That's what you want me to do?"

"No, what I want you to do is brainstorm. Anything that comes into your head, or mine, even as ridiculous as it might seem it gets blurted out. Do you have any idea how often the crazy ideas lead to really sane actions?"

"Huh, brainstorming. I can't even remember the last time I heard the word."

"Watch a teen flick." Kara wrote "laugh video" and "teen flick" in the sand and then said, "It's just the first ideas, and I write down every idea that we brainstorm—good, bad, or ugly—without any judgment. We'll save that for the end."

"So this isn't my assignment."

"No. It is just brainstorming ideas. You got one?"

"What if I want it to be my assignment?"

"We are brainstorming. You will get to pick one or two from our list. I've got another: sail your boat. That always gives me the feeling of freedom." Kara wrote "sail" in the sand.

"I like that too. How about I get a date on my own."

As Kara wrote "get date" in the sand, she said, "Ask Dr. Norris out."

"Hell no!" Rikk blurted and watched Kara stop writing. "Why do you assume I would ever ask Heidi out?"

"I'm sorry. I can't believe I said that. Does it help to know that I'm relieved that it made you irate?"

"Was that another poke?"

"I'm sorry. I wish it was. I don't know why I said that. Do you want to be done?"

"No. I just don't know how you could come up with that."

"I crossed the line. I guess I really hope you aren't interested in someone like her. But that had no place in a coaching session, and I feel so unprofessional for saying it. I'm sorry. We should quit."

"No. Don't quit. You aren't my coach, and I'm really curious how this brainstorming leads to action that I can take. I won't act sixteen, and you won't make erroneous assumptions about me. OK?"

"Ok."

"Now what do we do?"

"Keep brainstorming. From the 'Freedom' perspective, Lauren is the falling star and wants to see you in love and sharing your life with someone. What are some things you can do to move in that direction?"

"Take up a hobby."

Kara's smile radiated, and she said, "That's great. How about sky diving."

"Sky diving? Why sky diving?"

"You can meet new people, and I know it's not gender specific. By the way, coaches are notorious for coming up with the worst ideas, but their ideas have value because they can show their client what they really don't want. I usually write them down anyhow, but if you'd rather I don't, I won't."

"Fine. Write it down."

"How about checking out an online dating service?"

"You are full of bad ideas," Rikk smiled at her "Write it down, but write down 'Invite friends over for steaks on the grill.'"

As she wrote it down she offered, "Invite friends for a sail?"

"Hire a captain to teach me to sail," Rikk's unmistakable hint landed, and Kara's eyes shot open as though the idea was preposterous. She bit her lower lip and looked away.

"Sign up for sailing lessons," Kara muttered.

What the hell is her reason to avoid me? With a gruff note of mockery, he broke the silence, "Ask you on a date." Kara fumbled the stick. Rikk held her stare as he picked it up, handed it back to her, and said. "Write it down. All ideas, good, bad, and ugly are written down. No judgment."

Kara took the stick, exhaled, and wrote, "Ask K out." She at last asked, "Do you have any more ideas?" Rikk did not and neither did she. With a resigned expression, Kara recited the list. "Laugh video, teen flick, get own date, new hobby, sky diving, online dating service, invite friends over for steaks, invite friends to sail, hire captain, sailing lessons, and ask me out." The words scratched in the sand were starting to disappear from the mist that had turned to drizzle, and now a light rain started.

"Do I choose what I want to do?"

Kara flipped her rain jacket hood up, but Rikk only had his polar fleece jacket on. "Yes, you get to choose." Before he could respond, Kara's voice jittered while she tapped the stick in the sand. "Rikk, um, you've got an idea what coaching is now, but I need to end this complimentary session. I'm not comfortable with me on your list of choices, even knowing that I'm not your coach and you're not my doctor. I, um—I can recommend a few coaches for you to work with, if you like."

Rikk swallowed, and the lump in his throat almost made him choke on his saliva. He wanted to ask Kara out, but she had closed down. He thought about how she had him identify where he felt his pain last night and wondered where she felt hers right now. He stood up abruptly and said, "Let's go." Again he helped her up, and they hurried to his car.

⚜

Rikk opened the door for her and picked up the bakery bag. Once she was inside, he shut the door and walked around to the driver side. He held onto the door handle and stood out in the rain deciding how he'd say what needed to be said.

Kara stared out the passenger window and didn't turn to look at Rikk when he got in the car. He nudged her, handed her the bakery bag, and then inserted the key into the ignition. He leaned his head back and dropped his hands to his lap. He felt her eyes turn to him, but he kept his eyes on the steering wheel. At the same moment Rikk said, "Kara, I was your son's surgeon years ago," Kara blurted, "Rikk, you were Tate's doctor seventeen years ago."

Chapter 21

Kara

Silence prevailed as they looked at each other. Rikk picked up a cup of coffee and handed it to Kara. An odd mixture of relief and tension filled the car. Rikk pulled a scone out of the bakery bag for Kara before getting the other one out for himself. Not hungry or thirsty, the tepid coffee and scone gave Kara something to occupy herself with as she searched for what to say next. She hoped Rikk would break the silence, but rain started to pour down, and the windows began to fog up. Rikk started the car, waited for the windows to defrost, then backed out of the beach parking lot. When he got to the stop sign, he took a bite of his scone, and Kara shifted the car back into first gear. Rikk looked surprised and said, "No one has ever done that for me before."

"I'm sorry. Your hands were full, and I did it before thinking, or asking if you wanted my help."

"Kara," Rikk waited until she looked at him, "that was a compliment."

Kara sighed and relaxed. When they got to the intersection, Rikk drove straight through rather than turning toward the marina. Kara peered at him. In what seemed to be a test of both of their wills, Rikk didn't offer his destination and she wasn't about to ask. He drove over the Aerial Lift Bridge and through Canal Park. That is when Kara's interest piqued. "Where are you taking me?"

"Shanghai. It means abduction." Rikk grinned, and Kara knew he was waiting for her response, but she refused to comment—and she knew her broad smile and raised eyebrows conveyed her amusement.

"I thought you were going to take—no, Shanghai me to get a hot cup of coffee." Rikk smiled back at her but said nothing and took the freeway entrance to the east. After the gamut of emotions Kara had just experienced, from coaching Rikk to revealing her secret, and hearing his admission of their previous acquaintance, she was surprised how easy it felt to be with him on this mysterious quest. When he turned onto London Road, Kara, asked, "Where are you taking me?"

"My house."

"Why?"

"I want to show you something."

"What?"

Rikk laughed and reached over and squeezed her hand—a gesture Kara assumed Rikk made to reassure her of his honorable intentions. "I want to show you Lauren's mask."

"Oh! OK. What made you think of that?"

"I know this may sound strange, but when you shifted for me, I remembered the times that Lauren did exactly what I needed without my ever saying anything. I used to wonder if she read my mind, especially when we were at Altamira. Then I thought of her mask."

"And you acted on impulse?"

"Yeah. I had the impulse to Shanghai you." Rikk looked at her for a moment before he asked, "Would you have come with me if I had asked you to come see it?"

"I don't know. I—"

"You wouldn't have."

"I might have. If you told me why you thought of it, I would have."

Rikk pulled into the driveway of an English Tudor home on the shore of Lake Superior. As they walked into the house, the phone began to ring. He left Kara in the living room while he answered it. She scanned the warm and inviting atmosphere. Her eyes lingered on the fireplace mantle where a recent picture of Lauren and Rikk sat. Kara crossed the room for a closer look, picked the photograph up, and studied it.

Kara didn't notice that Rikk's phone call ended or that he was standing behind her. "That picture was taken a few of months before she was diagnosed with cancer," Rikk's hushed tone resonated with sadness.

When Kara turned to face Rikk, tears welled in her eyes. "Lauren is beautiful. I'm truly sorry that you lost your wife. You look so in love." Kara felt his body quake even though he stood a foot behind her, and she knew the flood gates could open. She had no expectations of him and hoped he could feel that. "Hey," she said as she swallowed her sorrow.

Trying to joke about it, Rikk's voice cracked as he said, "I didn't intend to burden you."

Kara hugged him, and with the picture in one hand she rubbed Rikk's back with the other. She held onto him tightly and whispered, "It's OK. This is your time and place."

Rikk cried briefly. It was obvious that reining in his emotions was a practiced and well-honed skill. He released Kara and walked away saying, "I'll get the mask." He pushed open a door off the living room, and Kara heard him open another door and blow his nose. He returned with an exquisite, hand-painted mask and handed it to her. They were discussing its intricacies when the doorbell rang and interrupted them. Rikk's face dropped as he checked his watch. "Damn! I did it again."

"What?" Kara frowned.

"I forgot about lunch with Barb and Joe."

"What? You forgot another date?"

"Damn! What's wrong with me?" He turned and walked to the door.

Kara wondered if this was Rikk's mode of operation, or if this was the release of his pent up stress. She also wondered what conclusion the Watsons would jump to seeing her at his house this morning.

Rikk followed Barb and Joe into the living room, and they acted as if they expected to see Kara there. It was only when Barb said, "Kara, I'm so glad you accepted Rikk's invitation to lunch," that she realized the Watsons didn't have a clue that he hadn't remembered to ask her. Further, she wondered if they were the match-making friends that Rikk was talking about earlier. Kara bit her lip, restraining embarrassed laughter, and faced Rikk. His fingers were raking through his hair, which lately Kara had noticed him do more and more.

"Kara, I meant to ask you this morning and, well, I forgot."

"And you forgot we were coming too?" Barb laughed. "Oh my, here is a new side of you I've never seen before. Do we need to schedule Alzheimer's tests?"

Joe just laughed and added, "This boat was supposed to be a destination for relaxation, not a distraction from reality." He walked over and slapped Rikk's back. "Maybe your friends need to be less demanding and distracting, so you can get on with your own life." As he said this, he winked at Barb.

"Joe, you and Barb have never been interfering. I'm at fault here."

Barb said, "You have a new boat and new people from the marina in your life. You are being too hard on yourself. Now, if we leave soon, we can make our reservation on time, and I ate a light breakfast hours ago in anticipation of lunch." Turning to Kara she added, "Kara, it would be so great to hear what it was like to live on a boat for seven years. I'm asking you to join us for lunch. Seven years? Is that right?"

"Yes," Kara said.

"I hope that yes was accepting the lunch invitation," Rikk's husky voice interrupted.

Kara realized that she wanted to spend more time with Rikk, yet she was frightened that she had already become far too involved. Although she revealed her secret to him, she didn't reveal all of it. Her gut told her to refuse, but her heart wanted to go. His persuasive expression was hard to refuse.

"Kara?" Joe said.

Joe drew her out of her thoughts, and she realized they all were waiting for her answer. "Yes." She said looking from Rikk to Joe. "Yes, I would love to go, but we need to stop at the marina, so I can get some cash."

"Kara, I'm asking you to be my date," Rikk said. Kara knew better than to insist she pay her own way since it was the first time he initiated a woman's company, and it was only lunch.

"OK, let's go, or we'll be late," Barb laced her hand under Joe's arm. "Do you want to ride with us?"

"No." Rikk blurted, "We'll follow." He looked to Kara to see if she objected to these arrangements. She nodded.

So much had happened that morning; Kara was numb from processing it all but simultaneously energized. After they pulled back onto London Road, Rikk reached down and squeezed Kara's hand, and in a hushed voice asked, "Kara, when did you recognize me?"

Kara stared into his searching eyes and wondered if she was ready for this conversation as she whispered, "Immediately." She cleared her throat to break the lingering silence. "How about you?"

"The moment I saw your eyes."

Kara shut her eyes, dropped her head back, and exhaled forcefully. "Why? What reason did either of us have for concealing our previous acquaintance?"

"Pride." Rikk signaled to change lanes. "I admit that I've come to expect former patients or their families to come up to me and talk to me, and most the time I'm embarrassed that I've forgotten who they are. I remember the patient's face, but not always their family and friends who are with them."

"But you remembered me?"

"I did. I guess I expected you to admit you remembered me first."

"Why?"

"I guess I've become so accustomed to being recognized that I expect it."

Kara smiled and touched his arm, "Please don't be offended, Rikk, but I would've ignored you even if you were a rock star, out of respect for your privacy and anonymity."

"You ignored me out of respect for *my* privacy and anonymity?"

"Yes, I did. Haven't you ever been annoyed when people interrupt your privacy when they recognize and greet you, or have you had a personal moment invaded and then lost because of an intrusion?"

"Yeah, I've been annoyed a few times, but sometimes it's nice to hear how your patients are doing."

"Well, I'm sorry I ignored you, but you could consider yourself on par with a rock star."

His grin burst out, and he said, "Are you comparing me to a rock star?"

"Yep! You are the rock star of surgeons," Kara said, then snickered. "But you'd never see me asking you, or anyone, for their autograph."

"Why not?"

"Too old!"

"I have people way older than you who come up to talk to me."

"Wow! You *are* the rock star of surgeons." Kara smiled at Rikk's laughter and then explained, "I imagine that the hardest part of fame for a rock star, movie star, or any famous person is people recognizing them where ever they go. I'd hate to go through my life restricted from being and doing as I pleased because people hounded me for their gain. I'd turn away and pretend not to see them, and hope for them that others do the same."

"I admire your respect for their privacy, and I'll forgive you for respecting mine even if I wanted your recognition." Kara's smile looked tired, and when she yawned and stretched, Rick said, "I will take you back to the marina if you would rather rest."

"What? Miss eating lunch with Dr. Rikkert Harmon, rock star of surgeons?"

"Yeah, the rock star of surgeons," Rikk said with exasperation in his voice as he nodded his head and laughed. "Maybe that's been Heidi's attraction to me all along."

"I would like to shut my eyes and rest until we get there. It is amazing how much a ten-minute nap can revive you." Kara wasn't going to revisit any discussion about Heidi. Her mind did rewind, though, and she had a gnawing feeling that more than pride prevented Rikk from disclosing their past encounter, but who was she to grill him. She had only revealed the part of her hand that she was comfortable showing since she did not know exactly where this "date" was headed. She hoped her admission would give her peace—peace from setting her secret free and peace that Rikk's interest in her was only as a friend. *Damn! Have we passed the friendship mark?* She really did not want peace from his interest. He was so much more than the man she had imagined, and she was so conflicted about him. How could this ever work?

Rikk pulled into the parking lot and Kara was looking around pensively. "Kara, are you having second thoughts about lunch?"

"I'm wondering where this is going?"

"What is 'this?'"

"'This' is the date. When I ended the coaching session, I felt you were going to choose asking me out on a date."

"I was, and I did when the Watson's showed up." Rikk sounded agitated and exhaled as he looked out the driver's side window.

"I know this is the date, I don't know where this date is heading."

"Are you having second thoughts about going on a date with me?" He turned the car off.

"I don't want to lead you to believe that I have more to give—I don't want to hurt anyone, especially you, Rikk. I don't understand what my path is and feel I need to find that before I—oh, I don't know what the hell I'm supposed to do right now."

"You don't have room for friendship?" Rikk's hands dropped onto his legs, and he scowled at her.

"No, that's not it. I don't want to—"

Rikk cut Kara off and with his sharp retort, "I'm not ready for anything more either, Kara."

Kara sat immobilized by her humiliation; she had assumed Rikk was more interested in her than he actually was. His remark stung, and she stared at her feet, wondering how she would get through lunch. "I'm sorry that I assumed you were."

Rikk brushed his hand through his hair, "Kara, I'm sorry that I was angry. You're the only person I've talked to—no, that I've wanted to talk to who understands what I've been through and where I am. Your attitude towards life and acceptance of what it has dealt you gives me hope that I will move past this disposition I can't seem to shake. I know you need to move on with your life. I can't believe how much your coaching this morning has shed new light onto mine. It really is good to see others peoples' perspectives instead of only mine. Last night I was going to ask you to go to lunch with the Watsons and me and then this morning too. But our conversations went other places, and I forgot to ask you. I've no idea where this 'date' will lead, but can't we just—" Rikk sighed.

"Be in the moment?" Kara noticed the tension drain from his shoulders, and he nodded. "Rikk, I'm sorry for jumping to the wrong conclusion. Actually, I'm embarrassed. I'm the one who preaches to be in the moment because you can't do anything about the past, and the future is in the future, so live this moment right now." They sat in the car in silence; at last Kara touched his hand. "We are—we *are* friends, aren't we?"

"Yes, we are friends. Are you ready to go?" Rikk pulled on his door handle, but turned to her before he pushed the door open. "Joe and Barb have been my constant support and lately have dropped many hints that I need to expand my circle of friends. They may be assuming our friendship is more, but they aren't the type to say anything to make you feel uncomfortable."

"Are you clairvoyant?" Kara unfastened her seatbelt. "I do like them. I just caught myself living in the future, worrying that they assumed that we are more than friends."

"Last night you made it sound as if it wasn't important what others think."

"I know it's none of my business what people think of me. I just don't want them to jump to the wrong conclusion for your sake." Rikk smiled at her, and Kara wondered if the terms of their friendship would work for her, or for him. Although her logical mind might be warning her to remain only friends, her heart wanted more. She had told herself she wanted Rikk to choose "Take sailing lessons" from the list. However, the one choice on the list that was stubbornly planted in her head was for him to ask her out. That is why she ended the coaching. Years earlier, she would've wanted Rikk to ask her out if her situation was different. But, seventeen years is a long time for millions of changes to happen. Kara's heart stung as it reminded her how the law of attraction works. Whatever your dominant thoughts and emotions are, you get—wanted or unwanted.

"What are you thinking now?"

No matter how she responded, she risked exposing how he captivated her. "Nothing."

"Nothing that you want to share?" Rikk said. Kara's eyes darted away and sent her answer to Rikk. He sighed and said, "You said you'd tell me later about the falling star that blazed across the sky."

"Oh, yeah, the falling star. Most times I make a wish—you know, wish upon a falling star. So I wished for clarity, which isn't that unusual for me to wish for. I rarely wish for material things. I had a weird sense that I'd get clarity, but it would come with difficulty. Just like seeing the stars through the city lights—they were diffused and dull compared to how bright and clear they are when you're in the middle of the ocean—or on Lake Superior. I just didn't want to share it with you and derail your coaching. That's all."

"Are you ready to go in?"

Kara sighed and said, "Yes, I'm ready."

Chapter 22

Kara

Lunch was long and leisurely. Barb started immediately to extract out Kara's story and asked the question that Kara had expected, "How did you manage to live for seven years sailing around the Caribbean?"

Kara took a deep breath. "Where do I begin? About seven years ago, my husband, Connor, and I had been working our daily nine-to-five jobs that had grown tiresome, and sailing in the same lake had lost its luster. Our children," she saw Barb's eyes rise, and quickly added, "Tate and Isabella, were out of the nest. We decided to turn in our comfortable, stable, and boring life for an adventure with the intention of returning to the real world after two years."

"Where are your children now?" Barb asked.

"Tate just graduated from UMD and moved to Oregon. He is working at a resort while he and his fiancée navigate their next career and life move. They are happy and dealing pretty well with the impatience and uncertainty of their careers and age. Maybe there will be a wedding date set the next time I talk to them."

"Were you in the Caribbean while your kids were in college?" Joe's question registered curiosity without judgment.

"We waited until Isabella was in college before we took off. The least we could do was allow her to graduate with the classmates she'd grown up with since grade school. Connor's family lived near Minneapolis, so she had family support close by. Both kids loved all their breaks because we would fly them to wherever we were. They'd bring their friends along, and sometimes we'd trade their hotel rooms for un-chaperoned boat nights. Moreover, we'd made it clear that if they ever needed us, we'd be there for them as soon as we found a flight home. It worked because both kids had family close by for emergencies."

"You must have raised some pretty independent children," Barb said. "Where is Isabella?"

"She just went to Australia with a friend from college. They are visiting his family, and I wouldn't be surprised if they are looking for jobs and applying at colleges to finish their degrees. Actually, I wouldn't be surprised to hear that they are engaged. She is the happiest I've seen her since she was a baby hanging off the side of the boat, dangling her hands in the water. If Isabella and her boyfriend could've figured a way to do it, they'd be living on *Genie's Bottle*, and I would be marooned on some uninhabited island."

"You must have been busy to get all the things necessary done in order to transition from working to living on a boat. You did all that while Isabella was still in high school? How long did that take you?" Joe asked.

"It took about a year to get it all together. We had our house paid for and rented it out. The monthly rent check covered our living expenses and then some. I'm a life coach, and that worked very well while living aboard and sailing the Caribbean. Connor also would take two or three trips back to the States each year continuing his consulting business. Our incomes from these ventures always provided money for boat repairs, equipment, and exploring the countries we visited. Connor was very innovative and was always helping other sailors and locals with fabricating the exact thing needed to make the repair or invent some new apparatus that made life better for them. It was an amazing life, to share what you had, giving without expecting compensation. Gifts were given to us without strings attached, and we gave the same way. The most generous people are also the happiest. We didn't have room onboard for anything but necessities, and it was freeing to have less. Have you ever heard the expression that your possessions possess you?"

Barb raised her eyebrows and joked, "That is a very un-American concept."

"My opinion is that buying everything you fancy, displaying it, insuring it, dusting it, stumbling over it, tucking it away rather than giving it away, and finally paying to dispose of it all has a huge cost that far exceeds the initial cost of the item. One day you wake up and realize that all these things are just taking up space in your garage, and cumulatively they become clutter and drain your energy. Connor and I appreciated things without purchasing them, but we weren't complete misers either. We just chose to buy original hand-crafted items that still spoke to us after we'd walked away from them for at least twenty-four hours. This encouraged us to use our brains and store the sights, sounds, smells, and all the sensations that we encountered. Anyhow, after six months we discovered that we didn't intend to return to our nine-to-five jobs and lives." Kara glanced at the ceiling and gave a soft sigh. "It was five of the best years of our marriage."

"I thought you lived on the boat seven years?" Joe said.

"Joe," Rikk started to answer for Kara.

"It's OK, Rikk, I'm fine telling them." Kara paused, "About two years ago, I had taken the dinghy to the village market while Connor stayed on the boat. He was replacing the zinc ball on the prop shaft when a jellyfish stung him. He went into anaphylactic shock and," Kara inhaled deeply and then evenly articulated, "he was gone when I got back from town.

They all sat silently waiting for Kara to continue. "So, after the funeral, I spent a couple of months at home, drifting through the paperwork that keeps you on some sort of course. One day I had everything done, and I realized I had a boat in St. Vincent that I needed to return to. I spent the next year aimlessly existing in the Caribbean with more company than Connor and I ever had before. I suspect both of my children orchestrated that. I finally realized that I had depleted my family and friends' benevolence of spending their vacations checking up on me and decided that I needed to move to the next chapter in my life. When I announced my plans to return, I had a waiting list of help to sail *Genie's Bottle* back to Marathon. I think they all were anxious to vacation somewhere other than the Caribbean; but they all wanted one last sailing trip in the southern latitudes." Kara grimaced with her smile and took a sip of water. "A friend of Dan's, the marina manager, was looking for a boat. Dan introduced them to me, and helped me sell *Genie's Bottle*. The buyer has rented a slip for *Genie* in Bayfield, so I'm delivering her there, and I've notified my renter that I'll be moving back into our house. I'm anxious to get off the docks and get *Genie* home and sold, and to set down roots."

Kara asked the Watsons about their family, and that led them into talking about their friendship with Rikk and Lauren. She realized that Barb and Joe were the supportive friends who would never force Rikk into awkward blind date situations. At the end of lunch, Kara excused herself to use the ladies' room, and Barb followed.

"What was Lauren like?" inquired Kara as they entered the ladies' room.

"Lauren was closer to me than any of my sisters. Rikk and Lauren became our closest friends soon after Joe hired Rikk. Lauren was always interested in my job. I would tell her about the kinds of problems that the people I worked with had, and she was amazing. She came up with intelligent and compassionate suggestions for so many of my clients. Then Zoey was born. She planned to return to her pre-baby job as a buyer for Genevieve's but was dragging her feet. She loved that job, and they loved her and her impeccable style. Lauren finally went back for a short period after her maternity leave had expired, but both she and Rikk wanted Zoey nurtured at home. Her old boss promised to find a position for her if or whenever she wanted to return. When Zoey entered kindergarten, she kept talking about going back to Genevieve's, but she would never pick up the phone. I finally told her, 'Lauren, from your non-action I can tell you don't really want to go back.' She confessed that she was more interested in what I do than buying jewelry, clothing, or anything else for that matter. Lauren said that after having Zoey, she realized how the materialistic things that had almost defined her happiness meant so little to her now. I asked her if she would like a job, and as soon as I found funding, I hired her to work with me in the community outreach program. She had an innate ability to see right through the cons of some people and hold them accountable; she also had the ability to heel the broken and desolate hearts of others. She knew exactly what to say to encourage them, to nurture their self-respect, and to help them regain their dignity and self-sufficiency."

"Lauren sounds like a remarkable person—and friend," Kara said.

"Indeed, she was a remarkable friend. Her death left a hole in so many lives, but none bigger than the hole in Rikk's heart. Their friendship was beautiful."

Kara was speechless. That is how she felt about her marriage and friendship with Connor.

"Oh, I hope I haven't scared you with my adoration of Lauren." Barb eyed Kara as they washed their hands. "Now, Kara McKee walks into Rikk's life, and I think he is torn between his discomfort with someone new and his undying loyalty to Lauren—who made it clear to him that she didn't want her memory to become a way for him to hide from life. She wanted him to live and love and find someone to share his life with. I don't know if that is you or not. I guess time will tell. The funny thing is, that bump on your head was unfortunate for you, and I'd never wish that pain on you or on anyone. However, if you look for a silver lining in the clouds, as I do, it may be just the catalyst that Rikk needs to break down the wall he has constructed to insulate him from living life. I believe your bump may provide you a silver lining, also—but I don't have any idea what it is."

Kara, mesmerized by Barb's information, nodded in affirmation. "Hmm, silver lining. I guess I'll just have to wait to see what it turns out to be." Barb's silver lining theory reminded Kara of her own belief that people's experiences that are unwanted often end up to be gifts. Sometimes those experiences provide the contrast needed to help them discover and achieve what they do want. She hoped Rikk would discover what he wanted from the two lists he had made last night. As she walked back to the table, she heard the voice of her authentic self whisper in her head, *Kara McKee, you tell everyone that sometimes those things that feel really bad end up being the catalysts for the most needed and best changes? Maybe you should make a couple lists.* Kara's stomach somersaulted, and she felt her heart twinge joyfully. She had been doing the opposite of what she had always instructed her children to do. She had been resisting what felt good, what felt right in her heart. Instead, Kara had been following her brain—her saboteur. Kara hadn't lied to Rikk; she just omitted some information. Actually, she omitted a lot of information. Damn her secrets. Damn how they prevented her from following her heart.

Chapter 23

Kara

The Watsons, Rikk, and Kara left the restaurant at three twenty, and on the way back to the marina, Rikk got a call on his cell phone. Kara heard half of this conversation:

"Hi, Honey, how are you?"

"Oh no! Zoey, I forgot. I'm so sorry. I can make it in a few minutes, but Zoey, I—hang on a minute."

Rikk muted the call and looked at Kara, who was trying to give him privacy. "Kara, this is my daughter, Zoey. I was supposed to meet her at the DECC for a circus."

"How old is your daughter?" Kara tried to imagine him having a daughter of an age who'd want her dad to take her to the circus.

"I have a date with my daughter, Zoey, and her children."

"You have grandchildren?"

"Yes, two. I was supposed to meet them at three fifteen and totally forgot. Would you like to come with us?"

"You have two grandchildren, and you forgot them and your daughter?" She shook her head and furrowed her eyes. "I agree with Barb; you might have Alzheimer's disease."

"You may be right. Listen, I know you are tired, and if you just want to get back to the boat, I will take you. But if you are up to being with my grandchildren at a circus, I would be indebted to you. Jacob and Maddie are disappointed that I'm late. It will only be a few hours."

She thought the idea of seeing Rikk with grandchildren was irresistible. "I think you're already indebted to me and Dutch for rescuing your boat. But don't you have to buy tickets in advance? It might be sold out."

"Zoey's husband, Eric, is sick, so he isn't coming. With me not there, Zoey is apprehensive about having both kids alone."

"Well, if you have a spare ticket, I don't think I could possibly pass up the opportunity to meet your grandchildren and daughter. Sure, I'd love to go."

Rikk un-muted the phone and said, "Zoey, I can be there in a couple minutes. I have a friend with me; she is a sailor. You'll get to meet her when I get there. You still have Eric's ticket, don't you?"

Kara thought that Rikk seemed happy by the prospect of seeing his family. She also was blown away that she was meeting them. A couple of minutes did not give her much time to contemplate or worry. When he hung up, she was watching him, smiling broadly and shaking her head in amazement.

Rikk said, "I don't know whether to thank you for the favor of consenting to come with me or prepare to defend myself for the tongue lashing I deserve."

"Just be glad that the drive is short, and I don't have time to properly torment you about forgetting your *two* grandchildren and your daughter." Kara laughed, "You have *grandchildren!*"

"Yes, I do."

"You've never mentioned anything about your grandchildren. I think I possess blackmail information."

"You wouldn't."

"No, I wouldn't," said Kara. "But actually, now that I think about it, keeping it quiet should render some payoff, say an ice cream cone or popcorn?"

"You need to set the stakes higher."

"You need to make the offense worse; then the stakes will be higher."

∗✦∗

Rikk parked the car, and they walked to the entrance. A little boy with red hair, freckles, and scabs on his knees and elbows tugged on his mom's arm and announced, "There's Grandpa!" The little girl with brown pigtails and bangs, cherub cheeks, and Band-Aids on her knees danced and squealed, "Bompa, Bompa!" Kara caught Rikk's joyful and proud expression as he knelt down with his arms spread wide open to give hugs to both of them as they dashed out of Zoey's hands. They ran into Rikk's arms and howled with delight as he hugged and kissed them. Kara stopped a few feet back as soon as Jacob spotted his grandpa and watched the reunion from a distance. Kara's eyes moistened as Rikk listened to Jacob and Maddie's excited news. She hadn't noticed Zoey approaching until she broke Kara's spell with her extended hand and introduced herself, "Hi, I'm Zoey. You must be my dad's friend."

Kara looked at Zoey and saw a beautiful young woman who resembled her mother. She blinked tears back and beamed her smile at Zoey. Kara shook Zoey's hand. "Hi, I'm Kara. Yes, I'm your dad's friend. Your children are beautiful."

"Well, thank you. They do have a lot of energy," said Zoey.

Picking up both grandchildren, Rikk stood and introduced them to Kara.

"It is so nice to finally meet you, Jacob and Maddie." Kara could not resist poking Rikk, so she added, "Your grandpa has told me so much about you." Rikk guffawed, and Kara reveled in his response, fully intending to keep it their private joke, she asked, "Jacob, how old are you?"

"I'm five, and I just lost a tooth."

"I see that you lost your front tooth. Where is that tooth?"

"The tooth fairy took it and gave me a dollar."

"What do you think the tooth fairy does with the teeth?" Kara asked.

"I don't know."

"I wonder if the tooth fairy would answer that question if you would leave a note for her when you lose your next tooth."

"I only can write my name, and my address," Jacob said.

"I bet you could ask your grandpa to write the question on a piece of paper, and you could wrap it around your next tooth. It looks like you have another loose one."

"I do, it's this one," Jacob showed her how far he could wiggle the front tooth that remained next to the space the fallen out tooth had occupied.

Maddie had been watching Jacob and Kara talk when she announced, "I have all my teeth. See?" She opened her mouth wide to allow Kara to inspect them.

Kara laughed and said, "Do you think you will lose your teeth when you are as old as Jacob?"

"No, only boys lose teeth," Maddie said. "I'm three. What's your name?"

"My name is Kara. How do you know only boys lose teeth?"

"Because I haven't lost mine." Maddie shrugged as if everyone knew that.

"Oh, OK," Kara could only agree with the effervescence of a three-year-old.

Rikk kneeled down again and released Jacob and Maddie, telling them, "You've both grown so much that I can't hold both of you at the same time anymore."

"Daddy can!" Maddie boasted.

"Your daddy has more practice than your grandpa does, Maddie," explained Zoey.

"What's wrong with Eric?" asked Rikk.

"He has the flu." Zoey looked at Kara and said, "I panicked when Dad was late—being the only parent with two very excited kids at the circus. They get so excited that they dart off the minute I look away. Then my own Dad forgot about us."

"I'm sorry that I forgot. I've had a couple busier than usual days."

"Oh, yeah, you got your sailboat! I suppose you've been preoccupied," said Zoey.

Rikk stepped toward Kara. "Actually that is how I met Kara. It is a long story, and to tell it now would deprive the kids of the circus, so I will tell you later how Kara got a huge bump on her head while rescuing my boat. I've persuaded her to be my sailing mentor. She owns the boat in the slip docked next to mine."

Kara noticed Zoey caught her father's affectionate glance at Kara, but thankfully, she ignored it.

Jacob was pleading to go inside, so Rikk grabbed his hand and Maddie took his other hand, and they started walking to the entrance. Zoey fell into place and walked with Kara. They did not have much opportunity to talk as the children consumed all of the adults' attention with their excitement over the circus.

While waiting for Zoey to buy popcorn, Maddie noticed a baby in a stroller. "Grandpa, can you get me a baby?" posed Maddie.

Rikk blushed and stammered, "Maddie, that is something you need to ask your mommy."

Maddie rejoiced in his answer, reeled on her heels, ran to her mom, and squealed, "Mommy, can you get me a baby?"

Zoey was trying to maintain her composure, but her laughter put Maddie in a huff.

With practiced, unemotional authority, Rikk said, "Oh, sweetie, babies don't come from a store. Having another baby is a big decision for your mommy and daddy, but not a decision for children to make." He looked up at Kara, who was doing worse at maintaining her composure than either he or Zoey. "Why are you laughing? What's wrong with my answer?"

"I love your answer, but I really love Maddie's response."

"What do you find so funny?"

Rikk's demanding stance did not coax her to reveal her answer. Kara grinned at Rikk and replied, "Later."

"You are like Queen Scheherazade. You enjoy keeping me in suspense."

"Then that must make you King Shahryar. I'm postponing the answer until a more convenient time tonight. Unlike Queen Scheherazade, I won't keep you waiting until tomorrow evening." Rikk looked perplexed. "Little pitchers have big ears," she replied to let him know she'd explain when his grandchildren were not present.

Kara looked down at Maddie and saw frustration bringing agony to her scrunched up and near tearful little face. "Maddie," Kara offered straightforwardly, "dolls are more fun than babies anyhow." Maddie's face brightened. "When you get tired of playing with dolls, you can put them away and go play with trucks." Maddie didn't look convinced that this was a great advantage, but she was listening. "If you had a crying baby, you wouldn't get to see the elephants dance, tigers do tricks, and people fly on the trapeze in the circus.

The smile returned to Maddie's face, and she turned to Rikk and exclaimed, "Grandpa, let's go in."

Zoey and Rikk's laughter gave approval to Kara arguments. Jacob was begging them to hurry, and they all began to walk to the entrance. Just as impulsive as a three-year-old could be, Maddie turned and started to run back toward the baby, but before Zoey could catch her, she dashed past. Rikk spun around, but Maddie had already sped past him and was heading towards Kara. Kara noticed a skateboarder coming from behind her and realized that he could not see Maddie through her. She swooped down, caught Maddie's arm, and reeled her around out of the path of the skateboarder. The young man on the skateboard didn't stop. Kara had a firm grip on Maddie's arm, but lost her balance and swayed down until she was kneeling next to her. Maddie, terrified by Kara's unrelenting clutch on her arm, burst into tears and reached up for Rikk. He kneeled down next to Kara and opened his arms to Maddie. Kara was a bit dizzy and wasn't aware that she still was gripping Maddie's arm until Rikk rested his hand on hers. She let go of Maddie and simultaneously lost her balance. She fell backwards and almost caught herself, but her momentum prevailed, and she continued to fall until Rikk caught her. Kara felt embarrassed, leaning on him while he soothed Maddie. He peered into her eyes and lowered his arm around her waist, pulling her into his body. Thankfully, Zoey reached the three of them, and Maddie lunged out of Rikk's hands for her. Rikk released Maddie and pivoted around to face Kara. He brought his other hand to Kara's waist until she regained her balance.

God, I hate this. Kara loathed the dizziness that came with a minor concussion. Her face burned red as she looked down at the floor. This bump had impaired her balance longer than she had thought it would, and her sail home might be difficult even with a crew. She dispelled that thought; she was only going to see herself capable and ready to sail *Genie* home. No negative thoughts; she would focus on her intention for an easy sail home. She reminded herself that if she could not leave the day after tomorrow, which was the next possible weather window, then something better would be in store for her. Kara did not want to discuss her bump or the dizziness and give Rikk a chance to be the doctor again. She looked up at him, then beamed her smile and said, "You passed the buck!"

"What?"

She knew Rikk had no idea what she was talking about and laughed. "When Maddie asked you for a baby."

"What do you mean?"

"Telling her she needed to ask her mommy for a baby. That is passing the buck."

"I guess I did pass the buck."

"Maddie's response was classic; she is precocious," Kara said and enjoyed Rikk's chuckle.

Rikk

In that moment both of them forgot to guard the space they rigidly maintained between them. Their faces were precariously close together. Both retreated to a comfortable distance. Rikk looked up and noticed Zoey, Maddie, and Jacob had gathered around and all peered down at them. Rikk helped Kara stand up. He released her arm and saw that she avoided his eyes.

The doctor in Rikk came out, and he leaned close and quietly said, "Kara, you need to sit down." Kara frowned and did not comment. "I know this injury must be hard for you, and you're not the type to milk it for sympathy. Don't push yourself when you need to rest and recuperate."

"Yes, Dr. Harmon. I guess I should have thought of that before I saved Maddie from being run over."

Rikk sighed. "I'm sorry for acting like your doctor, and I am grateful that you pulled Maddie out of harm's way. I guess it was selfish of me to bring you to the circus rather than to your boat."

"Rikk, stop. I reacted and caught her. But even if I'd remembered this knock to my head, I would have done the same thing." Kara sighed, and in a calm voice she said, "I guess you can't withhold your doctoring instincts any more than I can withhold coaching."

"I guess not."

✦✦✦

Jacob jumped up and down encouraging them to go find their seats. Kara looked at Maddie, who was snuggling in her mom's arms. She rested her hand on Maddie's head and gently soothed her, "Maddie, I'm so sorry for scaring you. Did you see the boy on the skateboard that almost ran into you?" Maddie's big tears flowed down her cheeks, and she nodded her head. "Oh, honey, I was scared too. I was afraid that he would run right over you. He was so big; I'm not sure we would find a Band-Aid big enough for all the scrapes that you would've gotten."

Maddie picked her head up off Zoey's shoulder and offered, "I have Band-Aids on my ouchies, see?" She pointed to her knees. Rikk watched Kara and admired her comforting way with Maddie.

"I do see that. I'm so glad you don't need another. I'd much rather see you playing with Jacob than you getting covered with more Band-Aids."

The announcements that the show was about to start blared from the loud speakers, and Maddie solemnly said to Rikk, "I want to see the ponies."

"Oh, good," said Kara.

As she said this, Maddie cradled Kara's face in her hands and said, "Do you want to see the ponies too?" She inadvertently brushed Kara's bruise. Kara flinched. Rikk unconsciously braced Kara with his hand on her back and answered Zoey's quizzical look.

"Maddie, Kara has an ouchie too. Something fell on her head and gave her a big bump—see?" Rikk brushed her bangs off her forehead to reveal the bump. It really hurts Kara when anything touches it, like you just did with your hands."

"It only hurts a little, and it doesn't hurt anymore, Maddie," Kara said.

"Ouch!" Zoey grimaced. "How did that happen?"

"That is the long story that can wait until later," said Rikk. "Now let's find our seats before this show starts."

"I want to see your ouchie," Jacob took Kara's hand and looked up at her. As Kara started to kneel down, Rikk slid his arm from her back and

203

lightly squeezed her bicep, then reached down and picked Jacob up. Kara brushed the hair from her forehead, so Jacob could inspect her bump. Jacob assured Kara, "My grandpa can fix your ouchie. Can't you, Grandpa?"

"Kara's ouchie is going to get better all by itself. It is just going to take a little time. Now, let's go find our seats before they start the circus without us."

✥

The children were mesmerized from the moment the lights went down until they came back up during the intermission. The crowd filtered out of the auditorium, and Zoey took Maddie to the bathroom. When they emerged, Rikk excused himself and walked to a concession stand. Jacob and Maddie spotted him and raced towards him. Each hugged one of his legs, and they danced and squealed while they taunted each other who would get the first ice cream cone. Diplomatically, he handed them their ice cream cones at the same time. Rikk handed Zoey hers, and while he waited for the last two to be given to him, he gave Zoey a nod. Rikk's gesture was a nonverbal communication that Zoey had learned to decipher long ago—it meant that her dad wanted privacy. Zoey and the kids meandered around the stands looking at all the circus souvenirs for sale. Rikk approached Kara with an ice cream cone, handed it to her, and warned, "You really don't deserve this payoff."

"Why not?"

"Don't you think telling Jacob and Maddie, 'Your grandpa has told me so much about you,' negates your payoff?" Rikk said as he placed his hand in the small of her back. They meandered through the crowds as they licked their ice cream cones, keeping close behind Zoey and the children who had moved on to concession stands. Jacob raced over to Rikk and Kara. His raucous laughter filled him with joy, and Jacob grabbed his grandpa's hand and yanked on him to walk faster and join Zoey and Maddie. "Mommy is going to buy a pony for Maddie and a motorcycle or a human cannon ball for me. But I don't know which one I want yet. Grandpa! Hurry, hurry!"

Rikk's attention diverted back to his grandchildren, but he took hold of Kara's hand and kept her in tow as Jacob dragged him over to a concession stand. "I think the motorcycle light is really cool, Jacob," Rikk said. He hoped he'd endorsed the right toy, and thought the human cannon ball might give Jacob ideas he didn't need to foster.

⚜

After the circus was over, the children, each holding one of Kara's hands, towed her around the concession stands looking at all the toys. Rikk and Zoey walked together close behind, giving Zoey an opportunity to quiz her dad about his new friend. Rikk told Zoey most of the story. Rikk knew Zoey read his interest in Kara more accurately than she let on. He wondered how Zoey would react to him spending time with Kara, or any woman for that matter.

"Dad, it sounds like you and Kara have had similar paths being that you both lost your spouses. I'm guessing she was as head over heels in love with her husband as you were with Mom. It sounds like both of you are suffering from broken hearts, and neither of you are interested in relationships at this time. But sometimes, Dad, the universe has different plans for us and presents us with what we need and want, and we don't even know it. When you think about it, the universe had a different plan for Mom and for Kara's husband too. So, if Kara and you are meant to be great supportive friends for a short time, or if it is going to develop into a deeper friendship, you will find out with time." Very much like Rikk had often done with her as a child, Zoey faced her Dad, placed her hands on his cheeks and stood on her tip toes, so her nose and his were as close as possible. She looked directly into his eyes and said, "And, Dad, if the universe wants Kara to be more than just your friend, I hope you will permit your brain to yield to your heart. I hope you'll be open to whatever comes." With that, she dashed up to Kara and the kids.

Rikk stood motionless. He was astounded by Zoey's perceptiveness and contemplated her words. When he noticed Kara walking back towards him, he dragged his hands through his hair as she approached, but remained speechless.

"You look confounded," Kara said. Rikk just shook his head and shrugged. "You look like I sometimes feel when Isabella's words sting me like a slap on the face. Usually she has told me something that I should've known or did know but had been avoiding its truth." He still didn't speak but nodded his head in agreement. "I see how much Zoey loves you and loves to share her children with you. You have an amazing daughter and grandchildren. You must be proud."

Rikk smiled at Kara and put his hand on her back; they turned to join Zoey and the children, and as they walked toward them, Rikk collected his thoughts enough to say, "I'm proud of them. Zoey reminded me of her mother, just now. I'm bewildered by how well Zoey knows me. I had no idea she was so intuitive."

It was almost six thirty. Maddie was getting cranky, and Jacob was over-stimulated.

"I think it's time we go home," Zoey said, and the children complained. They didn't want to leave their grandpa.

"How about I take you out to dinner?" Rikk said.

"No thanks. I already have dinner made in the Crockpot. Besides, I'm not sure how much longer Maddie's good nature will last before today's excitement takes its toll." As they said goodbye, Zoey reached out and rested her hand on Kara's arm, "Kara, it's been so much fun to meet you. I really hope that I have a chance to see you again in a more sedate setting, so you can tell me all about yourself and about sailing. Dad filled me in a little about you and how you got that bump on your head. I would love for Eric to meet you."

"Zoey, Kara is on her way back to Bayfield," Rikk said.

"Great, then you are practically in the neighborhood. That is only a little over an hour drive from here." She gloated as she said, "Hey, Dad, maybe you should consider hiring Kara to give you sailing lessons."

"There's an idea!" Rikk said, and immediately regretted his sarcasm.

Kara smiled at the two of them. "Wow, there are a lot of ideas flying around to consider. I'm sure the right ones will manifest by themselves. Zoey, I've thoroughly enjoyed meeting you and Jacob and Maddie. I'm glad that Rikk forgot his date with you. If he had remembered, I would've missed spending the afternoon with you."

"I'm glad too, and I hope I don't get struck by lightning for saying this, but I'm glad Eric was sick so we had a ticket for you. Love you, Dad. Call me sometime; we all are dying to see your boat."

The sky was filled with black thunderclouds when they walked out of the auditorium. Rikk and Kara dashed to his car as the rain began to plunk down in heavy droplets. Once inside the car, Rikk said, "Thank you for coming with me. I really appreciate how you snatched Maddie out of the path of the skateboarder—you've got quick reflexes. You know it takes a while for a concussion to heal and—"

"You're welcome. Rikk, I know it's going to take a while for me to get back to full speed, I just forgot. That's why I have a crew helping me sail *Genie* to Bayfield."

A change in the subject was needed. Rikk didn't want to spoil the mood, or talk about Kara's departure. "I'm glad Jacob and Maddie included you in their trusted friend circle."

"Me too. I spent the day completely different from how I expected. It was the most fun-filled time I've had in quite awhile." She yawned, and added through another yawn, "I'm so tired when I lie down, I won't get up until morning."

Chapter 24

Rikk

Rikk just smiled as his mind reverted to their meeting years ago. He wanted to ask Kara why she hadn't mentioned it before this morning, but it could wait. She was so tired, and actually, he was too. Rikk sighed and said, "One of these days I'm going to have to buy some things for my boat."

"Provisions," Kara said.

"Provisions. Does that include what I need for the kitchen?" he questioned.

"You mean galley."

"Yes, for the galley. If it rains all day tomorrow, maybe you could help me provision my boat?"

"OK, I don't have anything to do tomorrow except wait. I already have *Genie* ready to sail on Monday, but I need a few more provisions for my crew."

The sound of thunder rolled in from over the hillside when they pulled into the parking lot. They hurried out of the car, and the droplets turned into a sheeting rain. They ran to the portico roof off the lobby to get out of the torrential downpour. Kara was laughing as she looked at Rikk.

"What's so funny?" Rikk said.

"It is just these last days have been filled with accidents, calamities, and crazy events; now we are stranded under the portico, drenched and waiting for the rain to subside. I just can't figure out what we are putting out to the universe that is causing us to attract so many mishaps and awkward situations."

Rikk remembered what Zoey said before she dashed off to join her kids. What was it about the universe that Zoey and Kara seemed to believe? In what felt like a weak moment, Rikk wondered if the universe lined up all these events to keep Kara and him together. But for how long? And what would the nature of their relationship be? He didn't know, but he did know he couldn't reveal Zoey's thoughts to Kara.

"You look like you did earlier when Zoey was talking to you at the circus," Kara said.

"You have no idea how similar what you just said is to something Zoey told me at the circus."

"Really?"

"You both mentioned the universe. It is uncanny how you both talked about it like it was some divine force."

"Have you ever said, 'Small world?'"

"Sure."

"Simply put, it is an expanded version of that saying."

"What do you mean?"

"Well, after many years, two acquaintances run into each other in an unlikely location. Some people would say, 'Small world,' but others think everything happens for a reason."

"Maybe it's just chance?"

"Do you feel your meeting Lauren was just chance?"

"No."

"Divine intervention?"

"Maybe."

"Well, maybe the term 'the universe' is how some people phrase what others might call 'Divine intervention.' As for me, people of all religions, even those lacking religion, are all connected to each other, and their god or divinity is universal. My belief is that religions are all right—as in correct—for those they support spiritually, but they are all wrong when they believe their religion is the only right one."

Rikk stared out at the boats and wondered what he believed. He wondered if losing Lauren had made him so cynical that he didn't believe any of it. He looked back at Kara and saw curiosity, and he shook his head. He didn't know anything anymore.

"What do you think? What is the cause of the events that have kept me here?" she asked.

"I don't know what I think. When I asked you how you coped and stayed positive, you told me all about intending to get what you want by manifesting it with your thoughts. Zoey just warned me to not resist the power of the universe because it provides the right things to happen. Do you think the universe really gives you things by what you are thinking?"

"I believe in metaphysical phenomena, but I do not expect you or anyone else to believe as I do."

Kara's mischievous grin and laughing eyes warned Rikk that he should prepare for something unexpected. "What are you thinking, Captain McKee?"

"I wonder if there is any way to prove you get what you think about that will satisfy your scientific brain. How about a blind test, Dr. Harmon?"

"A blind test?" Rikk was doubtful but interested—or at least entertained.

"First you have to realize that my illustration is light hearted, and second, I can already prove it by something that happened this afternoon."

"You can prove it?" said Rikk.

"I can, but you have to listen with a sense of wonder and remember that the first thing I said was to take this lightly."

"OK, prove it to me."

"I almost bought a pint of ice cream at the Bay Side Market on Thursday morning, but I would've had to eat it all in one shot because I don't run *Genie*'s freezer. I decided that I could wait until I got to Bayfield because a whole pint would be more than I really wanted to eat in one sitting. Then when I was thinking of payoffs for keeping your forgetful-grandpa status a secret, I thought of popcorn or an ice cream cone. You didn't ask my preference and bought ice cream cones. So you see, I did get what I wanted. How's that for being scientific?" she said.

"I'm glad you don't expect me to take any of this seriously." Amused at Kara's loose application of science to rationalize her metaphysical beliefs, Rikk laughed at her example.

"Why not?" Kara smiled and said, "Just try this for me. Think of someone you haven't seen for awhile. This is really a silly thing, but it is amazing how often it works. They'll turn up in your life in some fashion. They walk around the corner, they call you up, some mutual friend tells you they just ran into them, or someone asks you about them. So did you think of someone?"

"Dutch."

"That is cheating; we both will see Dutch soon. You need to think of someone else that you haven't seen or thought about for a long time."

Kara and Rikk were standing at the edge of the roof, leaning against the portico post just inches from the transparent cascade of rain pouring off the eaves. Rikk stood quietly and considered her argument. He remembered someone from years ago, who had entered and exited his life when he was in med school. Rikk sighed.

Kara reached up and brushed away a raindrop trickling down his cheek. Kara froze, and Rikk knew it was because she had entered his personal space. Rikk waited to see if she'd back away, but something much stronger than her own will seemed to hold her there. He couldn't tell if she was about to run or if a desire burning inside her kept her there, but he wanted to cure the ache that she provoked inside him. Although Kara's words this afternoon said to stay platonic, her physical presence tonight urged the opposite. He resisted kissing her and tried to back off. But he touched her face. Her eyes closed when he leaned towards her, and then opened wide. He was not sure if they revealed longing or fear, but it would be hard to pull back now. He brushed his thumb over her lips. He watched her and waited for her to flee his presence—but she stayed. Her breaths quickened, and her lips relaxed and invited him. Her eyes shut as her body trembled. Rikk drew her into him and softly covered her yielding mouth with his. His head quieted, and his heart pulsed stronger as he kissed her deeper. The need this kiss stirred in him had lain dormant for so long he trembled at the power of its awakening. Kara reached up with her hand and brushed his cheek, caressing down his neck. He felt her lips part when she pulled him closer.

Desire overtook Rikk and suspended his awareness of every sensation except that of Kara. He could feel Kara's craving burn as deep as his. They tasted each other's kisses, caressed each other, and excited each other's needs that had been neglected and ignored for so long.

Rikk pulled away and watched Kara's languid eyes open. In a husky whisper he said, "Should I stop, Kara?"

She whispered, "No." Her eyes held his, full of expectation.

Rikk pulled Kara's body into his and watched her lids fall over her green eyes and her head drop back. His eyes shut as Kara's slender thighs brushed against his legs and her belly fell against him. He had no doubt she felt his arousal. Their kisses deepened, enticing each other, both eager to give as well as receive pleasure.

Rikk contemplated where they should go when their world was startled with the sound of someone approaching. Kara broke away and looked toward the familiar voice in raucous song. Dutch staggered past the lobby. When Dutch first saw them, he greeted them boisterously. "Good after—" He belched and squinted toward the sky. "Good evening to you." He stumbled on the sidewalk, catching himself before either Rikk or Kara could reach him. Then Dutch recognized them, and his good mood soured instantly. Kara flushed and diverted her eyes from him.

"God damn, Siren!" Dutch yelled as he glared at Kara. "You just luring the Doc away." Then he turned to Rikk and sternly warned him, "She's worse than the other one, Doc. The other one ain't going to hold your interest like Kara will. Both are Sirens, but Kara took you away."

As they watched Dutch venture toward the docks, Kara looked up at Rikk as her strained voice said, "Rikk, I don't know what I did last night to make Dutch so angry at me. I'm not—"

"Dutch is drunk, Kara. He isn't making any sense."

"No, this is more than just being drunk tonight. This morning he said the same thing to me, and that is why I walked to the beach." They saw Dutch stumble as he was walking down the dock. "Rikk, we have to help him." She darted out into the rain and ran toward the docks with Rikk passing her after a few strides.

Dutch swaggered as he was singing a song that neither Rikk nor Kara had ever heard before. "Charlie, where you been? Charlie, where you going? Charlie, isn't it time to be with me, Charlie, Charlie, won't you come b—" A giant belch cut the phrase off and sent his body stumbling dangerously close to the edge of the dock. Then he slipped on the slick dock planks. Rikk caught up to him just in time to grasp his arm, tug him back to the middle of the dock, and help him recover his footing. Rikk pulled Dutch's arm over his shoulder and steadied him as they walked to *Miss Sea*. Kara snuck in front of them and jumped aboard to open the hatch; then she offered Dutch her hand to help him onboard. At first, he gave her his hand, but before she clasped onto it, he jerked it back and went into a tirade. "No Siren's going to be on my *Miss Sea*. Get the hell off her! You no good Siren! You just get the hell off her."

Rikk saw how Kara appeared immobilized from the vengeance in Dutch's voice as he barked those vile words. He hated hearing her pleading tone when she said, "Dutch?"

"It's all right, Kara. I can help him," Rikk said.

The time that it took Kara to clamber off *Miss Sea* crept in slow motion. All the while, Dutch grumbled and complained about Sirens and someone named Charlie. Rikk managed to get Dutch onboard *Miss Sea* safely. He glanced at Kara standing in the rain, watching him as he struggled to help Dutch down into *Miss Sea*'s cabin. Lightning arced in the distant sky and seemed to mimic Dutch's angry state.

<hr>

Rikk re-emerged from *Miss Sea*, stepped onto the dock, and faced Kara. He began to wrap his arms around her.

Tension creased Kara's forehead, and then she pulled her arms up in resistance and stammered, "I can't figure out Dutch and—and what I did to him. What's going on?"

"What do you mean, 'What's going on?'" Rick demanded, scowling now down at her and feeling the impenetrable barrier that Kara's arms presented.

"Why are all these delays and disasters happening?"

Rikk didn't try to hide his anger, "Am I one of those disasters, Kara? Was that kiss a disaster?"

"God, no. That kiss was—" Kara gasped, and she was speechless. She cleared her throat, but her voice still cracked as she finally said, "That kiss breaks the terms of our friendship." He glowered at her, but before he could say anything, she held her hand up letting him know she needed to finish what she was saying. "I've never been able to do one-night stands. I can't give myself without giving my heart. I can't expect you to make a commitment after one red-hot moment, and I would never ask you to, either. I don't trust myself at this moment to know what my heart is telling me. We both are too vulnerable right now to go any further. Rikk, I know that this may not make sense to you, but I don't want to hurt you either."

The anger that flashed through Rikk and lingered in his glinting eyes didn't help his plight. "What makes you think you know what my heart feels or what commitment I'm prepared to make?"

Kara's voice quaked as she said, "I don't know my heart. You're so angry. That's a disaster."

Silence followed, and Rikk turned away and sighed. He could not influence Kara tonight to love him as he wanted to love her. He was frustrated, both emotionally and mentally, and now the most tormenting was his physical frustration. Lightning and thunder began to roll down again upon Duluth.

"Rikk, I'm so sorry. I really thought I was OK until Dutch showed up. I know Dutch is wrong about me luring you away from him, but maybe the universe keeps putting obstacles in my way to prevent me from making mistakes."

"Am I a mistake, Kara?"

"I don't know, Rikk. Maybe I'm the mistake."

"Maybe you are putting too much stock in Dutch's crazy behavior. He's drunk."

Kara tried to explain, "Dutch wasn't drunk this morning. Even though his words shouldn't matter, they do. A huge part of me wishes that what Dutch said didn't matter."

A lightning bolt struck very close, illuminating the bewilderment in Kara's eyes. Rikk's patience was fried. He could not stand seeing her this way, but he knew the incredible moment they kissed was gone. In frustration Rikk said, "Then choose to ignore them."

"Damn it, Rikk, are you so angry that you won't give me more time?"

Rikk broke the prolonged silence with a heavy sigh. "Do we still have a date for provisioning my boat tomorrow?"

"Yes, of course."

He came closer and placed his hands on her shoulders. He leaned over her and kissed her forehead, careful to avoid her bruise and bump. "Let me help you onto your boat."

"You don't have to; I will be fine."

He snorted a sigh and forced a smile, "Then get out of this cold rain."

"This cold rain is just what I need right now. Good night."

"Good night." Rikk slowly walked back to his car, letting the cold, pounding rain wash his desires and frustration away.

✦⊙❀⊙✦

The last few days for both had been a jumble of conflicting emotions and discovery. Rikk was exhausted and knew he needed to be alone to reassess his life. Kara had let her defenses down, and it was clear she wanted him, maybe even more than he wanted her. Then why did she let Dutch dictate her actions? Rikk had plenty of experience identifying when people were concealing something. He just wished he didn't care what she was hiding, or why.

Rikk swallowed hard as he recognized he had just caught himself pointing his finger at Kara for concealing something. Rikk remembered what Zoey told her children, and in that moment he realized that like his grandchildren, he had three fingers pointing back at himself. Rikk started his car and drove through the storm back to his house.

Chapter 25

Kara

Kara changed into her long-sleeved t-shirt and cotton knit pajama pants, then collapsed on the settee. Rain poured on and off all night. Every time she thought of turning on the cabin lights, an arc of lightning lit up the cabin with pure white flashes that blinded her and then disappeared as violently as they appeared. She was left in cold darkness with the incessant rain pounding on the hull. *Genie*'s cabin felt like Mother Nature was mirroring Kara's last three days in the marina—as if the storm was a gift given to teach her whatever it was she needed to learn. The brilliant light induced the kindred spirit she felt with Barb and Joe, Zoey, and the children and above all the feelings she had for Rikk. Following the lightning bolts, the growling, roaring thunder rolled over Kara and transported her into the depths of the falling boom's impact, the freezing isolation from Dutch's sudden alliance shift, the ambiguity of returning to Bayfield, and the uncertainty of Rikk's role in her life. The deepest black hole Kara faced was her fear of Rikk's reaction to her revealing the role he had previously played in her life.

The thunder rumbled through Kara, numbing every cell in her body and placating her weary spirit. She sat still and concentrated on the thunderstorm, and tried to push the memories of the past forty-eight hours out of her mind. Being present—not dwelling on the past nor looking to the future—came so easy to her a couple of years ago. She struggled to regain the present and wondered what had happened to transport her back to the person she had been years earlier, before she and Connor left their nine-to-five jobs and worry-burdened lives. The storm was perfect for her at this moment; every time her thoughts derailed to all the questions surrounding Bayfield, being detained in Duluth, and especially Rikk, another lightning bolt flashed and thunder rumbled. It brought her back to the present, to experience the power and energy of the storm. She shut her eyes and tried to meditate, but the fury raging outside was so intense that she opened them to watch Mother Nature's spectacular show through the portholes.

The rain pounding on *Genie's* deck at last passed out onto the lake, and the lightning and thunder gradually subsided. Kara shut her eyes again and this time succeeded in meditating, quieting her mind and spirit, and opening herself up to her higher consciousness. Her body tingled as she relaxed and allowed her mind to be transported to where it needed to go. The flashing of a latent lightning bolt ended Kara's meditation. Feeling calmer and more relaxed, she sat and stared into the pitch-black cabin. She felt Rikk's kiss and her eager response. Her body quivered, and she recollected the first time they met so many years ago under very different circumstances. Back then, she was attracted to him but never imagined she would ever have a relationship with him. In this moment, Kara realized that she had to explain the reason she hid their previous encounter from Rikk, and more important, she must reveal these things she continued to guard.

❧◈❧

The next thunderstorm rolled in with flashes of lightning and thunder in the distance. Kara only had Rikk's office number. She couldn't remember seeing a phone book in the lobby, but if the lobby computer was working she could look up his home number online. At least she could talk to him. She headed to the companionway. Just then, the lightning struck very close with blinding light coupled with a deafening crack that sputtered on and on. Kara took it as an omen to stay put and give Rikk some space. He had asked her to help provision his boat, so she knew she would see him in the morning.

Kara lay back down on the settee and wondered if Rikk was sleeping, or if he lay awake thinking of the lists. *That's right, I need to make my own lists.* She got up and spent the next few minutes doing exactly what she had Rikk do the night before. When she was done, she burned her list in the cockpit grill. The backdrop of her purging ritual was a black sky filled with lace-edged clouds that were illuminated by the moon. The storm had passed, and the sky was clearing. *Maybe Mother Nature is telling me something.*

217

Kara went back inside the cabin. She felt so disoriented with Rikk in her life, but it felt good to feel so alive again. Be that what it may, she realized she needed to follow her own advice and allow the obstacles in the way of her return home to actually provide her the correct path. She was ready to take a risk, be it a broken heart or a lasting relationship; it was better than the isolated existence she had chosen lately.

It was almost four a.m. She pulled the blanket over her head and rested her fingertips on her eyelids in an effort to relax them. Kara felt the relaxation drifting over her body and floated off to sleep.

Rikk drove into his garage, shut off the car, and sat considering the events that led up to this moment. How did something as simple as getting a boat complicate his life so much? Was he attracted to Kara, or was he only interested in a casual sexual encounter or a short-term, casual sexual relationship? She was getting to him. He shuddered. Kara was right, the moment of passion is not the time that a relationship commitment could be given or should be received. Why, then, did her words crush him? Rikk feared that he was already in over his head with Kara, and the fact that she didn't know the hold she had on him was infuriating. He held his tongue and stifled his response to control his anger. She misunderstood him. As he calmed himself, he considered that she might be right; his interest was in sex and not the repercussions of the next morning or either of their futures. But, if this was just lust, why did it take so much effort to restrain himself from barking that he didn't do casual sex either?

As Rikk reviewed their quarrel, he realized that Kara introduced the idea of casual sex to him. He had opened up to her that morning and admitted he wanted a relationship. He hadn't made one gesture to imply that he was interested in a one-night stand. If that is what she worried about, then maybe he needed to guard his own heart. She wasn't concerned about misleading and hurting him. She was only protecting herself. She was making her own choices and claiming they were for him. If he was willing to involve himself in a relationship that could end up painfully, that was his decision; it was not her responsibility to protect him. Yet there was a chance she may actually be protecting him, and that chance made her all the more attractive to him.

Rikk felt torn between betrayal to Lauren's memory and the torrent of feelings Kara's company stirred in him. This newfound euphoria was tainted with guilt. However, it felt good because along with the guilt he had laughed, smiled, played, and been more stimulated in the last two days than he had been in the last year and a half. He felt alive. In fact, the last few hours he had felt more alive than he believed possible, living instead of existing in a haze of self-pity and doubt.

Finally, Rikk got out of the car and walked into the house. He went to his bedroom, pulled off his drenched clothes, and slipped on a sweatshirt and flannel pants. He knew trying to fall asleep right now would be futile, so he went to the living room and switched on the fire and sat in the recliner. With the constant flame from the fireplace and the sporadic flashes of the lightning, he sat and thought about Lauren and wondered what she would want him to do. Was he falling for Kara? Maybe. Was Kara detained here to help him move ahead and start living again? Maybe. But maybe he was in Kara's life to help her move on and live too. Rikk drove himself mad thinking about the possibility of a relationship. All this was giving him a headache.

Rikk felt Kara was more affected than she knew or wanted to admit; she could not contain her passion completely, and the proof was in the passionate kiss they just shared. He wanted to ask her all these questions and considered driving back to the marina and demanding to talk to her. Instead, he went to the bathroom medicine cabinet, shook two aspirin out, and filled a glass with water. As much as he wanted resolution tonight, he did not want to push her away by insisting that she conform to his urgency. He would see her tomorrow since they had made a date to provision his boat. Rikk stared at his tired body in the mirror and winced at the exhausted face that stared back at him. Sleep should come easy. He walked back to the fireplace intending to shut it off and go to bed. There on the mantle sat *Be in Choice*. He picked it up and began to re-read the passages that Lauren had noted. He oscillated between reading passages and ruminating about what Lauren had written. Around four in the morning, he got up and shuffled into the bedroom. He collapsed onto the bed and fell asleep.

A reoccurring dream awoke Rikk. He used to have the dream before he met Lauren. It flashed a memory of a young woman who had walked into and out of his life when he was a graduate student. She was filled with so much energy and life that he would've found her attractive even if she was plain. However, she had natural good looks—was graceful and unpretentious. Her independent spirit captivated him. The desire that burned in his dream of her always made him regret not looking her up. She was the person that came to him when Kara asked him to think of someone that he had not thought about or seen in quite awhile. How many years had passed since he'd last had that recurring dream of her? Rikk laughed and wondered if it counted when the person appeared in a dream. He closed his eyes in anticipation of falling asleep and back into that dream. The sleep state came quickly. The dream did not return.

Dutch

Dutch passed out on the settee before the Doc even left the cabin. At daybreak Dutch awoke thrashing and sweating from nightmare. He kept chasing the towns folk, but they always managed to flee before he could reclaim what they had stolen. That same old dream had plagued Dutch for almost fifty years, yet the frequency and intensity had subsided over time. This time it ended the same as all the times before, except the Doc was doing the chasing, and Dutch had what belonged to him.

Dutch sat up and shuddered. He got it! He knew why this dream had re-occurred to him and why his role was reversed in it. *Damn, I'm an old fool!* Dutch shook his head and muttered aloud, "A damn stupid old fool." He got up and crept off *Miss Sea* and up the dock. It was five thirty, and the marina was dead quiet other than the sound of his footsteps squishing on the saturated dock planks. He went into the men's room and came face to face with his reflection. He stood looking at himself, sickened by the sight of a lonely old man who had become an expert at putting on a happy bachelor front. He could not believe what he had just done to Rikk and Kara, and he sure as hell didn't want either of them to look in a mirror when they were his age and see a lonely old soul looking back at them. His anger was misplaced. He directed it at Kara, but he knew that he had been an idiot. What he walked away from years ago always came down to his own bad choice when he looked at it honestly. He understood the meaning of the nightmare, and he understood why it happened again this morning. Dutch knew he didn't deserve Kara's friendship—or the Doc's for that matter—but he had to talk to her one more time. He had to tell her that he was wrong. He had to convince her that she was perfect for the Doc and the Doc was perfect for her.

The lobby door thudded shut behind Dutch. He walked down the dock, past *Miss Sea,* to *Genie's Bottle.* He listened while wondering if he should knock and wake Kara or let her sleep a while longer. He knocked softly. Dutch was relieved that she didn't reply; he'd have time to think about what he needed to say. He'd also have time to think about all that he needed to keep to himself.

Dutch went back to *Miss Sea's* cabin and made a pot of coffee. He poured a cup into an insulated mug and went up into the cockpit despite the drizzle that ushered in the day. It matched his mood, and the only way he was going to lift that was by making right what he had wronged. He was determined to sit there, despite the weather, and wait for Kara to wake up.

Chapter 26

Rikk

Sunday morning Rikk woke up at eight thirty to an incessant drizzle, but at least the thunderstorm had passed. He lay in bed wondering if Kara was already awake and if she was waiting for him to get there, or if she was having second thoughts again. On one hand, he understood her need to take it slow, but no amount of cold rain or sleep would relieve the ache in his body—or in his heart.

What caused Dutch's unexplainable switch? When Dutch finally succeeded at getting Kara to warm up to Rikk, why did he turn on her? *Hell, I'm the one who's been the antagonistic ass.* If Rikk learned anything last night, he learned that he had a choice in the friendship between all three of them, and no matter what happened between Kara and himself, he would make sure Dutch and Kara resolved their problem—they would remain friends.

⚓

As Rikk walked down the docks, he spotted Dutch poking his head out of *Miss Sea*'s cabin. As Dutch stepped into *Miss Sea*'s cockpit with a full cup of coffee, Dutch said, "Morning, Doc. Got something to say to you. I've been acting like a damn fool. I guess sleeping off this drunken binge brought me to my senses."

Rikk shook his head and dug his hands in his jean pockets. "What?"

"You heard me. I'm a damn fool, and I ain't proud of it."

"Dutch, what about Kara? She has no idea what she did to offend you, and neither do I. What made you attack Kara?"

"I ain't been seeing straight. I've been sitting out here waiting for her to wake up for a couple of hours already. I got to tell her what a damn fool I've been, plus a couple other things too."

"Is she up yet?"

"I haven't heard a peep outta her, no movement on her boat either."

"I'll go get her. You might as well get out of this drizzle. Do you have any more coffee made?"

"I'll make a fresh pot," Dutch said and slipped down into *Miss Sea's* cabin.

⚓︎

Rikk knocked on *Genie's* hull. Not hearing a reply, he boarded then knocked on the hatch. He opened it to see Kara lying on the settee with the blanket over her head. Rikk went into the cabin and was surprised she still hadn't stirred. He smiled wryly at her as he tugged the blanket off her head, and she squinted at him. "What time is it?" she asked. "Is it still morning?"

"Nine thirty. I thought you would be up already."

Kara sat up and stretched her arms overhead. "I couldn't get to sleep last night."

"I couldn't sleep either. I just kept running through everything that led us to this point."

"Rikk, I'm so sorry about last night. I almost went to the lobby to look up your number, but the lightning struck too close. I took it as a sign to stay put, that you needed your space."

"Oh, yeah? I almost drove back to talk to you too."

"I have so much I want to explain, and I don't know where to begin. I guess it took me a night of soul searching to get clarity—well, you're going to laugh. I made lists just like I had you do. When I found out what I was most miserable about, I figured out how wrong I've been and what I want."

"What are you most miserable about?"

"I was so afraid you might not come back today. I was afraid I wouldn't get a chance to tell you that even though I have uncertainties about myself, and you, these last few days I've been happier than I thought possible. I want—" Kara looked up and squeezed her eyes shut.

"What do you want?"

"If I could do it all over again, I would get hit on the head just so I could spend these days with you. All of it, except I would not have run away last night."

Rikk shook his head, "Kara, I didn't feel this way when I left last night, but you were right to stop us. It gave both of us time to consider what we were doing, our motives, and commitment."

Kara tossed the blankets aside and stood up. She folded her arms over her chest and said, "It wasn't fair of me to ask you to make any commitment last night any more than it would be for me to ask you for one right now. I can only take one day at a time and make the most of it. Why would I expect or ask more of you?"

Rikk wasn't expecting such quick agreement. "I spent the night deliberating my life with Lauren and how you've snuck in. Even though I still miss Lauren, I feel alive—completely disoriented, but definitely alive."

"Do you mean that?

"Yeah!"

"Rikk and Lauren alive?" Kara whispered as she looked deeply into his eyes. "That was the subject of your coaching from yesterday. Are you just saying that?"

"I wasn't thinking about my coaching session when I said that. Kara, I meant what I said. I feel Lauren with me, yet I feel alive and free for the first time since she passed away."

"Wow!"

"Is that all you've got to say, Coach?" Rikk grinned, then said, "I guess we both are ready."

"It feels a little odd to reach the same conclusion so quickly. What do we do now?"

"Kara, I don't want to push you. Hell, I don't want to push me either. Let's just go wherever we are taken."

"Live in the moment? What a great idea!" Kara said in a satirical tone, and then she looked at her reflection in a porthole. "I need a shower, bad."

"I like how you look when you need a shower."

Kara's apologetic grin covered her face. "I wish I already showered. I'll only take a few minutes, and you are welcome to wait for me here."

"Dutch is waiting to talk to you."

"Dutch wants to talk to me?"

"He has been up all morning, sitting in *Miss Sea*'s cockpit, waiting for you to get up so he can apologize to you."

"Really? He wants to apologize?"

"Yes, and he said he has some other things to say."

"Did he tell you what I did that hurt him?"

"No, but he's feeling pretty bad about his actions. He just brewed a pot of coffee and is waiting for us."

"OK. Can I take a minute to make myself somewhat presentable?"

"You look very presentable, Kara."

"Well, there's an opinion not shared by anyone else on this boat."

"If Dutch wasn't waiting for us, you'd have to fight me off right now."

"Hmm." Kara waved her eyebrows and grinned, "So, he's been waiting all morning? I suppose it'd be rude to keep him waiting any longer."

Rikk grabbed her around her waist, pulling her to him and whispered in her ear, "You devil."

Their lingering kiss grew greedy until Kara broke free, covering her mouth she stammered, "Teeth—brush—toothbrush. I need to brush my teeth." Gaining her composure, she added, "If we don't stop, *you'll* be the devil that kept Dutch waiting."

Rikk released her and sighed, "I'll wait for you with Dutch. I need some coffee." He turned for the companionway. As Rikk joined Dutch in *Miss Sea*'s cabin, he hoped Kara had any more intention of provisioning his boat than he did.

Kara brushed and flossed her teeth, washed her face, and brushed her hair. She threw on her jacket and moments later knocked on *Miss Sea*'s hull and waited until Dutch hollered for her to come aboard. An empty coffee cup sat on the table partially hiding Dutch's face. With his hands supporting his head and his elbows resting on the table, Dutch stared down into his insulated mug. Rikk filled the cup for Kara while she studied Dutch's comatose state.

Kara slipped into the bench across from Dutch and took a sip of her coffee. She finally broke the silence, "Hey, Dutch. How are you feeling this morning?"

"I got a damn headache, but I guess I deserve it," he mumbled and lifted his face to look at Kara. His eyes were watering, and his ashen face was filled with dread.

"Do you need an aspirin?"

"Geez, Kara, there you go again. Worrying about me instead of listening to what I got to say." Dutch paused and shook his head. "Didn't mean to yell, just got to—"

Rikk exchanged glances with Kara then calmly said, "Dutch, you have something to tell Kara?"

Dutch inhaled loudly. "I'm a big damn fool, and you ain't got no reason to like me, but I got something you gotta hear—you both gotta hear." His eyes fell on Rikk as he went on, "Doc, that doctor woman ain't right for you. Hell, I don't know if she's right for nobody."

Rikk didn't try to contain his laughter despite how serious Dutch was. "I have to agree with you, Dutch. I think most men she has tangled with would agree that she's a Siren. But why did you call Kara a Siren?"

"Because I was thinking only of me. I saw that high falutin' woman flash her smile at you, and I just didn't want you following her round like a bull sea lion chasing a cow in heat."

Dutch laughed along with Rikk and Kara, and the tension drained from his face. Rikk said, "But, Dutch, why did you call Kara a Siren?"

Agitated, Dutch growled, "Because I got jealous. I couldn't see no difference between Kara and that woman. Thought they'd keep you all tied up with them and you wouldn't ever use your boat."

Rikk didn't buy his explanation, at least not totally. Dutch certainly wasn't blind to how Kara resisted him. Something else had happened to make Dutch categorize her with Dr. Heidi Norris, but what?

Kara set her coffee down and shook her head, then said, "Dutch, I can hardly believe that you thought I would keep Rikk all to myself. I was doing my best to avoid him!"

"I ain't gonna explain no more. Guess that's why I ain't never married."

"That still doesn't make sense, Dutch. I still don't know why you worked so hard to get us together and then spun on a dime to get us apart when Dr. Norris showed up," Kara said.

Rikk saw the anger flare in Dutch's face and touched Kara's arm, warning her to quit pressing Dutch for more.

"I said all I'm going to say about this. I said I was sorry. Hell, you two were made for each other, even this damn fool could see it right off. Now there ain't nothing more to be said." Dutch got up and reached for the pot of coffee. "You want a refill?"

Kara handed her barely touched cup to Dutch. As he took it she smiled at him and said, "Truce?"

His eyes watered as he choked out, "Truce."

Kara stood and hugged him as Rikk watched and sipped his coffee. Then Dutch, in his jovial way, winked at Rikk. "Doc, how late was it when you left *Genie* Friday night?"

"Dutch!" She held onto his name and her eyebrows shot up. "You're entering dangerous territory."

"I stayed on *Genie's Bottle* much longer than I promised Kara I would," Rikk said.

"You sure came early yesterday morning," Dutch said.

"I woke up with more questions than answers," Rikk said and glanced at Kara.

Dutch quizzed them about their day and didn't allow either of them to skip over a detail. Rikk was wondering if he would ever have Kara all to himself. He looked at Kara a couple of times and was certain that she too struggled to be courteous, spending enough time with Dutch before they found seclusion. At last, Rikk asked Dutch, "Is it true that the fish really bite in this weather?" He hoped that Dutch would understand the hint.

Dutch winked at Rikk and slammed his coffee mug down on the table. "What time is it, Doc? I can't sit 'round here all day keeping you two company." He looked at his watch and added, "Ten thirty? I ain't caught no fish yet, and the morning is wasting away."

⁂

After they helped cast *Miss Sea* off the dock, Kara reminded Rikk she needed a shower. As Kara gathered her shower tote and clean clothes she said, "Rikk, if you really want to work on provisioning your boat but have no clue where to start, you could rummage through my galley and see what is in there that you could use. I may part with some of my cooking utensils."

"You don't have any problem with me digging through your stuff?" he asked.

Kara smirked at Rikk's question and started up the companionway. "I don't have anything hidden in my galley."

⁂

Rikk looked around the galley, but decided to wait for Kara. He perused the books on the shelf behind the dinette and pulled one off the shelf. It was *Be in Choice*. He opened it up, checking to see if anything was written in her copy. It looked brand new, as if it hadn't had a single page turned in it before this moment. He read the author's enigmatic dedication, again.

When Kara returned from the shower, Rikk looked up from the book and smiled appreciatively at her walking down the companionway. He had to make a conscious effort to contain his hunger for her. "Do you feel better?"

"Much."

Kara's shy smile captivated him, and made Rikk feel lecherous. The last thing he wanted to do was—well, was anything but touch her soft skin, breathe in her fragrant hair, and most of all taste her. He diverted his eyes back to the book and was about to ask if she had read it when a knock on *Genie*'s hull startled them.

It was Pete and Sophie coming to sign Pete on as crew to help Kara sail *Genie* back to Bayfield tomorrow. Rikk and Kara exchanged looks of resignation. Kara covered her mouth in attempt to conceal her laughter then answered that she would be out in a minute. Rikk listened as Kara worked out the details with Pete and commiserated with Sophie that she couldn't get out of work to join the crew. Now her crew was found. Rikk knew she could not postpone, no matter how much he wanted her to. The weather forecast called for the low to clear out today, presenting a five-day weather window to cross the lake. Kara arranged to leave at six the next morning. He put the book back onto the bookshelf.

By car, Bayfield was only a little over an hour away, but he wanted to see Kara more often than a distant relationship would provide. Rikk was dismal. Rikk didn't try to hide his disappointment when she came down into *Genie*'s cabin. "I don't want you to go. I'm just getting to—" He stopped in mid-sentence, and realized what he wanted wasn't what Kara needed to hear. "I know you have to go, and Bayfield isn't that far away. I'm just frustrated with all the interruptions we've had."

"I am too."

Rikk sighed deeply and said, "What do you have in your galley that you want to donate to my boat?"

Kara opened the top drawer and rummaged around in it, setting some of her most used cooking tools on the countertop.

Rikk picked them up, examined them, and put them in a shore bag that Kara dug out. She set out a handheld, wooden juicer, and Rikk grinned as he turned it in his hand. "What the hell is this used for?"

"What do you think it is used for?"

"I guess I was thinking more about what it probably shouldn't be used for."

"OK?" She drew out her question. "From the way you asked, I don't think I want to know what it *shouldn't* be used for, Dr. Harmon."

"You wouldn't believe the things I've seen walk through the emergency room door."

"I'm sure I wouldn't—and absolutely don't want to know all the whacky things you've seen."

Rikk laughed and continued to inspect it. "Well, what is it designed for?"

"It's a citrus juicer. It's great for squeezing lime juice into guacamole and French martinis. You cut the lime in half, dig out the seeds, and then use this to squeeze the juice into whatever you are making."

Setting it down, Rikk's hands embraced her hips. "Kara, as a doctor, I advise you to take these things over to my boat immediately."

"But you're not *my* doctor."

"I was hoping it wields some authority—or at least urgency."

Kara wrapped her arms around Rikk's neck and gently pulled his face to hers. "I think captains outrank doctors, don't you?"

"Depends on the situation."

"It's my boat."

Wrapping his hands around her lower back, Rikk closed the space between them. He gently nuzzled the nape of Kara's neck and kissed her ear. "Have you ever heard the term mutiny? It's when the shipmates commandeer the ship and toss the captain overboard."

"You can't commandeer a ship if the captain leaves on her own accord." Kara's whispering into his ear tickled him.

"Would the captain abandon her own ship?"

Kara nodded her head. "Only to commandeer another captain's ship."

"Sounds like piracy to me."

"It is." Kara shut her eyes and met Rikk's eager kiss with the intensity greater than he felt coming from her last night. At first, their kisses lingered while they caressed and explored each other. When Kara fell against the companionway steps with Rikk stumbling over her, they pulled themselves back up. Kara whispered, "No more interruptions. Deal?"

"Deal."

Kara peeked out the porthole and then turned back to Rikk and in a raspy pirate's voice said, "Coast is clear, Mate. Take these things to your boat. Give me five minutes. Hurry, before anyone else sees you."

Rikk loved Kara's rendezvous plans. "Five minutes! Why so long? Make it two."

"Four. Now go, time's a-wasting."

When Rikk pulled Kara in for a kiss, she shivered. He knew she felt his urgency, and he sure as hell felt hers. She pressed her fingertips over his lips and whispered, "Please, hurry."

"Make it three minutes, Kara."

"I'll try."

Kara

As soon as Rikk was out of her cabin, Kara dabbed on perfume and applied a touch of blush and mascara. She went to her berth and dug to the bottom of her drawer. She pulled out the lace bra and panties that still had the tags on them. She bought them in the village a few days before Connor had died. They lay untouched, and Kara only saw them when her laundry bag was full and her drawers almost empty. With the price tags still on them, their only use was a reminder to wash her laundry. She held them for a moment. *I always wondered if I'd ever wear these. I never dreamed it would be for you, Dr. Rikkert Harmon.*

Rikk

Rikk left the hatch open for Kara and leaned against the galley counter. He wondered why she needed five minutes and then agonized that they had already passed, plus a few more. He felt the slight listing of his boat and looked up to see Kara's bare feet stepping onto the cockpit seats. Her blue jeans hid the rest of her legs. The realization that he would soon see them—and more of what he had longed to see since she first waltzed into his world—sent a jolt through his body. She handed down the shore bag that contained a few galley gadgets. He then noticed why she kept him waiting. Kara's green eyes shined out behind her long dark eyelashes. Her blush, that wasn't entirely from the soft powdering of her cheeks, reflected a bashful yearning. The sage sweater Kara wore revealed her bronzed neck and defined collarbone that gracefully drew his eyes down to the lace peeking out under the fourth button she had left open. The bottom button, also left open, exposed the snap on her jeans. He took the bag from her and tossed it on the counter, never removing his hungry eyes from her. He reached out for her hand. Even though she didn't need his assistance, he needed to touch her—to draw her to him as soon as her feet hit the cabin sole. She gently bit her bottom lip as her eyes smiled at him. His voice croaked as he muttered hello. Then his senses filled with her delicate fragrance, intoxicating him. Kara dazzled Rikk; ten minutes ago, he embraced her on *Genie's Bottle*. In that short time she had transformed from alluring to goddess.

Rikk pulled Kara to him and devoured her with a ravenous kiss. His cell phone rang. Kara leaped from Rikk's embrace. "Damn!" Rikk scowled. He tore it from his pocket and noticed who was calling before he pressed the key to divert the call to messages. "It's Zoey. She'll leave a message." He set the phone on the counter and looked at Kara gazing at her feet. Without a word or hesitation, he took her hand and pulled her past the counter. They stood in the center of the OSQ's cabin. His eyes meandered down again to the three buttons fastening the soft sweater.

Rikk leisurely unbuttoned them and slid it off her shoulders. He paused briefly, appreciating the fullness of Kara's breasts hidden behind her delicate white lace bra. He drew her close and consumed her with his kiss.

At last, they found themselves in each other's arms. The world around them faded. No longer did they hear the waves lap against the hull, nor the seagull's incessant shouts, nor the humming traffic on Minnesota Point. Alone, fused together in their urgent desire, they made love to the rhythms of their souls—pulsing their sonata in their private universe.

Chapter 27

Kara

Rikk's cell phone rang again. Kara jumped with a start and laughed at their predicament. She could've fallen asleep in the comfort of Rikk's arms and was bummed that he hadn't turned his cell phone off. She reached for his jeans with the ringing phone in the pocket. "Who has the audacity to disrupt our tryst this time?"

Rikk read the name on the phone and sighed. "It's Zoey again. Kara, I'm sorry, but I know my daughter, and she'll come looking for me if I don't answer this."

"Then by all means, answer it. I sure don't want her to see me like this."

Raising his eyebrows and flashing Kara an appreciative smile, he said, "Does that mean you intend to stay like this for awhile?"

"Maybe." Kara's grin telegraphed her intention. The phone rang its fifth ring, and Kara snickered. "You better hurry up and answer it before she hangs up and jumps in her car." She went into the head to freshen up. She overheard Rikk's half of the conversation.

"Good morning, Zoey. What's up?"

"I heard it ring, but I had my hands full, and I haven't had time to listen to your message yet."

Kara stepped out of the head and slipped Rikk's shirt on. She went into the galley and started to remove the items from her shore bag while Rikk talked to Zoey.

"That's tonight? Are you sure? I thought it was next Sunday," Rikk moaned as he looked up in despair. "What is wrong with me? I can't remember anything."

"No, of course I'll call her. Did she sound sick?"

"And you're sure she is not going to make it?"

"What exactly did Grandma Lotte tell you?"

"No, I can call her and make sure she's all right."

"I, um—I'm on my boat. We just had breakfast."

"Kara and I." He looked at Kara and winked. He mouthed, "She likes you." Kara smiled.

"OK, what is the absolute latest time I need to be there?"

"Since Grandma Lotte won't be able to make it, is it too late to bring a guest?" Rikk captured Kara and drew her tightly into him.

Kara bent backward to look up to see Rikk's seductive grin as he hovered over her. She laughed as she wondered what this call was all about. She whispered, "Careful, you've got your hands full again."

Rikk choked back his chuckle. "Good. Hang on, I'll ask." Rikk dropped the phone away from his head and pushed the mute button with his thumb, not releasing his hold on Kara. "You aren't going to believe this. I should get down on one knee to ask you this, but there just isn't enough room."

Kara smiled, "Maybe if you let go of me, you could get down on one knee."

"I'm afraid you'll run away when I let you go, especially when you hear my question."

Kara looked at him and by the expression on Rikk's face and the disappointment in his voice; she realized they would not be spending the whole day in each other's arms. She wasn't sure where her answer came from, but she whispered, "Rikk, it would take a lot for me to run away from you now." She stretched up on her toes and kissed his cheek.

With more impishness than chivalry Rikk asked, "Will you be my guest at the Duluth-Superior Health Care Providers' Annual Benefit?"

"When?"

"Tonight."

"Tonight?" Kara was astonished.

"Yes, tonight. I know this is short notice." He grimaced, and then said, "I thought it was next weekend. You see, I've been captivated by this damsel and have lost all my wits."

"Maybe you've been captivated by a captain, and you've lost your mind, or at least your memory."

"I really will get down on one knee if you would go with me."

"Well, what kind of event is it?"

"It's a short program, dinner, and then dancing."

"Short program, dinner, and dancing? Tell me more."

"They'll have a few speakers, serve dinner, and a band will play anything from waltzes to rock and roll. It's like a wedding dance, except dinner is served in three courses to a room full of people in the medical profession," said Rikk.

"Help me understand this? Grandma Lotte can't make it tonight, so I'm your rebound date."

"I guess I didn't think of her as my date, but I suppose she was. I guess that does make you my rebound date. I would really like you to come with me."

"OK, what do people wear to this benefit?"

"Wait," Rikk said as he un-muted his phone and placed it back to his ear, "Zoey, I'm going to put Kara on, and you can tell her what to wear and answer all her questions." Then handing his phone to Kara, he said, "Zoey won't let you say no. It is great to have allies!" He kissed Kara before he gave her the phone.

With a smile that conveyed Kara had been coerced into this, she leaned against the galley counter and squinted her eyes at him. She knew getting out of it would be almost impossible. Other than the apprehension about what she'd wear, being the conspicuous date displayed for the first time, and being the only non-health care person in a room full of medical professionals, she was excited that Rikk had asked her to accompany him. Besides, she wanted to go; she wanted to be with Rikk.

"Hi, Zoey." Kara said.

Zoey was laughing, "You've got to love my dad's persuasiveness, don't you?"

"I guess," Kara said with laughter, and she shook her head all the while eyeing Rikk.

"Kara, it would be great if you could go, and I really want Eric to meet you. Barb and Joe will be there, as well as most of Dad's co-workers. I know that men have no consideration for advanced notice or the fact that it is Sunday, but I know that I could help you with anything you need. Do you have a dress?"

Kara clinched her lips together to hide her smile and listened to Zoey's convincing arguments. When she got off the phone, she announced, "I have a big date tonight, and I need to shop for a dress. You will have to excuse me, Dr. Harmon, as I have much to do and so little time in which to do it. By the way, what time are you picking me up?"

"Five. We have hours, Kara."

"Really? Because I need to go shopping, and not just for a dress, either."

"What else do you need?"

"First I need to find a dress, then shoes, and accessories."

"How long will that take?"

"It depends on how fast I can find a dress. I'll need to get started as soon—"

"I'll go with you and help you find one."

"Seriously? You want to go shopping for a dress with me?"

"I want to spend the entire day with you. Shopping for a dress isn't my first choice of ways to spend it with you, but I would rather shop with you than spend my day without you."

"I would rather spend the whole day alone with you too. But neither of our wants will happen as we've planned." She wrapped her fingers around his neck and said, "I am kind of excited to go on a real date with you though."

"And spend the evening with me?"

"If that is an invitation, I accept." Kara allowed her eyes to glance over Rikk's bareness and noticed Rikk's growing sign of arousal. She blushed and sat down on the settee. He sat next to her and playfully pulled her on top of him, and they kissed and caressed each other tenderly. "Rikk—"

Kara, breathless, called his name and again snuck her fingers to his lips. "I can't believe I'm telling you to stop because every fiber of my body wants to make love to you, again. But I need to shop for a dress. Besides calling your mom, you might want to check to see if you have the proper attire cleaned, pressed, and polished for this affair. You'd hate to be shown up by your date who's wearing a new dress and you're in a crumpled old suit, thread-bare tie, and dusty shoes."

"You needn't worry about my attire. Zoey picked up my suit a couple of weeks ago and had it dry-cleaned. She's informed me that she has everything I need, down to my socks and polished shoes, at her house, and she'll bring them over to me."

Rikk's phone rang again; this time is was Barb. The half of the conversation that Kara heard put a new spin on the afternoon.

"Hey, Barb."

"I just planned on saying a few words."

"Is it that big of a deal?"

"Well, Kara needs to shop for a dress and other stuff, so I guess I'll have time to throw something together."

"Why?"

Then Rikk pulled the phone away from his ear, and frustration covered his face. He whispered to Kara, "She's giving the phone to Joe. I have to say a few words."

"Words? What do you mean?" Kara asked.

Rikk raised his hand to Kara and held the phone to his ear, "Barb tells me that they think I need to make a speech. I just thought I would say a simple thank you and call it good."

"Yeah, Joe, I guess I will have time to write something."

"Sure, I'll put her on." Rikk then handed the phone to Kara. "Barb wants to talk to you."

Kara's half of the conversation was much less revealing to Rikk than his was to her. Mostly Kara said hmm, no, or yes and gave OKs. When Kara hung up and handed the phone back to Rikk, she explained her conversation with Barb, "Well, you are picking me up at the Watsons' home at four thirty for a sort of pre-game warm up. We'll have cocktails together before we leave."

"Why am I picking you up at their house?"

"Because Barb is picking me up at four, and I'm getting dressed in their spare bedroom. Barb doesn't think getting dolled up in my boat or the marina's shower rooms is appropriate for a formal affair. I, of course, declined—but she insisted and upped the ante with cocktails. Now that I know I have to find a dress suitable for a formal affair, the cocktails sounded like a great way to ease into this event." Kara's growing apprehension was evident in her voice as she asked, "What do you have to write? Are they the 'words' you have to say?"

"Yes, Kara, I have to write a few more words than I thought. The Health Care Providers' Association has just set up an annual continuing education scholarship in Lauren's honor, and they are making the first presentation at the banquet tonight" Rikk said.

"Wow, it sounds like quite an honor."

"It's really no big deal."

"Really? Because there are two things that I know to be true when people say the phrase, 'no big deal.' First, it always is a very big deal. Second, the universe does not recognize no or negatives, which is probably why it's always a big deal. Tell me more about this."

"They'll present me with a plaque, and I'll say a few words."

"Those few words are what you have to write?"

"Yes, but I'll just say, 'Lauren would be honored to know that this was set up in her name,' and things like that. It will be more about the recipient of the scholarship; they just want me to give a thank you from my family for setting up the scholarship in Lauren's name."

"Rikk, that is a very big deal."

"Well, it's a big deal to be there and thank them, but it isn't a big speech."

"But Joe called to tell you to write something. He must think it's at least a bigger speech than just a thank you."

"I think he just wants me to look prepared, so I will write it down and read it off the paper."

"Barb and Joe called just to tell you to write your few words down on a piece of paper so you look prepared? Are you sure they don't want you to write a few more words than you are planning to say?"

"Are you clairvoyant, or do you have really good hearing?" Rikk laughed. "They want me to say more than I planned, but they don't expect me to talk for more than a minute or so."

Before Kara could question Rikk further, the phone rang for the third time; this time it was Eric. Rikk's conversation was sparse, and his disappointment registered in his slumped shoulders as he gave brief answers that ended with, "Tell her I'll be there in half an hour." Raking his hand through his hair, he looked over at Kara and sighed heavily. "Eric said Zoey is melting down about my speech and has just talked to Barb. Apparently none of them think I'm taking this seriously, and they all feel I need to tell everyone about Lauren, about who she was."

"Oh." Kara sighed. "Well, it sounds like we both have our afternoons filled."

"So much for spending the day with this creature whose sexy legs are tempting me from under my shirt."

Kara hugged Rikk and soothed him, "This is important and a very big deal to Zoey and to all the others, maybe even to you? We'll get our time together after the banquet. I will personally shut off your phone."

"Damn, I really thought it was next weekend."

"Well, I guess it is too late to back out now," Kara replied.

"No, Kara, if you don't want to go, it's OK," Rikk reassured her with his words, yet his body language did not mirror his message.

"I do want to go. It's just that I always want all the information before I make a decision. I still would've accepted your invitation if you would have told me up front that you had to accept an award and give a speech."

"I'm sorry. I should've told you about the scholarship. But I didn't think I was expected to say more than thank you." Before Kara could answer Rikk asked, "Is this our first fight?"

"No, this is our first defining moment." Kara's intuition told her that something else was bothering him but decided to lighten up. "I think our first fight was after the boom fell on my head."

Rikk returned a grin to Kara, "Well, it's good to have that over. So you aren't too mad at me?"

"No, but I'm serious about wanting all the information before I'm asked for a commitment or opinion."

"OK, I respect that. I'll give you all the information in the future. I'm sorry I didn't. I've been dreading this banquet. I've keep pushing every thought of it out of my head. It's no wonder I thought it was next week."

"Why have you been pushing it out of your head?"

"I'm tired of being the pitied widower."

"Then stop being the pitied widower, Rikk. I hope you didn't ask me to be your date to stop being pitied. You do have to make that choice, though—all on your own. You know you don't want to be pitied, so what do you want?"

"I want to be treated like I was before Lauren died. People don't let me forget. They ask, 'How are you?' with that sympathetic voice and sorrowful look written all over their faces. How do you expect me to control what people say?" Rikk huffed a sigh.

"You can't control what anyone says, or what they think, or feel, or even how they act. All you control and can change is you. Sometimes I get those same questions asked in that sympathetic way about Connor. But I hardly get that anymore because I've chosen to answer in a way that conveys I've accepted Connor's death."

"So how do you respond to that question?"

"I tell them that I loved Connor and am so grateful that I have the memory of all the years we spent together. Connor's spirit lives in me through my memories of him, and his spirit also lives in their memories. I thank them for asking about me and assure them that Connor wouldn't want me to shrivel up and die by being stuck in the past any more than I'd want him to do that. I tell them that I love Connor as much today as I always have, and if I was given the opportunity to choose, he would still be living in this world with me."

"Do you think Connor chose to die?"

Kara had wrestled with that question over and over during the first few months after Connor died. The answer to that question was just too big to give at this moment.

Rikk broke the silence. "Kara, I can get this speech written in an hour and then come help you find that dress and all the other things you need."

"No! I learned long ago to shop by myself. It isn't that I don't like company; it's more that I fall into the 'detest to shop' category. That is why I never shop with anyone. I also hope I can sneak in a nap this afternoon. Do we still have a date following the benefit for some uninterrupted time?"

Rikk smirked at Kara's suggestion and planted a kiss on her laughing mouth. "Hurry and find that dress and take a long nap. It'll be the only sleep you'll get for the rest of the day."

"That sounds like a date that I'll want to rest up for." She blushed and wondered if she sounded too eager.

"Or we could just—"

"Don't say it, Rikk. I remember hearing you tell Eric that you would be at their house in half an hour and that was—geez, that a while ago. You have to call your mom too."

"Well, I could at least drive you to the mall and pick you up when you're done."

"I will accept the ride to the mall, but I will call a taxi for the ride back to the marina, so you can have time to write all those words that tell everyone what an amazing person Lauren was and how much you loved her." Kara hugged and kissed Rikk with playful abandon to ease his ego with her rejection of his shopping help.

He groaned, "I better get to Zoey's."

"After a few sleep-deprived nights, you might like a nap too." Kara said. She tossed Rikk his boxers and slipped into her panties before removing his shirt. They dressed quickly, sneaking peeks at each other and stealing hugs and caresses along the way.

"Kara, I didn't ask you to come with me tonight so people would stop pitying me."

"I know that. I'm sorry I said that, and I was just frustrated to hear you're feeling like the pitied widower. Really, that was not about you. It was about my own fears of being your first date." She grimaced, "I am your first date, right?"

"You're the first date that I've asked out. You're the first that I've wanted."

Kara smiled back at Rikk then crawled up the companionway. "I'll grab my wallet and shoes." As they walked up the dock, Kara entwined her hand in Rikk's, just as she had done a million times with Connor. She felt him looking down at her and realized her unconscious action; Kara dared to look up and was flooded with affection when he squeezed her hand then dropped it to put his arm around her waist. They walked to his car arm in arm, unabashed.

⚜

As Rikk started the car, Kara leaned her head on the headrest and shut her eyes. Her mind wandered to finding a dress that would be smart and elegant. She appreciated the silent ten-minute drive to the mall, giving her time to get centered. When Rikk pulled up to the mall entrance, Kara leaned over to kiss him goodbye. He held her tightly, lingering in the moment. Rikk's embrace sent surges down her, and she labored to suspend her craving for the man whose mere touch ravished her body and left her starving.

Rikk released Kara. "I'm not happy that I'm not spending every minute alone with you from now until you leave in the morning."

"Well, what is—is. You can spend time being unhappy or you can look forward to seeing me at the Watsons' in a few hours."

"I am. I'll see you at four thirty."

"You better be on time. I don't want to be kept waiting any longer for you than I have to." Kara said. With a fair amount of restraint, they kissed and said goodbye.

Chapter 28

Kara

Increasing in volume and speed, the alarm beeped with angry insistence at Kara to wake up. Before she lay down, she had moved it from the V-berth to the dinette so she wouldn't be tempted to push the snooze button over and over. Her tired body awoke as she stretched and contemplated how she could turn it off without getting up. Kara drew in a breath and anxiety replaced her exhaustion as she recalled the reason for her nap's end. *Geez, what did I agreed to?* She forced herself to sit up. She spun around to back her way out of the V-berth and scrambled to the dinette to punch the stop button on the irritating alarm clock.

Kara looked at her dress and shoes that only took her a couple of hours to find. She grabbed her shower tote for the second time this day and threw in a clean t-shirt and shorts. She munched on an apple and headed up the companionway. Dutch popped out of his boat and had to hurry to catch her as she walked down the dock. Although she didn't have time to spare, she was happy that he was back to his gregarious self. This Dutch was the same fatherly figure and friend she had come to love over the last couple of weeks.

"Kara, I'm sorry about interrupting the Doc and you last night," Dutch said.

Kara's face flushed. She didn't want to talk about it, yet appreciated that Dutch apologized again. He followed her all the way down the dock repeating his apology, keeping up with Kara's increased pace as she tried to escape this conversation. At the end of the dock, she turned to Dutch, gave him a kiss on the cheek, and told him, "Dutch, I have a date with Rikk tonight. He is taking me to some hospital-sponsored benefit dinner. Your only crime, if you want to own one, is pushing a reluctant couple of lonely hearts together until they found out they were fond of each other. All things happen for a reason, and you happened onto us last night, so we'd have time to figure some things out." She squeezed his arm and added, "The way you've been match-making, Dutch, I'm so curious about your expertise in the ways of love."

"Huh?" Dutch stopped in his tracks and fidgeted, "I just thought you could help him, that's all. I wasn't match-making." He took a breath, and a grin covered his face. "So you have a date. You go get ready, Kara. I got things to do. You get ready."

Kara intuitively felt Dutch's deeply buried and well-guarded secret was directly related to his playing cupid with Rikk and her. If she had the time, she would've chased him back to his boat and quizzed him. She smiled and said, "Dutch, someday you are going to tell me about the woman who broke your heart. But I don't think I have time right now to coerce it out of you." Dutch spun around and raced back to *Miss Sea*, pretending not to hear Kara.

⁂

Kara passed the ladies' room mirror and looked at her bump and black eye. While she napped, she had compressed her eye with a warm washcloth. The bump had shrunk to the size of a small flattened pecan since Thursday night, and the puffiness in her eyelid had dissipated. She would wear a bit more makeup than usual to cover the black eye, which already had faded to yellow.

⁂

As Kara left the ladies' room, she felt a little conspicuous walking through the marina. Her hair, pulled over to one side with gentle waves cascading down onto her shoulder, and makeup were uncharacteristic of her, especially in the late afternoon and so casually dressed. Kara wondered what all the early boaters readying their vessels for launching must be wondering about her. At least the dress bag slung over her shoulder and shoe store shopping bag she carried into the lobby indicated an evening out on the town.

Feeling apprehensive about fitting in with the medical crowd at the benefit, Kara sat near a window and watched for Barb. She never had any reason or opportunity to attend anything like this, and she was feeling much the same as she did decades ago attending her first prom. She feared that she would feel completely out of place, so she decided she would be the best listener tonight that she ever had been. Kara would say very little and keep her answers direct and to the point. She sighed, because she had yet to be shy—ever.

When Barb drove up, Kara dashed out to meet her. Barb asked her how she was, and Kara exposed her anxiety in one question. "What is this event all about?"

"It is a fairly important event for the medical community. It used to be a black-tie event, but attendance was dropping. It seems that loosening up the dress code has increased the interest. It is a one-hundred-dollar-a-plate dinner, and proceeds go to the charitable organizations that the Duluth and Superior area hospitals and clinics sponsor. There'll be a four-piece ensemble playing during the cocktail hour; then we'll be seated and served dinner. After a short program, the orchestra plays and later a band finishes off the evening. It is a fun evening."

"It sounds interesting," was all that Kara could say. That wasn't a lie, still she wondered how she'd fit in at an affair like this, which was so foreign to the boat shows or sailing parties following regattas that were always laid-back.

"You sound nervous," said Barb.

"I've never been to a benefit like this before."

"Well, what are you most nervous about?"

"I don't know how I'll fit into a group of health care professionals, whom I have nothing in common with, and not feel out of place." Kara saw Barb grimace.

Barb nodded her head and said, "I understand how you feel. I'd feel the same way if I went to a boat convention. Do they have boat conventions?"

Kara smiled, "Kind of. They have boat shows."

Barb laughed, "That sounds a little more casual, doesn't it? My guess is everyone will ask you what you do, and they'll be just as intrigued about what you've been doing the last seven years as I am. You seem to be a person who will be as interested in them as they are in you." She gave Kara a reassuring smile. "It might be an opportunity to learn about a field that you know little about."

"You are right. That is the way I should look at this," sighed Kara, "and I appreciate that you've given me a new perspective. I've been feeling, I don't know—all these people have a horde of letters behind their names, and I don't even know what they mean."

"It sounds like you're feeling intimidated?" said Barb.

"I don't know if that is it exactly; I guess it is part of it. It's just been my experience that when professional people congregate, they start talking about their professions and become self-absorbed." Barb did not respond. "Ugh! I hope I haven't insulted you or Joe or Rikk. I'm sorry. I feel so ridiculous. I've been in situations when people from one profession talk in jargon that is foreign to others. We are outsiders watching a conversation that we can't participate in. I just don't want to cower to the remedial corner of the room or make Rikk feel like he has to change the subject on my account."

"Hmm," Barb said. "If I was sitting around a marina with you, and another sailor started talking about boats, would you use terms that I may have never heard before?"

"Probably, but I hope that we would try to explain what we were talking about and include you or change the subject to something that included everyone." Kara noticed Barb nod, and then said, "What I worry about the most is feeling conspicuous."

"I think these health care professionals with a horde of letters behind their names will find you and the experiences you have had not only interesting, but exciting. So you very well may be conspicuous, but not for the reasons that you think. Kara, they are just people, even if they have more in common with each other than they have with you. You will meet some that you've described, but you will meet more who are like Joe and Rikk. You don't find Joe and Rikk self-absorbed, do you?"

"No, of course not," Kara said. "I'm so glad we'll have some time to chat at your house before we go to this," she exhaled and pulled a mock apprehensive expression, "so I can relax!"

"We'll have that cocktail right after we get dressed." Then Barb added, "Oh, Kara, I need to tell you that Rikk might not be picking you up at our house after all. He called me just before I got to the marina. Zoey is still polishing his speech, and Rikk hadn't left their house yet."

"He hasn't?" Kara was dismayed. "He said it wasn't a big deal; that he would only have to write a few words."

"Well, Eric called Rikk to remind him he was there when the hospital president told Rikk about the award and asked him to say some words. Since then, Eric has run into the president a couple of times and she's asked Eric how Rikk is coming with his speech. So Eric really believes it's a big deal."

"Wow," Kara laughed, "He doesn't think it is a big deal, and then he forgets it's tonight! Thank God he's got all of you watching after him."

"Joe and I have noticed how forgetful he has been lately. Really, it is out of character." Barb looked at Kara as she was turning into her driveway, winked and teased, "Joe and I have no idea what is occupying his mind lately." Barb snickered at Kara's embarrassed smile and continued, "If he doesn't make it to our house by ten to five, we're going to meet him at the Kitchi Gammi Club at five."

"I get asked out on a date, and I don't even know if he'll be picking me up!" Kara shook her head, "Can you believe that?" When Barb touched her arm, Kara blurted, "Thank you, Barb, for everything, and especially for easing my mind and reminding me to have a good attitude. If I look forward to having fun, I will. Sage advice my mom gave me that I, in turn, passed down to my kids. Now, if I can take my advice as well as I give it, I will have a great time."

⚜

Barb escorted Kara to the guest bedroom where she had set up the ironing board, then excused herself to get ready. Joe was mulling around the house, and if she needed anything, Barb instructed her to call for Joe.

Kara lightly steamed her black chiffon dress. The spaghetti straps curved into the scoop neckline. The princess cut draped close to her slender figure, and the panels cascaded fully from the waist to just below her knees. She clasped on a delicate gold bracelet, dangling gold earrings, and a gold chain with a diamond pendant from her great grandmother. In the dress shop, Kara had to choose between an ivory shawl and bolero jacket made of a sheer black organza with gold metallic flecks woven into the fabric. She opted for the jacket, so her hands would be free. She detested the inconvenience of keeping a shawl on her shoulders or keeping track of it when she took it off. Though the shawl draping off her shoulders produced a very sensual and tantalizing effect, her nerves won this battle, and she chose convenience and modesty. Her clutch bag presented the same problem of tracking but since it carried the basic requirements, like identity, money, handkerchief, and blush; she needed it.

Kara laughed and realized that even entertaining that thought was proof that she had lived on a boat way too long. After all, what woman attending an affair like this would not carry a purse? The fact was, she hadn't carried a purse in years, since she had very few occasions that deemed it necessary, or convenient. All things considered, it felt very feminine to dress up, and that outweighed any inconveniences—even the discomfort of wearing heels. She almost teetered as she turned into the hall from the spare bedroom wearing the black patent sling-backs that had tiny gold buckles securing the straps around her ankles. It had been quite a long time since she wore high-heeled shoes, and even though these were not very high, she needed some practice walking in them.

Kara carried her shore bag through the empty living room and set it by the door. It was four thirty, and she imagined that both Barb and Joe were finishing dressing, so she went back into the living room to wait. She paced around the room, admiring the paintings on the walls. She didn't notice that Joe entered the room and watched her for a moment. Kara faced the fireplace and gazed at the painting above it. Her arms fell at her sides as appreciation spread over her face. It was an original oil painting of the Duluth harbor. Although painted relatively recently, the era that it captured was the turn of the twentieth century. The architecture of the city had always drawn her to Duluth, but the painting captured the stately Victorian homes, churches, and the Central High School bell tower. Joe cleared his throat, and Kara turned around careful not to wobble in her heels.

"You look stunning, Kara. All eyes will be on you," Joe said.

"Oh, I hope you are wrong. Everyone will see my shiner. Just think of the scandal that will cause Rikk."

"Believe me, Kara, nobody will notice it. You've concealed it well. It's healing fast," Joe said.

"You found that dress today?" Barb raved when she entered the living room.

Kara smiled and said, "I just asked for the perfect dress to find me right away, and this is the first one I looked at and tried on."

"Whom did you ask, Kara?" said Joe with mirth in his voice.

"Yes, whom? I want to ask them the next time I go shopping for a dress," Barb said.

"No one in particular. I just put it out there, I guess."

"You put it out there?" said Joe and he gave an implausible laugh.

"Yeah, it's a little hard to explain. However, it is along the lines that if you expect to find what you want, you will; and if you expect to never find what you want, you won't. It's a bit like magic," Kara said and blushed, certain she'd have to explain herself further.

"You've got to share that magic trick with Barb," Joe said.

"Well, I apply it to whatever I want, not just shopping for dresses." She looked at Barb and said, "I want to have a great time tonight, so I will."

Barb winked at Kara and announced, "We all are going to have a great time tonight." Then looking at Joe, Barb added, "Now, how about that cocktail?"

"I will be the talk of the town tonight," lauded Joe, "for I will be escorting the two most beautiful women to the ball. What can I get for you, Kara? Wine, a cocktail, what's your pleasure?"

"Rikk isn't coming?" Kara asked Joe.

"He called just before you got here and said he was running late. He said he'd call back, but I haven't heard from him yet. Do you want to call him, Kara?"

"No, that's—" The phone's ring interrupted Kara.

Joe answered it, and then nodded his head confirming to Barb and Kara that it was Rikk. "Well, then we'll see you there." He watched Kara's shoulders slump. "She's right here. Kara?" He handed the phone to her and said to Barb, "I could use a hand making cocktails. Kara, we are having a Manhattan. Would you like that or something else?"

Kara took the phone from Joe, and inhaled and slowly blew out her breath. "A Manhattan sounds perfect." Barb followed Joe into the kitchen.

"Hello," Kara said, biting on her lower lip.

"Kara, I'm sorry. I just stepped out of the shower, and Zoey will be here in ten minutes to make sure I can get myself dressed properly. She said she had a couple ties and wanted me to try them both, so she could pick out the right one. I guess we men don't know how to dress ourselves if we are left to our own accord."

A thought shot through Kara, and she wondered if Zoey had second thoughts about her and was conspiring to detain her father, so Kara would decline to attend. "Does she really want me to come? Because I can take a taxi back to the boat."

"No, Kara. She is happy that you are coming. She said that a hundred times today. This award is extremely important to her. I suggested that she make the speech, but that just made her mad. I think this is her way to let everyone know how much we loved Lauren and how much Lauren loved life. I get the feeling she sees this night as a turning point for us, me especially, to embrace life with the same enthusiasm and joy that Lauren did."

Kara's voice cracked, "Are you going to say that in your speech?"

"No, Zoey wrote my speech, and it is more of a factual account of Lauren's life with a few funny stories, more like a eulogy. But I decided to quit arguing with her and do it her way since it means so much to her."

"You are very giving, Rikk. I'm glad that I got to hear *your* words. But you need to get your clothes on, so Zoey can pick out your tie. I'm hanging up on you now."

"Kara," Rikk hesitated.

"What?"

After a short pause he said, "Thank you."

"For what?"

"Thank you for understanding and being flexible. Thank you for not backing out, especially since I'm not picking you up."

Kara choked back her emotion and masked it with a joke, "Get dressed, Rikk, because I'm only going to be part of Joe's harem to the ballroom door. If you aren't there, I'll find my own chariot to take me home."

"I'll be there before you arrive, waiting for you. I promise."

"You better be. See you soon." Kara didn't wait for his response. She hung up the phone and looked up to see Barb and Joe walking in with drinks. Barb took the phone from her, and Joe handed her a drink. She took a sip and was relieved that it had a strong kick to it. Not quite knowing what to say she asked, "What kind of beverages will be served at this event?"

Joe responded, "They'll have wait staff bringing around wine and champagne, and there is a bar for mixed drinks."

Kara relayed her conversation with Rikk to the Watsons and then asked about the award honoring Lauren. Barb explained the association was working on it last year, but since it had only been five months after Lauren's death, Joe had persuaded them to delay it for a year. She explained Rikk's wounds from losing Lauren were too fresh, and Zoey's also. Joe added with a wink that the timing of it was perfect this year. The reason he believed it was perfect seemed to be a secret he and Barb shared. She looked at them for an explanation, but neither offered one. As Kara sipped on her drink, she asked, "Do they also serve hors d'oeuvres? I'm feeling the need to absorb some of this alcohol with food, so I can coast through the social hour."

"I *thought* my Manhattan was weak. I guess I gave you the wrong one, Kara. I'll get some snacks," said Joe.

When Joe left the room, Barb let out a little laugh and admitted, "I saw him make one stronger than usual and assumed that it was for him. If I know him at all, I know that he took the liberty to calm your nerves, especially since Rikk can't meet you here."

"Is that his idea of social medicine? Inebriate the fear out of me for the social gathering?"

"You are onto him," laughed Barb. "I don't suppose you had time to eat much today either?"

"Let's see, a cup of coffee, a handful of trail mix, and an apple. That was about it," said Kara.

"Well, I'll let him know he needs to reform his socialized health care program."

"Don't be too hard on him, Barb. His heart was in the right place, and he is bringing us snacks."

Joe walked in on the tail end of their conversation and pulled a defensive expression. "Were you talking about me?"

"Of course we were," Barb shot back her answer with a broad grin. "We were talking about your vigilante methods on socialized medicine, in the loosest sense of the term imaginable." Joe's eyebrows shot up; he clearly wasn't following Barb's banter.

Kara said, "It was more about your covert distribution of medicinal alcohol to ease my nerves tonight." Kara snickered at Joe's humiliated expression. "This drink is stiff, but it's helping me relax and be comfortable socializing, but I'm just a little worried that if I don't eat something I might crash and make a scene."

"Well, have some of this, and let it be known that I find no need for altering my distribution of medicinal alcohol." Joe handed Kara a plate with cheese, crackers, and mixed nuts on it. Then he raised his glass to them and took a drink.

Barb looked at Kara with an air of indignation, "I think he eavesdropped on us."

Kara flashed Joe a quick smile before she spoke. "I think he knows you very well."

❧❀⊙❁☙

They conversed until Joe looked at his watch and announced it was time to leave. Filled with anxiety, Kara stood up, smiled with resolve, and walked with them to the car. She realized she was clenching her fists when she opened the car door. Kara appreciated the constant conversation as they drove; it kept her engaged and her unease somewhat abated. The Kitchi Gammi Club parking valet opened the door for Barb and Kara, and from Joe accepted the car keys. Joe offered his arm to Barb and then his other arm to Kara and walked them to the main entrance. Once inside the door, he took Barb's arm and allowed Kara to walk in front of them. A couple called out to the Watsons and walked over to greet them.

Chapter 29

Kara

In the Club's entry hung an abstract painting in vibrant reds, oranges, and ambers that called out to Kara as she passed. Since Barb and Joe were chatting with others, Kara impulsively spun around and returned for a closer look at the painting. She stood mesmerized at the image, which on first inspection appeared to be two soaring flames. As she gazed at it, the obscured and silhouetted human figures emerged from each flame. They interlaced in a dance reminding Kara of traditional Latin American native dances. Many smaller flames of various heights appeared to be dancing around the two flame forms. Its sensual mood drew Kara to study it. She thought of Rikk and shuddered. Then apprehension filled her again, and she wished she were simply the guest of someone attending the event, rather than date of one of the speakers.

Kara was about to turn and rejoin the Watsons when Rikk's soft voice spoke her name. Startled, she turned to see him admiring her. She felt herself blush as she said, "Hi." Smiling at him, she looked down, self-conscious that all eyes in the hallway were on them.

Rikk shook his head and took Kara's hands as he stepped toward her. He cleared his throat and in a quiet, husky voice said, "My God, Kara, you look beautiful."

Looking into his eyes, Kara whispered, "Thank you." She became aware of the hushed tones that people were speaking in and then looked out to see that they, in fact, were the center of almost everyone's attention. Kara glanced at the floor, wishing to vaporize to anywhere but here. She forced herself to look up at Rikk and shivered as her eyes met his gaze. He squeezed her hands and stepped close to her. His smile radiated as she fixed her eyes on him. "You look very handsome," she said. Even his shy grin didn't ease her self-consciousness. She turned back to the painting to compose herself, then turned to Rikk and said, "I passed this painting, but the colors pulled me back. I was captured by—" Kara looked back at the painting.

Rikk, peering down at Kara, finished her sentence, "You were captured by the flames?" Kara blushed even more. Rikk added, "When I saw you turn back, I was afraid you were going to go look for that chariot."

Kara was mortified when she glanced around and saw they were definitely in the spotlight. She'd do anything to change the crowd's focus. "How is your mother?"

"She said she's just feeling blue. She suffers from SADD. She goes to Florida during the winter. I've tried to convince her to stay down there until all the spring weather has passed, but she always insists on getting back by at least the last week in April."

Before Kara could respond, Barb rescued them by suggesting that they make their way into the ballroom. Rikk placed Kara's hand around his arm and secured it with his free hand. As they moved toward the ballroom, the crowd resumed their conversations, and the commotion returned to its prior level. Many of the staff from Rikk's surgical department already were there. Rikk introduced his coworkers, ranging from the clerical workers to surgical team. By the way he provided personal information about each of them, it struck Kara that they all seemed to be a close-knit family of friends. They all were interested in Kara and gracious to her.

***

Dr. Heidi Norris made a grand entrance, securing a glass of champagne and calling attention to herself as she greeted everyone she knew with palpable exuberance. When she approached Rikk and Kara, she said, "Rikk, I left a message on your phone yesterday to call me. You must have been extremely busy on your sailboat this weekend. Oh, hello again, it's *Mrs.* McKee, isn't it? What a surprise to see you here. Rikk, isn't Lauren's scholarship being presented tonight?"

Kara admired Rikk's ability to remain stoic despite Heidi's attempts to maneuver him into escalating her big scene. Rikk's controlled and even tone, rumbled when he said, "It's Kara, Heidi. It is *especially nice* that she is here with me tonight *because* Lauren is being honored." He slipped his hand onto the small of Kara's back and drew her closer to him. He was scrutinizing Heidi and seemed to enjoy himself as he said, "Actually, we have spent most of the weekend together." Heidi's perfect smile twitched.

Kara smiled at Heidi and politely said, "It is nice to see you again, Heidi."

Heidi looked Kara up and down, her smile back in place. As supercilious as ever, she said, "Thank you." Heidi turned to Rikk and stepped in front of Kara as she deposited her emptied champagne flute on the table. Heidi didn't step back when she beamed her beautiful smile at a server passing by as she lifted another glass from the tray. "Rikk, have you thought more about the races they have every Wednesday evening? I remind you that I am an experienced racing crew." She laughed, tossed her head back, and glanced at her co-workers surrounding them. She failed to notice the forced smiles pasted on their faces while their eyebrows collectively waved like flags in the wind. "Racing is a fast way to perfect your sailing skills. I'm sure you agree, don't you, Kara? Or are you one of those cruising purists?"

"I do agree and have participated in loosely competitive races."

Heidi glanced at Kara and then batted her eyes at Rikk. "Do you already have your crew chosen?"

Kara watched Rikk turn red. "I'm not interested in racing, Heidi." He took Kara's arm, turned away from Heidi, and said, "Kara, I would like to introduce you to my assistant, Carol. With that, he whisked her off to meet one of the surgical nurses.

"Rikk, I'm OK with Heidi," Kara said in a near whisper.

"I'm not. I just don't want anything to spoil this night for you."

"Or for you and Zoey and Eric?"

"For all of us."

⚜

Zoey approached Rikk and Kara with Eric trailing close behind. She extended both of her hands to Kara and rather than shaking them brought Kara into an embrace as she said, "Kara, it is good to see you again. I'm so happy you came with Dad tonight." Zoey introduced Eric to Kara, and he seemed very relaxed and easy to be around. Between the Watsons,

Zoey, Eric, and Rikk, she was feeling confident that she would enjoy the evening.

Kara met several people and felt very much on display, but never self-conscious because of the considerate way they included her in all the conversations, bringing her up to speed on as much as they could. The wait staff wove through the room with trays of champagne and hors d'oeuvres.

A four-piece ensemble played during the cocktail hour, and people mingled on the dance floor. Kara noticed Barb and Joe keeping surveillance on her and Rikk, and when they both looked in her direction, Kara raised her glass to them. They smiled and approached with glee-ridden faces. Barb said, "I'm so glad you came, Kara. I was afraid for awhile that you were going to renege." Hearing this, Rikk looked to Kara for an explanation, but before either could speak, Barb answered his question, "If you've never been to one of these events and have no idea what to expect, that is one thing. But if your date is making a speech that he didn't even realize he needed to write and is writing it the day he is to deliver it, so he can't even pick you up, well, that is just a recipe for anxiety." Remorse spread over Rikk's face.

Kara wished Barb hadn't mentioned this to Rikk and was relieved that he didn't get a chance to respond. The chair of the hospital board was standing at the podium, and she was asking guests to take their seats. Rikk's colleagues sat at the reserved banquet tables close to the front of the room. When everyone was seated, the room quieted down.

The chair welcomed everyone and then began the program, "This year we are presenting an award created in honor of an employee who a year and a half ago lost her courageous battle with cancer. Lauren Harmon was an inspiration to all those who knew her, worked with her, or who just had the brief pleasure of meeting her direct eyes, genuine smile, and sincere greeting while walking down the hallway. I remember once I passed her in the hall; I was totally consumed in a problem I had. Rather than a simple good morning, Lauren sincerely and warmly asked, 'Hey, Beth, how are things going?' I automatically replied, 'Fine, Lauren. Just fine.' She said, 'Really? You're *fine*? Looks more like you've got the world on your shoulders.' Then without prying into my dilemma, she looked directly into my eyes and assured me, 'I'm guessing you aren't fine at the moment, but you will be.' And you *will* find the right answer to whatever problem you are mulling over.' Lauren saw through me and had the courage to let me know that I was not fine at that moment and graciously offered her confidence in me—confidence that I would find my solution."

"My dilemma worked itself out, and as things fell into place I recalled the encouragement that Lauren's simple and brief words gave me. Her few words were the catalyst that turned my attitude around, enabling me to look differently at the problem and come up with the right solution. Her spirit is an inspiration to all who knew her. During her hospital career, she worked diligently for all the people she consulted. Independent of her community outreach facilitator position, she conceived and developed the Lake Superior Health Collaborative. This program helps middle class families struggling with high insurance deductibles and premiums. Lauren would be pleased to know the idea she conceived is continuing to be molded into viable heath care alternatives for thousands of people in Duluth, Superior, and surrounding communities I pray that somehow she knows the achievements accomplished from what she initiated. Before I present the award to one of the many employees who have provided patient care exemplary of Lauren's spirit, I would like to call on her husband and our surgeon, Dr. Rikkert Harmon, to say a few words."

Rikk

As Rikk pushed his chair back, he scanned around the table and saw Zoey was beaming at him. Eric's supportive eyes diverted from Rikk back to Zoey as he clasped her hand. Joe was grinning at Kara who was observing Zoey and Eric. Rikk stood, took a step, and lightly touched Kara's shoulder. She glanced up and her smile sent encouragement to him. He walked to the podium, pulling a sheet of folded paper out of his inside jacket pocket. The board chair shook his hand and then sat down at the table in front of the podium.

Rikk cleared his throat, and with a hushed and cracking voice began, "For those of you who did not know my wife, Lauren, she worked in the outreach program under the direction of Barb Watson. About two years ago, she was diagnosed with cancer and after a brief battle passed away. Lauren would be very honored to—" Rikk stopped, looked up at the ceiling, and drew in a deep breath. He sighed, folded his paper, and put it back into his pocket. He looked at his daughter said, "I'm sorry Zoey, but I can't read this."

To the audience he explained, "Our daughter, Zoey, rescued me today from my ineptitude. I didn't realize—no—I didn't want to think about writing or giving a speech about Lauren. I've been pretty intent on working non-stop to prevent me from wallowing in self-pity. Lauren would be very happy with the speech that Zoey helped me write for tonight. However, sometimes you have to act on your impulses. To honor Lauren—to really honor her—I'm going to share some things she has taught me that I finally have *learned* in the last few days; things that she'd been trying to get through my thick skull since I first met her."

Rikk's deep inhalation and slow exhalation seemed to relax the house. "She spent her life trying to explain how practicing medicine compassionately was not synonymous with doctor-patient over-involvement. We split hairs over this issue—me on the side of detachment and Lauren on the side of affable connection. Lauren dedicated her life to touching the lives of all people, whether they were her clients, friends, or family." Rikk stopped, shifted his weight, and shifted direction in his thoughts.

"Lauren has been more present in my life these last four days than all the days since she left this world. After her death, I insulated myself from life. She didn't want that for me. In fact, she made a few requests just before she died that I've found almost unbearable to keep. She loved to read, and the last book she bought just prior to her diagnosis was *Be in Choice* by Audrey Lynn. The day she read the first few chapters, she told me about the story and even read passages from it. She kept telling me I had to read it. Then our lives were turned upside down with her cancer diagnosis. She didn't mention it again, or if she did, I wasn't listening. One week before she died, Lauren dictated to Barb Watson an inscription to me in the front cover." Then looking directly at Barb, Rikk said, "Barb, I've read her inscription a million times, but could never force myself to comply with her last request—to read the book. Last Thursday night I started to read it only because I didn't have many other options."

Rikk sighed, inhaled slowly. "When Lauren gave me the book a few days before she died, she made me promise her a couple of things. One promise I just fulfilled a few days ago. I bought a sailboat. It is something that I've always wanted, but Lauren's fear of water kept me from buying one. I guess my reasons for not buying a boat are a testament to Lauren's love and her incredible hold on me. Though Lauren often encouraged me to get a boat, I preferred to spend my free time with her and our daughter Zoey rather than pursuing something that I knew she would not share with me."

"Her second request," Rikk hesitated, then forced out the words, "She told me that she wanted me to remarry. I must have looked like death itself when she said that. I know I felt like I would rather die than be with anyone else. She teased me—even then! She read me and teased me. She said at least a sailboat would provide a mistress if the thought of marriage was too much to imagine right then." Rikk's voice broke as he said, "It was."

A hush resonated throughout the room, except for sniffles and shuffling as people dug for handkerchiefs to dry their eyes. Rikk felt a chill as if Lauren's spirit was telling him to lighten up. "My boat needs a name, but I promised Lauren I wouldn't name it after her. She said she wouldn't allow my boat to be a shrine to her. *Now* I have a nameless mistress." His gave a nervous laugh, and the audience's chuckles permeating through the room calmed him. "I also brought a new friend here with me tonight. Kara McKee is a sailor who rescued my new mistress from the wind on the first night I had her. I guess I'm not very good at keeping a mistress." Rikk felt Lauren's spirit again as he looked out over the faces and realized he had relaxed them by giving them a laugh.

"The next promise I made to Lauren is one that I've tried over and over to keep. I promised to read the book, *Be in Choice.* I just could never get past her inscription to me. On a few pages, Lauren scribbled my name in the margins. I reread these passages a few times, never sure if I reminded her of the character, or if she wanted me to be more like him. I think I understand at least some of her message now, even though I just got it this minute when I came up here to read this speech. I think Lauren wanted me to hear the author's message that we always have choices in every situation—and not just two choices. We have as many choices as we can *creatively* generate. We can change how we see, speak, act, and feel about everything—about everything in life that presents itself to us."

"Lauren's writing became more and more illegible as the cancer consumed her, so she started underlining passages when she was too weak to write. I called Barb today to confirm what I suspected when I finished the book in the early hours Saturday morning. Barb had read the last few chapters to Lauren in between long hours of drifting in and out of sleep. Barb told me how Lauren communicated through her expressions and frail hand gestures on the one passage that she wanted me to know the most. Barb circled it and wrote a note that said, 'Rikk, Lauren needs you to live this.' When I read that passage, I wrote it down and later stuck the paper in my pocket. I've been carrying it around since then." He pulled out and unfolded the page, took a deep breath and said, "That passage is, 'Live fully present in each moment, give love freely and unconditionally, choose in every aspect and moment of your life by following your heart and listening to your intuition. Be in choice.'"

"Lauren must have told me a million times, 'Rikk, you're not living your life when you sit back and let life happen to you; you're just existing.' I never really understood what she meant or what she expected from me. A few of you may know that I was sued a few years back. These are the times that you are actually happy to pay your malpractice insurance premium." Rikk was glad that brought a little comic relief to the audience. "I wanted to fight it and argued with the insurance investigator and lawyers. They explained that although it was likely that the case would be dropped, they estimated the cost of getting it to that point would be at least double the settlement. I was angry at Lauren for agreeing with them and did not understand her reasoning. She said she understood my need to be absolved of the charges, but also felt the long and tedious process to get to that point would be more life-draining than settling it and moving on. She tried to show me that I had more than the two choices I saw: one to fight and the other to settle. She said that just looking at the choices in different ways was making a different choice. After the suit was settled, I became, in Lauren's words, jaded. I was hurt and unconsciously began to treat my patients from the outlook that they were all potential lawsuits."

Rikk stopped as a new thought came to him, a thought that made him shudder. He knew then what he had to say. For Lauren, he'd repeat her words that he finally understood. Rikk smiled directly at Kara, knowing that if no one else understood them, she would. "It took a remarkably independent and self-reliant woman receiving a boom—in both meanings of the word—to her head to compel me to finally read *Be in Choice*. It was the catalyst for me to learn what Lauren had been trying to teach me since we first met. Isn't that strange? I'm the one who needed to get knocked on the head, but it happened to Kara McKee while she rescued my boat."

Rikk's pondering of his own words hushed the audience. He glanced back at Kara and composed his thoughts, "Another thing Lauren must've told me a million times was that although professional distance is absolutely necessary, aloofness is detrimental to both you and your patients. Ninety-two percent of communication is nonverbal, and reaching out comes in many forms. You never know how a simple compassionate look, a listening ear, or a reassuring smile can give encouragement to your patients. That is not over-involvement; it is just one person giving another person care. I don't know what was so hard about that. She was right; I let one bad experience jade my subsequent relationships with my patients."

Rikk paused and looked down at Zoey, then scanned each face sitting at that table and rested his gaze on Kara. He noticed her eyes had the deer in the headlights look and the color had drained from her face. He was not sure what she was feeling, but he had one more thing he knew he had to say. "The one phrase repeated often in this book is its title. I'm sure none of you will be surprised to learn that the first time it appeared, Lauren underlined it and wrote in capital letters," emphatically he pronounced each letter, "R-I-K-K, exclamation point." He brushed the corner of his eye. He drew in a deep breath and was relieved that the audience's laughter had given him a moment to collect himself. "After that, each time it appeared in the book she'd underline it. I guess she knew she'd have to drive the point home for me." His voice cracked, and he waited a moment for the audience to settle. In a hushed deliberate voice, Rikk said, "I hope this scholarship created in Lauren's memory and honor will inspire all of us in the medical profession to look for all the possible different choices to reach out—humanly, with honor and professionalism—not only for the benefit of our patients, but also for those of us who care for them. For every person that we encounter in our careers and in our private lives, let us all *Be in Choice.'* Thank you."

Rikk stood at the podium for a few seconds looking out over the audience, standing and clapping. Tears streamed down Zoey's radiant face, and her drenched eyes locked onto her dad's. Wiping her tears away, she stood clasping her hand over her mouth. Eric wrapped his arm around her and hugged her close. Rikk watched his daughter as his own eyes filled up. He diverted his gaze to Kara and noticed her pallid face and rigid posture. She bit her lower lip and fixed her eyes on his. As Rikk walked back to the table, Joe handed Kara his handkerchief with one hand and drew Barb into his side with his other. When Rikk approached, Zoey stepped to embrace her dad. Eric extended his hand to Rikk, shook it, and pulled Rikk in for a quick hug. Joe held out his hand, shook Rikk's hand, and then released Barb as she embraced Rikk. The others at the table stepped forward likewise, applauding Rikk for his unabashed openness.

Kara stood motionless, sneaking a few peeks at Rikk while straining to regain her composure, dry her eyes, and mostly just breathe. As others from surrounding tables also congratulated Rikk, Barb noticed Kara's ashen face and realized that she appeared ready to faint. Barb tapped Joe, and together they slid out Kara's chair and flanked her while they all sat down. Barb handed Kara the glass of water from her place setting as Joe rested his arm over her chair and steadied her by securing his hand around her shoulder. By then the rest of the table was seated except for Rikk, and a few eyes were on Kara.

Rikk turned to the table to see Barb attending to Kara and Joe in Rikk's chair. He then realized that Joe's arm supported Kara while Joe conversed with Heidi as if everything was normal. When Rikk put his hand on top of Joe's hand, Joe glanced up with a concerned expression. Rikk's look sent Joe confirmation that he understood Kara's predicament. With that, Joe stood up and Rikk slipped into his seat. Kara's eyes drifted up to Rikk who had moved in close to her, slid his arm around her waist, and took her hand in his other hand. "Are you OK, Kara?"

"I'm sorry, Rikk," she whispered, "I'm so sorry."

"Do you want to get some air?"

"No! No, I'm fine. I'm just a little overwhelmed."

"Maybe I should've read Zoey's speech?"

"No! It was beautiful. Lauren would have been happy with it."

"Yeah, I think she would've. Are you sure you are all right?"

"I would like to take my jacket off."

Rikk helped guide it off her shoulders and arms, watching to see the color returning to her face. He stared at her for a moment, admiring her almost-bared shoulders and the scoop neckline of her dress. As he placed the jacket over the back of her chair, he smelled her delicate perfume. He studied her but had no idea what caused her intense reaction to his speech. It only made her more intriguing. He leaned close to her, whispering in her ear, "No interruptions tonight."

Kara's cheeks blushed and her demure smile telegraphed she felt revived, and romantic. She leaned close to him and whispered, "I'll throw your phone in the lake the moment it dares to ring."

Rikk didn't have a chance to respond, as the president was beginning to award the scholarship. The presentation was brief, and the award recipient gave a short thank you. After a few acknowledgements and award presentations, the president introduced the keynote speaker. He joked that Rikk might consider a career as a motivational speaker if he ever tired of surgery; and then gave a twenty minute humorous and inspirational speech. As the president ended the program, the wait staff began to serve the meal. Barb and Joe initiated eating once all at the table had been served. Rikk released his hand from hers and moved his arm from around her waist to grasp her left hand. He let go of it only after Kara had taken her first bite of salad. All the time he was conversing with others at the table, his attention remained on Kara.

⁂

As they ate, Rikk's friends and coworkers quizzed Kara. She'd finish answering one question, and before she lifted her fork off her plate she had to field the next question about her sailing experiences.

"What did Rikk mean by both definitions of boom?" asked one.

Kara had just taken a bite of her salad, and held her fingers to her mouth motioning that she would answer after she had swallowed. Rikk, seeing her predicament, explained, "The boom is what the bottom of the sail attaches to, and it swings out from the mast; and *boom* is the sound it made when it hit her head." Laughter sounded from all at the table except from Heidi.

Heidi rolled her eyes and said, "The *foot* of the sail attaches to the boom."

The table became silent. Everyone stared at Heidi, then to Rikk and Kara. Heidi wielded command in this group, and Rikk could see most of them found it as overbearing as he did. Heidi took over the conversation at every opportunity by interjecting explanations of sailing terms. With an artificial civil inflection, she challenged Kara with technical sailing questions. Unruffled by Heidi's unrelenting nautical examination, Kara answered all her questions as politely and in easily comprehended terms so all those present would understand Heidi's questions as well as her own responses. Heidi seemed to resign to the fact she could not distress Kara with her questions, so she changed her tactic by diverting all topics discussed on the table to her own medical experiences at every possible opening. Barb, Joe, Zoey, Eric, and Rikk all maintained a polite, uninterested involvement in Heidi's dissertations and inquired about the families and interests of the others at the table whenever Heidi took a bite or a breath. Even though other subjects were discussed, Heidi continued to steer the conversation and send covert jabs in Kara's direction whenever possible.

One of the nurses asked Rikk, "How did your replantation surgery go?"

Before Rikk could answer, Heidi tilted her head and pasted her smile on. "You must feel so lost while we discuss medical procedures that you have no knowledge of, especially one that has a dual meaning. Replantation, Kara, to a landscaper or gardener means to cover an area of land with plants or transplant plants. I'm sure you know this. However, in the medical field, replantation is a term used when a surgeon reattaches a patient's severed limb. With the use of microsurgery to reconnect nerves and blood vessels, most fingers, arms, and toes can be successfully reattached."

Rikk turned red and was about to counter attack, when he felt Kara's hand patting his knee. He was impressed how dignified Kara was to Heidi's rude inquisition. Rikk set his fork down, reached under the table, and squeezed Kara's hand.

Kara dabbed her napkin to her mouth, smiled at Heidi, and calmly replied, "Thank you Heidi, for your concern about my feelings. Actually, for the most part, everyone is choosing terms that I do understand and, just like you, they're explaining those that I may not understand."

Heidi waved over a server pouring champagne, extended her glass to him, and said, "To the top, please." She sent her glamorous smile to the whole table, sipped from her glass and then tilted her head to Kara. "Choosing terms. Well, Kara, you sound like that book Rikk quoted. What was the quote, Rikk? Something about choice?" Heidi chuckled.

Rikk saw Kara bite her lip and stare down at the table. He wanted to tell Heidi she didn't have the capacity ever to receive the Lauren Harmon Scholarship and wondered if that was on Kara's mind as well. Without taking his eyes off Kara, Rikk said, "Choose in every aspect and moment of your life."

Barb said, "I think the point that the author was making is to listen to your heart and intuition to decide what choices are the right ones to make. It is a good reminder for those of us who have read and understood the message in *Be in Choice*. I highly recommend the book to everyone."

Kara did not look up; she swallowed and said nothing. The silence that followed was excruciating, though it was short-lived. Joe was leaning back in his chair, which he had pushed away from the table to observe the conversation. Unruffled and serene, he cleared his throat and said, "The band is tuning up. I think our department needs to be the first to make its appearance on the dance floor."

"I am looking forward to dancing with my favorite man," Barb winked at Joe and gave Kara a genuine smile as she played into Joe's tactful diversion.

Joe's eyes twinkled as he pursued her invitation, "Barb, may I have the honor of the first dance?"

"Oh, I was hoping you would ask." Barb playfully batted her eyelashes at him. "Let me check my dance card."

"May I suggest that we all finish our dinners and take to the dance floor," Joe announced to all at the table.

Heidi directed her genteel smile to Rikk and then flashed it to everyone at the table.

Rikk appreciated Joe and Barb's diversion from the conversation and for the peace that it instilled, giving everyone time to finish eating. The sooner Kara and he finished eating, the sooner they could escape Heidi's domineering presence.

❧❦❧

The band played classical music during their meal. When the next song started, Kara said, "This music always reminds me of Christmas."

"It's the *Waltz of the Flowers* from the Nutcracker," Barb said.

"Oh, sure. I remember ice skating to this when I was a kid."

Rikk stood and held out his hand. In a playful tone, he said, "Kara, may I have this dance?"

She placed her hand in his, "Yes, I would love that."

Rikk practically paraded her onto the dance floor, and Kara looked a little self-conscious. He figured for Heidi's benefit it was worth it. Rikk placed his hand on Kara's back and immediately began to waltz. Kara fell into step flawlessly with him, as if together they amassed energy from their united stand against Heidi's barrage of attacks.

"Kara, I'm sorry about Heidi—"

"Shhh. I don't want to spoil this moment by thinking about her," Kara interrupted.

As they danced the next few measures, their eyes held each other in wonder at their harmonized steps. They relaxed as the waltz charmed them away from the table conversation. Rikk drew Kara toward him while stepping in her direction. This initiated the first of a continuous string of twirling waltz steps. Kara easily followed Rikk's strong lead. Her dress whirled as they floated over the entire dance floor.

"I was hoping you'd ask me to dance, but I confess that I was worried. I wasn't sure if I'd be able to figure out the right steps." Kara said.

"Really?

"If the next music played is either a two-step or fox trot; I'm not sure I'll be able to pick up the correct step."

"I doubt you'll have any problem," Rikk said, pulling her closer to him.

As they wove around the dance floor, neither Rikk or Kara noticed the other dancers' glances. When the music ended, Rikk once again spun her around, this time a full revolution. She faced him bearing an impish smile. As impetuously as he had been to spin her moments ago, Kara pinched the skirt of her dress and curtsied to him. The laughter and clapping made both of them aware they had captured the attention of the other dancers near them. Rikk was amused when Kara blushed and shot him an embarrassed smile.

Kara looked flustered from the attention, and it reminded him that Barb had said how conspicuous she felt attending the benefit in the first place. On an impulse that he found inexplicable, Rikk spun her around to face the other dancers. Her toe grazed the floor, and she literally tripped over her own foot. He caught her and almost made her stumble go unnoticed. He saw the next wave of crimson rush onto her cheeks as she looked at the dancers still watching them. They were clapping, and now laughing at her stumble. Rikk's eyes remained fixed on her, and his grin staved off his own laughter. "Bow," he said.

"What?"

"Bow." He was proud to be with her, and felt happy. He hoped she knew it—he wanted her to feel it, and maybe she did. With merriment, she curtsied to those standing around them. It was stiffer with a smaller genuflection and noticeable embarrassment. Kara laughed and mouthed *thank you* to the other dancers. Kara opened her eyes wide to Rikk, telegraphing her need to leave the dance floor—and flee from the center of attention. He loved that about her.

Rikk wondered if she knew she had captured him. As far as he was concerned, he never wanted to be released.

As they walked off the floor, Kara said, "Thanks for catching me."

"Thanks for dancing with me," was all he said, but there was so much more for which he was thankful.

Chapter 30

Kara

Intermittent conversations with interesting people filled the night. Kara realized she enjoyed herself more than she'd imagined possible. She found most people she'd met led intriguing lives, both in and out of their professions. The evening was winding down, and many people were leaving. They had just chatted with the hospital chair and her husband, who were making the rounds to greet everyone before the event ended. Rikk had asked her to dance several times but, with so many people stopping to visit with him and share a story about Lauren, they had only made it back onto the dance floor once. Kara had learned a great deal about Lauren and her extraordinary compassion; she would've loved knowing Lauren too.

Kara excused herself to the ladies' room. When she walked into the powder room to refresh her makeup, she reflected on Rikk's speech. His words overwhelmed her, but she also rejoiced in his new maxim. This wasn't the time or place to tell Rikk how affected she was with his speech—or why. However, she knew she'd have to tell him soon.

Through the arched door to the restrooms, she could see a woman applying lipstick and talking to someone who occupied a lavatory stall. "You don't really think she's—" The woman pulled the lipstick from her lip and stopped mid-sentence when she noticed Kara. She stared for a moment, stunned silent. Kara waited for a lavatory to open with that sinking feeling that she'd interrupted gossip being said at her expense.

Heidi's voice sounded tipsy as it emerged from one of the stalls, "He is just like a little boy with a brand new toy and Mrs. McKee is more than happy to teach him how to play with it. She looks more than ready to fulfill his grown man desires too. I'm sure Mrs. McKee would make a entertaining adventure for him. She has the best of both worlds, like that book, what was it? Oh, yeah, *Be in Choice*. Rikk thinks she's a good choice, but besides sailing, what do they have in common? Nothing! She sure isn't in tune with Rikk's career. When he tires of Mrs. McKee, *and he will*, I'll be there. I'll be the one going home with him, spending our evenings discussing new procedures and difficult cases—not basic sailing terms."

"Heidi, um, you, uh" the woman stammered.

Kara was too taken aback to follow the advice of the voice in her head, telling her to say something—anything to Heidi—if only to help Heidi's friend out of a difficult predicament. However, she was too stunned to even swallow, much less talk or even move.

"What?" Heidi said to her friend but didn't pause for her reply. "And did you see her after he gave his speech?"

The woman whom Heidi was talking to stared at Kara. Mortification showed in her widened eyes as her mouth hung agape. She managed to send a sharp warning, "Heidi."

"She was so *overcome* with emotion! A bit dramatic, don't you think? How embarrassing for Rikk. I'm shocked that he fell for someone so intellectually beneath him. Hmm! I wonder if being beneath him is his choice or hers." Heidi cackled.

"Heidi, people's professions and lifestyles do not quantify their intelligence—nor do they give credence to your double entendre." She tossed her lipstick into her purse and looked apologetic as she left. Her heels clacked over the marble floor until they hit the carpet in the powder room. She pulled the door open with so much force that Kara grimaced. God, she didn't want a head-on collision when Heidi emerged from the stall. But before she could follow this woman out of the powder room, Barb came out of the other stall wearing a disgusted expression. When their eyes met, Kara froze. Anything Barb said would only result in an uncomfortable scene, and Kara was barely holding herself together after hearing Heidi's cruel words.

Before Kara could flee, Heidi emerged, and the three women stared at each other in a shocked silence. Kara heard Barb's voice tremble with restraint as she said, "Heidi, you need to grow up! Do you have any idea how utterly ridiculous you are? I didn't believe a professional woman with your skills could be so malicious. You have so much to learn, and I'm not talking about new procedures and difficult cases." Barb shook her head, and blew a heavy sigh out.

Kara turned for the door, but before she darted out, she saw Heidi actually lower her head. Kara fled the ladies' room. Her brisk flee to the exit doors was accompanied with hope that she could escape without bringing attention to herself. She didn't want to shed tears or give any energy to Heidi's words. Kara needed to escape for a few minutes and regain her composure. Heidi did not, and would not ever control her destiny. All the hurtful and manipulative ways of others could not ruffle her, unless she allowed it. As hard as she resisted—she had allowed Heidi to ruffle her. A bit of fresh air and solitude was what Kara needed to regain a peaceful, or at least an accepting spirit.

Kara sat on a bench outside the club, breathing deeply and regaining her poise. A fleeting thought crossed her mind to walk to Sir Benedict's Tavern nearby and call a cab. No, she would not run away, even as much as she dreaded going back in and seeing Heidi. She knew she couldn't walk out on Rikk like this. Being gracious to Heidi might just be the greatest challenge she'd face in her relationship with Rikk. She drew in a breath and resolved to take the high road. Kara stood up to return to the club when she saw Barb walk out the door. "Barb, I'm fine. It is never easy to hear what people say about you behind your back."

"No, but she's ridiculous and immature."

"I know. But I allowed her to get to me, didn't I?"

"Kara, I'm not defending Heidi, but maybe you can comprehend her juvenile behavior if you're aware of her life and what she gave up to become one of the best surgeons in the department at the youngest age that Joe's ever known. Heidi was not only the high school class valedictorian of a very elite private school; she was at the top of her class all through undergrad and med school. Being a woman in a still predominately male field, she's been forced to be competitive as all med students are, especially women." Barb sighed, "But she has taken competiveness to a new height and doesn't know how else to act. Like most new surgeons finally done with school and interning, she is working hard to establish herself in a practice. She's just waking up and discovering that she has had no life, and few social skills. Heidi—more than anyone Joe has ever worked with—*hasn't* had time to develop them. I'm probably less tolerant than Joe is, but in my estimation, her maturity level is ten or so years behind her age. I'm not sure why she fixated on Rikk, but *you* are the competition that is keeping her from what she wants. With about the only skill that she knows—and the one that has served her so well—she is competing with you for Rikk."

"Competing is her only social skill?"

"Just about. She's been competing—and winning—all her life. But she doesn't know what to do with the men she's dated once she's won their undivided attention. She's known around the hospital for subscribing to the catch and release program."

"Does Rikk know all this?"

"He does now, but not before Heidi turned her attention to him. Kara, this is Heidi's first medical practice. Besides working to be the best surgeon in a new practice, she is trying to fill the voids that are in her life. She started here about the same time Lauren was diagnosed with cancer. When Lauren stopped in to see Rikk, she met Heidi a couple times—both brief and forgettable. Heidi was aloof to everyone at first, especially to Rikk after Lauren passed away—probably because she didn't know how to act. Something happened at the beginning of this year, and she's taken an interest in him—a one eighty from how she was at first."

"So Heidi has been coming on to Rikk for months? How does he handle it?"

"Ignoring her is all he has strength or patience for. Joe has offered to talk to Heidi, but Rikk thinks she'll get the message sooner or later. Sadly, it's been later—actually never."

"I'm glad you told me this. Though, I feel about as ridiculous as Heidi has acted tonight."

"Hmm." Barb smiled at Kara, "Go easy on yourself, Kara. How often do you have someone who is so malevolent, spiteful, and—"

"Please stop," Kara interrupted Barb and shook her head. She forced a pleading smile.

"Stop?"

"Barb, to finish that sentence would be name-calling, and I don't want either of us to sink to that level. I understand her better and feel sorry for her. She's given up all the other areas of her life for her career. Wow! I have all kinds of negative things I could say about Heidi, and it would feel good to say them for a second. Then I would be doing exactly what she just did to me, and I'd feel guilty and defeated in the end. It's sad. It sounds like she lacks confidence in herself and drags others down to build herself up."

"You are right about the confidence. She has an abundance of it as a surgeon but really lacks it socially. It's really hard to witness such poor behavior."

"Well, if we're going to talk about bad behavior, I'd better examine mine. Don't you think it was pretty sophomoric the way I ran out of the ladies' room?"

"Oh, Kara, it's been a stressful day for both Rikk and you. Rikk didn't even remember he had this benefit tonight."

"All right, I admit it's been a stressful day for both of us. But it was so hard to hear Heidi say—almost verbatim—my fears that I told you in the car."

"Yes, I suppose it was. You've looked completely comfortable around everyone tonight, even with Heidi gunning at you every chance she's had during dinner."

"I've been very comfortable around everyone, except her." Kara blew out a cleansing breath. "She was successful in finding my Achilles heel, wasn't she?" Kara, comforted by Barb's words, was bouncing back from Heidi's attack. She reached for the door handle and held the door for Barb.

"Are you OK, Kara?"

"Yes, I'm fine. But it did take some of the luster out of the evening."

"Just don't allow her to spoil your night. I really am impressed with your ability to roll with the punches. We need more of that in this world."

"Well, I'm still feeling a little shaken by Heidi's words. Nevertheless, 'No one can make you feel inferior without your consent.' Eleanor Roosevelt said that, and those words are so much more powerful than anything that Heidi has said."

"You are strong," Barb said and grinned.

"I feel like I'm just getting my strength back. I don't know how I became so lost. I need to use the ladies' room, so I guess it's time to gather my courage and go back in."

Barb walked into the ballroom and Kara detoured to the ladies' room. Kara was relieved that the powder room and lavatory stalls were empty. She brushed her hair and washed her hands while she firmed up her resolve to be true to herself no matter what curve balls Heidi lobbed her way. She smiled at her reflection in the mirror, stood tall and pivoted on her toes, and then headed out the door.

With confidence, Kara walked back into the main room, smiling as she scanned the floor for Rikk. There he was, dancing with someone. With his back to Kara, Rikk's dance partner was hidden behind him. Kara smiled and felt a rush of joy. She loved dancing—although tonight it had been fun to dance with only Rikk. She hoped that there would be many dances in their future—and dancing with other friends too. She saw Barb and Joe a few feet away looking on. Barb looked irritated as she scrutinized Rikk. Kara followed Barb's gaze out to witness Heidi in Rikk's arms. Though his face showed annoyance, he nonetheless had consented to dance with her.

Kara's saboteur, Hisser, was laughing. His lethal weapon was the words he sarcastically spewed, *Be in choice, Kara, be in choice.* Those words activated her anger and jealousy, and mostly her fear that Heidi had manipulated Rikk. Maybe Heidi was right after all; maybe Rikk would tire of her once he learned to sail. Maybe she couldn't carry a conversation that would hold his interest, and he'd tire of explaining replantation and other surgeries to her. Kara's gut ached and her confidence dissolved. She turned quickly, hoping the Watsons had not seen her, and slinked back to the table where her bolero hung on the chair back. She sat down, staring at her lap as she tried to talk herself back to an accepting attitude towards Heidi. Instead Kara thought, *Screw Heidi. No matter how manipulative she is. Rikk accepted her offer to dance. Why would he do that?* Kara's head ached, and her heart felt stabbed. *Don't jump to conclusions.* She knew she should allow Rikk to explain, but this was more than she could take. Kara slumped and rested her forehead against her hand. Kara looked up to see Rikk approaching.

"Kara, there you are. Are you feeling all right?"

"Yes, I'm fine." Her words were cold and disingenuous.

"Fine?" Rikk mocked.

"I'm feeling tired, and my head is aching. Rikk, I've had a wonderful evening, but it is getting late, and I do need to get up early tomorrow morning to sail *Genie* to Bayfield. Would you mind taking me back to the marina?" Kara asked in the most unaffected tone that she could muster.

Rikk studied Kara for a moment as disgust washed over him. "You saw me dancing with Heidi?" Kara rolled her eyes. "Let me explain, Kara. Barb said Heidi—"

"Barb told you what Heidi said?"

"What?" He scowled at her, but Kara only shook her head at him. In an insistent tone, he said, "What did you say?"

"How could you dance with her?" Kara rubbed her forehead, and then winced in pain. In a steady voice she said, "How could you dance with Heidi after Barb told you what she said?"

Rikk sat down next to Kara and stared at the ceiling before his paced words demanded an answer. "What did Heidi say?" Kara gritted her teeth and glared, and he said, "Kara, what did she say?"

"Didn't Barb tell you?"

"Barb said she was going to encourage Joe to take disciplinary action against Heidi—better yet, fire her. I asked her why, and she said she'd tell me later. Then Heidi came over, and I took her arm and said, 'Let's dance.' She actually refused," Rikk said, spitting his words out at Kara.

Kara couldn't believe her ears. "You asked *her* to dance?"

"Not like that. Come on, Kara; this is Heidi we're talking about."

"Rikk, you don't owe me an explanation, and this is not the place to have this discussion anyway. Please, I just want to go back to *Genie's Bottle*."

"OK, let's go."

⚓︎

Kara stood up and rushed toward the door. Rikk stood transfixed for a moment. He grabbed her bolero that she left on the chair and walked fast to catch up to her. They walked in silence, and once they were outside, Rikk handed his parking stub to the valet attendant. She could tell he wanted to explain why he asked Heidi to dance, but she was not in a place where she could even listen. It took a lot to push her over the line, but when she was over it, nothing but solitude could bring her back. She hated that about herself. Rikk raked his hand through his hair. She looked away; she couldn't stand to see how hurt he was. When the car pulled up, Kara rushed to the passenger door. Before Rikk could open it for her, Kara opened it and climbed in. Rikk slammed it shut and walked around the back of the car. After driving a few blocks Rikk finally broke the silence, "Kara, I'm sorry. I never meant to hurt you."

"I know that, Rikk. I just am so tired. It really is a bad time for me to talk. I need a timeout, or I'm apt to say something that I will regret later."

The space between them felt insurmountable to Kara. Her headache wasn't caused by her bump, but it throbbed now for the first time since Friday. Kara felt confused. So much of the time she spent with Rikk felt as if she was going with the flow, but this moment she felt she was paddling upstream, fighting the current. Why did Rikk and her attempts for intimacy continually end with a detour? In a flash, she got her answer. Kara could not have an honest and open relationship with a man she most feared sharing her hidden identity with. Why the hell did this happen? What was she supposed to learn from this whole mess?

Rikk parked the car at the marina. They sat in silence. Rikk was unsure of where he stood with Kara, or if she wanted anything to do with him. Unsure about what to say, Rikk said, "Kara, I'll walk you to *Genie*."

"No. I really need—I really need a timeout."

"A timeout?"

"Yes. I really need a very long timeout."

"What does that mean for us, Kara?"

Kara shut her eyes and laid her head back onto the headrest. Her voice was tense but quiet as she said, "Rikk, please trust that the right thing for both of us will happen. Please."

"Aren't you even interested in listening to why I danced with Heidi?"

Kara shook her head, reached for the door handle and unlatched it but didn't open the door.

"What was it that you said about saboteurs being in control? You don't have to say anything, but you owe it to me to listen to my explanation," Rikk said.

"Rikk, I just can't do this. I don't belong in your world, and I really need to be alone right now."

"What the hell does that mean, my world? Kara, do you know how silly you sound? That's something right out of an outdated romance novel."

"Thank you." She glared at him then turned away.

"Well, I could say the same thing, couldn't I? I jumped into sailing without anything more than a life-long fascination with something I don't know hardly anything about. Hell, I had just started reading about it, and then I bought a boat. But I don't feel like I don't belong in your world because I—"

"OK, all right. It was stupid of me to say that. But there is more to my world you don't know about, and maybe—" Kara stopped and blew her breath out across her upper lip.

"Maybe?" Rikk waited for her to finish, but she stared out the passenger window. "Kara, don't I get to figure out who belongs in my world? I'm sorry I danced with Heidi."

Except for the quiet, insistent thud of Rikk's fingers tapping on his leg, emphasizing time ticking away as he waited for Kara's answer, the silence between them ensued. Her gaze fixed out the passenger window as Kara's shallow and reticent voice spoke, "You deserve someone who can understand your life."

"Like Heidi?"

Anger blazed as Kara spun around. "NO! Nothing like Heidi, but not me either. She is right about one thing; I don't have much in common with you. I don't have the courage to tell you—" She froze, shocked that she almost exposed her history. Kara was not in the state of mind to tell Rikk what she so carefully guarded from him. She felt herself shake. She recaptured her loose tongue in the nick of time, but not her calm.

"The courage to tell me what?" His knuckles turned white as he grasped the steering wheel. "You don't have anything in common with me? When did she say that? Is that what you thought Barb told me?" Rikk's face was red and he raked his hand through his hair. "That's bullshit, Kara. Heidi has only one thing in common with me. She only has one thing in her whole life. Every man she's dated has just been a project for her to advance the only thing she's got going for her—her career. She's the best surgeon we've got, but that's all she's got." He huffed, "And I can't believe you'd think I'm only interested in my career. Jesus! Do we have to have everything in common?"

Kara's forced breaths, deep and deliberate, slowed her heart rate. Once again composed, she said, "You're right—it is bullshit. Maybe you are right about my saboteur being in control. I can't ignore that almost every time you and I have begun to get close we've had an interruption. Maybe Heidi is just another one of those interruptions. I don't know what to make of any of it. Maybe this is as far as we are supposed to go, and we need to be thankful for what we have learned from each other. Maybe we shouldn't want more."

Rikk stared at Kara in disbelief. He shook his head and with a husky whisper, he said, "Maybe I want more."

Kara sat motionless. One push and the door would be open, and she would be out of there. "I honestly don't know what I want. I do know when things are right, they flow and come easily."

"I think our relationship has flowed easily. Could it be that all the interruptions are happening to keep you here so we can spend this time getting to know each other?"

"Or could it be that all the interruptions are happening to keep us from getting too close? Maybe I'm here just to get you unstuck. Maybe there is someone out there who is perfect for you."

"For God's sake, Kara, you couldn't be more wrong."

"Rikk, I'm so sorry, but I need time to sort it all out. Maybe we *are* meant for each other, and I really believe that it will happen if we are. I'm not a jealous person and see jealousy as a form of control, not love, or trust. So seeing you with Heidi tonight stirred a jealous emotion in me that I've rarely felt in my entire life. That bothers me, and I need to figure out where that came from. I don't want to try to control you, or anybody. I really do need a timeout, Rikk. Please understand. I know that I want—" Kara was petrified of telling Rikk what she wanted. Being petrified was an emotion she didn't tolerate.

Rikk watched Kara and waited for her to finish her sentence. When she started to push on the car door Rikk said, "Kara, tell me what you want!"

Kara did not look at Rikk and swung open the door. She ran towards the docks until she was out of the sight of Rikk's car. As she retreated down the dock, she heard his car peel out of the parking lot. She shut her eyes and whispered, "Drive safe, Rikk. Please drive safe." She blinked tears from her eyes and felt them trickle down her cheeks. God, she hated feeling like a drama queen, and she hated more that Heidi was right when she insinuated that she was one. A long timeout would be required to sort out the last four days.

Rikk

Rikk drove over the lift bridge and stopped for a red light. He looked over at the empty passenger seat and noticed Kara's bolero. He was livid that he hadn't told Kara what he said to Heidi, and furious that he hadn't made her listen. He needed her to know. The light turned green, and his tires squealed when he sped through the intersection. He took several deep breaths and slowed down. When he got to the intersection at Lake Avenue and Railroad Street, he knew he had to turn around. During Kara's self-imposed timeout, she needed to mull over what he told Heidi. He pulled into a hotel parking lot, turned around, and drove back to the marina. He grabbed the bolero off the seat and marched to *Genie's Bottle*. Rikk knocked on the hatch as he opened it, not allowing Kara a chance send him away.

Kara sat at the dinette facing the companionway, black mascara smudges smeared below her red swollen eyes, tears again began to well and spill over as she wiped them off her cheeks. She looked up at Rikk and an audible cry escaped her. She covered her mouth and snatched another tissue from the box on the table.

Rikk waited for Kara to compose herself before he told her what she needed to know. He was angry, but seeing her in agony made him ache. He walked over and knelt down at her side, and put his hand on her shoulder. Rikk felt Kara stiffen, and immediately knew he needed to give her space. He sat down across from Kara and set her bolero onto the table. "I brought you your jacket."

Kara nodded her head but did not talk.

Rikk leaned his elbows on his knees and sat in silence. At last he looked up at her and began, "Kara, I told Heidi—" Rikk paused and lifted Kara's chin, so she would look into his eyes. "I told her that you and I are seeing each other."

Kara nodded her head but still did not respond. She lowered her eyes again.

Rikk felt as if he were dying as Kara's words about his world replayed in his head. "Tell me why you feel that you don't belong in my world?"

Kara dabbed her eyes and blew her nose. She looked like she was trying to formulate her thoughts, trying to choose the right words. Rikk was growing impatient, "Please, Kara, talk to me. Tell me what that means. What world do you think I live in that you don't belong in?"

She blurted out through tears, "It's not your world, or you, or your career, or the f-ing medical profession, or even Heidi. It's me—it's my world. You won't like me once you get to know who I really am."

"That has got to be the most ludicrous thing you've ever said. That's definitely your saboteur talking."

"Well, maybe my saboteur is protecting me!"

She sounded so childish Rikk knew he should back off, but he couldn't let Kara get by saying something that he knew she didn't believe. "It isn't protecting you. Isn't that what you said? People sometimes *think* their saboteurs protect them when they are really tricking them to play small?"

"Rikk, we have known each other for four days. It has been a whirlwind, starting with making the best of a bad situation to physical attraction. It has been one calamity to the next, and now we are both caught up in the thrill of sensuality."

Rikk glared at her, "The thrill of sensuality?" He paused and scowled, shaking his head, "Is that what you call falling in love?"

Through the new flood of tears Kara croaked, "This all has happened so fast. I need time. I need to get this damn boat delivered and some normal routine established at home. I need to get on my feet."

"When you have all that done, do you think I won't like you?"

"You see, you insist on arguing, and I'm saying things that I regret. I can't think, and I don't even know why. I'm jealous over Heidi—jealous! Over Heidi! I'm on a damn yo-yo. I think some space and time is needed by both of us to figure out what we want, and how we really feel about each other."

"Kara, when I met Lauren I knew instantly that I couldn't live without her. I've never met a woman other than Lauren who turned my world upside down like that. I never thought it possible to find another. Lauren is gone, and I haven't stopped missing her, not even in the last four days. But you've turned my world upside down, and I'm feeling things again that I haven't since Lauren died."

"Oh, Rikk, maybe we were put into each other's lives for a short time to help each other—you to start living again, rather than just existing each day filled with loneliness and grief. I need to figure out what my next career move is. Tomorrow morning I leave for Bayfield, and you will go back to your job. If our paths are meant to cross again, they will."

"So this is it? One minute you want some time and the next you expect me to walk out and wait and see if our paths cross again?"

"Rikk, you don't know me that well. You've seen me struggle to stay on my best behavior. You think you love me, but there are so many things you don't know about me. Maybe I'm wrong to say that I don't belong in your world, but you know so little of my world—of my life. I worry that our lives are not compatible."

"Compatible? When you let down your defenses, you seem incredibly compatible to me."

"There are things about me that would send you running in the opposite direction."

"What things?"

"Things that I don't like to even think about."

"You make it sound like you are some kind of a criminal."

Kara said nothing, just shook her head, and stared at her hands. At last she whispered, "No, not criminal. But they are—"

"What?"

"I don't know how to explain. They are just things I'm not proud of. They aren't anything bad, just things I'm embarrassed to admit."

"Kara, we all have things we are embarrassed to admit. That is no reason to turn your back on me."

"Rikk, please, please let me have some time." Kara buried her face in her hands and shook her head, then whispered, "Please."

⚜

Rikk stared at her. He shook his head and looked away. There it was, on the shelf, the book *Be in Choice*. Rikk took the book and opened it to the dedication. He looked at Kara who sat motionless with her eyes transfixed on her lap. He pondered what to say next, but the voice in his head kept insisting that he go with his gut feeling. He gave in to the voice and spoke, "Kara, the dedication in this book sounds so much like the things you've told me, and finally I am starting to understand them. Let me read the dedication to you, and then I promise I will leave if you want me to." Kara froze while Rikk began to read.

To my readers:

Fifteen years ago, I had a chance encounter with a stranger. The circumstances of our brief association gave me infrequent meetings with him, and always in the accompaniment of other people. I'll never know if he knew the impact his quiet reserve, his warm but guarded smile, and his patient, kind manner had on me.

Years later, his small and sincere gesture inspired a character who began to evolve into *Be in Choice*. At times, I've hoped he innately knows he has helped someone without ever knowing whom, why, or how he did it. I have no ridiculous notion to divulge this to him.

For a few years, I thought of him often, until I discovered the Seven Essene Mirrors. When I came to understand the third mirror, I understood my long-held memory of him was a mirror back to me of something that I had lost as a child and had given away as an adult.

As for me, I've worked hard to change the things in my life that have been unfulfilling. Thankfully, a friend introduced me to attracting all that I wanted into my life—like health, loving relationships, spirituality, career satisfaction, and even abundance. Applying my friend's wisdom, I've discovered not only what I want but also how my choices are responsible for the changes I've made and the person I've become. Most important though, it helped me learn that I create the life I deserve *by choice—not by chance.*

We all mold and form our lives by our choices. Some choices we make by default; that is, we don't know we can choose something different. Some we make unconsciously; that is, continuing down the same path because it's always been done that way, or we choose not to choose and let others choose for us. Either way, we're afraid or too passive to make a different choice. However, the best choices are those that we make consciously; that is, we choose by tapping into our intuitive wisdom and spirit to discover our authentic path.

My wish for all who read this novel is you find the courage to change your life and make new choices that bring you the goodness you deserve. I hope everyone will be kinder, more caring, and giving in all the encounters that they have. What may seem a chance encounter may instead be a synchronistic opportunity for you to choose your actions consciously. I hope you enjoy *Be in Choice,* and I hope it propels you on your own authentic journey long after you've read it. Most of all, I wish for all of you that you be in choice, so you may attract all that you desire and deserve in your life.

Audrey Lynn

As Rikk read the last few lines, Kara turned away. He watched her as he waited for her response. "Kara, the last part sounds like things you've said." Kara looked mortified. "Is there something about this book—something between Connor and you? Is that why you clam up every time I mention Lauren and it in the same sentence?" Kara fidgeted, looking down. "Oh. It's confidential. You know the author—you're the author's coach."

Finally Kara whispered, "Rikk, I really need to be alone. I'm leaving at six tomorrow morning. I need to get some sleep."

"Kara, I understand that you can't reveal your clients any more than I can reveal my patients. I'm sorry that I didn't figure that our earlier. That's it, isn't it?"

"Please, Rikk," she pleaded.

Rikk rose and walked to the companionway. He turned to see Kara blink tears from her eyes. He combed his hand through his hair, and this time his voice was angry. "I guess I should be happy for these last four days; happy that you've shown me that I can feel love again. But your actions contradict your beliefs, Kara. You've helped me see that I get to choose what I want and what path I go down. Up until now, you've been a great example of practicing what you preach. But if you're so damn sure that you want a timeout, then why are you sitting here bawling?" He watched despair consume Kara, yet she remained silent. In exasperation Rikk hurled his words like a spear, "Be in choice, Kara."

Kara covered her face with both hands and sobbed aloud.

"Kara, can't you see that what you want is right in front of you?" Rikk waited, giving her one last chance to invite him back. He wanted to hold her and comfort her. He wanted to be with her, but she did not want him. Anger welled inside of him until he could no longer contain it. "Kara, you don't know what the hell you want." With that, he stomped up the companionway, slammed the hatch, and jumped off the boat.

Kara

She couldn't erase the memory of Rikk's incredulous eyes, seeking an explanation from her. Her inner voices were competing for her attention. The virtuous voice, unlike her saboteur's voice, had her best interest at heart and whispered to Kara to run after him—to come clean with the truth and let the pieces fall where they may. The burden would be lifted no matter his reaction. Her terror-filled saboteur voice insisted that disclosing the truth would only bring her disapproval and humiliation from Rikk. She was completely bewildered. How could she tell him? She needed time to get her bearings. If they were meant to be with each other, she knew something would bring them together again. She heard his steps recede as he stomped down the dock. When the dock was silent, she said, "You, Rikk. I want you, but you don't know who I am. If you did, you wouldn't want me."

Chapter 31

Rikk

Rikk didn't sleep much after leaving Kara. Lying awake in bed while Kara occupied his mind was going to give him an ulcer. He had been so careful since Lauren died to guard his heart from being hurt again, but Kara broke into it and claimed a vast part of it as her own. Now she had abandoned it. If Kara called him, he'd tell her he couldn't trust her. She wouldn't get back into his life. *Oh, fuck! That's not what I really want.*

Rikk stared at the shadows created from the dim city lights that seeped into his bedroom, and he thought about his list that Kara had him make. No matter how hard he tried to keep his eyes closed and shut down all his thoughts of her to fall asleep, he only became more frustrated. He looked at his alarm clock, and watched it tick off minutes for hours. Even more frustrating was accepting that Kara's presence in his life had made many of his wants come true. At last, he knew now how he wanted their relationship to be—trusting and open yet honoring her client and his patient privileges. He'd clearly state his terms and allow Kara to choose him, or her silence.

The last time he remembered looking at the clock on his nightstand was at three in the morning. The cumulative lack of sleep over the last few days rendered Rikk physically exhausted and emotionally spent.

Kara

God, Kara was feeling so alone. In the past, she had felt that Connor was with her any time that she needed or wanted him. Tonight, more than ever, she wanted a memory of him to somehow guide her. Kara got up and

284

poked around the boat looking for something to remind her of Connor that would give her insight or a clear idea of what she should do.

As Kara rummaged around, she took off her dress and changed into the wicking base layer that she would wear on the trip home. She packed the dress, bolero jacket, and shoes away. All the while Kara wondered if she'd ever have a chance to tell Rikk the whole truth, and if he'd understand why she had protected herself by withholding it. Even though she'd never been dishonest with Rikk, Kara felt like she'd been deceitful to him by concealing the truth from him. She pulled out her jewelry box and tucked her necklace, bracelet, and earrings into their compartments.

When Kara shut the lid, her eyes caught on a wooden item that she'd forgotten about. It was a small rosewood canoe paddle that Connor had carved and then meticulously etched the word "Downstream" on it. He had given it to her when she wrestled with the thought of quitting her job even though it had grown stagnant. When Connor gave it to her, he told her to keep it in her pocket, and any time she felt uncertain about their cruise, to rub on the paddle like a worry stone. Every time she touched the paddle it would remind her to listen to her built-in guidance system—her emotions. When the idea to cruise came to them, they were still learning how their emotions guided them. They learned to identify the right path to take by understanding that their body's sensations were the reactions to their thoughts and actions. When they felt thrilling chills, tingly and good, they knew they were on the right path, but if they felt uncertain or queasy, they were on the wrong path.

Years earlier, when Connor and Kara started to pay attention to their bodies' responses to their emotions, they were amazed at how they were led to make the best choices and take the right actions. They finally understood that the universe provided all they needed and wanted when they let go of their paddles and floated downstream with the flow of the river. When they were open to the gifts offered, they jumped to receive the opportunities that manifested. Leading up to the day of their departure, Kara carried the paddle with her always, and it led her to their cruise. Whenever she felt uncertain when deliberating a complete career change and a new life void of the nine-to-five job security net, she'd take out the paddle and examine her fears. Hisser was present then, trying to keep her "safe." In reality, Hisser was scared and tried to keep her cemented in her stagnant life. She wondered why she stopped carrying it and then remembered that once in the Caribbean she rarely wore anything that had pockets.

Tonight Kara set the paddle on the galley counter and put the jewelry box away. It was late, and Kara was mentally and emotionally exhausted. Once again, she was wide-awake. She knew she could begin to quiet her brain by engaging in rudimentary activity. Although Kara had been ready to leave for days, she decided to recheck all the last-minute things on her passage preparation list that she'd relied on Connor to do all the years they sailed. She missed him. She also realized that a gift given from his death was the knowledge that she could stand on her own. Hell, she *was* standing on her own. Was it right to want more? And, what the hell was "more?"

Kara turned on the marine radio to listen to the weather forecast. The winds would be three to five knots from the north-northeast in the morning. If they were more northerly, they might be able to motor sail with the sails close-hulled. The winds were forecasted to clock around to east-southeast. That would push the low front out of the area and bring in warmer and dry weather. However, as the winds clocked to the east, they'd have to drop the sails and motor into the wind. With luck, the winds would clock around quick and build as they continued to the southeast. The mid-afternoon forecast called for south-southeast winds building to ten to fifteen knots. If the weather forecast proved true, later they would be able to sail on a close reach at about six knots. Providing the winds continued most of the day and into afternoon at that strength, the three of them would sail into Bayfield by four or five o'clock.

When Kara had all the preparations for the trip done she sat down on the settee. She rested her head on the back of the cushion, staring at the ceiling as her thoughts returned to Rikk. Why had all this happened? Then she realized what "more" was. It was standing independent—and at the same time standing with someone and sharing her life with that one person. She looked at her watch and groaned; it was two thirty. She pulled a blanket over her eyes and drifted off to sleep.

Kara woke with a start as she felt *Genie* slightly heel over as someone boarded her and gave three insistent knocks on the hull. Kara's alarm hadn't gone off, and she was disoriented. *What time is it? Oh, God, is this Rikk?* Her heart pounded, and she wasn't sure if she was afraid it was him, or afraid it wasn't. Kara watched the hatch open. It was Dutch. He was stepping down the companionway as she pushed herself up from the settee.

"Dutch, what are you doing?" Kara couldn't contain her shock that he barged in without an invitation.

Dutch interrupted Kara and began his stern lecture, "I ain't gonna let you sail away from Doc without telling you you're making the mistake of your life."

"It is convoluted, Dutch, and thorny."

Dutch growled at Kara. "Hell, everything's thorny."

"Oh, Dutch, if you only knew. Some things are just too complex to explain. Even if there is no intent to hurt anyone, sometimes your actions and words just do. At times, less is best. This time, Dutch, less *is* best," Kara sighed and shook her head.

"Less is best? Sounds like you got a secret."

"I guess I do."

"Everybody got a secret, Miss Kara, but the thing is—usually ain't no big deal to nobody except the person keeping it," Dutch dabbed his watering eyes as he spoke with regret.

Dutch's remorseful voice echoed through Kara. She shivered. She had never heard Dutch call her Miss Kara before now. *That's it! That's the missing clue.* Kara saw Dutch clearly.

"Charlie! Who is Charlie, Dutch? You were singing a song the other night about Charlie. Is Charlie a woman?" Misery washed over Dutch's face and gave away his long-kept secret. "Dutch, who is Miss C? Who is the C?" Dutch fidgeted, and Kara pressed him, "That's it, isn't it Dutch? S-E-A was how you disguised capital C. The woman who broke your heart, Dutch; her name begins with C, doesn't it? Her name is Charlie." Kara was proud of her detective work, until she saw that she'd been oblivious to Dutch's discomfort.

Dutch

Dutch sat down on the companionway stairs, with his elbows on his knees he cradled his forehead in his hands. Kara kneeled down next to him, rested her hand on his shoulder, and said, "I'm sorry, Dutch. You don't have to answer."

Dutch knew the time had arrived to reveal his secret. He swallowed hard, but couldn't ease the pain in his throat. He knew that telling Kara what had caged him nearly his entire life would make that lump in his throat a little more bearable, and just maybe he could make her see what she was doing to herself, and to Rikk. "Kara, I ain't never talked to nobody about this and never planned to neither, but I can't just sit around watching you do the same stupid thing I did to Charlotte. Her daddy owned the bank in the town I grew up in. I came from the wrong side of the railroad tracks, so they forbid her from seeing me. Didn't stop us; she'd sneak down to the river behind their backs. She got pregnant and wanted to run away with me, but I didn't have two nickels to rub together. I knew she'd never make it scraping together an existence with me, and it wasn't fair to ask that of her, especially since that ain't no way to raise a child."

"Dutch, you have a child?"

Dutch nodded yes and returned his head to his hands. He told himself that grown men don't cry, and then coughed to get his voice back. "They sent Charlie to live with some relatives in Florida to hide her pregnancy, and then her uncle arranged a marriage for her with some rich, spoiled trust funder. I left town—had my family and hers madder at me than a swarm of hornets after you kicked their nest. Never went back, neither. I ran into a classmate some years later; he filled me in. He said Charlie got married and had a baby boy. Told me Charlie and the child spent summers at her parents', but her husband never came with them. Nobody has seen him for years; they don't think they are married anymore. Guess Charlie never talks about him or even goes to town much."

"Have you ever tried to contact Charlie?" asked Kara.

"Listen to yourself, Miss Kara! You hear my story and right away you ask if I'd ever contact her. Don't you see how you're running away from the Doc just like I ran away from Charlie? There's one big difference between us. Times have changed, Kara. Ain't nobody worth worrying about who gives one damn what side of town you come from anymore. It's what you make of yourself that counts. What you've done with and without Connor says more about your character than you give yourself credit for. Damn it, Kara, Doc's all in rut over you, and you're fluttering all over him."

"I think it's too late, Dutch. I'm guessing you overheard us last night. You heard how angry he was when he left. You don't know my past or how it will affect Rikk."

"You're making assumptions about Doc. I know one thing for sure, Kara, you leave this marina this morning, you be making the mistake of your life. Getting back ain't gonna be easy, either." Dutch stood and plodded up the companionway and off the boat.

She is as goddamn stubborn as I am. Well, I'll talk to the Doc. Hell, I owe it to him after all I put him through. He'd get them together if it was the last thing he did. It sure as hell was the most important thing he'd ever do.

Chapter 32

Kara

Kara stared out the porthole as Dutch strode up the dock towards the lobby. She shivered as she contemplated all that Dutch had said. Her gut ached. She knew he was right, but Dutch had no idea of what she hid or how Rikk unintentionally magnified it. Her alarm clock buzzed. She pulled her polar fleece on, lit the stove, and placed the teakettle on it.

The rosewood paddle, sitting on the counter, caught Kara's eye. She picked it up and rubbed it. It gave her clarity and a sense of calm. It became clear to Kara that she didn't fear Rikk; she feared divulging her past to him. Kara wanted to cancel the voyage to Bayfield and find Rikk, but she couldn't. Since Rikk would be working today, making the voyage was the right choice and she'd use the timeout to figure out how she would reveal all that she kept hidden. *My emotions guide me to do the right thing if I only choose to listen to them.* This time the right thing was not going to be easy because she didn't have any control over Rikk's reaction. Her mom's voice played in her head and reassured her with her message, "Always follow your heart."

Kara ground coffee beans, and then put them into the press pot. The tea pot whistled and Kara filled the press pot with boiling water. As the coffee steeped, she went topside to disconnect the shore power and stow the cord. For the first time in a week, Kara wanted thunderstorms and fierce winds. She wanted an excuse to stay, but the weather was good. She needed to trust the universe and know the perfect time and opportunity would present itself for her to reveal who she was to Rikk.

The sun warmed Kara as she admired the sky's brilliant display as the morning sun rose over the houses on Minnesota Point. It was filled with golden hues that were laced with soft magenta veins. Kara removed the dock lines, except for one bow and one stern line, coiled them, and then tossed them into the cockpit. She was about to step onboard *Genie* to stow them in the line locker when she stopped. She crouched next to *Genie*, and held onto the lifeline, resting her head on her hand. With her other hand she rubbed *Genie's* hull, and whispered, "OK, *Genie*. It's been a long time since I've asked you for anything. I need some help confessing my past to Rikk. Please look into his heart; if he loves me, help him understand why I've kept my secret. Please help him forgive me and find a way to love me again." She rubbed *Genie's* hull again and whispered, "And if he doesn't, please help me find a way to accept this and move on. Thank you, *Genie*."

At the sound of footsteps, Kara bounded to her feet. "Good morning," Ted said, "I brought you a cup of coffee." He handed the coffee cup down to Kara.

She watched him take a sip of coffee, and then scrunch his face. She smiled and asked, "How is it?"

Ted frowned, "Bad. But it's as good as you can get at the gas station by my house."

"From the face you pulled, I think I'll pass. I appreciate your thoughtfulness, but I have a press pot that's ready to be pressed. Feel free to dump yours out and have some of mine."

Ted stepped aboard with his backpack. Pete shuffled down the dock and stared at *Genie's* hull. Kara said good morning, and Pete sleepily replied good morning not changing his stare. "Not a morning person, are you, Pete?" Kara offered.

"No."

"Does coffee help?"

"Only sleep."

"Did you work late last night?"

"Yeah, I went to bed around three." Pete said.

"I guess you are tired. Let's get your stuff on board, and *Genie* out on the lake. Then you can go down and sleep. We'll each take two-hour shifts, so you can get four hours of sleep before your turn at the helm."

That brought Pete out of his exhausted state, and he stepped onboard. Kara turned on the instruments, while they stowed their backpacks. When they came topside, Kara started the engine while Ted removed the sail cover and attached the mainsail halyards. Pete took the fenders off the lifelines and threw them into the cockpit, and Kara stowed them in the lazarette locker. Kara let them know she was ready to go. Ted crossed back onto the dock and freed the last two lines from the cleats. Pete went up to the bow, coiled the bowline, and lashed it onto the lifeline. Ted walked *Genie's Bottle* out of the slip, jumping on at the end of the dock as Kara backed her out.

Kara looked over at Rikk's OSQ; her heart felt stabbed, and a spasm crunched her stomach. *I'll be back, Rikk, to tell you everything and let you decide if we have a future.* That statement lessened the pain, and she gave all her attention to navigating. Kara put *Genie* into forward and headed toward the marina opening, then looked at her watch; it was six twenty-five. Ted stood in the cockpit, grabbed his coffee cup from the wheel's drink holder. He took another swig without making a face, and looked back at Kara. She watched him drink and decided that the sooner she downed her coffee, the quicker it would bring some energy into her brain and body. She hoped it wouldn't aggravate the ache in the pit of her stomach. "How many times have you gone out of this harbor?" she asked Ted.

"You mean this year?"

"Well, I meant in your life, but from the way you answered I guess that this year might be a better question."

"My parents keep their boat on B dock. They've had a boat ever since I was a baby and have kept one here since I was about ten. I sail their boat more than they do; in fact, I think they'd have sold it if I didn't use it so much."

"I suppose I should hand the helm over to you since you have more experience here than I do." Kara said.

"It is kind of nice to stand around and let someone else steer. Besides, from what Dan told us, with all the countries and ports that you've been in, you have a lot more experience than I do."

"All right, I can see you are going to make me work. I am counting on you to speak up if you see a problem." Kara said. As they took *Genie* out of the marina she found out Ted was in his mid-twenties; he had sailed all his life with his parents, and had worked in the yard in the spring and fall when extra help was needed launching and hauling out boats. He supported himself with odd jobs and spent as much time as possible crewing boats in the winter in the Caribbean. Summers he worked in the boat yard and sailed and crewed on racing boats on Lake Superior.

She picked up the handheld radio and hailed, "Aerial Lift Bridge, Aerial Lift Bridge, Aerial Lift Bridge this is the sailing vessel *Genie's Bottle*."

"*Genie's Bottle*, this is the Aerial Lift Bridge. Six-eight," was the operator's response.

"Six-eight." Kara dialed it in on her radio. "*Genie's Bottle* on six-eight. Can you lift the bridge for us?"

"I'll give the bridge a lift. Aerial Lift Bridge monitoring on sixteen."

"*Genie's Bottle* monitoring on sixteen."

Genie's Bottle slipped into the canal and passed under the lifted bridge. Kara steered *Genie* out into the lake, and they settled into the voyage. Pete went below to sleep when Kara gave him the nod. A few hundred yards past the canal, Kara checked the wind direction and noticed that Ted was also looking at the wind indicator. The winds were almost due north.

"In the boat that I race on, we would raise the sails in this wind, but it is a lighter-built boat and designed for speed," Ted said.

"*Genie* needs about eight knots of wind to give her a push." Kara checked the wind speed. It was hovering between seven to eight knots. "We might pick up half a knot with the sails until the winds clock to the northeast and is on the nose. Let's raise them." Kara and Ted raised the sails and trimmed them close-hulled. If the winds clocked all the way to the south-southeast, as forecasted later in the day, then they would be able to shut the engine off and just sail.

Ted demonstrated his competence as a sailor, but Kara was more impressed with his respectful attitude and easygoing nature. Ted and Kara talked for a while about sailboats and their sailing experiences. It was almost eight o'clock. Kara would turn her watch over to Ted around nine. She told him to crawl down into the cabin, and she would call him for his watch. Kara had an hour to herself with the sun skimming on the rolling waves with warm golden light. The gentle breeze blowing down over the dodger was a complete contrast to the violent winds that brought her out of *Genie*'s cabin the night the boom fell on her head. She looked back and watched downtown Duluth shrink in the distance; the tight restrictive feeling in her chest grew, screaming at her to turn back. Ted and Pete would think she was insane if she turned *Genie* around and sailed back to the marina.

Kara purposely changed her thoughts to what she would do when she arrived in Bayfield, but Rikk and the events of the last four days crept back into her mind. She dug out the headphones and MP3 player and listened to music. She listened to a set of songs she hadn't heard in ages and sang along to keep her mind engaged and alert. She was glad that the engine was on, so her crew wouldn't hear her sing.

Chapter 33

Kara

It was quarter to nine, and *Genie* was making good headway. Kara would be turning over the watch to Ted in a few minutes. She was glad for the diversion that listening to music provided her, but then a song from her teenage years played. Jim Croce's "One Less Set of Footsteps" brought her thoughts screaming back to Rikk. The chorus made her shudder: "And you've been talking in silence, but if its silence you adore, there'll be one less set of footsteps, on your floor in the morning." Kara felt the serendipity of choosing a playlist that included a song that described exactly what she'd been doing.

When Kara's cell phone rang, her heart jumped at the hope that it would be Rikk. She unzipped her pocket and read the name on the cell phone. "Hi, Robin. Thanks for calling."

"Don't sound so disappointed, Kara. What's going on?"

Kara's breath quaked as she exhaled and let down all her defenses. "So I can't even say hello without you hearing distress in my voice?"

"Did you really think you could hide it from me?"

"I guess that's why I called you."

"Are you looking for me to be your coach or your friend this morning?"

"Both. But maybe lean more toward friend while I tell you what is going on." She told Robin the tale of Dr. Rikkert Harmon, leading up to and including the events of the tumultuous last week. Robin interrupted her a couple times for clarification and details and to ask a couple significant questions that caused Kara to hear her saboteur's voice.

"OK, Kara, now I'm putting on my coach hat. What do you really want right now—no limitations?"

"I want to talk to Rikk. I want to tell him everything."

"I hear that in your voice, Kara. What will telling him everything give you?"

Her reply came instantly, "Peace. It will give me peace and freedom from hiding and from shame."

"You sound lighter just saying that. But I want to hear more about the shame you feel."

Kara considered this question, "What do I feel ashamed about? Wow, where do I start?" she said and gave a wry laugh. "Well, I'm ashamed that I've been giving my saboteur way too much energy—that I've been living in the past, and that I've been petrified of the future. I've only been in the moment with Rikk a fraction of the time. Those times have been so incredible, so downstream. I *know* better than this, or at least I should have known better. The only way I can have a relationship with Rikk is to tell him about my past."

"What will revealing your past give you?"

"I can't forge a relationship with him if I'm wondering when my secrets will seep out. He needs to know, so he can decide if he wants to continue to see me. I need to tell him even if it means our relationship is unsalvageable. I owe it to him to explain my actions. He might fear all women after the way I've treated him." Robin remained quiet and listened. Kara knew Robin was being patient, waiting to see if she had any more revelations. She did, "I love him, Robin. I've tried so hard not to, but I love him."

"When are you going to tell him?"

"Tonight—or tomorrow."

"Kara, is tonight soon enough? Sounds like waiting will give your saboteur time to talk you out of it."

"Rikk's at work and probably can't take my call."

"Doesn't he have voicemail?"

"It's hard enough to call him, let alone leave a message. I want to hear his response and not wonder if he deletes my message without listening to it."

"What was the name of your saboteur, the snake?"

"Hisser," Kara said. "So you think he is in control now?"

"I think he's been slithering rampant for the last four days. I think the longer you delay making that call, the harder it will get. Kara, I'm taking off my coach hat for a minute—as your friend I want to share one of my experiences with you. Right after my husband and I had our first big fight after we got married, he went for a drive. A few hours later, he left a voicemail for me. I was too angry to hear what he was saying when I first listened to it, but something that he said kept me coming back to replay it. As I calmed down, I was able to hear his pain and sorrow—and finally the point that he had tried to make in the argument." Robin paused, then said, "Now I'm coaching again, how does your message depend on his response?"

"What I have to say doesn't change—" She sighed, blowing air across her top lip. "It doesn't change even if he listens to it and never wants to see me again. My message is the same. I guess I have to let the cat out of the bag and hope he likes cats."

Robin laughed. "I have a crazy feeling that he loves cats. Kara, what will give you relief right now?"

"Calling him, and leaving a message if he doesn't answer." Kara's mood lifted, and she felt the knot in her stomach release. "At least I'll have said what I need him to know, and then I'll trust that the right thing will happen."

"Now you sound like the Kara I know. I guess you've sent Hisser packing, so when are you going to call Rikk?"

"Well, my watch is over pretty soon, so my next watch will be in four hours. I'll do it then, if my crew isn't in the cockpit."

"Kara, has Hisser slithered back to you? How many more years are you going to wait?" Robin's irritation was undeniable. "I'm not sure if I'm wearing your friend's hat or my coaching hat at the moment, but I'm all for you taking a few minutes to think about the main points you need to make. I know you and your tendency to over-analyze things. Don't you think five minutes would be more than enough time to figure out what to say?"

Kara blew a cleansing breath out, "You're right," she paused a moment. "I know what I have to say."

"Then make the call, Kara, and above all, speak from your heart."

"OK, Mom." Kara snickered and knew Robin understood her inference.

"OK? When will you call him?" Robin was relentless.

"As soon as we hang up."

"Will you let me know you've called him? Oh, hell, Kara, don't keep me in suspense. Let me know right away. I have a client calling. I have to hang up. Leave a message as soon as you talk to him. Bye."

Robin didn't wait for Kara to say goodbye before she disconnected the call. Kara stood bewildered and stalled shutting her phone because as soon as she did, she promised to start dialing Rikk's number. A muffled ringtone came from the cabin, and she saw Ted rise. He pulled his cell phone out of his pocket and turned off the alarm. After he hung up the phone, he looked out the hatch and called to see if she needed anything. She didn't, and then he went to the head.

Kara shut her phone and saw that it was eight fifty-five. She opened her cell phone directory and found Rikk's office phone number. It took her a moment and a deep breath to push the send button. As she listened to his phone ringing tones, Kara's fear that Rikk had already quit on her peaked, and she reminded herself to release the thought and replace it with what she wanted. *Rikk understands and forgives me. He wants to see me and drives to Bayfield as soon as he can.* The call connected, but she got his voicemail. She panicked as she listened to Rikk's outgoing message, but forced herself to wait for it to end. At least she'd apologize—she'd clear her conscience—and cling to hope.

Chapter 34

Rikk

Rikk got to the hospital at seven Monday morning and made his rounds, then went to the clinic. He stared out the window at the lake and realized that Kara had had consumed all his thoughts. It was seven fifty, and he felt so drained. He shook his head hoping to release his memories of Kara. One minute everything had been amazing, and the next he was taking her back to the marina.

Although Rikk needed a cup of coffee, the thought of seeing the staff bothered him after last night's debacle. However, he knew he couldn't hide from the world, so he might as well get coffee. He felt as ragged as he did when he was an intern. As he suspected, many of his colleagues in attendance at last night's benefit made comments about how much they enjoyed Kara. How would he ever get Kara off his mind when everyone he worked with was so excited about her? This would be a long and trying day. His hand was in his pocket, fumbling with a sheet of paper tangled among coins. It was his list of what he wanted that he wrote onboard *Genie's Bottle* on Friday night. He wondered if it was even possible to get what he wanted. He took his coffee and returned to his office. Relieved that his first patient had arrived, he welcomed the distraction of work.

Rikk was treating his last patient of the morning when he went to his office to look up a medication. A message had been left on his voicemail, and he pushed play. Rikk yawned and stretched as the irritating computer voice said, "You have one new message left on Monday, May seventeenth at eight fifty-five a.m." The sound of Kara's voice punched his gut, and he slouched down into his chair.

"Rikk, you were right about everything. I haven't been practicing what I preach; I haven't been following my emotions that feel so good when I'm with you,"—He heard Kara's voice falter and then a long breath as if she were trying to regain her composure.

She continued, "Oh, God, this is going to sound crazy, but have you ever heard the Zen term, satori? Roughly defined, it's the moment of presence when you stop listening to your saboteur and all the ridiculous scenarios that it plays in your head. Satori is the moment when you stop living in the past or future and become present in the moment. I had a satori this morning. I realized that I have been hanging on to things in my past and looking forward to Bayfield but not sure why. I've been paddling upstream the whole time. You were right. I could not see what was right in front of me. If I only could've been present in the moment, I never would have felt so lost. I know I've hurt you, and I wish I could turn the clock back to make different choices. Please, Rikk, please give me a chance to explain. Rikk, I need to—" he heard her hesitate and in a quaking voice, she said, "Rikk, I have something in my past that I need to tell—"

A deafening clunk interrupted Kara, followed by a piercing grinding over the hum of the engine. Her message was still recording, and he heard her swear and then he heard a muffled thud that sounded like she dropped her cell phone onto the cockpit cushion. The engine stopped and he could hear distress in Kara, Ted, and Pete's voices, but he couldn't make out what they said. Then the phone went dead.

Chapter 35

Kara

"Oh, SHIT!" Kara said as she reached for the engine switch and dropped her cell phone on the seat.

"Cut the engine!" Ted yelled as he burst through the head's door at the same time that Kara switched it off. Ted flew into the cockpit.

"What in the hell was that?" Pete yelled out and a second later scrambled out of the cabin.

Kara was looking overboard, "Damn! We hit a deadhead." She pointed at the floating log bobbing vertically off the port side of the stern.

"It sounded like it hit the propeller," Ted said.

"The way it ground when it hit, I think it could've bent the prop shaft," Kara said.

"Yeah, a bent prop shaft would grind like that," Ted said. "The through-hull packing might have been ground out some."

"What happened? What made the boat shudder like that?" Pete asked when he arrived in the cockpit.

Ted said, "Besides diving, the only way to check it out is to start the engine again. A bent prop will cause some vibrating, but a bent shaft will—"

"I need to check the bilge. Pete, take the wheel." Kara rushed for the cabin, but Ted was the first to get there and pull up the bilge floorboards. The bilge didn't appear to be filling with water. "Leave the cover off, so we can keep an eye on it," Kara said.

She led the way back to the cockpit and took the wheel. "We are going to turn around and sail back. I could start the engine again, but if the prop shaft is bent, it will only bore out the cutlass bearing and increase the chance of taking on water. We'll sail on a broad reach, and if the wind switches east-northeast, we'll have to run wing on wing." Kara looked up at the wind indicator, and said, "Prepare to jibe."

At the same time Kara gave the order, Ted said, "If we jibe—" He stopped and sent her a heartened smile. "I guess you already planned to jibe."

She nodded at him and appreciated his confidence in her seamanship skills, and even more, she appreciated having complete confidence in his. She eyed Pete and answered his confused expression. "Jibing will keep the boat speed up."

Kara and Ted instinctively flung into action. Kara said, "Pete, Ted's going to bring the jib across. I'll watch the main sail and tell you when to ease it." Pete's deer-in-the-headlight expression telegraphed that he needed more explanation. "After the boom comes across to the port side, I will tell you when to ease the main sail—to let it out. You're going to ease the mainsheet a little at a time—but don't uncoil it from the winch. Watch the main sail and wait until it starts to luff, then you will come over and push the boom out until it fills with wind. Keep low when we jibe, so you don't get knocked by the boom when it comes across." Pete nodded his head in agreement.

"OK, jibe ho." Kara turned the wheel starboard gradually, keeping the sails filled and her speed up.

When the sails started to luff, Ted yelled, "Jibe ho!" He released the jib sheet from the starboard winch, grabbed the boom and slowed it down as he crossed to the port side of the cockpit. Ted wrapped the jib sheet around the port winch and pulled the jib to port, then inserted the winch handle and cranked it until the jib was trimmed.

Meanwhile Kara said, "Pete, when Ted pushes the boom out over the water, ease the main." Pete let it out too far, so she called out, "Pull it in, Pete. Go slow, just a few inches at a time and watch the sail. Pull it until you just get the luff out of it. I'll tell you when to stop." Kara noticed that Pete was still a bit wide eyed, but he was rising to the occasion.

Ted watched the mainsail as Kara continued to guide Pete until he'd trimmed the mainsail to a constant smooth line, without any luffing on the leech side. Kara lined *Genie's Bottle* up with the Lift Bridge in the distance and felt optimistic they could shoot through the canal on a broad reach, providing the wind remained out of the north.

Then they all looked at each other and took a breath. Kara said, "I'm going down to check the bilge and call the marina. Ted, you're in charge of the sails. Pete, take the wheel and keep us on this course." She went down and checked the bilge. Although relieved it wasn't filling, Kara knew it was too soon to feel relaxed. She had not heard the bilge pump come on but knew she had been too preoccupied to listen for it.

"Minnesota Point Marina, Minnesota Point Marina, Minnesota Point Marina, this is *Genie's Bottle*." It was a little after nine a.m., but they did not respond immediately. She hailed them again; this time Dan answered. "*Genie's Bottle*, this is Minnesota Point Marina. Switch to channel six-eight."

Kara responded, "Six-eight," and switched the radio channel. "Minnesota Point Marina, *Genie's Bottle* on six-eight."

"Go ahead, *Genie's Bottle*"

"Dan, we just hit a deadhead. It sounded like it hit the prop. I cut the engine immediately, but I'm concerned that the prop shaft was bent."

"Did the engine grind?"

"Yes, and the boat shuddered. Ted and I think the cutlass bearing might be damaged. So far, the bilge pump has not come on. I just turned around, and we're sailing back. Can you check with the Army Corps of Engineers to see if any ships are scheduled go through the canal in the next few hours?"

"Sure, I'll check with the Corps and get back to you. Do you think you can make it all the way in, or should I get someone out there to tow you?"

"At this point we are making good progress, and I think we'll make it. I know I can call Dutch if I need a tow. Is he around there somewhere?"

"I haven't seen him yet this morning. Let me check with Jessie and see if he's been in for coffee." After a few seconds, he came back on the radio and said, "Jessie hasn't seen him all morning, but I don't see *Miss Sea* in her slip. Do you want me to check around and see if anyone knows where he went?"

"No, he's probably fishing somewhere out here. I bet he's listening to us right now. He'll call me as soon as we hang up. At this point all I need to know is when the next ship is scheduled to go through the canal. Can you find that out for me?"

"You got it. Minnesota Point Marina monitoring on sixteen"

"*Genie's Bottle* switching back to sixteen."

Kara ran up the companionway to see Ted trimming the sails and looking at the wind indicator. In the short time she'd been below, the wind was clocking around to the east, and the sails were beginning to luff in the following wind.

"Oh, crap!" Kara said, "It looks like we are going to have to go wing on wing."

"Jib to port?" asked Ted.

"Yes, I'll hook up the whisker pole, and you can get the preventer ready. Pete, you stay at the helm and keep us on this tack for now." Kara flew up on deck and latched the whisker pole to the padeye on the port toe-rail track while Ted rigged the preventer onto the boom and starboard toe-rail track. Ted came to the cockpit and eased the jib on the port side until Kara grabbed the jib's clew and latched it to the other end of the whisker pole. As she did this she said, "Pete, time to jibe. Steer to port. Ted will sheet the main in until the wind brings the main to the starboard, then he'll let it out, and you're going to steer back to starboard."

Pete followed Kara's instructions even though uncertainty spread over his face. When the boom was centered over the cockpit, Ted pushed the boom across and eased the main. As Pete completed the jibe, Kara crossed over the deck and took up the preventer's slack so the boom was held on a broad reach. Kara looked back at the jib and when she turned to Ted, she saw he was waiting for her to cross back to the port side. He eased the jib while she fully extended the whisker pole. Pete watched from the helm as Kara returned to the cockpit. The wind filled the sails, and *Genie* started gaining speed.

Kara gave Ted a nervous smile and said, "Nice job," when she came back to the cockpit. Kara tweaked the jib's sail trimming while Ted did the same on the mainsail. She looked at Pete and could see he was impressed by what they'd just done. She said, "So this is wing on wing, Pete. They call it wing on wing because the sails look like dragon or butterfly wings with the jib and main on opposite sides of the boat. With the wind on the stern, this is how you catch as much wind as possible." Kara grimaced at Ted and said, "I've never wished I had a spinnaker more than right now." She wasn't surprised by Ted's wry smile and shrug.

Kara was about to check the bilge and figured that Ted must be telepathic because he slid past her, down into the cabin. She followed him down the companionway, and they agreed that so far Genie's shaft packing was holding up. They went back topside and breathed. Ted's sailing experience would be better used trimming sails, so Kara kept Pete at the helm. She said, "How are you doing, Pete?"

"I know you taught Sophie and me to jibe, but everything feels different—I'm sure it's because Genie's Bottle is a bigger boat."

"Yeah, and we are sailing with a defined purpose, not on a leisurely cruise," Kara said.

"Racing fate is more like it."

Pete's word choice, 'fate', landed like a sucker punch. "Pete, I'm OK with racing, but the fate part needs to change. I'm putting out that we're racing to arrive safely at harbor."

Even though things were working out, Kara had seen and heard too many stories of captains with overly inflated egos who did not prepare for the worst and relaxed into *hoping* for the best; then the worst-case scenario happened, and a disaster that could've been prevented became reality.

If the prop shaft was broken, it could fall out leaving a two inch hole in the bottom of the hull. The batteries would run the bilge pump, but would they last all the way back to the marina? Of course, if the prop shaft did fall out, she could start the engine, and it would run the bilge pump faster than it would run off the batteries. But what if the bilge pump failed? *Genie* would slowly start sinking. She got the manual bilge pump handle hooked up and a five-gallon bucket out of the lazarette locker as a precaution. But with the slower tack going back to the marina, would they make it bailing water manually? Although Dan would send out someone to tow or rescue them, the Coast Guard would be able to pump water out of *Genie*.

Kara picked up the handheld radio and hailed, "Coast Guard, Coast Guard, Coast Guard, this is *Genie's Bottle*."

Moments later the Coast Guard reply came across the radio, "*Genie's Bottle*, this is the Coast Guard. Switch to channel twenty-two."

"Channel twenty-two," replied Kara. As she switched the radio dial, she noticed Ted and Pete's expressions of surprise. She smiled reassuringly to them and in a calm voice said, "The devil plays with the best-laid plans."

"Coast Guard, this is the sailing vessel *Genie's Bottle.*"

"This is the Coast Guard, *Genie's Bottle*, go ahead."

"I'm under sail, heading toward the Duluth harbor. I hit a deadhead and possibly have a bent or broken prop shaft. I have engine but cannot use it for propulsion since the prop-shaft packing may be damaged. My position is about sixteen miles northeast of the entrance. I'm planning to sail through the canal on my present tack and turn into Minnesota Point Marina. I believe I can do this without assistance. I'm just informing you of my situation and intent."

"Are you the captain of the vessel?"

"Yes, I am Kara McKee, captain of *Genie's Bottle.*"

"*Genie's Bottle*, are you taking on water?"

"Negative. We have been monitoring the bilge since we hit, and the bilge pump has not run, nor do we see indication of water coming in. I have the bilge cover off and will continue to monitor it."

"*Genie's Bottle*, how many people do you have on board?"

"There are three of us, including myself."

"Do you have personal flotation devices on board?"

"Yes."

"Have every person on board put on a personal flotation device."

"We'll get them on."

"What are your GPS coordinates?" Kara read off their present coordinates and gave a description of the boat. "Stay on channel twenty-two, and we will call you every fifteen minutes. If you do start taking on water, inform us immediately, and we'll send our rescue boat for you. Do you have any other concerns at this time?"

"No, I'm confident that we'll make it into the marina, and I've already notified them of my return, so they are expecting me."

"Once again, contact us if you start taking on water or have any problems. We'll call you in fifteen minutes. Coast Guard monitoring on twenty-two."

"Thank you. *Genie's Bottle* monitoring on channel twenty-two."

From the expression on Ted and Pete's faces, Kara suspected they thought calling the Coast Guard was unnecessary; she hoped they were right. But she'd answer their unvoiced question, and said, "I would rather have them standing by with their rescue boat and water pumps if the shaft packing fails than let my ego risk losing *Genie's Bottle*. Dan could send someone out to save us, but the Coast Guard could save *Genie*."

❦

They settled into sailing on a slow tack. Pete remained at the helm, and Kara and Ted kept a vigilant eye on the sails, trimming them with the slightest fluctuation in the wind. The cabin radio remained on channel sixteen, and they could hear other vessels hailing each other. Kara was tempted to go down into the cabin to hail *Miss Sea* from her cabin radio, but figured it wouldn't take long before Dutch would hear another boater's conversation and discover that *Genie* was heading back. With her handheld radio on channel twenty-two, standing by on the Coast Guard's monitoring schedule, she was content to wait for Dutch to call her. Things were going well, and since Dan had offered to send someone out to tow her if Dutch didn't show up, she'd delay hearing Dutch's, 'I told you so' she was sure he'd say. Her intuition told her that if, or when, she needed Dutch, he would show up.

The wind remained constant, as did their speed at three and a half to four knots, allowing them to make steady progress. Just prior to the Coast Guard's check-in calls, they'd check the bilge. For the next two and a half hours a quiet nervousness prevailed as they sailed slowly, but steadily, back to the canal.

At eleven forty-five they heard the radio in *Genie's* cabin squawk, "*Genie's Bottle, Genie's Bottle, Genie's Bottle*. This is *Miss Sea*."

Kara raced into the cabin and pressed the radio's transmit button, "*Miss Sea*, this is *Genie's Bottle*. Switch to six-eight."

"Six-eight." Dutch came back on the radio and said, "Kara, I just heard chatter on the radio that some boat hit a deadhead and is on a monitoring

307

schedule with the Coast Guard. I knew it was *Genie* even before I switched to twenty-two to listen. I'm on my way, but it's gonna take me awhile to get to you."

"Where are you?"

"I'm by Spirit Lake."

"Really?"

"Yeah, just decided to let *Miss Sea* take me somewhere far from the big lake. Didn't want to have to watch *Genie* run away from the port she was meant to stay in."

Kara turned away from Ted and Pete and choked on the lump that formed in her throat. It was clear they were intrigued by Dutch's 'run away' innuendo. She tried to eliminate the sorrow in her voice, but it came through despite the three deep breaths she took before she said, "*Genie's* coming back, Dutch. She's bringing me back."

"Never underestimate the powers of these ladies of the sea, Kara. They have minds all their own, and your *Genie's Bottle* got some magic tricks tucked in her sails too." Dutch laughed then said, "You ain't the only one who makes wishes and rubs on her hull."

"Dutch! What did you do?"

"I didn't get anywhere reasoning with you this morning, so I had to do something." Dutch's jovial laughter was cut off when the radio transmission ended.

Kara's incredulous voice said, "Now you're meddling with magic!" She laughed and turned to Pete and Ted and caught their smiles and failed attempts to look disinterested.

"Like I said, had to do something! Kara, I'll give you a tow when I get there. Just throw me a line."

Kara couldn't believe that she laughed, but she figured the stress of the situation must have needed to find a release valve, and laughing was better than crying. The first thing that came into her head was the rule of towing at sea. If the periled vessel throws the line, they are also relinquishing ownership of their vessel to the towing vessel. "Dutch are you trying to commandeer *Genie's Bottle*?"

"Haw, haw, haw," Dutch's laugh bellowed over the radio. "Well, if you're making jokes, you ain't bobbing out in the lake like a duck."

"No, we've turned around and are running wing on wing and doing about four knots. We are keeping an eye on the bilge and haven't noticed any water coming in. I'm doing fine and should be back," Kara looked at her watch and said, "around twelve thirty—one o'clock."

"Well, I'm coming out and will escort you in, just in case the Anemoi—ain't that what you called the wind? In case Anemoi peters out."

"Anemoi, god of the four winds, is going to bring me back to Duluth. It seems that he wants me to work hard to get there though."

"Just like I told you, getting back would be hard."

"I know, Dutch, I know."

"Well, he'll bring you back, but I guess he's giving you some time to figure a couple things out. I'm on my way out to tow you in if you need me."

"Thanks, Dutch. *Genie's Bottle* out."

⚓

The Coast Guard continued to call them every fifteen minutes, and their radio conversations continued to repeat almost verbatim.

It was twelve fifteen when Kara spotted Dutch coming through the canal.

Dutch pulled up alongside Kara and throttled down so he could yell to her, "Kara, do you want me to throw you a line?"

"No. Just stay a couple hundred feet behind me. I don't want to stop now, and so far things are going good."

He pulled away from *Genie's Bottle* and turned around to follow her.

Chapter 36

Rikk

Rikk's heart was thawing as he listened to Kara's voice message—against his head's protests. His mellowing feelings screeched to a halt at the sound of the engine grinding and the alarm in Kara's voice as her message played. He didn't know the extent of their peril from the muffled exchange between Kara and her crew, but he heard the distress in their voices. Then the message ended. Rikk had no idea what he should do. He looked at his watch; it was twelve thirty-five. His head raced, but he was immobilized.

The knocking on his office door snapped him back to reality. Dazed from the message Kara left and annoyed with the interruption, his reflex words erupted, "Come in."

It was Joe. "Hey, from the looks of it, your evening ended on a sour note. Barb filled me in on what happened in the ladies' room last night. I think it's time I have a talk with Heidi and—"

"Joe. Listen to this." Rikk felt his heart pounding. He had no idea what Joe had just said.

"Rikk, what the hell is wrong? You look—"

"Just listen!" Rikk pushed play.

When Joe heard Kara's voice, he smiled. "It's good to hear that she left a message. Barb thinks Kara is good for you, and you are good for her."

Rikk fast-forwarded to the grinding noise. "Wait. Listen to this." He didn't mean to snap. Rikk watched Joe's smile fade and concern wash over his face as the message played. Rikk's eyes fixed out the window, when he heard himself say, "I've got to find her."

"Rikk, have you called her?"

"No, I heard her message just before you came in."

"Wouldn't she call the marina or the Coast Guard to get help if her boat was in danger?"

Rikk's brain tumbled in slow motion—bewildered and alarmed—and helpless. Finally, Joe's questions seeped in. He pressed the call back button on his answering machine and heard the ring tone several times before her cell phone's recorded answer played. Dread filled Rikk when she didn't answer. Pulling his cell phone out of his jacket, he fumbled to get the directory to pull up the marina's number. He felt the complete powerlessness that his patients and their families feel with a diagnosis of a disease they know nothing about. Now it was his experience. Rikk did not know how to save her or if she even needed saving. He had no idea where she was now, and it had been three and a half hours since she left the message. He just wanted to go to the marina and find her there. If Kara wasn't back, he would get Dutch to fire up *Miss Sea* or get the Coast Guard out looking for her. He just couldn't sit here and do nothing. He needed to get to Kara.

"Rikk, I will get the rest of your appointments covered or rescheduled. You're not going to do anyone any good in your state. Just go."

Rikk looked up from his phone.

"You should leave now. Don't waste any more time here. Just go."

Rikk hesitated to accept the offer for only a moment, then said, "Thanks, Joe."

"Just let me know how she is, Rikk. We all have fallen in love with her too."

A stunned gaze overcame Rikk. He stared at Joe and felt the punch his statement rendered. He left the office as fast as he could without running. It felt like a monumental effort to command his legs to take every step; it seemed to take an eternity to get to the parking lot. His frustration mounted as the marina's phone repeatedly rang.

At last, the casual female voice answered, "Minnesota Point Marina."

"This is Rikk Harmon. Has Kara McKee called on the radio?"

"What?" The surprised response of her voice seemed to deem him crazy.

"Kara McKee left your marina this morning, in *Genie's Bottle*. She left a message on my voicemail, and something happened, and they may have turned around. They hit a deadhead, I think, and—"

"Just a minute." With that, Rikk heard the receiver clunk as she set it down. He plugged his ear buds sync cord into his cell phone and then placed the buds into his ear before he started his car. Over the background noise he heard her page Dan to answer his call. "Dan will be with you in a minute," said the woman. Before Rikk could say anything, she put his call on hold.

He was pulling out of the parking ramp onto Third Street. Under minimal traffic conditions, it was a ten-minute trip to the marina from the clinic. Rikk labored through traffic that seemed heavier than usual. Finally, Dan came on the phone, "This is Dan."

"Dan, this is Rikk Harmon. Kara called and left a message, and then something hit the boat. Have you heard from her?"

"Yeah, Rikk. Kara is coming back in under sail. We just heard her tell the Coast Guard she's almost at the canal entrance."

"Is she taking on water?"

"No, if she were taking on water, the Coast Guard would be out there pumping water and towing her in. She should get here in a few minutes."

"Does Dutch know what's going on? He could go out and tow her."

"Rikk, relax. Dutch is following her, but she is making good time and is doing fine. He might give her a little tow in the marina after she has dropped her sails, and I've got a couple guys waiting on A dock to catch *Genie's Bottle* at the slip."

"Where is the Coast Guard?"

"She called them, and they have her on a fifteen-minute monitoring schedule. As long as she isn't taking on water and doesn't request a tow, there is nothing more for them to do. Kara is good, Rikk, she'll be able to do it; and she's smart enough to know when she needs help."

"I'm on my way down. I'm turning onto Lake Avenue now. I'll see you in a couple of minutes."

Rikk forgot that the street repairs began today, and apparently so had everyone else. The flaggers directing traffic looked as harried as he felt. Of course, one driver refused to follow the flagger's directions and went down a street that was barricaded off. He made the already slow traffic come to a stop. If Rikk thought it would do any good, he'd pound on his horn and vent his frustration along with several other motorists who were registering their anger. Everything that could've possibly detained him from reaching the marina had occurred. Finally, he had crossed over US Interstate 35 onto Canal Park and turned right onto Railroad Street. When he turned left, back onto Lake Avenue South, he saw the lift bridge rising. It could be lifting for Kara coming in or for a laker. Traffic was backed up for blocks, and Rikk was stopped next to the Lake Avenue Cafe. He wouldn't be able to see if it was *Genie's Bottle* or a ship without parking and walking up to the lift bridge. He contemplated doing that, but when the bridge went all the way up, he guessed it was probably a laker coming or leaving. He hoped Kara wouldn't have to wait for the laker to pass through the canal before she could enter it. He looked at his watch. It was a little after one. She might already be back at the marina. *God, let her be back.*

Kara

Kara took over the helm as they approached the canal. The wind had continued to clock east, now it was out of the southeast. She looked at Ted, "Have you sailed through the canal before?"

"Once. The winds get fluky at the canal entrance, making it tricky to sail through."

"Broad reach." Kara called out the order looking at Ted and trusted that he'd let her know if he thought they'd have any problems.

"Broad reach." Ted confirmed Kara's order, and followed it by immediately going up on the deck to prepare to release the whisker pole and preventer.

"We've got our bases covered with Dutch ready to give us a tow if we need it. Pete, are you ready for this?" Kara asked.

"Let's go for it." He seemed to brighten at the prospect of sailing through rather than getting a tow.

"Broad reach it is. Let me call the lift bridge for the OK."

Kara switched the radio to channel sixteen, "Aerial Lift Bridge, Aerial Lift Bridge, Aerial Lift Bridge, this is *Genie's Bottle.*"

The Aerial Bridge operator responded and informed Kara that a laker was due to leave in thirty minutes, but he would lift it for her as long as she had Dutch there to tow her if she couldn't make it through under sail. Kara was grateful that he allowed her a lift instead of waiting for the laker to leave first. Without this break, they'd be forced to circle near the entrance and wait, meanwhile *Genie* would lose speed, and that'd pretty much guarantee towing. Kara switched back to channel twenty-two to continue monitoring with the Coast Guard.

"Pete, you are going to bring the jib across when Ted releases the whisker pole. Get the starboard jib sheet ready on the winch."

Ted handed the preventer back to Pete and was unhooking the whisker pole as Kara steered into the canal. She directed, "Pete, release the port jib sheet and bring the jib to starboard." Ted came back into the cockpit and took over trimming the main sail. They maintained *Genie's* speed through the canal. The waves lapping onto the corrugated steel walls of the canal and the wind filling the sails were the only noises made until they were nearly through the canal.

The Coast Guard called, "*Genie's Bottle, Genie's Bottle,* this is the Coast Guard. What are your coordinates?"

"Coast Guard, this is *Genie's Bottle.* We're at the west end of the canal and will be starting our tack into the St. Louis River basin in a minute. We are going to make it into the marina without assistance."

"*Genie's Bottle,* remain on channel twenty-two and give us a call when you get to the dock. Coast Guard monitoring on channel twenty-two."

"Affirmative, Coast Guard. *Genie's Bottle* monitoring on twenty-two."

The wind had decreased a knot, but Kara knew they would gain enough speed as she pulled the sails close-hulled when she turned southeast toward the marina.

"The winds change directions off the land once we get through the canal. They tend to go south when the wind is out of the southeast out on the lake. A south wind would be the best direction to get into the marina without a tow from Dutch," Ted said.

"Let's hope the wind gods give us the south wind. I know Dutch would love to tow us in, but I'd love to bring *Genie* back on her own accord."

"So far Anemoi has done his part to get us back. He hasn't made it too hard." Ted grinned.

"So you know Anemoi." Kara relaxed and wondered what else his quiet eyes and reserved manner knew. She had a feeling he had a wise old soul, and his being *Genie's* crew was another synchronistic blessing.

"Ted, when we get past the marina entrance, release the main sheet and let the sails luff. If it is slowing *Genie* down too much, just drop the main. Pete, get ready to pull the jib in, fast. We'll need to keep up the speed to turn upwind to the dock. Wait until I give the signal. You can pull up the lazy jacks now, and get the fenders and dock lines ready." Kara's adrenaline rushed. She knew she had a small margin for error to keep the speed up enough to make it to the end dock but slow enough to coast in to a stop. She knew Dan would have plenty of shipyard technicians ready to catch her, but she would prefer to make it as easy on everyone as possible. At least with so few boats launched in the marina, there wouldn't be many motoring around in the dock channels. Dutch would always be able to catch a line to either tow her to the dock or slow her down if her approach was too fast.

Kara steered *Genie's* bow towards the marina entrance, feeling confident and triumphant. Now merely a few hundred yards away, she would deliver *Genie* safe to the dock, and after taking care of matters at hand, she would call Rikk again.

In that moment, she remembered Rikk's question: why didn't she have friends help her sail *Genie* to Bayfield? Her answer was not untrue, but there was more to it than she admitted. She wanted to stand at the helm and with the assistance of her crew, get *Genie* to the dock unassisted. *Why, Kara?* Her answer came as spontaneously as her question. *To prove to myself that I can be on my own—no more family and friends checking on me.* Stomach acid rose in her throat as she felt so alone, and it wasn't what she wanted at all. She needed to call him and tell him who she was.

"Oh, damn," Kara muttered. Both Ted and Pete shot her looks of alarm. She bit her lower lip and said, "Sorry, I just remembered I was on my cell phone when the deadhead hit. I tossed it aside. I'll find it later." Her eyes searched the cockpit for it.

"I shut it," Pete said. Her phone had slid down between the cushions. He found it and handed it to her.

As Kara stuck it into her jacket pocket, *Genie's* stern passed through the break wall into the marina. "OK, let's drop the sails. Pull the jib in, Pete, fast." Ted released the main sheets, letting the main sail whip around free in the wind like a giant flag. Everything was going as planned. They spotted a couple marina employees on the end of A dock about a hundred yards away, waiting to catch *Genie's* dock lines.

Kara started to make the turn toward the dock when they heard the sound of water gurgling, and the bilge pump started to run. Kara yelled, "Oh, shit," She jumped up on the stern seat to look below as Ted scurried down into the cabin.

"The water level is rising fast." Ted's calm demeanor changed to alarm.

"Is the bilge pump keeping up?"

"No!" Ted said. "The water's gaining."

"We need to get lifted now." Kara was too far from the boatlift to shout to Dan that she needed to be lifted right now, especially over the trawler motor idling in the lift. She grabbed the handheld radio, switched the channel back to sixteen, and hailed, "Minnesota Point Marina, this is *Genie's Bottle*. We just started taking on water, and it's coming in fast. We need to come right into the lift."

Jessie's voice came on the radio, "*Genie's Bottle*, switch to six-eight." Jessie was gone before Kara could say she didn't have time to switch channels.

Kara switched to channel six-eight and prayed that enough boaters were listening to get the message to Dan before the woman could relay the message. She didn't follow Coast Guard protocol either; she didn't have time to hail the Coast Guard. They would never make it before she would be in the boatlift slip. With a calm forcefulness, she clearly articulated, "This is *Genie's Bottle* on six-eight. I need you to inform Dan that we're taking on water and we need to get hauled out. I'm going directly to the boatlift. I need him to get that trawler out of the boatlift, so I can come in. I need to be lifted immediately. *Genie* out." Kara steered *Genie* back towards the boatlift slip as *Genie's* speed started to slow.

Dutch was just entering the marina and sped up to her, yelling, "Kara, where you going?"

"*Genie*'s taking on water. I've got to get lifted, *now!*"

"Throw me a line."

"No! Go tell Dan I need to bring *Genie* in to be lifted." Kara was relieved that Dutch sped off without a discussion.

The employees tossed the dock lines to the motor boat as it backed out of the lift slip. A few boaters were flocking to the slip with a noticeable amount of commotion. Although no one on *Genie's Bottle* could understand their words, it was evident that the message of *Genie*'s peril got to Dan and the shipyard techs.

Someone handed Dan a handheld radio, and he answered, "I heard you, Kara. This boat is leaving so come right in, and we'll lift you." He passed the handheld back to the boater and started directing her with his hands.

Dutch had turned around and came back to help. He yelled again, "Throw me a line."

"No, we are coasting in fast enough, Dutch." Kara looked at Ted and Pete standing on the deck ready to fend *Genie* off the slip's wall. "We *are* going to make this." Their expressions showed they had no doubt that they would.

"Can you slow down any?" came Dan's direction.

Kara steered an "S" pattern to slow *Genie* down as the boat leaving the boatlift sped out of the way. "Backwind with the main," was all Kara needed to say, and Ted grabbed the boom and pushed it out over the water, filling the sails with wind that pushed back against *Genie*'s forward motion. Awe replaced Pete's puzzled look.

When *Genie* was about fifty feet away from the slip, Kara gave the instruction, "Drop the main." Ted pushed the boom back towards the stern, and the sail luffed in the wind as Pete released the main sheet, and the sail flaked into the lazy jacks. Kara steered into the lift as Ted and Pete tossed the dock lines ashore, bringing *Genie* to a halt. The techs quickly positioned *Genie* over the lift straps and immediately started hauling her up.

Chapter 37

Kara

Exhausted, Kara collapsed on the stern seat and rested her head on the wheel as *Genie's Bottle* emerged from the water. A broad smile covered Pete's face and he said, "That was one hell of a sailing lesson." She gave him a weak smile and shook her head in disbelief.

Pete jumped down to the dock and watched *Genie's* hull emerge. Kara knew Ted was doing his best to ignore her as she slumped back down and rested her head on the wheel again. He worked his way back to the cockpit as he tied the sail to the boom and pulled the lazy jacks down. Ted's calm voice brought her back. "Kara, let's go take a look."

"*Genie's Bottle, Genie's Bottle, Genie's Bottle*, this is *Kismet*," both the handheld and cabin radios screeched.

Kara jumped and held her breath while her predicament began to focus in her fogged mind. She exhaled and picked up the handheld radio. She didn't know this boat and had no idea why it would be calling her, other than they had been monitoring the entire calamity and wanted to know if she was still afloat. When she looked at the radio she realized that *Kismet* had hailed her on channel six-eight, and she hadn't changed back to channel twenty-two. "*Kismet*, this is *Genie's Bottle*. Go ahead."

Kara heard the voice from *Kismet* say, "The Coast Guard is hailing you on twenty-two; they've called twice now. Do you want me to tell them where you are?"

"Oh, crap!" Kara said under her breath. She pressed the talk button on her radio and said, "No, I'll give them a call. Thanks for letting me know, *Kismet*. *Genie's Bottle* switching to twenty-two." She switched the channel, but before she could call the Coast Guard, she heard them hail her.

"*Genie's Bottle, Genie's Bottle, Genie's Bottle*, this is the Coast Guard."

"Coast Guard, this is *Genie's Bottle*. We have just pulled into the Minnesota Point Marina." Kara's voice started to crack, so she took a deep breath and went on, "We got a little busy and didn't have a time to call you. We started taking on water when we passed through the marina's entrance. I suppose you heard me when I switched to channel sixteen to let the marina know we needed to be lifted immediately."

"Yes, we left when we heard you request to go right to the lift."

"I'm sorry that I didn't call you, but I didn't have time for the correct protocol. We had to keep going; we were just too close to stop. We made it. They are lifting her right now." Kara looked out toward the entrance and saw the Coast Guard rescue boat approaching the marina.

"Our rescue boat will be there in a minute to check on you. Coast Guard monitoring on channel sixteen."

"Thank you for monitoring, Coast Guard. *Genie's Bottle* out."

The Coast Guard entered the marina and slowly motored to the transient dock near boatlift slip.

Ted reached his hand down for Kara, and she took it and stood up. They jumped down to the dock and saw what the techs were looking at. The prop and its shaft were gone, and prop-shaft packing had been routed out. Dan said, "We'll haul her out and get her onto stands, Kara, but it is going to be a few weeks before we get her into the shop. It's a busy time of year." Kara shook her head in agreement and started to contemplate what her next move would be. She felt nauseated.

Kara walked off the dock and watched the lift bring *Genie's Bottle* completely out of the water and up the boat ramp. The Coast Guard crew had walked up, and the captain of the Coast Guard boat spoke, "Are you Captain McKee from *Genie's Bottle*?"

"Yes."

"Is everyone who was on your boat on shore?"

"Yes, we made it to the lift slip. *Genie* began taking on water right after we got into the marina. They got the straps lined up perfectly and started lifting her immediately. Thank you for checking on us."

"You are one hell of a captain, Ms. McKee. We'll be looking forward to seeing you back out on the waters." He and his crew walked back to their boat.

❧❀❧

As Dan and Kara started walking to the shop, she kept her eyes glued to the ground. She wanted a minute of privacy to check her cell phone for messages. *Genie* would be repaired, and she would get to Bayfield in due time, but now all she wanted was to talk to Rikk. As they approached the lobby, Kara noticed a small crowd of feet.

"Hey, Captain McKee," Sophie called out. Kara looked up to see her, Pete, and Ted with a couple shipyard mechanics and techs, as well as a few boat owners who had come to watch the spectacle. "Sounds like you gave Pete the sailing adventure of his life! I hope you haven't given him a taste for that kind of drama. I want sailing to be relaxing, not a white-knuckled thriller at the tiller."

"Sophie, what are you doing here? Didn't you work the midnight shift?"

"Yeah, but I decided to sleep on *Whisper* today rather than at home while Pete here," Sophie smiled up at him and patted his chest, "was sailing with you. All the commotion woke me up, and I saw *Genie's Bottle* sail back through the marina entrance. I ran here in time to see her pulled out of the water and my Pete safe on the dock all hyped up and wide eyed." She stretched onto her toes and kissed Pete's cheek.

They all laughed and poured more good-natured ribbing on Pete. Kara was getting compliments for the skillful handling of her boat, especially in the compromised condition *Genie* was in at her arrival at the lift. Kara's tarnished confidence began to rebound as Pete told his animated version of their trip back to the marina. The other marina staff and boaters asked questions and gave their opinions based on the communication they had followed on their marine radios between *Genie*, the marina, and the Coast Guard.

Ted stood back, listening and adding a few bits of information here and there. Finally, he directed his gaze at Kara and said, "You're one damned skilled captain."

320

Kara's appreciation showed in her warm smile. "I'm so lucky to have had you for crew. I always knew that I could hand *Genie* over to you, and you would get us back. Ted, you are one damned skilled sailor too. Thank you."

Pete piped in, "Any time you need a crew again you can call me."

"Thanks for jumping in and doing everything asked of you perfectly." Kara laughed at Pete's blushing face.

"If you ever think about racing, Pete, you'd be great," Ted said and slapped his back. "Just let me know, and I'll find a boat that needs crew.

Then to both of them Kara said, "I would not have made it without the two of you. You were the perfect crew."

Dutch, who oddly had not said anything yet, surprised everyone when he said, "I reckon you got unfinished business to do." He wrapped his big fatherly arms around Kara and held her in his secure embrace.

Kara sighed. Her emotions were ragged. She relaxed in the comfort of Dutch's arms and wanted to stay there at least until the crowd dissipated. When Dutch released her, she clutched his jacket, not ready to face whatever came next. He gently pushed her away from him and spun her around to see what he had spied over her shoulder.

Rikk was approaching the crowd from the parking lot. Kara gasped when she saw his determined stride lengthen towards her. She felt herself relax as tears pooled in her dried out eyes. Kara whispered his name, "Rikk!" The crowd split as they moved toward each other.

Rikk

They clutched each other, and Rikk felt Kara's body shudder as her adrenaline dissipated. Rikk leaned back to look at her. "Damn it, Kara, you drive me crazy." He put his hand under her chin and drew her head up to his, tenderly kissing her without regard to Kara's consent. He felt her easy and unabashed reply. Rikk pushed her away when he became aware of Sophie and Pete howling with merriment and encouragement. Sophie was singing a lyric from *The Little Mermaid*, "Go on and kiss the girl." Without hesitation, Kara's lips met Rikk's in another long and fervent kiss. A symphony of cheering and taunting from the witnesses accompanied their moment. Rikk laughed at Kara as she regained her composure.

Rikk whispered, "I just named my boat." He didn't know if his unexpected remark surprised him or Kara more, but her quizzical grin peered up at him. Before she could ask what the name was, he said, "*Satori*."

"*Satori*! That is a great boat name." Kara wiped tears off her cheeks a satirical grin spread over her face as she said, "Do you think all this happened just so you could find a name for your boat?"

Rikk's heart burned with intensity he hadn't felt in months. "I found way more than a name."

Kara reached her hand around his head, pulled him close, and whispered, "I hope you mean you found me." He answered her with another kiss, and felt her semblance of control strip away. Rikk heard the crowd whistling and whooping like a college bar at closing time. Kara shyly gazed at him and said, "*Satori*! Maybe we could sneak away on *Satori*?"

<hr>

Someone who had just arrived at the marina approached asking about the commotion, and several stories began. As Ted and Pete answered questions and relived the events, Kara and Rikk wrapped their arms each other's waists.

Dutch broke the silence. With a twinkle in his eye he asked, "Kara, since you ain't got a place to stay while they's working on *Genie's Bottle*, you could stay on *Miss Sea*."

"Oh, you are a scoundrel, Dutch." Kara blushed as she looked up at Rikk.

"Kara has a place to stay," said Rikk. With his free hand, he brushed the hair out of her face and gently kissed the faded bruise on her forehead. He held her close and watched her shut her eyes and rest her head on his chest.

After a few clumsy seconds, Dan announced that they all had a lot of work to do and needed to get back to it. He escorted Kara and Rikk into his office to discuss *Genie's* repairs.

Kara and Rikk walked out of the building into a beautiful warm day with a five—to ten-knot east-southeast wind. "Do you have to go back to work?" Kara asked.

Rikk discerned hope in Kara's voice and silently thanked Joe. "I should call in and see if all my patients are rescheduled." Rikk called his office and learned the rest of the day was clear. He was about to hang up when he remembered Joe's request. He glanced at Kara to see her waiting. "One last thing," he said. "Can you put me through to Joe's office?" He grabbed Kara's hand and playfully pulled her in for a quick kiss as he listened to the outgoing message on Joe's voicemail. "Joe, Kara is fine, but her boat needs repairs. They've hauled her out, and it will be a few weeks before they can get her into the shop. I'll tell you all about it tomorrow. Thanks for getting my appointments rescheduled. Oh, and, uh, we're spending the afternoon sailing my boat." He turned off his phone and stuffed it back into his pocket.

Jessie, who was standing in the ship's store doorway, interrupted their kiss. She called out, "Um, you are Kara McKee, right?"

"Yes," Kara said.

"We just got some of your mail addressed to the marina." With that, she handed Kara a small stack of letters.

Chapter 38

Kara

Kara thanked Jesse and paged through the mail. She stopped when she came across a business-sized envelope made from high quality, white paper. She felt like she was finally floating downstream and everything with Rikk was perfect until this letter reminded her of her past. The trepidation she had previously felt rushed back into her. She looked at Rikk's tired but tranquil face. He smiled a brazen look that telegraphed his craving. Kara couldn't start fresh with Rikk if she was still holding onto her past—a past he might find too bizarre. "Rikk, I've got to tell you something. I was starting to tell you when the boat hit the deadhead."

"What is it?"

"Can we go to the beach?"

"How about to *Satori*?"

"No, there's too big of a chance for interruptions. Besides, it will give me a chance to read this letter while you drive."

"OK," Rikk replied.

⚜

Kara opened the letter and read it. She sighed and looked out the car window.

"Is it bad news?"

"No. In many ways it is good news."

"Does it have anything to do with what you need to tell me?"

"Yes, a lot. Everything."

324

"Everything?" Rikk pulled up into the parking lot.

Kara sprung out of the car and inserted the letter back into the envelope as she waited for him to step out. Time slowed, yet her mind raced to find the words she needed to say. "I'm sorry for prolonging this; I just needed to get out of the marina. Too many people and distractions for me to even begin to tell you—"

"Tell me what?"

She blew out a breath and started to walk down the boardwalk to the beach, shooting Rikk a side glance that invited him to follow.

Rikk caught up to her, and they walked several steps together before he said, "Kara, nothing you can tell me will change how I feel about you."

"Some secrets need to be kept, but this one has to be revealed. I'm just scared you will never understand."

"What won't I understand?"

"What I do."

"What do you do?" He stopped walking and waited for Kara to answer. Though she also stopped, she continued to look out at the lake. "Kara, what do you do that could be so bad that I wouldn't understand?" He didn't wait long for her answer. "OK, what is the worst thing you could do? Are you an assassin?"

"No," Kara fretted and turned toward him. Still struggling to find the nerve to explain, Rikk's question had lightened her mood and made her realize there were a lot worse things that she could do.

"Then what? A foreign spy?"

"No," she smiled, but before she could answer, he pressed on.

"A traitor? Have you given military secrets to the enemy?"

"Rikk!" She sighed, and the tension came back into her face. "I—Oh, man, I—"

"Have you embezzled retirement funds?" Rikk teased as he stepped forward. "Robbed banks?"

"NO! Shut up and listen! I'm a writer!" Kara thrust the envelope at Rikk and sputtered, "Here, read this, and you will understand."

The return address was from HB Editing. He glanced at Kara. As he pulled out the letter, his stunned expression asked his question before his words tumbled out. "You wrote *Be in Choice*?"

Kara just nodded and said, "Yes. I used a pen name."

"Why?"

Kara didn't answer. Rikk saw the discomfort in her face but could not hide how bowled over he felt. He opened the letter and began to read it.

⁂

Dear Kara,

I've just gotten off the phone with a producer from the *Suzie Sibley Show*. They have selected *Be in Choice* for this summer's book club. They would like you to make a guest appearance as early as possible. I told them you've been very adamant about publishing your book under your pen name, Audrey Lynn, even though I made every attempt for you to publish it under your own name.

Kara, please consider the *Suzie Sibley Show* interview. Since you're settling back in Bayfield to write as well as coach, this could be a perfect venue for you to reveal you're Audrey Lynn, especially considering how it would launch your popularity and boost your career.

If you haven't noticed, *Be in Choice* is still climbing the bookselling lists. With you coming forward as the author, it could give you more opportunities in publishing your next work.

Please call me as soon as you can to discuss this. It would be a wonderful way to start the new chapter in your life.

Sincerely,
Susan O'Day
Editor, HB Editing

⁂

Rikk finished reading the letter. All the while Kara kept her eyes fixed on his. Rikk looked out over the lake and then at the letter before his baritone reverberated through Kara. "Why didn't you tell me when I asked if you had read the book?"

"You read the preface to me last night. Oh, god. The preface—"

"What about it?"

"Do you have any idea how humiliating it is for me to admit to you that you are the man who was the inspiration for Jack? And then Lauren's last request while she was losing her battle with cancer was that you read the book." Kara noticed how her words jabbed Rikk, but she needed to release this secret from her. She breathed and drew on her fighter instinct to finish. "Why, Rikk? Why was it so hard for me to admit this? Because I didn't want to know if the real man was anything like the man I imagined him to be. Because I learned early in life that the subject of my infatuations almost always proved to be a figment of my imagination and far from who the person truly was. I'm too old for silly fascinations, and I didn't want to contemplate being wrong—or worse, being right."

He folded the letter and inserted it back into the envelope.

"And because I thought it would be impossible for this man to ever understand how impacted I was from our brief encounters—and because I never wanted to fall in love with him."

"So am I the man you described in your preface?"

"Yes. Rikk, when you were Tate's doctor. I was young, times were tough, and everything about you seemed so attractive. The logical side of me thankfully prevailed. I knew I could never act on my attraction. In fact, I always forbade myself from looking at your left hand to see if you wore a wedding band. The possibility of you being single frightened me too much to look. I forced myself to keep my eyes on your face." Kara laughed, "That wasn't a hard task." She was glad that Rikk smiled at that. "The last appointment that Tate had I invented a conflict, so Connor would take Tate to the appointment."

"Huh," Rikk nodded his head as if he just found the missing answer.

"When I recognized you on the dock last week, it was more than I could handle. In the early years, Connor and I were struggling to find our way to love each other without trying to change each other. When I was frustrated with my marriage, I'd imagine you to be whomever I wanted you to be—most often a saint to whisk me away. Deep down I think I knew you weren't what I really wanted. I wanted a happy marriage with Connor, but when things were difficult I'd let my imagination run and I cast you as the leading man. As Connor and I figured things out and everything started to click between us, I rarely thought of you—and when I did it usually was when Tate's surgery was mentioned. While we looked for pictures for Connor's funeral, I stumbled upon a picture of Tate in the hospital. That's when you returned and lurked in the background of my mind. A few months later, a story started brewing inside of me, and once again I cast you in the lead role. I finally let go of you by writing *Be in Choice*. Then Thursday morning there you were, standing in front of me. You were the last man in the world that I wanted to come face to face with."

Rikk looked stunned and stood motionless. Kara shook her head and thought how she wouldn't know how to respond if the tables were turned. She might as well finish—she wasn't sure she'd ever get another opportunity to say all she needed him to hear. "I was so attracted to you back then; I often wondered, what if I'd pursued you. A few years after Tate's surgery, I learned about the Third Essene Mirror, and then my attraction made sense. I finally accepted the fact that I'd never forget you, and I finally understood what you mirrored back to me. Through writing the story about the character, Jack, who I'd created around you, I released the hold my memory had on you. Rikk, I don't know how to explain this to you. This character you inspired grew until he stepped into a story." Kara paused, but she could not look at Rikk. "There, my secret's out. I'm so—I don't know, embarrassed doesn't even begin to describe it." Kara stood motionless and waited for his response. At last, she lifted her eyes to meet his penetrating gaze. Her fear seemed to come true. "Rikk, all I wanted to do is get out of the marina as fast as possible when I saw you. Then your boom hit my head. I never intended to become part of your life."

"Why did you publish it under a pen name?"

"I'm not exactly sure. I guess I was feeling the urge to move back to Bayfield and didn't want to risk you ever finding it and wondering if it was you. I never wanted to burden you like that. I'm sorry—sorry I didn't tell you sooner. I just didn't have the nerve to face you."

"I'm stunned, Kara. I inspired Jack?"

"Yes."

"I'm actually flattered. I'm not sure what to say. I guess I can kind of see how I would be the last man on earth that you would want to run in to."

"You do?"

"Yeah, but this doesn't change how I feel about you."

"Really?"

"Yes, really."

Rikk's shy smile allowed Kara to breathe. She said, "I guess Dutch was right; secrets are more about the person keeping them than about anyone else. It is humiliating for me to remember and admit how often I wondered about you, and if we ever would've been compatible under other circumstances. I never planned to bring my imagination of you to life in a book."

"I don't know or have facts to support this, but I'd guess you're far from the first who did such a thing."

Kara turned back to the lake and whispered, "I've been such a drama queen."

"I've seen worse drama queens." Rikk's laughter danced in his words. He closed the gap between them and handed back the envelope to Kara. When she took it, he drew her to him.

"Maybe in junior high," Kara said and clenched her teeth and screwed her mouth into a guilty as charged expression.

"Maybe you were a little bit of a drama queen," Rick kissed the top of her head. "I may be ignorant, but why even tell me this?"

"That I'm a drama queen?"

"No. That I inspired Jack."

"Just like the medical profession, I keep confidences with my coaching. But my writing is something that I want—no, I *must* be able to share with the most important person in my life. I cannot imagine having a relationship with you and having to worry about hiding the source of the royalty payments that I receive."

"So that's why? So I don't learn where your money comes from?"

Kara freed herself from his arms and began to walk down the shore. "Rikk, if what you say is totally true, but you intentionally withhold some information, does that make it a lie?"

"I don't know. What do you think?" Rikk walked next to Kara.

"For me, it's a lie, even if whatever is hidden doesn't matter. When you don't trust someone enough to let him know everything, I feel you are controlling the outcome. If all the information comes out later, by withholding information you've manipulated the situation, and it will undermine the relationship."

"Then I have something I need to admit to you. Doctors experience the same feelings that the rest of the world does, and sometimes we are attracted to our patient's mother." Kara stopped and saw his reticent smirk widen into a smile.

"Me?"

"You. So many mothers do all the talking for their children, but you encouraged Tate to answer my questions. He was a shy child, and when he didn't answer, you would answer for him and then check with him to see if you had said it right. You treated Tate with so much respect, yet you didn't expect him to be a grown up nor did you baby him. Besides being a great mother, you were so attractive and smart. My heart missed a beat every time I pulled Tate's chart off the examination room door because I would get to see you again, even though I'd never do anything because of my attraction. I was married, and Lauren and I were happy. Yet I'm human, just like you, and I wondered what it would be like to know you."

"Is that why you didn't say anything about being Tate's doctor?"

"Worse. I was offended. So many patients recognize me that I guess I expected you to, but when you acted as if you didn't, I was hurt. My wounded ego wouldn't allow me to admit I remembered you first. Now I understand why you avoided me. At least as much as an available man can, who runs into the beautiful and now-available woman who intrigued him years ago."

"It feels like some perverse sort of destiny has brought us together."

"Perverse?" questioned Rikk.

"Well, perverse may not be the exact word, but, my best-kept secret is out. Not only out, but you know that I stole your face, body, and your mannerisms to create my character, Jack. I don't know if you can understand this, but it was unfathomable for me to ever think that I would be telling you that you are the one whom I couldn't forget—and consequently inspired a character I created."

"Kara." Rikk reached out and drew her back to him. Kara clutched Rikk, and he held her until she released the anxiety she held in her body. "I'm flattered. Hell, I'm even turned on. But, you do know that I'm not Jack; I'm not the man you have imagined."

"Of course, Rikk, that is why I never wanted you to know. I explained that in the preface."

"I just want to make sure that you don't expect me to be Jack."

"Rikk, you are not Jack. You are alive and real, and so much better than any character I could ever create in a story."

"Lauren thought Jack was pretty great. She wanted me to be more like him."

"Are you sure? Maybe she saw you were like Jack; that you had gotten lost from the man she knew you to be. Maybe she wanted you to find your way back to your authentic self."

"Was that the point of the story?" Rikk grimaced and looked as if he regretted asking that question. "Kara, I guess I didn't get that because of all the comments that Lauren had written in the book. I guess I was trying too hard to understand everything she was telling me to get your overall message."

"Yes, the point was how imperative it is to find and reclaim your authentic self in order to live a fulfilling life." Kara smiled at Rikk, who looked as if he finally understood Lauren's real message to him. "Rikk, I'd be a fool to try to change you. I'd be a fool to try to change anyone except myself. I love you the way you are."

Rikk

For Rikk, the serene silence holding them felt like a magnetic field. They were like polar opposites, incapable of breaking away from each other, even if they wanted to. Rikk let out his breath and watched Kara close her eyes. She stretched her face to his, and they sealed their bond with a gentle yielding kiss. Kara kept her eyes closed long after the kiss ended while Rikk studied her face. "Do you have any other secrets?" he whispered.

"No. There are many things you don't know about me yet, but I have no other secrets."

Rikk scanned the lake with a distracted glance. He saw—and felt—how free Kara was now that she'd released her secrets. He wanted to feel that same freedom and wished she'd ask if he had any secrets. But would

Kara understand his reasons for keeping his secrets? *Hell, do I understand them?*

She reached up and touched his cheek and her eyes looked as they were searching for reassurance. "Are we all right?"

"Yes," he gave her a heartening smile.

"Where do we go from here?"

"I don't know, Kara, but they got the sails on *Satori* this morning, and I know one hell of a captain whose boat will be out of commission for a few weeks. It's time to take *Satori* out on her maiden cruise."

"It's time." Kara slipped her arm around Rikk's waist, and together they walked to the car.

Rikk checked for oncoming traffic and observed Kara. He wondered if Kara was as anxious to be alone with him as he was to be alone with her again. Although sailing would provide the privacy that he craved, he didn't know how long he could contain his hunger for her. But he did know that *Satori* was the perfect place for both of them to be. It contained no memories of either Lauren or Connor and no ghosts that his house or *Genie's Bottle* might have.

⊹⊱◈⊰⊹

When Rikk turned the car off, Kara touched his hand and broke the silence. "Rikk, can we try to get *Satori* off the dock as quickly as possible?"

"Are you in a hurry?" He tantalized her with his suggestive grin.

She blushed and her words tumbled out. "Yes, and you know it." Then she asked, "Aren't you?"

Leaning in close to Kara, Rikk caressed down her cheek onto her neck, and slid his fingers around her nape. He raked his fingers through her hair and gently tugged on a strand of hair and examined it's ends while he controlled his breath. Uncertain if Kara would be comfortable at his house, he whispered, "We could go to my—"

"When you taking your boat out, Doc?" Dutch shouted out as he walked to the car.

Both startled and reeled away from each other. Rikk looked towards Dutch, then back at Kara staring down at her lap with a guilty grin on her face. "Right now, Dutch, right now."

"You need a hand with anything, just let me know."

"Dutch, I'm sure that Kara and I will be able to handle this by ourselves." Rikk noticed Dutch watch Kara get out of the car with the eagle eyes of a father hawking at his teenage daughter after he just caught her in her first kiss. Rikk eyed him and shot him a stern warning; Dutch nodded his head as if he acknowledged Rikk's claim for privacy.

"Got some research to do, Kara. I ain't gonna go back out fishing today. Just got to unload my truck. Taking some stuff to *Miss Sea*, that's all. Then I'm gone," Dutch said.

"Research?"

"Yep, and I got the feeling you two want to be alone, anyways."

"Thank you," Kara said to Dutch with a shy smile. Rikk walked around to Kara, wrapped his arm around her waist, and hugged her close to him as they walked to *Satori*.

Dutch kept to himself while he rummaged around in *Miss Sea*. He had thrown a duffle bag into her cockpit, but said no more to Kara and Rikk as they prepared to sail. Rikk and Kara removed the sail cover, started the engine, and in no time were removing dock lines from the cleats.

Kara fended *Satori* of the dock as Rikk backed her out of the slip, and then she jumped onboard. Rikk had just turned *Satori* toward the marina opening when Dutch ran up *Miss Sea*'s companionway and hollered out, "Doc, what you gonna name your boat?"

Kara picked up Rikk's handheld radio and hailed, "*Miss Sea, Miss Sea, Miss Sea*, this is *Satori*." Dutch hurried back down into *Miss Sea*'s cabin, went to his radio, and answered Kara's hail. "*Satori*? This is *Miss Sea*, six-eight."

"*Satori* on six-eight."

"What kind a name is *Satori*?"

Rikk pulled Kara between him and the wheel. He engulfed her in his arms and kissed her neck before she replied, "*Satori* is a perfect boat name."

Taking the radio from Kara, Rikk said, *"Miss Sea,* can you keep a secret? I named her *Satori* to remind Captain McKee to live in the moment, just in case she gets cold feet and catapults into the future or revisits the past, again. *Satori* is monitoring on sixteen." Kara's punch landed on Rikk's arm.

As Satori motored past *Whisper,* Sophie grabbed the air horn and gave it a toot. She hollered out, "Hey, *Satori!* What kind of sailing lessons is Captain Kara giving? And, what is this living in the moment? Be careful, you two."

Pete emerged from the cabin and grabbed Sophie around the waist and shouted, "Never mind her; she's a sucker for a love story."

Rikk looked at Kara and laughed as he said, "Sorry. Secret's out." Then another horn joined in and a few more horns blasted from the far corners of the marina.

"Careful what you say over the radio. These sailors are a noisy lot, all monitoring on channel sixteen to be the first to get the scoop and pass it on."

Rikk throttled up *Satori* and winked at Kara, "I hope it makes headlines in the marina's newsletter."

Chapter 39

Kara

Turning west into the St. Louis River basin, Rikk and Kara raised Satori's sails. With nowhere particular in mind, they sailed where the wind took them. Rikk was eager to learn, and Kara was enjoying sharing her skills with him.

Steering with one hand, Rikk cradled Kara with his free arm between him and the wheel. As they sailed, Kara relaxed into Rikk's solid body, with the comfort of his arm surrounding her waist. His warm breath fell over her neck when he nuzzled her head. When he stole a kiss they both were distracted, but the sound of the sails luffing brought them back. Kara would take over the wheel and steer back on course, filling the sails with wind again. Rikk kept one hand on the wheel, but it was obvious to Kara his attention was focused on her. He pressed his body gently into hers, and Kara felt Rikk's arousal as his hand holding her close to him began to caress her. She shuddered. His hand traveled down her belly, and under her jacket and t-shirt. Kara emitted a groan as her body arched at Rikk's touch. She forced herself to speak, "Rikk, we need to stop." Her voice croaked as she tugged herself back to the responsibility of sailing his boat. "I've had one harrowing experience on the water today; I'm not going to have two."

Rikk swallowed and brought his attention back to sailing, and his hand back to Kara's waist. "Let's go back to the marina."

"I think it is a perfect time for a lesson on setting an anchor, don't you?" Kara snuck under Rikk's arms. She needed to create space between them and to divert her attention. Her heart and body ached for Rikk, but she needed to cool her jets, and help him cool his too. Kara retrieved the chart of the St. Louis River basin from the cabin. They found two designated anchorages on the St. Louis River basin side—one on each end of Minnesota Point; or they could sail out onto Lake Superior to drop *Satori's* anchor. With winds out of the east, anchoring on the leeward side of Minnesota Point was the logical choice. Since they had tacked and were sailing back towards the marina, they decided to anchor at the Duluth end of the basin.

It only took a few minutes for them to get there and set the anchor. The gentle sound of budding leaves rustling in the wind muffled the negligible residential noise. Rikk disappeared into the cabin. Kara pulled off her polar fleece jacket, stepped out of her shoes, and stripped off her stockings. She kicked her feet up on the opposite cockpit seat and faced the sun.

"You look relaxed," Rikk said as he came up the companionway with the bottle of wine, two glasses, and the corkscrew they commandeered from *Genie's Bottle*.

"Oh, I'm getting there."

He uncorked the wine and poured them both a glass. Raising their glasses, Rikk toasted, "Here's to *Satori*."

Kara added, "And to years of incredible sails and all the great times she'll bestow." They took a sip, and Rikk sat down next to Kara. While Rikk took off his jacket and shoes, Kara shut her eyes, raised her glass slightly, and whispered, "And to big bumps that knock you to your senses."

"And to *Genie's Bottle*, who turned you around and brought you safely back," Rikk said.

A wry smile fell on her face when Kara remembered her wish on *Genie's Bottle* this morning and Dutch's hint that he'd done the same. It was a story that she couldn't wait to tell Rikk—but she would wait.

Kara set her glass on the wheel's cup holder and took Rikk's glass from him without protest. Rikk pulled Kara to him and kissed her, teasing and exploring. Kara's body tightened as Rikk kissed her neck.

"We need to watch the anchor for awhile before we get too distracted and make sure the anchor doesn't drag. See Enger Tower up there? That is one of the dead reckoning points we'll use." Kara picked out a couple more points. "We'll look out every five to ten minutes or so at each of the points. We can see if *Satori* is dragging anchor or holding by checking her position to the reference points."

"For how long?"

"Since this is a designated anchorage, it probably has great holding ground. We are also in the lee of the Minnesota Point, so we're well protected from the wind. We need to keep a close eye on it for half an hour."

"That long? Is that all we can do?"

"No, we can check the tension on the anchor, but that only tells us that it has dug in. If the sand is too soft, the anchor will plow through the sand as the waves or current float *Satori* out."

"Then what?"

"Then we anchor again or go back to the marina, but it felt like it was holding. In the meantime we drink a glass of wine, snuggle a bit, and wait."

After a while, Kara lay down on the cockpit seat. "I might as well soak up some of the sun's heat and vitamin D while we wait."

"I can't stand watching you lie there. Are you trying to frustrate me further?" Rikk's scheming smile reignited Kara's desires.

"You could join me. We could take a nap while we wait." Kara laughed at his immediate acceptance of her invitation. They snuggled under the warm sun and blue sky, but napping wasn't on their radar. Every few minutes Kara popped her head up to check the anchorage reference points, and Rikk would sit up and complete a full scan.

Kara looked at her watch, then whispered, "Time's up."

"Come here." Rikk drew Kara close. He kissed her ear and brushed his lips down her neck. He pulled her up as he stood, and they retreated into *Satori*'s cabin.

Hunger or love—Kara wasn't sure what possessed her more while she unbutton Rikk's shirt and he slid her bra straps off her shoulders. He nuzzled her neck and soon they tumbled onto the settee. Kara returned his kisses and caressing with eagerness. They were alone, and even though they were surrounded by two nearby cities, they might as well have been floating in the middle of the ocean. They were free to satisfy their urgency to love each other, wholly.

Chapter 40

Kara

The honking of a flock of geese flying overhead woke them. Kara wiggled off Rikk, "I'm going to check the anchor." She slipped on Rikk's shirt and climbed the companionway stairs into the cockpit. She looked 360 degrees around and spotted her land reference points. She jumped when her cell phone rang. Kara picked her fleece jacket up off the cockpit floor and wrestled her phone out of the pocket. It was Robin.

"Robin. Hi." She whispered, "I can't talk now—" Before she could say more the flock of geese landed a few hundred yards from *Satori*, honking and splashing in the water.

"What's that noise?" Robin said.

"Geese landing."

"Where *are* you?"

"Robin, I have so much to thank you for and want to tell you all that has happened today, but this is really not a good time for me. Can I call you tomorrow?"

"Are you OK?"

"Oh, God, Robin, I'm so much better than OK. I'm so happy I can't even begin to tell you."

"Are you with Rikk right now?"

"I am."

"In Bayfield?"

"No, we're in Duluth."

"Duluth?"

"On his boat."

"Oh, well, then I've got to go. Kara, call me tomorrow night because I have clients all day. I'm going to hate waiting to hear from you, but you sound better than you have in years."

"Robin, I'll call you tomorrow night. Bye."

"Can't wait. Bye."

Kara kneeled down and tugged on the anchor chain, reassured it had dug in. When Kara returned to the cockpit, Rikk was waiting there, wearing only trousers, and holding up her wine glass. She took the glass of wine and wrapped her free hand around his neck. "Thanks," she said and took a sip.

"Kara, I never imagined I'd see a woman walking on *Satori*'s deck so scantily dressed, let alone, in the middle of the day."

Kara blushed and admitted, "It comes from years in the Caribbean when most days you can hardly stand to wear even a swimsuit."

"I look forward to more of that." They sipped their wine, kissing, embracing, and teasing while they basked in each other's company until their glasses were empty. They lay back on the seat and once again dozed off.

An hour later, Kara awoke and raised her head off Rikk's chest. Rikk stirred and squinted through his eyelids. "How many days has it been since you've slept?" asked Kara.

Rikk groaned, "Since the day you appeared on the dock."

"I could stay here forever, Rikk, but I need to use the head." With that, Kara disappeared into the cabin. Rikk sat up, and gathered his and Kara's socks and shoes. He then brought them down into the cabin and set them on the settee.

When Kara emerged from the head, she hugged and caressed Rikk. Their hunger for each other had only begun to be satisfied. Rikk's hands lingered on her bare skin emerging below his shirt, but a growl sounded from his stomach and prompted their decision to pull up anchor.

⁂

Rikk steered *Satori* into Minnesota Point Marina. As *Satori* entered the slip, Kara jumped off onto the dock. They secured *Satori* on the dock cleats, and together they put the sail cover on and closed her up. *Miss Sea* bobbed in the next slip, and Kara said, "Dutch calls closing your boat up and leaving it at dock 'putting it to bed.' Hey, don't you wonder what his research is and how long he is going to be gone?"

"As much as I like Dutch, I'm glad that he is doing research and is not here. I'm sure it's personal business. Anyhow, I'm not willing to share you with him tonight." Then his stomach growled. "Kara, aren't you hungry? We could eat at Bellisio's." Kara raised her eyebrows in consideration but didn't answer, so Rikk asked, "How about going to the Lake Avenue Cafe or Black Woods?"

Kara gave no reply as she was contemplating Rikk's suggestions. Then her stomach growled and broke the silence.

"Where would you like to go?" he asked.

Although Kara considered all of his suggestions, she offered her own. "I have the makings for a great meal onboard *Genie's Bottle*. Do you have a grill?" Kara did not wait for his answer as she spotted his amusement with her offer. "We could make penne pasta and grill fresh green and red peppers, mushrooms, broccoli, carrots, and pea pods in olive oil and fresh herbs. We can stop at the market and get salmon or lake trout to grill. You can grate cheese, right? We can make a great dinner."

Rikk's derisive laugh preceded his proposal. "Or we can call Thai Krathong and order takeout?"

"Yes, I suppose we could. But all those fresh vegetables are just screaming to be devoured."

Rikk stayed his course and shook his head, "Or we could stop at a number of fast food joints along London Road?"

"Food can be very sensual when prepared by hungry sailors."

"Ok, let's raid *Genie*'s icebox and galley. If I didn't know better, I'd say you want to keep me secluded."

"What? Keep you all to myself? Perhaps you know me better than I thought," Kara said.

They loaded groceries and Kara's overnight duffle into the back of Rikk's car and headed across the lift bridge. The smell of food cooking from the Canal Park restaurants permeated the air, drenching the convertible with aromas that made their mouths water. Rikk announced, "Kara, I need to eat something now. I can't wait to cook something."

"Would an ice cream cone tide you over?" Kara said. "I'll buy if you walk to the lighthouse with me."

"You drive a hard bargain."

"I'll take that as a yes."

At Grandma's Boxcar, a train car converted into a food stand, Kara bought two cones. They strolled along the Lake Superior boardwalk and down the concrete canal pier to the lighthouse. Without thought, Kara placed her hand in Rikk's; the silence between them was tranquil, comfortable. Skaters and bicyclists infused energy into the crowd, weaving in between the couples, families, and groups of teens all basking under the early evening sun that warmed the air and cast its subtle illumination over the lake. The ice cream satisfied their immediate hunger and squelched their growling stomachs.

❧❀❦❀☙

While Rikk drove out of Park Point, Kara daydreamed. Resting her arm on the convertible's door, she pressed her hand into the wind and let it flap the direction that the wind chose. As they neared Rikk's house she noticed a slight scowl on Rikk's face. She cleared her throat, but he didn't seem to hear her. She bit her lip, trying to think of a gentle way to approach her question. The car slowed for the final traffic light, and Kara's quiet voice was just audible above the engine. "Rikk? Are you all right with this?"

"What?"

"Are you all right with this?"

"With what?"

"Bringing me to your and Lauren's home?"

Rikk reached over and took Kara's hand. "I am."

"Are you sure? Because there are other options besides this, and if you're not ready, it's not right."

"Kara, I was thinking about how odd it will be to have someone besides Lauren in the kitchen cooking. I want you there; it's just that the first time will be—" His voice trailed off, and Kara was tempted to help him find the words to finish his sentence, but she knew she'd never learn Rikk's answer if she provided it for him. She waited, searching his face for a clue. The light changed, and traffic began to move. "It will be different. It's a change—a good change."

"I'm never going to be Lauren."

"No, I don't want you to ever try." After a moment he asked, "Won't it be odd for you when I'm at your and Connor's home?"

"Yes, I suppose it will, though I've hardly been there in seven years, so my memories aren't as fresh as yours. But it will be odd," Kara said.

Rikk pulled into the garage and shut off the engine. He sat looking at the door, then turned and leaned his back shoulder against the car door. "Are you all right spending the night here with me?"

"I think I am. I mean, I want to spend the night with you, I just don't want you to be uncomfortable with me sharing your—" Kara stopped herself and looked away. Rikk tugged her hair. Heat rose up her crimson cheeks and she felt timid. Rikk brushed the back of his fingers across her cheek and smiled at her. Kara cleared her throat, and said, "You do have a guest room, don't you?"

"Let's make dinner and afterwards let our sleeping arrangements take care of themselves."

"Oh, I get it. Let's be in the moment."

"Yeah, something we both need to do more often."

They each grabbed two shore bags filled with *Genie's* provisions. Kara was transferring her bags to one hand, so she could carry her duffle bag too.

Rikk shook his head at her. "Don't you believe in two trips?"

"I guess it isn't that far. I'm used to walking a distance, so it's become instinctive to carry as much as I can to minimize my trips."

Rikk

"I'll get your bag later. I need some real food." Rikk unlocked the door, and Kara followed him into the kitchen. He gave her a quick tour of the kitchen, locating the cutting board and knives. "I'm going to change my clothes and get the charcoal out of the garage." He left her to prepare the vegetables for grilling.

"Rikk?" Kara called out after she had all the vegetables chopped and marinating.

"In here." Rikk answered her from his bedroom. Kara walked to the door and Rikk noticed her shy smile when she saw him putting clean sheets on the bed. Her cheeks flushed, and without any explanation he knew he'd conveyed their sleeping arrangements to her. "Would you mind giving me a hand?" Rikk's question eased the moment. He tucked the fitted sheet corners around the mattress then flung out the top sheet to Kara. Together they pulled the blanket up and folded the top sheet back over it. When they pulled the bed spread on top the bed, he watched Kara as she spotted her duffle bag that was hidden under it. She looked at Rikk, smiled, but didn't speak. "Pillowcases," he said and tossed her a pillow and a case. When Kara glanced back at her duffle, Rikk said, "I brought it in when I got the charcoal out of the garage." Rikk put the pillowcase on the pillow, tossed it on the bed, and walked around to Kara. He waited until she put her pillow on the bed; then he took her hand and walked out into the kitchen.

It was an odd moment, Rikk thought, for both of them—not bad, nor uncomfortable, just odd. Rikk wanted Kara there with him. Even after all her indecision and fears, he invited her into his whole life and was pleased that she had accepted.

They talked about sailing and foods while they cooked. Kara found a candle and placed it next to the place settings she had arranged on the kitchen bar. She cut a few lilac branches off the bushes in the backyard. The lilacs, which had only started to bud out about a week ago, permeated the room with their intoxicating fragrance. She put them into a water pitcher while Rikk finished grilling the salmon and vegetables. Kara tossed the grilled vegetables into the penne noodles and grated Asiago cheese and Rikk opened a bottle of wine and poured their glasses. Towards the end of the meal Kara asked, "Rikk, do you think cupid's arrow could ever strike Dutch's heart?"

The out-of-the-blue question brought an astonished grin to Rikk's face. "After all the blind dates I told you about and your belief in the law of attraction, I hope you aren't thinking about match-making for Dutch?"

"No. I was just thinking how wonderful it'd be for Dutch to spend his last years with someone. Companionship must be important to him, the way he pushed us together."

"Kara, there is something that I can't quite figure out. It is easy to see why Dutch called Heidi a siren, but why you? What made him so mad at you, and how did he get over it all of a sudden? He is back to treating you like a daughter."

"Prodigal father?" Kara said and shrugged.

Rikk's eyebrows rose. "I don't buy that."

"I guess I reminded him of something that was painful, and he took it out on me."

"Is this confidential?"

"It is. Dutch insisted on talking to me before I left this morning. He tried to convince me to stay—to stay because of you. Our conversation is confidential, but I will say that I guessed what had been bothering him."

"Do you think he is not fishing today because of it?"

"I don't know what his mission was today; I'm just happy he had one." Kara's smile suggested agreement.

"You look happy. Now what were you saying about me knowing you better than I thought? Something about having exclusive access to me?"

"I think it was about secluded access to you for the entire evening."

"You've gotten your wish, Kara McKee."

"You're too easy—and—I need a shower. May I use your shower?"

"Yes, of course. You don't have to ask. You can make yourself at home here."

Kara stood up, kissed his cheek, and said, "Thank you." She took their plates to the kitchen sink, and Rikk followed and insisted on doing dishes. Kara went into the master bathroom and took a long shower. Rikk thought about all that had happened in the last five days. He thought about Dutch, and about how Kara wondered if Dutch would find someone now that he had successfully pierced both of their hearts with his cupid's arrows. Most of all, his thoughts were on how Kara had released him from his loneliness. Nothing, he hoped, would change that.

Kara

Rikk knocked on the bathroom door, "Here's a robe," he said as he hung his robe on the hook.

Kara stepped out of the shower, dried off, and donned the black plush robe. She combed her wet hair and applied moisturizer to her face and body. How long had it been since she last felt excited about her future—a future including Rikk? Drowning in Rikk's bathrobe, Kara joined Rikk in the living room. He was looking out the window at the lake. As he turned, Kara sat down on the couch. Rikk's eyes were riveted on her exposed neck where his robe gapped apart. When she crossed her legs she felt the robe slide open. Kara watched his eyes meander down her thigh.

Rikk crossed the room. He took Kara's hand, pulled her up, and led her into the bedroom. He stepped behind her, standing so close they were almost touching—yet he maintained the most excruciating and minuscule distance between them. Kara felt the intense heat radiate from his body. Rikk tugged the robe's belt and the knot gave away leaving the ends dangling from the belt loops. Kara's eye's fluttered as the robe draped open. He floated his finger scarcely above her skin, tracing over her cheek, drawing down her chin, and outlining her neck—daring never to make contact with her skin. All the while, his chin grazed her ear and the heat from his breath warmed her cheeks. With agonizing leisure, Rikk eased the robe off Kara's shoulders. She quaked as it skimmed down her back and fell to her feet.

Kara never expected making love would feel this natural or this whole again. The one aspect of her life she had been ignoring, Rikk revived by his satisfying of her desires; with tenderness she hadn't expected. She hoped that she gave Rikk the same passion she'd just received.

Kara collapsed onto Rikk's encircling embrace, and tears welled in her eyes. She tried to squeeze her tears back, but her body shuddered, and tears rolled down her cheek onto his arm.

Rikk soothed Kara with his caresses and whispered, "It's OK, Kara. It's OK." He reassured her, "Crying is a natural emotional release."

"I know," Kara whispered, "I know." She also knew that living in the present was the explanation of her release. She felt alive. Living in the past and then in the future these past couple of years, she rarely had lived in the now. "Rikk? You do know these are tears of joy, don't you?"

"Yeah, I know." Rikk pulled a pillow under Kara's head, caressed her, and kissed her forehead.

Cradled in Rikk's arms, Kara's thoughts drifted off. She listened to Rikk's relaxed, deepening breathing and watched his serene expression until he fell asleep. She realized that she just had an amazing satori—a moment of presence on so many levels. It was the first of many she knew were going to follow. Lulled by the beating of Rikk's heart, her eyes closed and she dozed off.

The mumbled words of Rikk's sleep talking awoke Kara. The first few sentences she couldn't make out, but after Rikk's self-satisfied chuckle Kara made out his words, "Third time's a charm." She listened for awhile, hoping that he'd say more, but he didn't. Was she the charm; and if so, what did he mean by the third time? Kara wanted to wake him and ask him about his dream, but she decided it could wait until morning. She snuggled up to him and fell into a peaceful sleep.

Chapter 41

Kara

Tuesday morning the phone rang and jolted Rikk and Kara out of their slumber. Rikk's eye squinted as the dawn's rays gleamed through the window and illuminated Kara. She clenched her eyes closed to shut out the sun. He fumbled to reach the phone, but when he answered it he realized the ring was from a cell phone. It took three more rings to clear his grogginess enough to realize it wasn't his cell, but Kara's.

"It's yours," Rikk said.

"Are you sure?"

"It's not my ring," Rikk said with a laugh. Then the alarm clock, playing the morning news program's theme song, joined her ringing cell phone. "But that's my wakeup call."

"Who'd call *me* this early in the morning?" Kara groaned an squinted at him.

Rikk was already pulling the blankets back and sitting up. He turned his alarm clock off and put his bathrobe on before he stumbled into the bathroom. Rikk found Kara's jacket with the phone ringing in its pocket hanging on the door hook and handed it to her.

The caller ID said Minnesota Point Marina. Kara took the phone and pulled the blankets over her head as she answered it. "Hello?"

"Kara, this is Dan. Sounds like I woke you up?'

Still exhausted, Kara tried to sound alert, "Um, yeah—what is it, Dan, has something happened to *Genie*?"

"No, *Genie*'s fine. I know six is a little early to call, but you are usually are up before I get here at quarter to. Sorry I woke you."

347

"It's OK. Why did you call?"

"I just listened to a message from a long-time slip holder who just bought a boat and needs a crew to bring it from Chicago to Duluth. I thought you might be interested in a delivery since *Genie's Bottle* is laid up and all. Here's the thing; his wife was coming along, but their daughter broke her arm last night and needs her mom to help her with her new baby and toddler. The boat will be launched today and he needs to sail first thing tomorrow morning because he has to get it here before the first weekend in June. With a perfect weather forecast these next few days, they planned to drive to Chicago this morning. So you will need to decide in the next few minutes."

"Geez, Dan. I don't even have my eyes open yet." Rikk walked back into the bedroom, pulled the blankets off Kara's head, and mouthed the word "coffee?" Kara nodded and pulled the covers back over her head, and then said, "Can I call you back?"

"Sure, but can you call back in fifteen to twenty minutes. He needs to find someone and get on the road. If I don't call right back, he'll start making calls and find someone else."

"He sounds uptight."

"No, Kara, he's great. He's laid-back. Here's the other thing, his other daughter is getting married in a few weeks. They are letting the newlyweds sail the boat on their honeymoon in the Apostles."

"What a dad and mom! OK, I think I can. I mean, what else do I have going on? Oh, man, let me call you back. I have to get a cup of coffee and wake up a bit."

"Sounds good, Kara. Hey, he asked for you after he heard about your return to the marina yesterday."

"Really?" Kara was surprised. "Sounds like you are putting pressure on me."

"Just a little. He's a great sailor, and he's got a great boat."

"What is it?"

"It is a newer Tartan 43."

"Oooohh," Kara said as she shut her eyes visioning how beautiful Tartans are. Impulsively she said, "OK, I'll do it. Is he a good sailor?"

"Kara. You will love him. He is a lot like Dutch, but he comes in a more polished wrapper. His name is Jim Bolt, and he's a salt-of-the-earth-guy."

"Dan, is anyone else crewing for him?"

"Ted wants to, but I can't spare him for that long this time of year. Jim is a good customer and a super guy. I wouldn't be calling you at this hour of the morning if he wasn't."

"OK, sign me up."

"Great. How long will it take you to get ready? Should I have him call you?"

"Let me think. Yeah, but give me a few minutes to go to the bathroom and break it to Rikk, OK?"

"Oh yeah, you and Rikk. That's good, huh?"

"Yeah, it's good." She smiled, "It's great. Um, but I've got to go. Give me fifteen minutes before you have him call me."

"Thanks, Kara. Hey, I really am sorry about stealing you away from Rikk."

"OK, OK. Dan, now you're embarrassing me. I'll see you in a bit." Kara dragged the blankets off and slipped out of bed to hang up the phone when Rikk returned.

"What did Dan want?"

"Hang on. I have to go to the bathroom." Kara closed the door and sat down on the toilet. She groaned and cradled her face in her hands. "What did I just do?" she murmured aloud.

Rikk asked, "What?"

"Hang on; I'll be out in a sec." She washed her hands and splashed water on her face. She willed herself the courage to break the news to Rikk.

Kara walked out to see Rikk pulling socks, underwear, and a t-shirt out of the dresser. She walked up behind him, hugged him—resting her head on his back, and latched her hands in front of him. He unclasped her hands and spun around to embrace her. Kara stood up on her toes to kiss him. The spark ignited, and they toppled onto the bed. Kara snuck her fingers over Rikk's lips and said, "I have to tell you what Dan wanted." She exaggerated an apprehensive look and wiggled out of Rikk's tight embrace. Rikk's frown prompted her courage. "Dan called to ask if I would crew on a boat coming from Chicago. The owner has to get the boat here before his daughter's wedding on the first weekend in June." Kara relayed the story to him and was relieved he wasn't upset.

"When do you leave?"

"Actually he is going to call any minute now, and Dan said as soon as I can get my stuff together we'll be on our way to Chicago."

"Oh." If Rikk attempted to hide his disappointment, he had failed.

"I know. I made a snap decision. I suppose I could tell him no," Kara said.

"No, that would be unreasonable after you already agreed. It's just that I thought you would be around. I'm selfish to expect that you stay here with nothing to do." Rikk sat up, swung his feet to the floor, "I'm just not ready to miss you."

How could Rikk say the thing she'd love hearing the most and the least in the same sentence? Kara sat up next to him. "Oh God, I'm not ready to miss you either. I probably would've gone to Bayfield today or tomorrow anyhow. I have to do a walk-through with the renter and see what needs to be painted or repaired before I move in."

"Weren't you planning on staying here until *Genie* is fixed?"

"Yes, but I do need to take care of my house. You didn't expect me to stay here the entire time they are fixing *Genie's Bottle* while you're working. You do have to go to work this week, don't you?"

"Yes. I have a long week. I expect that they have rescheduled most of my appointments from yesterday to Thursday—my day off. Kara, I didn't expect you to stay here all that time. Although the thought of holding you captive does have a certain appeal." Rikk ran his hands through his hair and sighed. "When will you get back?"

"I'm not sure; I didn't even think to ask, but I would guess that if he wants to get back as soon as possible, he'll push it. It will be week and a half at least, weather dependent, of course. My guess is he'll want to—or need to get back to help with his daughter's wedding preparations. He wants to leave Chicago tomorrow morning."

Rikk dropped back onto the bed and pulled Kara down beside him. He rolled onto his side towards Kara and supported his head on his elbow. "So do you think you will be back by Memorial Day weekend?"

"Yes, I would think I will be back for sure by then. Do you have the weekend off?"

Rikk swung his legs over hers and drew her arms above her head, gently pinning them to the mattress. "I want to keep you here all to myself, Kara. I'm tired of sharing."

"I can still say no."

"No, I'm being selfish. A week and a half is a long time to be wondering what trouble you're getting into."

She grabbed her pillow and hit him. "Rikk, I'll dream about you day and night. Will you dream about me?"

"You have no idea, Kara—no idea how much I've dreamed of you."

"Were you dreaming of me last night?"

"Why do you ask?"

"You were talking in your sleep." Kara laughed at the guilty look that crossed his face. "You said 'third time's a charm.' What were you dreaming about?"

"I may have been dreaming about you," Rikk said and then kissed her.

It was obvious to Kara that Rikk had no intention to answer her question. "You were dreaming of me! Admit it!" He just laughed; elevating her curiosity. Kara's phone rang again, and Rikk reached to pick it up. Kara grabbed his arm and stopped him. "What does 'third time's a charm' mean?" He laughed again, then picked up her phone and handed it to her. He left to shower, and Kara made her plans with the boat owner.

Chapter 42

Kara

It was two thirty on Friday afternoon, May 25th, and Kara hadn't seen Rikk in eleven days. She laughed at how giddy she was to see him and wondered if the obsessive compulsiveness of a new romance ever felt anything but sophomorically lusty and urgent. She muttered, *Note to self—try to act your age.*

<hr>

Kara and Jim Bolt were a couple miles from the canal entrance when Kara turned the helm over to him. They'd been motoring in a thick drizzle, but Kara was grateful for the almost perfect weather they had until yesterday morning. The low-pressure system moved in on this last leg of the trip and was moving through the southwestern tip of Lake Superior, central Minnesota, and northern Wisconsin.

<hr>

Once the Tartan was secured at dock, Kara checked in with Dan to see if there was any update on *Genie's Bottle*. She found out that *Genie's* repairs were on the schedule for mid-June. She had called Rikk that morning, and they had planned to meet on *Satori* after work. When they talked, Kara thought Rikk would arrive at the marina before her, but with the favorable winds they made better time than expected—despite the continuous drizzle they sailed through today. She stood outside the marina office and considered sitting around on *Satori*. Waiting for Rikk for an hour and a half after she'd been on a boat for the last ten days with minimal stops and only two layovers lacked the appeal of stretching her legs and taking a vigorous walk—even through the drizzle.

On her hike, Kara lost herself in the smells, sights, and sounds of Minnesota Point. It reminded her of two weeks earlier when she walked past *Satori*, newly delivered on the trailer—and of her re-encounter with Rikk. Although she had talked to him daily since she left for the sailboat delivery, she couldn't wait to be with him.

Kara crossed the Aerial Lift Bridge and US Interstate 35 overpass lost in her thoughts. Excited to reunite with Rikk, she trekked through the city before she realized how far she'd gone. She discovered herself waiting for a light on Third Avenue. How she got downtown, yet remembered little about walking there, mystified her. She stopped and deliberated between turning east or west. East led to the clinic where Rikk worked. Was she crazy to walk that direction? She reasoned that Rikk would see her walking and pick her up if he was driving to the marina. She pulled her cell phone out and called him, hoping he was done with work or would be soon. His voicemail answered, so she left a message and walked east.

Kara found herself standing outside the clinic. Strands of wet hair framed her misted face, and rivers meandered down her slicker. She wasn't sure what Rikk would think of her barging into the clinic like this, but she'd leave a message with the receptionist and wait at the coffee shop for him. God, she hoped he hadn't already left, and their paths had already crossed. It was four thirty when she walked into the waiting room. The receptionist's surprised look made Kara realize that she was pretty much soaked through. She glanced around the waiting room to witness all the eyes in the room focused on her dripping torrents onto the carpet. She looked at the raincoats filling the racks and a few opened umbrellas drying in the corner; these people were all very dry. She felt herself flush but cleared her throat and said, "Hi, I was wondering if Dr. Harmon is still here?"

The receptionist's eyebrows shot up into her hairline as she considered Kara's question. A caution-laden voice replied, "Do you have an appointment to see Dr. Harmon?"

"No, I—I don't, I—" Kara felt the heat rising in her cheeks, and took a deep breath. "I'm a friend of his, and I got into town a little earlier than

I expected. I just thought if he was here—I guess I should tell you who I am. I'm Kara McKee—um, and I just walked here from the marina." Kara was stammering and felt silly for coming to his office. She was about to turn and walk out but decided to explain herself. She took a deep breath and in a composed manner started over. "I called and left a message for him. I'm sorry; I should've waited for him to return it. I'll wait for him to call me." She turned toward the door, and the receptionist asked, "Do you want to leave a message?"

"Oh, um, yeah, um, you can tell him Kara McKee stopped to see him and that I got back a little early." Kara turned again for the door.

"Kara, is that you?"

Kara turned and saw a nurse she'd met at the benefit. She smiled and said, "Yes. Hi, it's Carol, right? Did your son get the art scholarship he applied for?" They had commiserated about their college age children when Carol mentioned she'd spent the day helping her son with his application.

"Oh, how nice it is of you to remember. Yes, he did. So you are back from your trip. Does Dr. Harmon know you are here?" Carol asked.

"No, actually, I left a message on his cell phone, but I haven't talked to him yet. I was out walking—after being cooped up on a boat for ten days I needed to move, and—well, I ended up here. I must be crazy for coming here without talking to him first," Kara said, "but is he still here?"

"Yes, he has one more patient. I think he'll be done in about half an hour. Let me tell him you're here," Carol turned and almost walked into Rikk.

"Dr. Harmon, Kara is here," Carol said like a gleeful hen clucking as Rikk's eyes met Kara's. Rikk stared at her for an awkward moment. Kara, certain that she had done the wrong thing, looked down trying to figure out how to disappear. Rikk took a step forward and grinned at her. Kara glanced back at him to see the laughter in his eyes that always enchanted her. She breathed a sigh of relief and beamed while biting her bottom lip. She looked away, feeling self-conscious, because she'd just seen the face she had longed to touch for days. Rikk bent down and talked to the receptionist in a quiet voice, all the while keeping his eyes locked on Kara. He straightened up and smiled at her. He raised his voice so she could hear him. "And have Kara wait in my office." She knew that devious grin pasted on his face revealed how glad he was to see her. He shook his head and to her he said, "I'll be done in twenty—twenty-five minutes."

∗∘◉∘∗

Kara walked into his office, looked around, and removed her wet slicker. She spied pictures on his desk and strolled around it to get a better look. She sat down, picked up the picture of Zoey, Eric, and the kids, and studied it for a while. She picked up the picture of Lauren holding Zoey when she was a toddler. She hoped that she'd be successful at always honoring Zoey's memory of Lauren—and Rikk's.

Kara gazed around his office walls and noticed his doctorate diploma hanging above his desk. She stood to read it. He graduated from the University of Minnesota Medical School a couple years after she had attended the U. *Wow. Rikk was there when I was.*

The doorknob turned, and Rikk walked in and caught her standing behind his desk, looking at his diploma. "Are you checking to see if it is authentic?" Rikk teased.

"No," Kara stood up. "Hey, I'm sorry if I've caused you any embarrassment. I wasn't thinking. I just started walking and ended up here," Kara shrugged. "I couldn't wait to see you."

Rikk laughed, "I don't know why you'd think you caused me embarrassment." He walked across his office, took Kara in his arms, and kissed her.

When they parted, Kara's wet locks stuck to Rikk's cheek. Kara laughed and asked, "Even if I walk in looking like a drenched rat?"

"You always make a stunning appearance, dripping wet or dry," Rikk taunted.

After a moment considering whether to give Rikk's joust attention or not, Kara decided on a different tack. "You know, this diploma does look forged." She grinned, and then stepped away from Rikk looking back at his diploma. "I was just sitting here, patiently waiting for you and decided to snoop at your pictures. Then I noticed that you graduated from the U. Do you know we were there at the same time?" Rikk stepped away from Kara. His grave expression surprised Kara. "What's the matter? Did I say something wrong?"

"No, Kara. I guess I have a secret I've withheld from you." Rikk's fingers on both of his hands raked his scalp. His voice was tense and metered. "When I was finishing my graduate program and had just been accepted into medical school—" His shoulders slumped while he shook his head.

"What happened, Rikk?" Kara searched his eyes for an answer to his abrupt mood swing. "What is it?"

Chapter 43

Rikk

Rikk cleared his throat and said, "I was a teaching assistant in a chemistry lab. After class let out, a campus tour guide walked in. She was looking for a newer lab to show to some foreign professors and dignitaries who were visiting from a university in Brazil. Her smile lit up the room—her warmth engulfed me. She told me she wanted to show them the newest, most modern buildings and labs, and she asked if she could show them my lab at approximately the same time next week. God, those seven days passed slowly. The following week she returned with the dignitaries and an interpreter, and my heart leaped when I saw her again. She was so alive and casual; she was professional but so comfortable in her skin. She spoke to them, smiling and peering directly into all of their eyes as if they understood every word she said. Then the interpreter relayed her information to them as she focused on all their faces. She introduced me, and explained I was the TA for the lab session that just ended. I managed to put a couple of coherent words together before one of the professors asked the interpreter to ask her if she was a student in this lab. All eyes were on her when the interpreter asked the question." Rikk sighed and took in Kara's astonished expression.

Damn it, why didn't he tell Kara this before? And why did he tell her now? Rikk knew very well why. He admired Kara's strength for disclosing that he'd been the inspiration for her book, and, like Kara, he wanted the freedom from the burden of keeping a secret. He also knew keeping it to himself would make it fester and grow. She deserved to know that he had concealed a secret too. If she discovered his secret, a wedge would be driven between them, especially with her feelings about concealed facts being lies. Whatever happened, he had to free himself of his secret's weight and let her choose their fate.

357

"Kara, you looked at the professor who asked the question and laughed. You should have heard the surprise in your voice. You said, 'Me? No! I'm majoring in English. I'm glad to be done with the twenty science credits I need for my degree.' The interpreter laughed at your answer before he relayed it to the group. Then they all laughed and joked with each other. I always wondered what they were saying, but I could see how enchanted they were with you. Kara, they fell in love with you, and I just stood back and watched with my tongue tied. I wondered for quite awhile why I didn't ask for your name and number. Every time I thought about finding the office that arranged tours and looking you up, I was sure you had more guys lined up at your door than you wanted." Rikk stood motionless waiting for Kara to respond.

Kara sank into his chair but maintained eye contact with Rikk. She caught her breath and had to remind herself to breathe—three times—before she whispered, "So, that—that was you?"

"You remember me?"

Kara continued to stare at Rikk and nodded. She was speechless as she watched Rikk frozen with defeat overtaking him. Kara diverted her eyes out the window.

Rikk kneeled down next to her and looked up into her chagrined face. "Kara, I'm guilty of keeping a secret too, and hope you can understand why."

"When did you recognize me, Rikk?"

"The first time was the moment that I saw you and Connor, right after Tate's surgery; you were waiting in the family room. Kara, you looked so familiar, but I wasn't positive until later when I came to check on Tate. I ran into Connor just outside Tate's door. He was going to get coffee. You had stayed with Tate, so I was showing you his incision and discussing his care. You were standing on the other side of his bed. I asked if you could see the stitches, and you said no. I had you come around next to me for a better view, and your head almost touched mine while you looked at it. As I explained the protocol, you looked up at me, and our eyes seem to lock. My heart missed a beat, Kara, and I froze. I was sure you did too. At that moment, your face became perfectly clear. Kara, when I was at the U, I had been so busy with my first quarter of med school I didn't have time to try to find you. But I never forgot you." Rikk's eyes dropped down, and in a quiet voice he said, "You have no idea how many times your smile shone in my daydreams and actually some very erotic night dreams too."

Kara stared at Rikk. "Is that what you meant when you said I had no idea how often you dreamed of me?"

"Yes."

"Wow," Kara said in a hollow voice. "I don't know what to say."

"Kara, I stepped out of my boat, and you were standing on the dock. You recognized me but acted as if you didn't. The truth is that it hurt. This was the third time you appeared in my life, and this time you couldn't wait to get away from me."

"Third time's a charm," Kara's voice seemed to echo off the office walls. "You talked in your sleep and said 'Third time's a charm.' I knew you were dreaming of me from the guilty look on your face that morning. Is that what your sleep talking was about—the third time we met?"

"Yes. In the dream I confessed that you had captured my interest the first and second time we met, but I hadn't captured your interest until the third time. You said third time's a charm and kissed me. I laughed and said it back to you, and then I woke up." Rikk shook his head and looked up at the ceiling, then blew out a deep breath. "Kara, I wish I could have been as easy going when we met on the dock the day Satori was delivered as I was in that dream. My self-pity tainted everything, and your reaction to me—I don't know. I couldn't handle you rebuffing me."

"Is that why you were so surly?"

"Surly? Yeah, I guess that's how I acted. You kept trying to avoid me, and it felt good to irritate you. It didn't take long to see that you were flustered whenever I was around."

"So it was fun for you to annoy me?" Kara's voice was almost a whisper.

"Fun? I'm not sure that it was exactly fun, but it started out as revenge, and before I knew it I was way over my head."

"Revenge?"

"Yeah, revenge. I dreamed about you every time our paths crossed. This time, when I had the chance to get to know you, you avoided me like I had done something terrible to you."

"Why didn't you tell me this after you read the letter from my editor?"

"Geez, Kara! You wrote a book about me. That blew me away."

Kara gazed out the window as silence overtook Rikk's office. "You said it kind of turned you on."

"Yeah, it did—still does. I didn't know, Kara, I was afraid."

"Afraid of what?"

"Afraid you wouldn't forgive my surly behavior."

"After I told you that you'd inspired Jack?"

"I'm sorry, Kara. After I read that letter from your editor, I actually hoped you would ask if I had any secrets. You didn't ask, and I didn't have the courage to tell you. Besides, I wasn't sure how you would take me telling you that I remembered you from a chance encounter twenty-five years ago when you only remembered me from seventeen years ago. I was afraid that now after we finally were together, telling you this would push you away, and you'd be gone forever."

"I'm sorry. That must have hurt." Kara took a long breath and held it, then slowly let it out. "I do remember you. I just never put it together that Tate's surgeon was that lab TA. Rikk, I walked by your lab a couple of times after I gave that tour, hoping that I would run into you."

"You did?"

"Yes."

Rikk stared at the floor, shaking his head and wondering why things between them took so long to work out. Would the third time be a charm for Kara and him. At last he said, "I'm sorry I lashed back at you like a vengeful seventh grader when I recognized you on the dock."

"Well, revenge is a few steps up from insecurity." Kara stood up. "I really hurt you, didn't I?"

"That's because you didn't act like a seventh grader; you didn't react to my revenge."

"But I did. I just stopped myself from doing it in front of you—at least most of it."

"You reeled me in, Kara."

Kara covered her eyes and face as she half laughed and said, "I think you reeled me in."

Rikk drew her hands into his, peered into her face, "Remember when you asked me to think of someone while we were standing under the lobby roof?"

"You thought of Dutch."

"That is who I told you I thought of. But when you said that I needed to think of someone that I hadn't thought of in years, the vision of you standing in the lab with Brazilian dignitaries smiling and laughing flashed through my brain."

"Oh."

"I suppose that was cheating, since you were standing right there."

"Cheating? I don't know. Your higher conscious mind brought that memory back to you. What did you think about that vision?"

"That is what is really odd. It was more a feeling that just washed over me."

"A feeling! Rikk, that is the woo that I believe in."

Rikk sent her a light-hearted, sardonic grin. "Yeah, I know."

"Well, I don't care what you believe in or if you ever even somewhat see this through my eyes." Kara laughed and shook her head. "I believe those feelings are the woo, and they happen to everyone. If people pay attention to those feelings, they'll see that it is their emotions and intuition guiding them to where they want to be."

"That doesn't prove your woo theory correct, but I knew—I felt that it was our time."

"Our time?" Kara's words escaped in a whisper. She blinked and exhaled.

"Is it our time, Kara?"

"I'm, I'm—" Stillness prevailed. She whispered, "Do you have any other secrets?"

"None." Rikk blurted the answer out. Softer he added, "Do I have a chance?"

Kara's smile turned into quiet laughter as she held Rikk's penetrating gaze. "I don't believe in chance—not like that anyhow."

"That's right. You believe in choice."

"Yes, I believe in choice. But the opportunity to make choices springs from the synchronicity of those chance encounters."

Satori, Rikk thought to himself. He felt they both were being in the moment, even with the shock of their past he'd just revealed. He hoped Kara would rather be with him than anywhere else. "I choose to be with you." Rikk paused and hope filled his voice as he asked, "What do you choose, Kara?

"You!" she whispered. "I hope you are prepared for the ride of your life."

"Somehow, I don't think anything could prepare me for that ride with you."

"Oh, hell, I suppose preparing would take all the excitement out of it. I got a feeling life will always be interesting for us—interesting and steeped full of new bearings adjustments and course changes."

"Change is good, Kara,"

"Yes, change is good. Change is great!" She kissed him.

May 28, 2007

Kara

Memorial weekend raced by with Rikk and Kara spending the weekend sailing *Satori*, lounging in her cabin and cockpit, and exploring their pasts and planning their future—but dwelling in the present. Monday evening they docked *Satori* and packed leftover groceries and their clothes. Kara and Rikk had only seen Dutch once, early that weekend. They were putting the sail cover over *Satori*'s main sail when Dutch came bustling down to *Miss Sea*.

"Dutch, where have you been all weekend? Hey, look at how handsome you look!" Kara whistled at him, while giving him an admiring look-over.

"I been taking care of personal matters," Dutch replied with a wink.

"Personal matters?" Rikk's side glance seemed to ask Kara for an explanation, but Kara didn't know what Dutch's wink meant either. "Is everything all right?" Kara said

"Let's just say I took my own advice." Dutch changed the subject, "Now, tell me how, what's her name, *Satori*? How'd she sail?"

Rikk and Kara proceeded to fill Dutch in with the sailing adventures that they had over the weekend. Kara excused herself to use the marina restrooms, leaving Rikk and Dutch to regale each other with their boating adventures.

≈≈⊛≈≈

When Kara neared the end of the dock, she noticed a black Lincoln Town Car pull up and park. The driver got out and opened the door for a petite and dignified older woman wearing charcoal dress slacks and a white cardigan over a white silk blouse. Kara heard the woman say, "Please, wait

363

here, Vincent." Her dark sunglasses did not disguise her pensive expression. She stood motionless, as if she were trying to will herself to take a step. At last she walked towards the docks, then stopped and looked back at her car.

Kara smiled at her and intuitively felt the woman needed a welcoming boost. She walked up to her and said, "Pardon me, ma'am. You seem to be looking for directions. Can I help you find something?"

"Oh, yes, thank you. I'm looking for the C dock."

"Go down B dock, straight ahead, and then C dock intersects on your left."

"Thank you." The woman forced a smile, and took a couple more steps.

"Are you looking for someone in particular? I know many of the boats on C dock; maybe I could help you find the one you're looking for."

"Oh," she heaved a sigh, "I'm not even sure that I'm ready to find my friend."

"Hmm. Well, if you need any help, I'd be glad to point out your friend's boat."

"Thank you." She passed Kara, giving her a nervous smile. "Your directions have already helped me."

✦✦✦

Kara chided herself for being the nosy sailor that she was, but her curiosity piqued about this woman and she couldn't help but wonder what her story was. After Kara used the restroom, she hurried back to *Satori* to help Rikk finish packing their bags and putting *Satori* to bed. She was surprised to catch up to the woman, who was standing at the intersection of B and C docks. The woman gave Kara an anxious glance and turned towards her. Kara sent her an encouraging smile and thought the woman looked as flooded with apprehension as Kara felt when Rikk stepped out of *Satori*'s cabin a couple of weeks ago. Kara said, "Are you all right?"

"I'm just a little nervous."

"You look nervous." Kara, trusting her intuition, blurted out, "Have you ever heard that ninety-two percent of the things we worry about never happen?"

She gave Kara a rueful smile and said, "Yes, I have heard that."

"Most of the time our worries are not only unfounded, but they also are completely the opposite of what *is* true."

"Oh, dear, I've lost all my courage. It's been so long, so many years. I don't know what I was thinking—" Her voice drifted off as her body tensed.

An astonished whisper burst from Kara. "Miss Charlotte?" She guessed this woman's presence had to be the result of Dutch taking his own advice. This was why he'd missed a weekend of fishing—this was what he researched.

Shock filled the woman's face, and her voice was hoarse. "I beg your pardon? Have we met?"

"No, please let me explain. I'm Kara McKee, a friend of Dutch's. You are Charlotte, aren't you?" Kara paused as Charlotte confirmed this with a nod. "Please, let me put you at ease. Dutch confided in me and told me about you, but only because Dutch couldn't bear to watch me risk sailing away from the man I fell in love with. Dutch has never stopped loving you, Charlotte. He has guarded his love and memories of you from everyone he knows, until a few days ago. It was only because I had guessed he was still holding a torch for someone that he finally was able break through his hurt and silence. He still loves you. Dutch didn't want me to make the same mistake he had, so he told me about you."

Charlotte's color drained from her face. Kara continued, "Dutch was trying to save me from making a terrible mistake. I was leaving when I had every reason to stay. When Dutch tried to talk some sense into me, I guessed that his boat, *Miss Sea*, was actually named after you. He couldn't risk naming it Miss Charlotte because you meant so much to him that he couldn't even bring himself to talk about you. So, he cleverly disguised your first initial C with the word Sea—as in the Mediterranean Sea. It's a long story," Kara said as she looked toward *Miss Sea* and offered her arm to Charlotte. "Here, take my arm; let's walk together, Miss Charlotte, and I will take you directly to Dutch." Kara realized that Miss Charlotte was having a hard time following all that she had said, so she added this explanation, "Dutch just mentioned that he was busy taking his own advice this weekend. I'm guessing that advice was to contact you."

"Oh my, I—I'm not sure I—I can go through with this," Charlotte stammered.

"Dutch is a wonderful man. He is so light and happy this evening, much more than usual, and he's looking very handsome too. You've come all the way here after so many years. Are you really willing to risk walking out now when you are so close to finding him after all this time apart?"

"I'm not sure if Dutch will even like me anymore."

"If you leave now, Miss Charlotte, when will you ever have another chance to find out? Your intuition has guided you this far. Please allow it to take you all the way to find out how you feel after you meet him again." Kara said as she grasped Charlotte's hand that rested it on her extended arm. "Let's walk." Kara said, and escorted Charlotte down the dock.

Dutch was standing in *Miss Sea*'s cockpit talking to Rikk as Kara and Charlotte approached the boats. Rikk had just tossed their canvas shore bags from *Satori* onto the dock. Kara patted Charlotte's hand as they walked down the finger dock next to *Miss Sea*. Rikk looked up as Kara and Charlotte approached. He was speechless as they walked to *Miss Sea*.

When Dutch saw astonishment spread over Rikk's face, he turned to see what caught Rikk's attention. Dutch and Charlotte's eyes met and they both held their breaths, their faces frozen in uncertainty. Dutch's knees wobbled and he caught himself on *Miss Sea*'s deck rail. Charlotte gasped for air as her eyes darted between Dutch and Rikk. Kara supported her as she teetered.

Rikk looked onto the scene in utter confusion. He finally managed to say, "Mom? What are you doing here?" Charlotte's eyes left Dutch, and remorse washed over her face while silence fell over all of them.

The awkward stillness ensued until Kara quietly said, "Dutch?"

Dutch scurried off *Miss Sea* onto the dock and reached his hands out to Charlotte. She rested her hands into his, and neither spoke. Tears welled in Dutch's eyes while Charlotte's tears escaped and meandered down her cheek as they stood—stunned silent by the surreal moment.

Kara gasped. Now she knew why Dutch treated her so coldly the night Heidi showed up on the dock. It wasn't Heidi or her, either. It was the story Rikk told about his mom playing in the rain and the mud; that was the reason for Dutch's personality switch. Now she understood why Dutch called her a Siren too. Now she understood why Dutch's role as cupid had changed in an instant to jealous stepmother with a poison tongue. She pulled her eyes off Dutch and Charlotte, and watched Rikk drag his hand through his hair while confusion surged through him. She walked over to Rikk and watched his eyes study Dutch and his mom. She smiled at him, and with all her intentions, she sent him silent reassurance. She stepped onboard *Satori* and hugged Rikk as they watched Dutch and Charlotte's reunion.

"*What* is going on?" Rikk's hushed voice demanded Kara's answer.

"I think I just figured everything out, but I think we should wait a moment for Dutch and Miss C to tell us." Kara nodded towards Charlotte as she purposely slipped the clue to Rikk. It really wasn't her story to tell, but she knew the truth was about to surface and didn't see the harm in easing it to Rikk. She also wanted Dutch and Charlotte to experience the magic of their reunion without Rikk demanding to know their story.

"*Miss Sea?*" As Rick repeated Kara's clue, she knew the fog in his head began to lift by the astonishment that swept over him.

Dutch finally spoke as he gently pulled Charlotte into his embrace, "Charlie, you are still the most beautiful woman I've ever seen." Charlotte laughed through her tears and embraced him. Dutch and Charlie hugged, laughed, and heaved sighs.

⚓

"*Miss Sea* is named for my mom?" Rikk asked Kara.

"I think so." It was all that Kara could say through tears and the struggle to maintain her composure.

Rikk was shaking his head, and a confused and impatient frown crossed his face. "Kara?"

"Rikk, this is their story to tell, but remember when I told you that Dutch woke me up early the morning I left on *Genie* for Bayfield? He came in and scolded me for running away from you. That is when I guessed that the song he was singing about Charlie—" Rikk looked confused, so Kara explained, "The night we first kissed under the portico, and Dutch came by singing a song about Charlie." Rikk nodded. "Well, the morning I was leaving to sail *Genie* back to Bayfield, he was trying to convince me to stay in Duluth and patch things up with you. That's when I guessed the Sea in *Miss Sea* actually was Dutch's way to name his boat for Charlie incognito."

Rikk shook his head in disbelief, "But how does he know my mom?"

"Please give them a minute to enjoy their reunion. I know they'll explain all this to us."

"Huh." Rikk sighed.

Kara was certain she had it all figured out and had to prepare him for another revelation. "Be open to other surprises Rikk. Remember what satori means, being fully present in the moment. Let your mom and Dutch have this moment."

"Their satori?" Rikk's shell-shocked voice muttered as he watched Dutch and Charlotte release each other and look over to him and Kara.

"Yes, their satori. Let the past be the past." Kara was watching him and hoping that he was prepared to hear what she was certain was coming.

"Rikk," Charlotte said, "Dutch and I are old friends—well, actually more than friends." She looked at Dutch for approval and encouragement. "We were in love, and my parents separated us." She turned back to Dutch and said, "I loved you so much, Dutch."

Dutch wrapped his arms around Charlotte, and Kara wasn't sure if it was to steady him or her. "I was a damned fool, Charlie. A yellow-bellied fool to walk out on you and our son."

"Son?" Rikk asked.

"Your dad," Charlotte flushed. Then she looked at Dutch's watering eyes and seemed to gain the courage. "Rikk—Oh, Rikk, Dutch is your dad."

"What?"

"Your grandparents arranged for me to marry your father. It was never a marriage of love; it was their way to hide the disgrace of their daughter's pregnancy by a man—" Her voice faded off.

"By a man from the wrong end of town," Dutch finished her sentence. "I figured out who you was when you told that story about your mom letting you play in the mud puddles—your grandma yelling, 'Charlotte Marie.'"

"Rikk, I'm sorry I never told you. I guess I never expected that Dutch would be in your life. I didn't think I would ever see Dutch again," Charlotte said. Dutch squeezed Charlie, and it seemed to prop both of them up after they revealed their tumultuous past.

Kara patted Rikk's back and sent him a compassionate smile. "I don't know what to say," Rikk responded with a slight tremor in his voice.

"I been hating myself for forty-seven years for running out on you. Ain't never forgiven myself for not raising my own son. When I figured out you was my son, I wanted you all to myself. That's why I called Kara a Siren and treated her so bad."

"It's OK, Dutch; I forgave you already and see no reason to revisit it." Kara looked into Charlotte's eyes before she settled her eyes on Rikk. "We only have this moment. The past is gone, and the future will unfold just as it should. But this moment is ours, and we all have our own choice about how we spend it." Kara released her arm from Rikk and crossed from *Satori* to *Miss Sea* and then onto the dock next to Dutch and Charlotte. "Miss Charlotte, I'm in love with your son, and I'm so honored to meet the woman who raised such a good and caring man." She glanced at Rikk who was following her. "I'm so happy that you and Dutch have reunited."

"Rikk, I didn't know you had a girlfriend." Charlotte's approving smile seemed to erase some of the tension Kara could feel in Rikk's body.

"Well, it just happened in the last couple of weeks," Rikk said.

"Charlotte, it has been a whirlwind romance, but our lives have crossed repeatedly over twenty years," Kara said.

Rikk stepped off *Miss Sea* onto the dock, and Charlotte opened her arms to him. As they hugged, she said, "I'm sorry, Rikk. I'm so sorry I never told you the truth. This must be very hard for you to understand."

"Mom, I don't know what to say. How do you take the news that the father that you barely knew isn't your biological father, and someone you just met a few weeks ago is? I don't know—"

"Please forgive me. You have every right to be upset."

"I'm not upset! I'm shocked. You can't expect me to not be shocked."

"If it matters at all, I'm shocked too. I wouldn't have come had I known it'd bring you pain."

"Mom, it isn't bringing me pain. I just—"

"Miss Charlotte, Dutch, I hope I'm not being too impetuous to suggest this, but I'm wondering if you'd like some time to get reacquainted. Rikk probably would appreciate time to process all that he's just found out. I know Rikk is very curious about your story, but you all will have plenty of time for that, right? Rikk needs time to come to grips with this news as much as you need time to sort out your past and present." Kara hugged Rikk. "I'm going to run down and get a bottle of wine off *Satori* for you. Enjoy it while you catch up on all the years," Kara said. All three remained silent, but their consent was mutual.

Before Kara left, she shook her head and cast her ironic smile onto all three of them. "Synchronicity! All of our paths that have either converged, ran parallel, diverged or intersected over the years—and now we've all collided in the month of May!" She entwined her fingers in Rikk's hand and smiled up at him, "Rikk and I have an ongoing discussion about law of attraction, and with all that's just happened, I'm dying to find out what Rikk thinks about my beliefs. We could have dinner tomorrow night at Rikk's house if that would be OK with you, Rikk?"

Looking a little stunned, Rikk blinked and said, "Sure, that sounds like a great idea."

"It won't be gourmet, but I don't expect the meal to be the main event, either." Kara's suggestion was perfect. She watched everybody relax, as they accepted her invitation.

Rikk

When Kara disappeared into *Satori*'s cabin, Charlotte squeezed Rikk's hand, "I hope you are in love with this young woman."

Rikk inhaled, "I *am* in love with her, Mom."

"How did your lives cross before?" Charlotte asked.

"I guess I've got some secrets too." Rikk didn't know how this news would change his life, but he knew it would. If he could accept Kara's secrets and she accepted his, he knew that time would help him to understand his mom and Dutch's secrets. Right now, he didn't even know how he felt. "Mom, I don't know what this all means to me—to any of us, but I like Dutch."

Charlotte's eyes filled with tears. "I don't know what it means, either. Thank you for telling me you like Dutch. I guess I never stopped liking him."

As Rikk and Kara carried the canvas bags off the dock, Kara said, "So many hidden treasures have been uncovered through the release of our secrets. You know, our secrets cause fears that have kept us disconnected. All these reunions are the definition of synchronicity. Can you see the law of attraction at work here?"

"Kara, I'm not convinced." Rikk shook his head. "I can't wait for you to explain it to me."

"Since that morning I left with Jim Bolt for Chicago, I've talked to Dutch on the phone daily." Rikk's eyebrows shot up, and Kara laughed at his curiosity. "He called to check up on our progress every morning of our delivery, and our conversations drifted from his meddling in our affairs to me encouraging him to meddle in his own. I've encouraged him to pursue his dreams. My guess is he's been thinking about how it would feel to see Charlie again. Although he never mentioned Charlie specifically, he did come to understand that you get what you feel. He must have done a gigantic amount of thinking and feeling what it would be like to see her again because here she is. That is the amazing power of manifesting."

"You think he got her here just by thinking she would show up on the dock someday?"

"Not just thinking, but feeling how it would feel. I bet that he visualized meeting her again over and over."

"That simple? Just thinking, feeling, and visualizing?"

"And taking inspired action," Kara said. "Listening to his intuition, and acting on it when he felt inspired; that's all taking inspired action is. I don't know what he did, but when he left Friday to take care of personal business, he was lighter and happier than I've ever seen him before. He looked pretty inspired to me."

"So he had to actually do something like write her a letter or call her."

"Yes. Whatever he did, Charlie is here. My guess is that your mom had never stopped pining over Dutch either. Rikk, it is kind of like you knocking on *Genie*'s hull until I opened the hatch so you could apologize to me in person. You called it an impulse, but what's acting on an impulse other than taking inspired action?"

"Hmm." He gave her a sardonic smile and let his skepticism show.

"Inspired actions are taken when you feel something is right, like when you feel it in your gut. Your higher conscious sends a message, 'Hey Rikk! This feels really good—you've been wanting this for a long time—maybe you want to take action.' And if you can act on it before your saboteur tells you to play it safe, you've succeeded in getting—or at least getting on the road to getting what you've been attracting with your desires. It's just like you did by your incessant knocking on *Genie's* hull."

"So you are saying this is the law of attraction at work? The same law that brought you back to Lake Superior and into my life?"

"Exactly!"

When they reached Rikk's car, he unlocked the trunk. After getting the bags loaded, he leaned against the car. Kara stood in front of him and reached up to give him a hug. "You know what, Kara? This may sound crazy, but in this moment I'm having difficulty thinking about Dutch calling my mom Charlie."

"Really?" Kara said, "Well, if that is what you are having a hard time with, how are you doing with calling Dutch Dad?"

"Geez, Dutch is my dad!" Rikk just shook his head. "I can hardly believe that. What else is going to change this month?"

"Change is good. You said that not long ago. We all just need to remember that change is good, and being in choice about the change is even better."

"I never expected so much change so damn fast. In everyone—" Rikk shook his head.

"You can't stop change. When those friends tried to match-make for you and Dutch for us, it was annoying and unwanted. Remember what you most wanted when that was happening?"

"I wanted to find my own date, and make my own choices."

Kara flashed Rikk a wicked smile, and then hugged him tight. "Do you know what the best thing about the law of attraction is, Rikk? It defies age; it works from the moment you are born until the moment that you leave your physical body."

"Whoa, I thought we were talking about change. How did we jump from change to law of attraction?"

"The law of attraction is all about change, and how we attract the all of the changes we experience. That is why our thoughts are so important."

Rikk shook his head and said, "Kara—"

"What?"

"Thank you."

"For what?"

"For sharing the law of attraction with a skeptic. I've seen miracles happen over the years, and I still don't know what I think about them. However, I think about my woeful life just a month ago when I was wishing for a change, but thinking it would take a miracle to change my life. Since my belief in miracles was non-existent, I couldn't see my life happy again."

"You said 'was non-existent.' Does that mean you believe in miracles now? Or at least in the possibility of them?" Kara said.

Rikk smiled and nuzzled his cheek to her forehead. "You and I feel like that miracle. I suppose Mom and Dutch feel like a miracle has happened to them too. I'm just not sure how their miracle affects me and the rest of us."

⚜

Rikk's cell phone rang. It was Zoey. She asked if Kara was with him and told him to put his cell phone on speaker.

"Dad, Kara, you'll never guess the surprise I have for you. You need to come over to our house to find out what it is."

"Oh, Zoey, have I got a surprise for you."

Kara lightheartedly elbowed Rikk's ribs and said, "Shush! That is Grandma Lotte's news to tell."

They set a time to visit Zoey, Eric, and the kids later in the week and Rikk would invite Charlotte along if she was ready to share her surprise.

⚜

Rikk and Kara drove out of the marina in silence. The canal bridge was up, and a laker was passing underneath, forcing the traffic to stop. Kara reached over to Rikk and brushed her fingers over his cheek. A sheepish smile replaced his absent gaze as he turned and looked at her.

"What are you thinking?" Kara asked.

"I was just thinking how my life has changed since the first of May."

"May Day," Kara said as her thoughts went back to the beginning of the month. "Why? What happened on May Day?"

"I ordered *Satori*."

"Oh?"

"Yeah, I woke up from sort of a dream. I sent the email to OSQ Yachts. I had a signed purchase agreement and the down payment wired to them by the end of the day."

"Do you have regrets?"

"No. I was just thinking how my dream told me my life would change. I remember that I didn't want it to change, but maybe I really did subconsciously. I knew it needed to change."

"Was it your subconscious or higher conscious? I think your higher conscious was asking for a change?"

"Aren't they the same?"

"Yes and no." Kara thought for a moment, then said, "I think people see their subconscious as mystic feelings they don't understand. When they learn about their higher conscience they understand how it communicates through their body with sensations and through their mind with thoughts that seem to appear out of the blue. Anyhow, what was your dream about?"

"Someday I'll tell you about that dream. For now, I'm astounded with all the changes this month has brought."

"It *has* been a month of changes." Kara smiled then looked out the window.

Rikk took her hand. "My mom and Dutch, I never expected anything like that."

Kara watched the ship as it passed under the canal. Her reflective tone mirrored Rikk's. "I first spotted Dutch on May Day. He came to the boat yard, put his ladder up to *Miss Sea*, crawled into the cockpit, and stayed there all day. He didn't talk to anyone; he just watched people getting their boats ready for launching. I thought it odd that he sat there all day and didn't work on his boat. Then the next day it seemed as if he had blossomed. The gregarious Dutch that we both know emerged. After he quizzed me about my sailing adventures that brought me to the marina, he asked me about Sophie and Pete. I thought it so strange that he was so relieved that I talked them out of buying a boat riddled with problems sitting on stands next to *Genie*. You know, I still wonder why he didn't come down off *Miss Sea* and talk to them if he was so concerned." The bridge began to lower as the ship's stern cleared it.

"Maybe he'll tell you someday."

"Maybe, or maybe he'll get to keep it his own secret. Either way, Sophie and Pete have a good boat and their lives have changed in a great way since May Day too. Dutch and your mom's lives are changing as we speak."

As Rikk drove, all that Kara had just told him about Dutch churned in his head. "Has Dutch ever told you why he was so reticent on May Day?"

"Not really. He did say that it wasn't his day to save anyone when I asked him why he didn't stop Pete and Sophie from buying that boat."

"Is that all he said?"

"No, he said that it was his day with *Miss Sea*, always has been since he got her. It is an odd way to celebrate the anniversary of the day his family gave *Miss Sea* to him, isn't it?"

"It's a little more than odd."

"Why?"

"Last year Vincent mentioned Mom's strange behavior on her first visit after returning from Florida. That was the first weekend in May. He said that her mood gets pretty low every May first. My head was in my own worries and I dismissed it. But now that I think back to when I was a kid, Mom was morose for days right before and after May Day. She has always had somewhere to go on May Day since I can remember, but she never told me where she was going. The babysitter wouldn't even tell me where she went. In high school and especially in college, I was gone during her gloominess. I just forgot about it." Rikk looked at Kara stare in the distance. He knew she understood his deduction. "I think it's an odd coincidence that both Mom and Dutch seclude themselves on May Day."

"That is a coincidence." Kara smiled at him, "Well, Sherlock, what are you going to do about that coincidence?"

"What do you think I should do?"

"Absolutely nothing. I think we both know that it's a pivotal day in their lives, but I think it best to let them choose to either reveal why it is or keep it their secret."

"You're right. But it's going to drive me crazy."

"The whole month of May has been a crazy one for all of us. Crazy good—but crazy."

"That it has been! Tell me about your crazy good month, Kara? How has it been for you?"

"Hmm, let's see. I was scraping *Genie*'s hull when I met Sophie and Pete, then I met Dutch, then you came back into my life, and then your boat whacked the top of my head." Kara laughed at Rikk's injured expression. "The month certainly has ended in an unexpected and amazing way. When I arrived in Duluth with *Genie*, I never expected I'd feel so in love, and certainly not by the end of the month." Rikk laced his fingers through the tangles of Kara's hair at the base of her neck; he pulled her toward him. The horn honking from the car behind interrupted their lingering kiss, and that initiated a choir of horns blaring with pulsing dissonance. Rikk pushed the clutch in and shifted into first gear. The tires rumbled across the bridge's grated platform, but Rikk wasn't drawn out of his contemplation of the month's changes.

When they approached the next intersection, Kara asked, "Rikk, are you in a hurry to get home?"

"Not really. What do you have in mind?"

"I don't know. How about taking a drive up to Palisade Head? Or we could climb Enger Tower, or—" Kara smiled, raised her eyebrows in a challenge. "Do you have any ideas?"

"Do you want to look out over the lake?"

"Not necessarily, I just thought it might be nice to digest all this from a different perspective."

"Are you coaching me?" Rikk teased her, even though he liked the idea.

"No, well, maybe a little. Dutch and your Mom's news is big for me, and huge for you. It feels like sitting on the crest of a ten-foot wave with the bow and rudder out of the water, just waiting to see which way the ocean is going to send you. Once the boat starts down the wave, the rudder goes back into the water; and *then* you get the steering back. Then you get to make *your* choice."

"Hmm, that's an interesting analogy, but not exactly how I feel about Dutch and Mom."

"Yeah?"

"Yeah, it's like my rudder is out of the water, but it isn't even my life. So, when I get my rudder back in the water, what choices do I get to make?"

"You get to choose how you feel about their news and their reunion. You get to accept them, support them, or not."

⚜

At last, Rikk said, "Let's go to Split Rock Lighthouse."

"Split Rock?"

"Yeah, have you ever been there before?"

"Once, years ago."

"I just saw an article about it and thought I might like to sail past it someday. I don't know. It just came to mind."

"Then it must be the place you are meant to go. It's a perfect choice."

Rikk looked past Kara's wise eyes into the knowing smile that had jump-started his heart. He saw her caring soul that guarded his freedom to choose, and encouraged him to do so—consciously. "You know, I just read somewhere to 'Live fully present in each moment, give love freely and unconditionally, choose in every aspect and moment of your life by following your heart and listening to your intuition. Be in choice." He grinned at Kara's smiling eyes. "Wise words, don't you think?"

"I think they need to be revised," Kara said.

Rikk's eyebrows shot up, and the grin melted from his face. He wondered if he'd ever be able to predict what was going on in her mind.

Kara

Kara laughed and squeezed Rikk's hand resting on the shift. Life is supposed to be fun, and being in the moment with Rikk was fun. She looked into his expectant eyes and offered her amendment. "You are never too young; you are never are too old, and it is never too late to be in choice."

Even though Rikk smiled, he said nothing. His wrinkled brow telegraphed that it was a quandary for him.

"You don't like the revision?"

"I do—I think it's great, except that a while ago you gave me an assignment to make two lists, and one of the rules was that I couldn't use no, not, or never on the list of what I want. I guess I'm surprised you would use never three times in your revision."

"Oh! *You're right!*" Kara laughed at her deviation from her own beliefs. She loved that Rikk picked it up and pointed it out to her. "I wasn't walking my talk."

"I'm sorry. I think it's a great revision."

"Well, I appreciate your holding me accountable, and I agree with you. I need to state it in a positive way; the way I'd like people to hear and remember it."

<hr />

As Rikk drove east on London Road, Kara looked at the Victorian houses and thought about how to rephrase her revision. The words rambled in her head along with her thoughts of Dutch and Charlie's reunion and their revelation to Rikk. She was glad he chose to drive the Scenic Highway 61 instead of the expressway from Duluth to Two Harbors. Although this section of Highway 61 wasn't as sheer as the coastline beyond Two Harbors, she loved seeing Lake Superior's tranquil waves lap the rugged shore as they drove in silence. Kara knew if Rikk was ready to talk about the astonishing information he'd just received, he would. She'd wait until he was ready.

They skipped the interpretive center at Split Rock Lighthouse State Park and walked directly to the lighthouse. As Rikk gazed out at Lake Superior, Kara broke his solitude with a hushed voice, "Rikk?"

He faced her and grinned, and while he hugged her he said, "You've figured out the revision, haven't you?"

Kara smiled and hugged him tight. Then she said, "Of every moment between your first and your last breath, *now* is the perfect moment to be in choice."

Live fully present in each moment,

Give love freely and unconditionally,

Choose in every aspect and moment of your life

By following your heart and listening to your intuition.

Of every moment between your first and your last breath,

Now is the perfect moment to

Be in Choice

Berta Bauer

About the Author

Berta Bauer is a writer, life coach, and owner of Light House Coaching and Retreats. She has embarked on coaching in recent years, yet her lifetime of varied experiences and careers have molded her. They have drawn Berta to coaching and writing, which are the instruments she uses to help people embrace their individuality and diversity, while Berta's champions their freedom to choose to live life their way.

Berta and her husband live along Minnesota's north shore. They enjoy their panoramic view of Lake Superior, with the Apostle Islands, their favorite sailing destination, beckoning on the horizon. They have sailed on Lake Superior for fifteen years. Berta and her husband are in the early stages of developing retreat programs to provide others an opportunity to experience the inspiration Lake Superior provides, while writing, meditating, or reconnecting with their inner spirit. Visit her website: www.bertabauer.com to learn more about coaching, writing, meditation classes, and retreats.

A Preview of Genie's Bottle Sequel:

Satori's Voyage

May 28, 2007

Rikk trivialized Zoey's excitement with his news that Grandma Lotte had a surprise too. Maybe Zoey was being juvenile, but it irritated her that Kara wouldn't let Rikk tell Zoey what it was. When Rikk said he'd invite Lotte to dinner, she felt her father's micro-managing sneaking into her life again. He hadn't done that since she graduated from high school. She was grateful for how close they had become in the years since then, and even more since her mother's death. But today "Dr. Rikkert Harmon–The Almighty" brazened through like he did when she was young. What was happening to her family? This month started with eerie feelings that she hadn't even shared with Eric. Sure, she was relieved—no elated that her dad met Kara and seemed happy again. Now, with all her grandparents congregating without an occasion to mark, Zoey felt uneasy. More than uneasy. All this activated her mama bear instincts, but Zoey didn't know who needed protecting. She wished she could talk to her mom about her anxious feelings and all the eerie things that had been happening—like the swing. What the hell was up with the kid's swing set?

OK, Zoey, let's be logical and analyze the facts. Zoey had called her dad as soon as she hung up the phone with Grandma Claire and Grandpa Henry. She didn't tell him that she'd just talked to her grandparents, or their exciting news. All Zoey told her dad was she had a surprise that she'd only tell Kara and him in person, and then invited them over to dinner later in the week. It was silly, but Zoey wanted was to surprise her dad, just once, the same way he and her mom had surprised Zoey all her life. Why did including Lotte diminish Zoey's announcement of Claire and Henry's news? She loved every minute she'd ever spent with Lotte. Whenever all three of Zoey's grandparents were together on birthdays, anniversaries, weddings, baptisms, and other family occasions they always seemed amicable. Today, her head ached at the thought of them all together again.

When Zoey was young, the time she spent with either her mom's parents or dad's mom had always felt like a circus train bringing fun adventures to town. But for reasons she couldn't explain, both grandparents' news, arriving at the same time, felt like two competitor circus trains heading to town on the same track. The trains crashing, taking casualties, felt imminent. But who? Eric, or their kids? Was it Dad or Kara? Maybe it was one of her grandparents?

Claire and Henry's announcement felt doom laden instead of exciting, and Zoey didn't even know what Lotte's surprise was. But, no matter how hard she tried to calm herself with logic, Zoey couldn't shake her trepidation.

Zoey connected her cell phone to the charger; sat down, and stared out the window at the swing set. The swing jiggled again as if someone had just touched it, yet no hint of breeze was in the air. That had happen so often since the beginning of month. It first moved on its own volition on May Day. That morning she noticed it sway when she and the children were across the yard, picking lilacs for her mom's grave.

At the cemetery, Zoey wiped the dust off her mom's headstone, then they put the flowers in the vase next to it. The lilacs mirror reflection off the black granite monument appeared peaceful.

That night the lilacs reflection reappeared in Zoey's dream. The inscription, Lauren Harmon, February 26, 1960 ~ December 3, 2005, carved on the headstone faded into May 1, 1960. The lilac reflection spread across the shiny monument and then a wooded area with a river running through it materialized over the lilacs. A translucent image of a young and beautiful Grandma Lotte, that Zoey had seen years before in an old photograph album, appeared near the river. Lotte's melancholic gaze always mystified Zoey, as did the fact the photograph seared into her brain when she first saw it.

That dream haunted Zoey daily since then. At first she remembered it every time the swing rocked when no one was near it. Now, every time she looked at the swing set, the dream replayed in her mind. What happened on May 1, 1960 to Grandma Lotte—and why had she invaded Zoey's psyche?

Zoey missed her mom's wisdom and reassurance. Heck, Mom would laugh at Zoey's imagining her grandparents as trains about to collide, and especially that there would be casualties.

Damn! Zoey's stomach churned and she knew it was telling her that something was about to happen. Then she remembered all the times her mom told her, "Zoey, pay attention to your gut instincts, and always follow your heart. Your heart will guide you through all of life's struggles and deliver life's abundant gifts to you." Yet, right now Zoey felt something was looming, and her heart wasn't guiding her like her mom promised it would. *This is just crazy! I'm letting my mind run away with itself.*

The phone rang and broke Zoey's trance. It was Eric. She'd tell him her surprise. Maybe telling him would ease her mind and restore her excitement that she felt only minutes ago.

⚜

This excerpt from *Satori's Voyage* by Berta Bauer has been set for this edition and may not reflect the final content of the book.

CPSIA information can be obtained at www.ICGtesting.com
Printed in the USA
BVOW041741280312

286278BV00004B/1/P